Handbook of NLP

Other books by Harry Alder

Gower Publishing Ltd
The Ultimate How To Book (1999)

How To Books
Achieve Twice as Much in Half the Time (2001)
Don't Stop Smoking until You've Read this Book (2002)
How To Live Longer (2001)
Quick Fix Your EQ (2000)
Remembering Names and Faces (2000)
Say it with Pictures (2001)
Tracking Down Your Ancestors (2002)

Kogan Page
Boost Your Intelligence (2000)
Mind to Mind Marketing (2001)

McGraw Hill
NLP for Trainers (1995, part of worldwide Training Series)

Piatkus
Corporate Charisma (1998)
Masterstroke: Use the Power of Your Mind to Improve Your Golf (1996)
NLP for Managers (1996, two editions)
NLP in 21 Days (1999)
NLP: The New Art and Science of Getting What You Want (1994)
The Right Brain Manager (1993, two editions)
The Right Brain Time Manager (1995)
Think Like a Leader (1995)
Train Your Brain (1997)

Handbook of NLP

A Manual for Professional Communicators

HARRY ALDER

Published by
Gower Publishing Limited
Gower House
Croft Road
Aldershot
Hants GU11 3HR
England

Gower Publishing Company
131 Main Street
Burlington, VT 05401–5600 USA

Harry Alder has asserted his right under the Copyright, Designs and Patents Act 1988 to be identified as the author of this work.

British Library Cataloguing in Publication Data
Alder, Harry
   Handbook of NLP : a manual for professional communicators
   1. Neurolinguistic programming
   I. Title
   158.1

   ISBN 0 566 08389 2

Library of Congress Cataloging-in-Publication Data
Alder, Harry.
   Handbook of NLP: a manual for professional communicators / Harry Alder.
      p. cm.
   Includes bibliographical references and index.
   ISBN 0-566-08389-2
    1. Natural language processing (Computer science)–Handbooks, manuals, etc. I. Title.

QA76.9.N38 H364 2002
006.3'5–dc21

2002024458

Typeset by Bournemouth Colour Press, Parkstone
Printed and bound in Great Britain by MPG Books Ltd., Bodmin, Cornwall.

Contents

List of Exercises

List of Figures

Preface

Many hundreds of books exist describing the principles and techniques of NLP, and extolling its benefits. Most of them originate from so-called certified NLP 'practitioners'. These disciples form part of what has grown into an influential, worldwide movement which, according to some, rivals orthodox psychology in its record of successful personal change methods. 'Outside' writers also abound, many of whom have applied the principles and methods of NLP in their own fields, such as sales and management training, sport, education and business. You can usually recognize these non-establishment books, characterized by less NLP jargon and optimistic claims, and lacking the parabolic prose that many 'NLPers' adopt. Few of these identify with the therapeutic background of many practitioners. Some 'outsiders', however, undertake formal NLP certification, but continue in their own line of work, leaving them with a foot in both camps. A handful belong to the different schools that any fast-growing movement attracts – in this case, typically, mainstream cognitive psychology, where NLP theory and practice might well put traditions and livelihoods at risk.

At the receiving end, NLP readers have no less disparate needs and perceptions. Expectations and loyalties vary as much as dress, accent, education and professional background. Many readers will have undertaken a short introductory training programme, or read articles on the subject. Others will have heard about it from a friend or colleague. Most have minimal knowledge of the subject and seem to come to it with a fairly open mind. Some want a 'quick fix' in an aspect of their lives in which they believe that NLP has registered some success. Some wish to further their self-development and cannot afford to ignore a subject that has invaded the Positive Thinking world so quickly and comprehensively. Others, working in the field of psychology, training or counselling, perhaps, need to stay abreast of current thinking, whatever their attitude to the subject and its adherents. Inveterate learners, seekers after life's meaning and the simply curious – all help to swell the ranks of NLP readers.

In planning an NLP handbook, I had to consider what approach and form it should take in this complicated environment. Clearly, it should offer more than one specialized application of NLP – training, golf or selling, for example. Although more detailed, such specialized texts do not provide comprehensive coverage. A genuine handbook should embrace all the main topics included in NLP training around the world. It should also function as a more-or-less DIY working manual, regardless of the particular interest of the reader.

Most NLP writing features a gung-ho, 'can do' style. I must admit to a characteristically English aversion to overstatement and gung-anything. None the less, I respect enthusiasm when quoting other people's experience. Likewise, if something works especially well for me personally, enthusiasm will no doubt show. Most importantly, NLP's concern with communication calls for what book jackets tend to call an 'accessible' style. The practical nature of much of the subject requires examples and applications to business and personal life. But at the same time, its unique view of the human mind deserves careful, step-by-step explanation and discussion, and minimum corner-cutting. It must communicate, not least, the sometimes controversial principles, or 'presuppositions', that form the foundation of NLP methods. It certainly should not take the form of verbatim transcripts of seminars – complete with parenthesized laughter – that some of the early works of the founders did. A book differs from a live training event, and each fulfils its own function.

Some scientific and academic readers bemoan the lack of high-level research and published papers in the field of NLP. To cater for such readers, I would have needed to pepper my prose with footnotes, references, qualifications and reservations that most readers would rather do without. But purists and sceptics want more than this anyway, demanding a level of scientific method that NLP simply does not aspire to. In any case, satisfying the typical reader, who looks for something 'accessible' and enjoyable, requires a stylistic balancing act.

My own background as a businessman, one-time accountant, management consultant, corporate trainer and artist makes me far from your average NLP writer. However, I confess to undergoing Master Practitioner training, and also to having written a number of NLP books and articles over the years. So, like some of the 'outsiders' I have referred to, I have a foot in both camps. To the NLP faithful, I shall probably sound like someone skewed towards objectivity and criticism rather than the familiar, upbeat NLP style. Newcomers, on the other hand, may detect an enthusiasm for the subject, based on what I have seen it achieve in my business and personal life. Some might even observe a little anti-establishment anarchy.

Far more important, perhaps, I have tried to present the complex terminology and weightier 'truths' with enough energy and emotion to keep the average reader awake for long enough periods to derive real personal benefit. My interest lies in the big changes that readers can experience from a little beginning in the mind, just as the flapping of a butterfly's wings can apparently affect the weather on the other side of the world. NLP scores well on personal change. Sometimes the smallest 'intervention', such as in attitude and belief, can affect a person's behaviour and achievement fundamentally – and history in turn. Even adopting a few key principles can make an impact on a person's life. I consider such a possibility justification for this, my latest, and thickest, NLP volume.

The butterfly effect applies not just to meteorology, but also to the neurology of your brain and the behaviour that inevitably follows. It starts with you reading this page at this particular moment in your life. Who knows where it might take you? From this point, you will start to make your own cosmic waves, and, I hope, discover in your tiny wings untold power for change and achievement. An optimistic belief for both of us, maybe, but listen to the story anyway.

What the book contains, and how to use it

I have divided the book into two parts. Part 1 deals with various NLP subjects, each chapter covering one or more topics. Some of the titles, and many of the main headings, use NLP terminology. I will explain each term as it occurs, but a fuller explanation appears in the glossary. For a full introduction to NLP (or refresher programme, if you already know something about it), work through Part 1, which covers all the principles and methods you will need to put it all into practice. It also includes many examples that will help you in the specific applications described in Part 2.

Part 2 deals with popular NLP applications, under chapter headings no doubt more familiar to you than some in the first part:

- Training
- Selling
- Negotiating
- Interviews and appraisals
- Coaching
- Speeches and presentations.

You will probably want to use your NLP skills in familiar functions such as these. In any event, from the examples given and the references back to Part 1, you can easily adapt your Part 1 learning to just about any field of behaviour. But whatever your immediate needs, by reading on through Part 2 you will extend your knowledge of NLP, as some of this material applies to professionals practising in these areas. With the benefit of this extra exposure, a few things you have learnt will probably fall into place better, and you may acquire some ideas that you can use in your own line of work. The selection of functions dealt with in Part 2 by no means exhausts even the common applications of NLP. However, I have chosen those applications that I think will meet most readers' needs most of the time.

Once you understand the principles and techniques, you will soon start to apply your knowledge to different aspects of your life, and think of new applications and benefits. For instance, what you learn under 'Negotiating' and 'Interviews and appraisals', you can also use in other types of interpersonal communication – perhaps with a little common-sense adaptation. You will find overlaps between the chapters anyway, such as between 'Speeches and presentations' and 'Training', between 'Selling' and 'Negotiating', and between 'Interviews and appraisals' and 'Counselling'. So any learning and practical experience will repay, in the form of the many ways they can benefit you, the time invested.

Rather than provide a comprehensive step-by-step instruction manual, Part 2 will acquaint you with some common, practical applications of NLP that you can use on a day-to-day basis in these or similar areas. These applications relate primarily to work, but you will need little imagination to apply them to personal and other contexts. If none of the Part 2 functions interests you, Part 1 will serve as a stand-alone introduction and reference, including more than enough practical exercises and applications for everyday communication, self-development, problem-solving and personal achievement.

With this simple learning strategy in mind, I have done my best to write in painless prose. To keep everything on a 'What do I do with this?', and, more important, 'How can I benefit personally?' level, I have not hesitated to use multiple examples where necessary. I also list, at the end of the book, some useful further reading and other NLP resources, so, if you want to, you can venture deeper into the subject and investigate other points of view.

Enjoy an exciting journey of discovery, then, into the biggest wilderness still unexplored by science: the human mind – your own, and those minds you want to understand and influence.

HARRY ALDER

Acknowledgements

I wish to thank David Norman, a leading British internationally certified NLP trainer and Master Practitioner, for his valuable help in the technical editing of this book. He is Chief Executive of David Norman Associates, specialists in director- and board-level development and transformation.

E-mail: DNorman.DNA@dial.pipex.com

HA

Principles and Practices

Introduction to Part 1

Part 1 covers all the topics you need for an introduction to NLP. As subjects, they appear in no particular order of importance. However, I suggest that you read the chapters in sequence, as they form a planned learning programme, and each builds on what has gone before. The topics relate very closely in nearly every case, so the 'full picture' will not emerge until towards the end anyway. Readers already familiar with the subjects and terminology may choose to use this part as a handbook and for reference, dipping into the chapters as appropriate.

I introduce the topics and explain any terminology at the beginning of each chapter. As with many specialist areas, some jargon comes with the subject. I have not included jargon just because it appears from time to time in NLP writings and seminars. For example, to 'representational system primacy' (presumably the more popular 'sensory preference' or already jargonized 'primary representational system [PRS]') I gave a summary thumbs down. It means the sense you prefer to think in, such as seeing or hearing. In some cases, however, we commonly use the words in a different way, and this can cause confusion. So, although I express Part 1 themes in lay language as far as possible, I have retained jargon that has a specific NLP meaning where I have already explained that meaning. However, I don't explain a word every time I use it – hence the importance of reading the chapters in the order presented. For a quick introduction to some of the topics, you can refer to the glossary at the end of the book. Otherwise, you can use it as a handy reference source to recall terms encountered in earlier chapters.

1 *The Nature of NLP*

NLP stands for Neuro-Linguistic Programming. Although at first intimidating, considering the individual components of the term it goes a long way towards describing what it means.

'*Neuro*' relates to the mind or brain, the central nervous system, and in particular the senses with which we feel, see, hear, taste and smell. Through these we communicate with the outside world, but we also 'communicate' with our inner selves through memory and imagination.

'*Linguistic*' means just that, and refers to language – both verbal and non-verbal – as an important element in thinking as well as communication.

We commonly use the term '*programming*' in relation to software and the personal computer. With NLP, you can identify the 'programs' that run your behaviour, including habits and unconscious behaviour. You can also program the way you think (*neuro*) and speak (*linguistic*) to attain greater competence in whatever you do.

The mental processes of perception, memory, learning, creativity and suchlike all involve neuro-linguistic programs. Together, they account for our behaviour and how and whether we achieve our desired outcomes. NLP definitions don't adhere to a specific standard, and its followers often struggle to explain it. Some describe it as an attitude. The founders, Richard Bandler and John Grinder, defined it as:

The study of the structure of subjective experience.

For most people, this begs further definition and you will meet the ideas of a structure and 'subjective experience' a lot as you get to know the subject. It has also been referred to as 'the art and science of personal excellence'. Much of NLP concerns interpersonal communication, but it goes far beyond orthodox communication theory and in particular majors on non-verbal communication. NLP also places emphasis on self-understanding, or intrapersonal intelligence (intra = within) – a main feature of so-called emotional intelligence. So its impact extends beyond communication to self-development at many levels. Its claims lie not in art or science, however, but in its successful, practical application in the lives of ordinary people striving for excellence.

The ABC of NLP

In broad terms, NLP covers:

- communication
- internal experience
- how language affects us

- modelling excellent behaviour
- how we use our brain.

People often associate NLP with fast-change techniques. In fact, techniques merely represent the *products* of NLP, which provides a *model*, and a modelling process. We base many techniques on what we call the NLP model. This describes sensory inputs – sights, sounds and feelings – filtered by generalization, deletion and distortion, for coding and storing subjective experience as a structure, or personal map of reality. NLP models a person's perceptual map. Moreover, the NLP model doesn't focus on repair, as do orthodox psychological approaches, but positive change, or *generation*. It sees people as whole and 'perfect', rather than broken, pathological specimens.

NEUROLINGUISTICS

The more historical term 'neurolinguistics' refers to an area of study in general semantics. Alfred Korzybski used the term in 1941, seeing it as key element in understanding the limitations of language and how we each build our 'maps' of the world. Significantly, as we shall see throughout this book, he distinguished the 'map' of our personal perceptions of the world from the 'territory' of external reality.

This linguistic connection exemplifies just one of the many features of NLP drawn from different disciplines and based on concepts familiar in some other context. Among other things, NLP expands, consolidates and develops neurolinguistics as previously understood.

SCOPE AND SCHISM

The scope of NLP has expanded since its inception in the 1970s, as others, as well as the founders themselves, have added important new streams of thinking. The main areas it has affected are:

- education
- training
- business
- counselling
- health
- therapy
- creativity
- personal change
- sports psychology.

The lack of a standard definition, of the sort that a professional body might agree upon, does not imply any lack of rigour on the part of the original propounders of the ideas. Rather, it reflects the fact that NLP has grown like Topsy, and its followers add new topics and interpretations continually. These developments form an essential aspect of the very adaptability of an evolving subject. The NLP scene can appear somewhat anarchic. For this reason, orthodox definitions may become stretched according to the school of thought prevailing, and the axes individual writers and practitioners have to grind.

The science of personal excellence

Some definitions have gained wide acceptance, such as 'the study of subjective experience' and 'the science of personal excellence'. As a behaviour science, NLP consists of:

- a system of knowledge – an epistemology
- methods and processes for applying knowledge and values – a methodology
- tools with which to apply the knowledge and values – a technology.

It draws on linguistics, neurology and cognitive science, and seeks to synthesize a number of theories and models into a single structure.

NLP contains a set of principles and distinctions which enable us to identify thinking patterns and behaviour, in people and their relationships. In particular, it enables us to identify those forces in our lives that work unconsciously, and the mental structures that control them. We can then use this knowledge to make *changes* to the way we think and behave.

MODELLING EXCELLENCE

NLP originated in what we term *modelling*, and this remains a central feature. Modelling entails identifying and emulating special competence, or so-called 'excellence', such as we find in outstanding achievers in every walk of life. The simple idea is that:

> If anyone can do it, so can I.

Modelling exemplars of human excellence demands copying of a specialized and technical kind. The 'I can' philosophy in NLP differs from the positive thinking and affirmations we have become familiar with, and which sometimes seem naïve in comparison. Modelling includes not just observable behaviour, sometimes down to micro-muscular level, but also the 'behaviour' of the mind, its mental structures and programs.

Through different techniques, a NLP 'practitioner' seeks to model, then emulate or replicate, how a person thinks and feels. The 'practitioner' tries to understand *how* rather than *why* they exhibit competence, or 'excellent' behaviour, and enjoy the success that invariably follows. 'How' includes mental patterns and programs, rather than the unique and personal *content* of thoughts and feelings. Thus, in a major departure from conventional therapy and problem-solving, NLP techniques can remain 'content-free'. This increases their scope and simplifies the processes.

SENSE AND SYSTEMS

NLP largely embraces the theory and practice of communication, which in this context includes communication with oneself, or self-knowledge, as well as communication with other people. Two important principles run through NLP:

- The phrase 'the map is not the territory' encapsulates the first. We respond to the world around us through the five senses and how we perceive things. This involves a complex set of filters, which turn outside reality into subjective experience – in other words, 'experience' unique to the person and based upon their beliefs, values, feelings, life experience and so on. We then *act* according to our filtered map of the world – the only world we know. *We cannot know reality* because of the way our mind structures and processes it as 'experience'. Our mental map seems like reality, but in fact can never equate to reality, or the 'territory'. The NLP presuppositions in the next chapter reflect these important fundamental concepts.

• These processes inter-relate with other systems, both inside the person and also embracing the people around and the wider environment. We act not independently, but systemically and holistically. So we cannot isolate any part of these systems – such as a specific behaviour – from the rest.

Art or science?

NLP practitioners refer to the subject as *both* an art and a science: an art, in that it largely calls for special skills, such as we use, for example, in interpersonal relationships and modelling behaviour. In particular, it demands acute observation skills akin to those of a patient portrait artist, and the listening skills of a dedicated counsellor.

Similarly, you need special, craft-like skills, as well as knowledge, to program your mind to do what you want it, and the rest of your body, to do. NLP concerns some highly subjective aspects of people which don't lend themselves to the absolute laws and predictability we associate with scientific method. The human mind, of course, doesn't provide the best scientific laboratory.

The label 'science', on the other hand, signifies a well-researched field of knowledge with a credible intellectual pedigree. It has drawn, for instance, on linguistics, computer programming, cybernetics and psychology, and, less directly, on several other disciplines. Moreover, its methodologies, although applied to the highly individualistic human mind, have evolved through as near to scientific method as human subjectivity allows. However, its history has an even shorter span than that of the young and equally 'soft' science of psychology. NLP, as a science, struggles to rank with the physical sciences, or 'harder', modern maths- or computer-related disciplines such as artificial intelligence. As we shall see, this relates more to the inherent subjectivity of the subject, and the role of the unconscious mind, than to any lack of rigour.

Some practitioners make quasi-scientific claims about the models they use. I noticed once the following bold claim: 'Because these models are formal, they also allow for prediction and calculation.' I make no such claims, and nor do peer-reviewed, learned journals respected in the scientific world, in which NLP writings have rarely figured.

NLP adopts a highly practical approach, and in this sense characterizes an art or craft that requires special skills as well as theoretical knowledge. It emphasizes change in behaviour, and involves testable processes. It differs from more conventional approaches to behavioural science both in its direct interventions in mental processes and in the shorter timescale of achieving change.

Art or science? – Take your pick. This hands-on, DIY subject stands or falls by its impact on individual people's lives, however we classify and define it. But the 'art or science' debate reminds us that both sides of our brain work continuously to fulfil different and sometimes paradoxical functions. As well as doing its ordinary 'thinking', the human mind has subjective and unconscious characteristics that play an important role in internal and external communication. These compare with other 'right-brain' characteristics in the familiar 'left brain/right brain' logical/intuitive distinction. NLP, from the vantage point of its multi-disciplinary origins, takes such a bicameral, or two-brained, view of the mind-body and its relationship with the outside world. It adopts a holistic perspective, making allowance continually for the lack of absolutes in its fickle human subjects, yet drawing on the infinite richness and potential of the human mind.

Embryonic growth

The founders and early NLP disciples have documented the growth of NLP well. If a new reader, it has finally reached you. If a veteran NLP reader, you have already contributed to its extraordinary early growth. Hailing from California, NLP has straddled the world like other US-originating movements, yet it promises a far longer life. After about a quarter of a century, it seems to maintain the characteristics of embryonic growth, and no lack of evangelistic zeal among NLPers.

Its growth partly stems from the impact of the Internet. Much of the development of ideas now happens online, through e-mail lists, chat groups, practitioner training Web sites, and the dissemination of articles covering every nuance of the subject. Growth has also resulted from the social relationships and networks that its adherents form in live seminars and 'practice groups', and through the Practitioner and Master Practitioner accreditation process.

'GEE WHIZ' EFFECTS

NLP practitioners have also documented and marketed the benefits. Its techniques often display what seems to professionals and business people a 'gee whiz' character, with extraordinarily fast 'cures' and life changes. None the less, after an initial appraisal, its claims seem to invoke little scepticism. It suffers from no shortage of sincere anecdotal testimony, whether of ten-minute phobia cures or the instant reversal of life-long debilitating habits. Research documentation covering its theoretical bases has proliferated rather less, however. As we saw earlier, few published papers reach the main scientific journals – though, in view of the hybrid nature of the subject, one wonders in which publication they might appear.

BENEFITS AND APPLICATIONS

NLP commands little acceptance in more orthodox schools of psychology. Described as 'better felt than telt', this implies an indictment neither of its effectiveness nor of its acceptance in fields with less direct rivalry, such as business, corporate training and personal development. People seem to test out and realize its benefits more quickly than in conventional applied social science. At the same time, its more lasting, readily testable results attract people looking for results rather than theoretical purism. Some of the more commonly claimed benefits include:

- Control the way you feel.
- Think positively.

- Adopt goals that motivate you and direct your energy.
- Overcome negative effects of your past life experience.
- Replace unwanted habits with more useful ones.
- Attain competence in skills you have seen others acquire.
- Develop confidence.
- Think creatively.
- Learn from others – skills as well as knowledge.
- Communicate effectively with others, such as work colleagues, clients, friends and family.

NLP offers an effective methodology for human change. More and more benefits come to light as new applications emerge and a larger following of people incorporate its principles and techniques into their lives. You may well discover new applications and benefits yourself. By way of example:

- Diners Club trained its managers and representatives in the customer service area in NLP skills for handling customer and internal communication. The programme resulted in a 254 per cent increase in customer spending, and a 67 per cent reduction in customer loss. This transformed the Customer Service department, previously a cost centre, into a revenue-producing part of the organization.

- BMW in England modelled the communication patterns of its top 1 per cent in sales performance. After determining the successful behaviours of these salespeople, the company taught the skills to every salesperson in the organization. Sales of a newly introduced model greatly exceeded projections.

- American Express trained 24 line managers from all over Asia to become transformational trainers. With no previous training experience, these employees became the heart of 'American Express Quality Leadership', an area-wide initiative to encourage every employee to take personal responsibility for quality in customer service.

- Fiat modelled the leadership skills of its finest formal and informal leaders. Subsequent management training focused on the skills uncovered in the modelling process.

The origins and development of NLP

NLP builds on the ideas of Gregory Bateson (an anthropologist), Noam Chomsky, and Alfred Korzybski (both linguists), Milton Erickson (usually cited as the father of modern hypnosis), and several others to different degrees. Richard Bandler and John Grinder developed and synthesized some of these ideas in the 1970s and established the term 'neuro-linguistic programming' and the ubiquitous abbreviation, NLP.

Grinder came from a linguistics background, and Bandler from maths and gestalt therapy. NLP established itself quickly in the public domain as a generic label for ideas that spread eventually well beyond those of the co-founders. In their first work, *The Structure of Magic, Volumes 1 and 2* (published in 1975 and 1976 respectively) they identified the verbal and behavioural patterns of Fritz Perls, the creator of gestalt theory, and Virginia Satir, an internationally recognized family therapist. Their next book, *Patterns of the Hypnotic*

Techniques of Milton H Erickson, Volumes 1 and 2, published in 1975 and 1977 respectively, followed work modelling Erickson's methods. Widely acknowledged as one of the most successful hypnotherapists of our time, Milton Erickson founded the American Society of Clinical Hypnosis. He made an important contribution to psychiatry, and some of his ideas and behavioural models have become part of NLP. We will discuss the Milton Model, based on that early modelling, in Chapter 12.

Some of the philosophy and methods of these outstanding communicators, and their practical skills as 'modelled' by Bandler and Grinder, comprised the early ideology and practice of neuro-linguistic programming. Others, such as Connirae and Steve Andreas, Judith DeLozier, Robert Dilts, Tad James and Wyatt Woodsmall, played an important role in the early growth. Anthony Robbins did much to popularize the subject. Scores of others made a major impact, and many hundreds have contributed in a smaller way to the richness and vitality of the ideas, models, techniques and applications. This army of enthusiasts added, and continues to add, specialist applications to the main body of methodology. Rather than propounding original theories, they normally adopt it as part of their professional practice or ordinary work and life. Some have specialized in public training towards Practitioner and Master Practitioner certification. Others train in-house, in industry, commerce and the public sector. These do not always use the NLP label, let alone some of the quaint terminology of specific topics.

Others have made a mark in writing, whether through books, the plethora of NLP journals and newsletters around the world, or online over the Internet. Some have turned their NLP skills to counselling, caring, psychiatry, coaching and other one-to-one applications. As with corporate training, the term 'NLP' doesn't always appear in these cases, although well-accepted NLP methods and precepts play their part, whatever the label. All this makes for a growing, vibrant movement, and the body of knowledge and skills I have tried to encapsulate in this book. The seminal principles of this 'change technology' take the form of the NLP presuppositions we will explore in the next chapter.

NLP schools of thought

As with any field of knowledge and practice as diverse as NLP, different schools of thought have evolved, and practitioners and followers come from very different backgrounds. First, let us describe some broad divisions.

THERAPY

Many practitioners have a background in therapy and counselling. They typically use the techniques as tools for change in a therapeutic, professional–client/patient relationship. You will notice this from reading many of the books on NLP, some of which comprise transcripts of live seminars and verbatim therapist–client exchanges. These not only assume that the reader has the same sort of background or purpose in learning about the subject, but tend to discourage the DIY, non-professional approach. Whilst many of these followers began in the field of traditional psychology, they now often rival colleagues practising the old methods. Rather like ex-smokers, they now champion the replacement of 'slow, misguided' therapies. Others, such as those from a business background, didn't have time for softer functions such as psychology in the first place, so have no interest in professional in-fighting. The growing number of Practitioner training programmes and seminars that reflect these tendencies, and utilize the jargon, indicates the dominance of this NLP school of thought.

ACADEMIC

NLP furnishes a wealth of theory for those concerned about its intellectual pedigree and its standing in the world of 'harder' sciences. Whilst NLP has produced scores of techniques and has a strong practical tradition, it can also proliferate models, flow charts, cybernetic systems, principles and presuppositions and carefully woven arguments. This school of thought, or academic camp, welcomes detail, objectivity, scientific method and logical testing, and prides itself on preserving the purism of original concepts. The smallest part of a system or process can mean a life change, and the search for such a behavioural variable can motivate like alchemy.

CHEERLEADER

Cheerleaders favour the fast changes and good feelings that NLP promises. This positive-thinking, fun-loving camp comprises body, soul and mind DIYers from very different backgrounds that have typically tried a few other super-remedies in their time. They form a sociable bunch that enjoys stage performances and the buzz of belonging to a fast-growing movement. For many of these, what works in a crowd doesn't seem to have the same effect on Monday morning. Their theoretical knowledge can seem embarrassingly shallow to pragmatic observers – let alone sceptics – even though many of these disciples follow the Practitioner certification route and offer to act as professional therapists. The international NLP trainer Anthony Robbins probably best epitomizes this camp.

NEW CODING

In co-operation with Judith DeLozier, co-founder John Grinder developed what he describes as NLP New Coding. They presented their ideas in a book entitled *Turtles All the Way Down*, in 1987.

New Coding draws heavily on Gregory Bateson's work in the area of systems theory, and reorganizes NLP methods based upon the key concepts of:

- states (of mind)
- conscious and unconscious relationships
- perceptual positions (such as first and second person)
- multiple descriptions (systemic characteristics)
- perceptual filters.

This differed from the old or 'classic' code, mainly based on specific behavioural and linguistic distinctions. The New Code emphasizes relationships between systems, and elements within systems, and so takes a systemic approach, now sometimes referred to as Systemic NLP. Some of the New Code concepts appear in later chapters.

Many consider these eclectic groupings part of the vitality of NLP, which welcomes new thinking and applications. Take them as stereotypes, of course. Many thousands of NLPers continually use what they have learned in order to do a better job in their personal lives and various professions. For them, and in context, it works. Business trainers, for instance, increasingly adopt NLP techniques without adhering to any camp, and in some cases without giving credit to the NLP source of much of their material (if they know it). The same applies to successful salespeople, teachers, academics, sports coaches, and many others whose work involves interpersonal communication and the human mind.

Armed with the definitions and background information presented in this opening chapter, we can now explore the main ideas of NLP. The next chapter explains the principles – or 'presuppositions' – on which NLP practitioners base all their practice. These provide a foundation for the change techniques described throughout this book.

2 *Principles and Presuppositions*

NLP adheres to certain operating principles, or axioms, known as *presuppositions*. These underlie the various methods and techniques that you will learn throughout this book. Much of the practice of NLP would not make sense without an understanding, and some level of acceptance, of a number of presuppositions or 'truths'. They reflect the definitions of NLP given in Chapter 1 inasmuch as they do not comprise a definitive list, and tend to differ in their wording. They also differ in the importance NLP practitioners accord them.

Some presuppositions, like 'the map is not the territory', which I cover at some length in this chapter, will seem to crop up ad nauseam. These – perhaps half a dozen or so – form in effect the NLP 'canon', and together serve as the foundation of most of what you will learn. Along with dozens of other presuppositions you will also meet less frequently, they constitute the precepts and principles of NLP.

Nevertheless, they do not represent inviolable laws like Pythagoras's theorem or Einstein's general theory of relativity. For one thing, they don't submit to scientific proof, nor can you consider them 'true' in an objective way. In this sense, you can liken them to economic 'laws'. These, although widely accepted, depend at best on *people* acting in a certain way – which they often don't.

Presuppositions build upon other presuppositions. None applies independently, and only together do they form a wide, adaptable theoretical framework for the subject. Besides, evolution of thought and adaptation rank high in NLP. In accepting a presupposition, you don't ignore what you have already presupposed. Knowledge adds to knowledge, and understanding to understanding, cumulatively.

Such an incremental approach to learning applies as a principle (in the usual sense) of NLP, although not uniquely so. We can only master driving a car, for instance, a little at a time. 'Incremental learning' in NLP may only become apparent when you have to suspend judgement for the moment, while presupposing another 'truth', without which you would have difficulty accepting the former presupposition. This calls on a skill we all have – imagination. In this case, you may have to pretend the truth of more than one apparently opposing idea, such as the pain and pleasure of a memory, compared with the sensory characteristics that created it.

The dozens of other presuppositions I referred to have appeared over the years as add-ons. Depending on the school of thought – which abound in NLP – some have 'added on' more than others. These reflect the development of ideas from widely different contributing disciplines that I have referred to. In some cases, they clarify or support an existing core, or 'canon' presupposition. In others, they assume the status of a new theory, principle or precept. However, you will meet presuppositions that seem to say the same thing in a different way.

NLP has not fixed its presuppositions in number, and they often differ in the precise terms in which people express them. I cited one for each day in my book *NLP in 21 Days*, but here I will introduce a few *en bloc*, as they form a good introduction to a handbook on the whole subject. Others appear throughout the book, as the topics require, but not necessarily identified as essential presuppositions.

Presuppositions don't come in a pecking order of importance, with the exception of 'the map is not the territory'. This seems to have assumed the status of NLP watchword and battle cry, and identifies NLP within the social sciences. You will come to place your own value on presuppositions as you rank them for 'common sense' and in answer to the question, 'How can presupposing this benefit me?' Most will seem self-evident, so you won't have to do much presupposing.

In this chapter, I introduce some of the core, or seminal, presuppositions I described as 'the canon', although no such definitive group has yet emerged formally. Later in the chapter, I describe what some call the 'NLP model'. This will help to explain the 'neuro' part of neuro-linguistic programming, as well as throwing light on some of the main presuppositions. Finally, I explain 'ecology', and its importance in NLP.

Try to apply the presuppositions to yourself and your own experience. In particular, apply what you learn to your whole self, as well as in the contexts of your job, family, self-development or a particular role you play in life. We all tend to consider a new idea in the context in which we meet it. New perspectives and applications usually mean new opportunities. So open your mind to discoveries that will benefit you more than you might have imagined.

Introduction to NLP presuppositions

By 'presupposition', I mean something that has to hold true for a statement or phenomenon to make sense. As we shall see later in the book, we presuppose things all the time. It seems an efficient way to cope with human life. We don't have time to check every chair we sit on, so, even with a few collapses over a lifetime, it makes sense to presuppose their structural integrity. NLP uses a few fundamental presuppositions that will help you to both learn and bring about change more effectively.

As applied in NLP, this seems to me a contrived (or, euphemistically, 'purposeful') use of the word 'presupposition'. I use the term elsewhere in the familiar sense that we all do constantly, as in the chair example. It occurs, for instance, in the Meta Model described in Chapter 12. Everyday presupposition, for instance, reflects the fact that we presuppose 'reality', when in fact our understanding occurs in the mind as a personal map, metaphor, pattern or *representation* of reality.

In the special canonical sense, the term 'presupposition' applies to a few important principles or 'truths'. Unsupported scientifically, these require temporary *pretence* or acceptance to make sense of further learning based on them. They serve the purpose of principles, or even laws, as most people use the words. Fortunately, we all have the ability to suspend belief (or to change a belief), and it often pays off. You retain the choice to revert to your former 'presuppositions' (or principles), or presuppose something else as experience suggests, so accepting a few interim 'presuppositions' will not damage your health.

THE MAP IS NOT THE TERRITORY

'The map is not the territory' – the key presupposition of NLP – originates from a statement made in 1933 by Alfred Korzybski: 'Think of the "map" as your mind, or your view of your world.' This mental map represents how we see or perceive things; what things mean; how we 'code' what we see, hear and feel for; how we make the memories that we can recall later, or that might spring into consciousness as insights and ideas. Your mental map portrays the way the world seems to you, and no one else.

Perceptual filters

We each construct and maintain such a map each waking moment. It comprises the few billion recorded, sensory stimuli we call 'experience'. Our maps vary, obviously, due to our different upbringings, backgrounds and values. More specifically, they differ because of the way we have unconsciously *interpreted* the sights, sounds and feelings of a lifetime, and the *meaning* and relative importance we place on them. These high-speed interpretations all translate into beliefs, attitudes and transient feelings. NLP refers to *perceptual filters*. Raw sensory data has to pass through these filters before it translates into 'understanding' and 'experience'. In short, this map consists of whatever makes you think what you think and do what you do. It forms your record of thinking it and doing it. It comprises your reality.

Think of the 'territory' as the 'real', physical world 'out there'. That world consists of course, of no more than the energy sources that produce the light waves we see, the sound waves we hear, and the bouncing molecules that translate into the smell and taste of a newly baked pie. From the scientist's point of view, *only* this world 'exists'.

Creating reality

The territory of the material cosmos doesn't mean 'reality' to you and me, although scientists might view it as such when they can handle and measure it in the laboratory. Indeed, outside the confines of your map and mine lies a depressingly colourless, tasteless world without sensation, meaning or purpose. Drive away from a beautiful rainbow and it ceases to exist, *for you*, except in your mind – the only place it ever came close to reality. We create reality and meaning as we draw our own unique, rich map of the silent, invisible, soulless, territory outside. Extraordinarily, each personal map, whatever a person's education, rank or experience of life, has no better claim than any other to 'reality'.

It follows, in this case from incontrovertible scientific 'facts', that these concepts of 'map' and 'territory' relate to separate and very different realities:

- an inside world of consciousness, experience and personal, subjective reality
- an outside world of material objects and forces.

In other words: *the map is not the territory.*

Some people find this hard to accept. It means that nothing qualifies as 'real' or 'true' other than as you make it so in your personal world view, or map. It means you have to accept a few billion *other* equally valid 'realities'. It means that you make our own reality. We all do – a humbling proposition for the lord of species. Whatever words we choose, it relegates reality to a figment of the imagination. None the less, from any point of view, we can describe the human mind as staggeringly complex, awesomely vast in capacity and rich in quality.

If it helps, don't consider this first presupposition 'true', but simply potentially useful. In any case, your 'truth' only applies in your personal map of the world. It ranks no more valid (or true) than mine, your brother's or a neighbour's down the street. And it has precious little relationship to real 'reality' and true 'truth' in the soulless territory outside. Put another way, reserve judgement, at least until you have the knowledge to try things out for yourself. Accept this presupposition for the time being, as you accept that your chair won't collapse, and proceed to the next one and the additional useful information you will learn. In any case, don't lose any sleep, and enjoy a journey of childlike discovery as you map out your world.

THE MEANING OF A COMMUNICATION IS THE RESPONSE IT ELICITS

The 'map and territory' presupposition imposes a special meaning on communication between people. To transmit understanding, you have to somehow gain access to the map of the other person. As the communicator, wishing to communicate something, you will have some object or other in mind, of course – a purpose, goal or objective (even if it all happens unconsciously), for instance to inform, persuade, shock, impress or question.

A 'successful' communication means simply that you achieve your purpose. Success need not relate to the actual message you transmit, such as the words you say. Nor need it depend on the medium you adopt, such as the telephone, e-mail or body language, and any technology you employ. The proof of the communication 'pudding' lies in the *transfer of understanding* 'eating'. The transaction takes place between minds.

The power of silent communication

In some cases, a person may appear to do nothing, yet clearly communicates something ('I could tell by the way she looked…'). Silence, for example, may 'communicate' indifference, boredom, deep reflection or animosity. The slightest, unconscious nuance of body language or voice inflection can similarly communicate with a power the most eloquent words cannot command. If you like, the communication takes place in the eye of the communicatee – the person to whom you intend to communicate something, or, in NLP-speak, within their map of reality.

This departs a long way from orthodox communication theory, which typically focuses on three elements:

- Message
- Manner
- Medium.

NLP concentrates on the *effect*, or outcome – including the emotional effect – of the communication. Defining communication according to this presupposition, however, those three Ms may hardly enter the picture. The *effect* of a communication, or the response you obtain, on the other hand, always does. The response confirms the effectiveness of a communication, gives it meaning, and forms the basis for success or failure. In the words of the presupposition: *the meaning of a communication is the response it elicits*.

Measuring communication success

It follows that you can best measure a communication by the extent to which it achieves your objective or purpose. A good speech, a concise e-mail, or clear instruction may each result in an ineffective communication. A silent glance, on the other hand, may communicate worlds between two people in rapport.

NLP explains communication in this map-to-map or mind-to-mind dimension, and you will learn more about the techniques for true communication in Chapter 6. Using the NLP 'technology of interpersonal communication', we can bring disparate individual maps closer together to produce a synergy of meaning and understanding – a relationship.

YOU CANNOT NOT COMMUNICATE

Although this presupposition makes the same point as the previous one in a different way, it has a different emphasis, and provides a useful rule in its own right when it comes to interpersonal communication. Poor communication ranks high on the list of human failings, leaving in its wake a trail of spoilt marriages, estranged children and the bloodiest wars. Moreover, self-justification seems to reign. Each party blames a breakdown of communication on the other party. The communicator insists:

- I told you so-and-so.
- I said exactly ...
- I made it perfectly clear.
- You knew what I meant (you could read my mind).

The communicatee retorts with:

- You didn't say that.
- You said so-and-so, not so-and-so.
- I knew what you thought (and intended to communicate) anyway (more mindreading).
- I knew what you meant.

Of course, we switch from communicator to communicatee role all the time, and so share the same frustrations and self-justification.

In the light of these presuppositions, we begin to understand that we don't give much conscious thought either to the nature of a communication, or to what we specifically want to communicate. In fact, it may not matter what message we insist we have transmitted, the words or gestures we used, and so on, however much we 'spell it out'. The response to, or effect of, a purported communication defines its effectiveness and your success.

This seems hard on the poor communicator who unknowingly offends the communicatee without realizing that they ever communicated in the first place ('I never said a word.'). The fact remains that they *did* communicate, as the 'response' or result clearly bears out – hence the blunt reality, like it or not (and that depends on whose foot wears the boot), that *you cannot not communicate.*

Common communication sense

With a moment's thought, this communication principle tells us no more than common sense. Sitting after dinner for half an hour 'not saying a word' can have a powerful effect on a partner, who may think:

- There's something wrong.
- S/he's deliberately ignoring me.
- S/he's in a bad mood.
- S/he's guilty about last night.

The list could go on and on. This applies in a group as well as a one-to-one situation.

The person currently in the role of communicatee *feels* and/or *believes* that they have understood the message communicated. Strangely, when in the role of communicatee most people conclude that the other party cannot communicate. 'That's your problem.'; 'It wasn't my intention to make you feel that way.'; 'I can't help the way you feel.' This presupposition means that we can't avoid affecting somebody by our behaviour in their immediate presence.

This imposes, surely, an impossible burden. Nevertheless, accepted in the right spirit, the presupposition can help to change attitudes and heal communication breakdowns. Simple *awareness* does wonders for a relationship: 'How will she feel?'; 'How will he interpret my behaviour/non-behaviour?' We can all put ourselves in somebody else's position – we usually expect them to do the same.

Of course, we still get it wrong, as we can't read minds. But this simple presupposition will tip the balance heavily in the direction of better communication and relationships. It provides a useful working assumption for trainers, salespeople, and other professional communicators. How many times have we made a judgement about a public speaker, trainer or sales representative before they entered their communication role – say, when in the foyer, asking the secretary for an appointment, taking the wrong parking space? They *communicated* unknowingly all the time, as we all do. You will often have a greater impact on a person when not in a 'formal' or conscious communication mode.

This leads to another presupposition that says the same thing in a slightly different way. I have included this one because it adds an important, if controversial, feature of communication.

THE RESPONSIBILITY FOR A COMMUNICATION LIES WITH THE COMMUNICATOR

I referred above to a person *wanting* – consciously or unconsciously – to communicate something to another person as the communicator. The outcome, desire or goal originates, and *responsibility* for the communication response lies, with the person 'wanting', or having, a purpose or outcome. The success or failure of the communication outcome resides in this person. The communicator has a purpose, or reason, such as to:

- impart information
- influence
- persuade
- impress
- question, for example to gain information
- pass the time of day.

This usually makes sense when you have a *conscious* outcome. In this case, you will succeed in a communication in so far as you achieve your purpose or objective, and fail in so far as you don't. Responsibility for unconscious communication intentions relates also to the presupposition that 'you cannot not communicate'. We live much of our lives unaware of our moment-by-moment intentions, although every behaviour has some intention behind it. So, knowingly or unknowingly, we may affect somebody else's feelings and life. This presupposition implies that we have responsibility for that, just as we hold them responsible for unthinkingly forgetting our own feelings.

As we saw earlier, achieving an effect or purpose invariably incorporates an effect on the other person, the communicatee, and not just the transmission of a message – an input. In other words, in communicating, you want the other person to *change* in some way. The change might relate to their feelings, beliefs or behaviour, or all of these.

Importantly, such a change in others can bring about *your* intentions. As purposeful beings, we have responsibility for our purposes, goals and intentions. These include communication goals as well as any others. This seems most obvious in the case of a conscious, perhaps formal communication, such as job appraisal. But even in the case of a casual conversation, you may have a clear purpose in mind, such as to console, warn, inform and so on, and also the effect you want to produce, such as gratitude, pleasure, remorse or caution.

Even when we communicate unknowingly, we fulfil our own unconscious 'intentions'. Into the bargain, we reap any effect we have on another person by our words, manner and behaviour. So not only can we not *not* communicate, as we saw in the previous presupposition, but we need to take responsibility for what we *do* communicate, for better or worse.

Two-way process

This seems singularly unfair on the communicator, but in fact, we all play this role more or less all the time. Interpersonal communication operates as a two-way process. For the purpose of establishing principles with regard to a single 'communication', however, we need to distinguish *at any moment* between the communicator and the communicatee. In practice, if the person you communicate with doesn't pay attention, that will not hold good as a reason for not achieving your objective. It becomes your job to gain their attention, do what you have to in order to transmit your intention into their minds, and elicit the response you intended – to affect, in some intended way, their feelings, beliefs and behaviour. But they have the same responsibility if they want to change anything by communicating, such as in their response to you (which forms a new 'communication').

On balance, it makes sense to have control over what you want to achieve, and to take responsibility for your actions, especially when they concern other people through communication.

PEOPLE CREATE THEIR OWN EXPERIENCE

We experience the outside world through our five senses. Not until an experience 'registers' something in your brain have you truly experienced it. Although we employ staggeringly complex optical mechanisms to see, we in fact see with our brain. Several aspects of sight, such as colour, movement and position in space, somehow synthesize to create what we perceive as a glorious sunset or a familiar face. As it happens, with all this impressive optical hardware, our perception *software* often lets us down. For a stark example of this, notice the extraordinarily differing experiences of 'witnesses' (experiencers) at a road accident. In other words: we see what we *think* we see, and hear what we *think* we hear. We create, *in our own minds*, whatever we see, hear, and feel – what we experience.

Human experience comprises more than direct sensory recordings of the physical, outside world. We also experience daydreams, memories and a whole kaleidoscope of fleeting thoughts. We imagine, remember and experience a 'real', vivid, inner world. Most of all, we experience that subjective, mystical state we call consciousness – the awareness of 'being' and thinking. We *self-create* experience, or re-experience whatever 'exists' out there in a way that makes sense or meaning.

For instance, when developing ideas, solutions, emotional experiences, insights and suchlike, we recall memories, and synthesize the most faint or distant brain recordings. And most of our mental goings on happen on 'autopilot': *we don't think about thinking.* But nobody else creates these private thoughts in this unique way – least of all the inanimate world of energy waves that provide the raw material. Other people form their own experience subjectively. Hence the presupposition: *people create their own experience.*

The implications of this presupposition affect what we mean by 'consciousness' and the very meaning of life. The ability to create and change experience gives us all an extraordinary power over our own lives and future. You can make such changes, and create experience to order.

THERE IS NO FAILURE, ONLY FEEDBACK

We learn by experience, but by a certain *kind* of experience: by *not achieving* what we set out to achieve – in other words, by making mistakes, or by missing rather than by hitting the 'target' we aim for. So-called successful people seem to understand this aspect of human achievement. Their success lies in what they have done, or attempted to do, more than other people have. That means they have made more mistakes, and learnt more in the process.

Every time you correct a 'miss', you increase your chances of achieving your target – your chances of success. We use feedback to carry out the continual steering process towards targeted outcomes. 'Hit' or 'miss' recognition provides *information* or learning. You learn about what happened, and the extent to which you missed the target. Next time, by making allowances for behaviour that you have learnt through feedback results in a 'miss', you grow progressively nearer your goal. With practice, you establish the habit of success.

The cybernetic process loop of aim–miss–correct–aim again–improve happens unconsciously when you learn a skill such as driving a car or tying your shoelaces.

Failing to succeed

Looked at in this way, we don't 'fail' – or indeed 'make mistakes' – but simply obtain feedback information about every behaviour. If you do it more, you will improve and succeed more. Specifically, you will tend to miss your target by less and less, until eventually you succeed consistently. In that sense, we never fail. But whether true or not, the presupposition can help the process along. Quite simply, you learn what happens when you do something, and do something different to arrive at a different result.

In the day-to-day cut and thrust of life, this may not seem so. Yet however catastrophic the result of an action or behaviour, you gain some useful information – for instance, what happens when you do or don't do, say or don't say something. With this new knowledge, you have a valuable resource you can use next time round – a down payment on future success. The process of succeeding involves improving by learning from your 'mistakes'.

This presupposition applies to all learning, and relates to the cybernetic or 'self-steering' nature of all our habitual behaviour, which we will cover in more detail in the next chapter. It may mean a change of attitude and self-belief. Upon reflection, the above feedback/learning process *obviously* takes place, yet we often label the result emotionally as failure. In some cases, 'I failed' translates to 'I am a failure', and that adds or confirms a powerful, insidious failure self-belief. As it happens, the human condition of 'all-round failure' doesn't appear often statistically, but none the less provides a popular self-fulfilling label. At worst, failing means: 'I failed in achieving that specific purpose' but the important lesson is not to do it that way again.

This presupposition will help you to view your behaviour objectively, and thus learn from it:

- I didn't fail.
- I learned that if I do so-and-so, so-and-so happens.
- I will therefore do something different – something I estimate will give me the result I want next time.

In general, you will gain more benefit by considering the negative feedback of your behaviour positively than by seeing it negatively as having 'failed' – or, even worse, as 'being a failure'. As the Positive Thinking gurus have told us for half a century, language with negative or disempowering connotations can unconsciously affect us for the worse. It doesn't take much effort to change a few words, or to see the glass as half full.

PEOPLE HAVE ALL THE RESOURCES NECESSARY TO BRING ABOUT CHANGE

The seeds of change and fulfilment lie inside you. The unique and massive store of experience that constitutes your map of the world provides practically unlimited resources to meet present life challenges. This treasure trove resides in your unconscious mind, but you can access it whenever you need to, and thus bridge the gap between your conscious and unconscious self. As we have seen, so-called 'failures' account for much of our learning, and every one provides a resource for the present and future. Of course, you need to acquire particular knowledge and skills and call upon outside resources *en route* to some of your goals. However, you can think, learn and do whatever you have to to obtain resources that for the moment you don't have inside. These acquired resources will help you achieve specific outcomes: your internal store of resources provides you with a natural goal-achieving ability.

Surprise yourself

These innate learning, goal-achieving resources provide the valuable core resources with which you can bring about change. In all too many cases, people don't realize what resources they have in themselves. Sometimes, when faced with a crisis or very demanding task, you surprise yourself – 'I didn't know I had it in me.' But that usually happens by accident. You might never have resorted to your own resources after some deliberation. By presupposing that you can face any crisis, challenge or new situation and drawing on your inner resources, you will start to fulfil your true potential. Awareness of your self-sufficiency will boost your self-esteem and increase your level of achievement.

PEOPLE MAKE THE BEST CHOICES GIVEN THE RESOURCES AVAILABLE TO THEM AT THE TIME

Your mental map consists of your values, beliefs and feelings, and on these you unconsciously base all your behaviour. We all do *well* within the confines of our map. We *succeed* within the boundaries of our present knowledge, beliefs, values, strategies and other mental patterns or mindsets. To others, a person's behaviour may seem bad, misguided or ill informed, especially though the eyes of an older person who boasts a bigger and perhaps richer experience store. However, they too can only perceive through a limited, filtered reality, which has no better claim to truth than anyone else's. Experience does not equate to empowering, useful resources, just as knowledge does not equate to wisdom. A willingness to change and learn from feedback experience counts for more than decades of experience.

If you judge people and their behaviour from that perspective, their map of reality constitutes the only blueprint for life they possess. You will probably find that they have achieved more than at first appeared. Indeed, their 'system' worked with extraordinary efficiency and consistency. Likewise, by understanding your own thinking structures better and opening up choices, you will create new resources, and thus new choices.

BEHAVIOURAL FLEXIBILITY MEANS MORE CHOICES: ALWAYS BETTER THAN NO CHOICE OR LIMITED CHOICE

'Flexibility' means you can create choices and unlock latent resources within yourself. You will always make the best choices given your resources, but you can increase those resources through flexibility and learning from feedback. You can start to control your attitude to change, and create new options, by harnessing the cybernetic system you use unconsciously. Use the simple maxim: *choice is better than no choice.*

BEHIND EVERY BEHAVIOUR LIES A POSITIVE INTENTION: IN SOME CONTEXT, ANY BEHAVIOUR HAS VALUE

As we saw earlier, even seemingly misguided or useless behaviour has some purpose for the person, which we can call a 'positive intention'. Most of our behaviour happens unconsciously in the form of habits, of course. Identifying any intentions or meaning behind these will prove a wise investment in self-knowledge. Perhaps you can achieve what you want in an easier, quicker, more satisfying way, for instance. We will deal with the idea of positive intentions in greater detail later in the book. For the moment, imagine separating your behaviour from 'you'. What positive purposes might it fulfil? And does the purpose hold good in your life today, or has the habitual behaviour outlived its usefulness?

WE COMMUNICATE AT BOTH CONSCIOUS AND UNCONSCIOUS LEVELS

Some of the earlier communication presuppositions incorporated this principle. It echoes Freud, Jung and others, and like the other presuppositions, does not originate from NLP. However, through NLP we do gain further insight into the structures and processes of thinking, so we can communicate better in both dimensions. Chapter 12 covers language models to help access the unconscious mind, and to bring to the conscious surface what a person would not have otherwise communicated. Likewise, through visualization and trance (see Chapter 13), you can not only communicate with your unconscious, but also bring about neuronal changes that affect your behaviour more effectively and permanently than orthodox psychological interventions.

THE MIND AND BODY FORM PART OF THE SAME CYBERNETIC SYSTEM

Making explicit what we have implied all along, this statement reflects the holistic emphasis of NLP, and the *systemic* theme that has developed since the initial models. Thoughts go hand in hand with feelings, or emotion. And emotion means movement, at many levels, in the body as well as physical happenings in the brain. Body and mind act in concert to bring about your intentions.

The NLP model

The presuppositions above described how people create their own experience. We experience the world around us through our five senses: seeing, hearing, feeling, smelling and tasting. But we 'register' and store these sensations only after unconsciously filtering them in a number of ways. In particular, we tend to omit or delete much of the available information. Other sensory information we reject or amend or distort. And, although perhaps understandable in view of the vast quantity of available data out there, we generalize and make all manner of approximations. As a result of all this mental filtering, we experience *subjectively*. You and I represent the world we perceive through our senses in a personal, unique, generalized, distorted and very incomplete way.

Figure 2.1 shows what we usually call 'the NLP model'. A model simplifies something too complex to fully understand, so it can never begin to fully represent, let alone replicate, the real thing. The nearer we get to accuracy, the more complex the task of understanding. On the other hand, the simpler the model, the less accurately it can represent reality. If you can replicate outcomes, or predict, from a model (like the multiplication tables, or $e = mc^2$ or a scale-model Spitfire), you have a good model. If, from the model, anybody with appropriate skills can obtain the same results, even better.

The NLP model doesn't quite fit the three times table category, but it makes the job of understanding the structure of experience much easier. You can make improvements to this and any model you come across as you grow to understand and use it. For the moment, it illustrates the first presupposition: 'The map is not the territory.'

On the face of it, generalizing, deleting and distorting real sensory information doesn't seem very rational. In fact, the process happens largely unconsciously, so we don't treat it as part of our rational thinking with which we reason logically. In any event, even when we consciously think about what we see, hear or feel, we tend to rationalize only *whatever we perceive*, based on what we feel or believe 'true'. Our beliefs, comprising also values, attitudes and mindsets, evolve over a lifetime of experience, the product of the varied influences of people, circumstances, and events.

WILD APPROXIMATIONS

The NLP model describes a most sophisticated filtering system. We make do with what seem

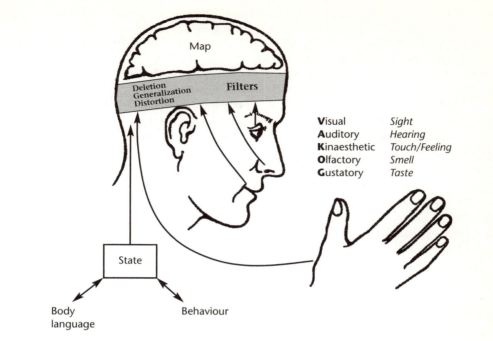

Figure 2.1   The NLP model

like wild approximations in data process terms, and make extraordinary cognitive errors every waking moment. Yet the system operates incredibly quickly and provides clear survival advantages. Sometimes, rough guesses are enough. For example, maybe that flying brick wasn't meant for you, or it wasn't a grizzly bear after all – but better safe than sorry, classify the sensory input assuming the worst, and behave accordingly. Fortunately, the system works rapidly enough to classify inputs to cope with emergencies, provided you have a classification pigeonhole ready. With this system, we *sense* potential danger, however incomplete or generalized the data. And we do it sufficiently quickly to live to talk or write about it.

ANACHRONISTIC SUPER-SKILLS

Over time, we become very good at this sensory guesswork. It incorporates the billions of earlier perceptions (filtered representations) and their cumulative effect on our present beliefs and character. However, in most cases 'survival' no longer justifies our behaviour, such as an angry response to a verbal insult or criticism. Anachronistic super-skills to avoid getting eaten may no longer help, and we make wrong interpretations and decisions.

The NLP model makes us aware of how we go about our lives in the absence of any conscious, corrective intervention in our thoughts and behaviour. This awareness, at worst, provides choice. You can freely believe one thing or believe something else. You can choose to see matters from another perspective, such as how the other person sees things through their own equally unique filtering system. Such an attitude does wonders for interpersonal communication, racial harmony and international peace, as well as your nerves and well-being.

DECODING

There remains the problem of interpreting other people's maps of the world. As we saw earlier, true communication operates mind to mind. But at least you now know the task in hand. By allowing for the process described in the NLP model, you can avoid the major communication failures that cause so much human misery and pain.

Mental filtering has the effect of coding sensory inputs into a personally acceptable, or credible form. NLP attempts to decode the three elements for change: *generalization*, *distortion* and *deletion*. In other words, how sights, sounds and feelings become experience, feelings, belief, insights and 'truth' – what makes a person tick.

Perhaps even more important, you learn to decode your own unconscious sensory coding and thus gain priceless self-knowledge about how you 'tick' yourself. You can now choose to classify or interpret (code) what you see, hear and feel differently if you can consciously identify a better or more useful meaning. Put simply, you learn to see situations from different perspectives, especially concerning other people, their motives, feelings and 'maps of the world'. You can now respond with awareness. You have greater control over your thoughts and consequent behaviour: control over your life.

Ecology

The term 'ecology' occurs often in this handbook, and I have judged it important enough to include with the principles and presuppositions of NLP. The term derives from the biological sciences, and relates to the whole person or organization as a balanced, interacting system. An ecological change takes account of other parts of the system and connected systems.

NLP concerns change – in behaviour and the way we think. Even small changes can have wide repercussions as we consider each part of our life, and the systems with which we interact such as other people, organizations and the wider community. For example, what might seem a 'good' change because a person overcomes 'bad' behaviour might turn out not to give the satisfaction they expected. The behaviour probably served some unconscious intention. It gave pleasure (or caused less pain) in an area of life not associated with the behaviour.

For example, seeking attention underlies the behaviour of some people. Certain behaviour attracts attention – so the behaviour 'works'. However, we may not choose such behaviour rationally, or even consciously. Indeed, we may wonder why we do it at all. In some cases, a person more or less denies the behaviour, or at least its mental origins. Attempted suicide, for example, and teenage antisocial behaviour, often have underlying causes or 'intentions' such as to win attention and respect. This usually applies also to psychosomatic illnesses, and explains the well-known links between physical symptoms of illness and psychological needs, intentions and beliefs. Behaviour encompasses all the hard-wired subsystems of the mind-body system. It works convincingly. So 'gaining attention', or any such unstated intention, will form part of any ecology check when setting goals.

SYSTEMIC CHANGE

Change in any aspect of behaviour or state can have almost unlimited effects on other parts of the body-mind system, and the larger systems we inhabit. Our complex body-mind systems consist of a lifetime of experience and a vast array of neural brain patterns. These patterns, in turn are made up of a few million synaptic electro-chemical connections. All these networks interconnect in some way, even if years apart in their origin as memories, and even when we place them in very different compartments of our lives.

These inner 'systems' include the different roles or identities we adopt from time to time and in different contexts. They include all the attitudes, temperaments and values that go to make up that identity. For example, a person might play the role of father, daughter, team player, clown, scapegoat, nurse, unpaid counsellor and so on. They might think and act in a family, work, social or self-development mode. Our behaviour might reveal the introverted, peace-loving, fiery, jealous, caring, sensitive, gregarious or comical part of ourselves. Change happens systemically, and we need to manage it ecologically, rather than in isolation.

All these 'subsystems' pursue what can seem like an independent outcome or purpose. Indeed, in social and family systems we have come to accept that 'you can't please everybody'. Yet, when making personal changes – which typically just apply to one or a few of our parts – we usually don't notice the ripple effect. The indirect repercussions of an outcome often come later anyway. Thus, a rationally positive change may produce a counteracting negative effect, sometimes out of all proportion to the expected benefits of the change.

This describes just yourself – your own system. In fact, an ecology check then embraces people with whom you associate in any way, in so far as you might affect their lives, and they in turn might affect you by the resulting change in them (and so on and on).

The ecology principle clearly extends to organizations such as where you work, or with which you associate in your hobbies, interests and social life, for example clubs, family, schools, hospitals, and professional life such as associations and societies. In particular, we should apply an ecology check to work outcomes. Often, we pursue goals in a job description, or accept implicit behaviour in adopting the company culture and values, that conflict with our personal values and desired outcomes. Ecology, like the butterfly effect, embraces everything and everybody that might have an impact on you and your life.

3 *Models for Success*

The idea of goals, objectives, aims and suchlike pervades the fields of business, management and personal development. NLP refers to 'outcomes'. The term, used generically, embraces goals, intentions, desires, responses, effects and so on. It emphasizes *change*, and the *effect* of some intervention, such as a communication. This chapter describes some important goal-achievement models that you can apply to every area of your work and personal life. They form the basis of many of the NLP change techniques you will learn later.

Goals and purposes

NLP focuses on outcomes in a practical way. As a result, or effect, an outcome takes precedence, whatever the process, underlying theory or *content* of a communication or any other behaviour. Chapter 2 introduced the presupposition, 'The meaning of a communication is the response (or outcome) it elicits.'

Historically, we have emphasized goals in such concepts as management by objectives (MBO), which concerns the outward process of setting and sticking to (mainly) organizational goals. However, the promulgators of MBO, like many management gurus, paid little attention to what goes on inside a person's mind. This includes personal motivation, the effect of other, perhaps conflicting, goals, and many other subjective factors. NLP takes account of this. It addresses, for instance, how your beliefs and values affect your goals, and the part 'unconscious intentions' play in your behaviour. It offers what we can call a 'technology of goal-achievement'.

To succeed, you need to set an outcome internally. You programme it 'neuro-linguistically'. Eric Berne, the author of *Games People Play*, said: 'Outcomes are determined at the psychological level.' They happen in the mind. The way we set and pursue outcomes can have as much effect on our success or failure as the content or nature of the outcome itself. A 'well-formed outcome', which I describe in the next chapter, has a better chance of success. In this chapter, I will refer to some general goal methodology applied – to different degrees – in NLP.

THE PURPOSE OF LIFE

The human goal-achieving tendency illustrates itself in words like 'purpose', 'vision' and 'meaning'. At the high-level, abstract end, we talk of the Meaning, or Purpose, of Life. At a day-to-day moment-by-moment level, we don't do anything without a reason or meaning, or without seeking to achieve a purpose, however irrational our behaviour seems to others. The NLP model set out in Chapter 2 helps to describe the process whereby we try to make meaning, or perceive what happens in the world. As 'meaning makers', we constantly seek out reasons (sometimes called 'excuses') for every phenomenon, every experience, every sensory representation. We ask, in effect, 'What does this mean to me?' or 'What should I do?'

On the other hand, we don't usually think *consciously* of everyday desires and tasks as fulfilling a purpose or having a meaning. We perform many of our actions on 'autopilot', or out of habit. None the less, we will usually furnish a reason (excuse) for what we do once we consider it consciously, such as with hindsight or when questioned. In other words, we justify our behaviour. Often, the true reason relates to some bigger or higher goal in a hierarchy of outcomes.

HIERARCHY OF OUTCOMES

At the top, we usually find abstract goals such as happiness, pleasure or fulfilment as Figure 3.1 shows. At this ultimate level – usually limited to longer-term outcomes – these take the form of 'life' purposes, or what, to an individual person, gives meaning to life.

Various intentions, or 'stepping stone' goals, may lie between our present and a desired state, such as health, fame or wealth. We perceive these as necessary to bring the ultimate happiness high up on our hierarchy of outcomes. Similarly, short-term tasks – right down to our daily 'to do' lists – contribute to intermediate goals like gaining a qualification or a better job, which in turn promise financial security and ultimate happiness.

These higher goals and purposes also relate to our values and beliefs – the things we deem important, good, right, worthwhile, beneficial or true. Keep this distinctively human search for purpose and meaning in mind as you consider other ways that you can approach, set or choose, and achieve, your desired outcomes.

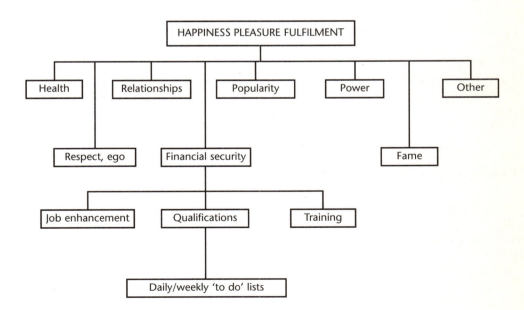

Figure 3.1   Hierarchy of goals

Cybernetic success

Like the ubiquitous word 'outcome', the term 'intention' has its own significance in NLP. The last chapter introduced the presupposition: 'Behind every behaviour lies a positive intention.' This means, in effect, that everything we do somehow aims to bring about a purpose or goal. That makes us goal-achieving beings, if you like. We each exhibit this human, cybernetic aspect of goal-achievement. Our behaviour has the elements of a cybernetic system, in that we:

- pursue a target
- receive feedback information
- continually steer towards the target, based on that information
- make corrections as we go, using an independent power source.

Like a central heating thermostat, once you set the target, the system operates automatically. Similarly, most human behaviour happens unconsciously – we don't have to 'think' about it. Indeed, the most vital of all human processes, like breathing and pumping blood around the body, and a score of other extremely effective neuro-physiological systems, operate as cybernetic systems. For example:

Target:	body temperature
Hit or miss?	feeling hot or cold
Correction:	too hot – sweat; too cold – shiver to create heat
Power source:	body organs, fuelled by food and drink.

These processes follow continuous cybernetic cycles all the time. In these cases, thankfully, genes or other hard-wired mechanisms 'set' the targets. That means that for critical life systems, we don't have to decide optimum survival operating targets as in a business plan. For our 'hit-or-miss' measuring devices, we boast the most sophisticated sensors – *senses* – second to none in the material world. The human power source, which runs almost maintenance-free, lasts a long time by any standards. Moreover, the whole system runs on a variety of cheap fuels available at our local supermarket.

Any consideration of outcomes in NLP falls within this universal human cybernetic context. The cybernetic model, like the NLP model, throws light on many aspects of our behaviour, and in particular the role of the unconscious mind.

Unconscious intentions

We can describe these physiological cybernetic targets as innate, *unconscious* intentions. Other intentions, not so 'hard-wired', also operate unconsciously. For example, you have probably heard the expression 'an accident waiting to happen'. Sometimes a person seems prone to behaviour contrary to their conscious, rational will. A strong habit usually perpetuates such behaviour, and ensures its outcomes.

THE PERFECT SYSTEM

The process happens as efficiently and consistently as any conscious resolution. Yet most people deny that they 'want' the outcomes that their behaviour habitually brings about. A person may describe the outcome as 'bad' or somehow undesirable according to their values. It therefore doesn't make (logical) sense to adopt it. Another person invents a rational explanation for their behaviour. In either case, outcomes, as NLP applies the term, don't always follow logical, consciously set intentions. Nor do they come with moral trappings. A person can achieve a foolish, evil or ill-informed outcome as effectively as a wholesome one. Like a central heating system you set at the wrong temperature, or a missile you program on the wrong target, the 'system' works consistently – in the case of the human mind-body system, some would say perfectly.

We considered the unconscious intention of gaining attention. A teenager starting to smoke may have the unconscious desire for independence from authority figures such as schoolteachers, parents or the government who issue cigarette health warnings. Or perhaps they want the respect and admiration of peers, to feel grown-up and so on. We invariably harbour such intentions unconsciously, whatever 'reasons' we give for our behaviour.

In other cases, a person – perhaps older and wiser – might want to throw off the smoking habit and pursue their intention as a conscious goal, long after the original intentions that provoked the behaviour. However, unaccountable failure in their attempts to quit probably means some underlying, conflicting intention remains: perhaps avoiding gaining weight, obtaining relief from stress, social reasons and so on.

Such intentions form cybernetic targets no less powerful than a strong, conscious desire to achieve a goal. Indeed, in bypassing the conscious mind, such an intention may have all the more efficacy, and accounts for the strange power of habits in our lives.

POSITIVE INTENTIONS

NLP calls these unconscious intentions 'positive', in the sense that we – our whole mind-body system – *positively behave* in such a way as to bring these unconscious intentions about. Because we have come to perform such acts unconsciously (like riding a bike, putting the kettle on, or twisting our hair), they don't seem like true intentions or targets. We don't monitor and reflect on them as we might do conscious thoughts and actions. This adds further to their power in a person's life – no rational, conscious part of us raises an objection. So we often need another person to point out, say, a bad driving habit or mannerism – which they usually do.

NLP, in its goal-setting criteria, seeks to identify these 'positive intentions'. You then have the choice of continuing with them, but now on the basis of a rational, *conscious* choice. Alternatively, you may find you can achieve the same intention by other, more acceptable, perhaps more pleasurable, and equally motivating means. For instance:

- A smoker might fulfil the 'positive intention' of relaxation, or maintaining body weight, in a different way.
- A gambler might achieve the 'highs' of risk-taking, or any benefits of gambling behaviour, through a different pastime or occupation.
- A hypochondriac might receive the sympathy and attention that now forms their 'positive intention' through some other behaviour, and do without the unpleasant symptoms of illness.

- A burglar might experience the adrenalin rush, and whatever positive intention impels them, in other ways and without the drawback of occasional state accommodation.
- A bullying boss might find ways to gain respect, recognition or whatever drives their behaviour in a more effective way, without the damage to relationships.

To make a conscious choice, you need to *identify* positive, though unconscious, intentions. Remember the presupposition (paraphrased): 'Choice is better than no choice.' Once you identify intentions – or behavioural tendencies – alternative behaviour that will fulfil these positive intentions literally 'comes to mind'. We will explore how to identify these in the next chapter.

GOING INSIDE

For the moment, think of areas in your life in which you have not achieved what you had hoped for, yet you cannot account for your failure. You've tried, but know you can achieve more. Or think of any behaviour that you would rather do without, but somehow it seems just a part of 'you'. Think about whether you pursue underlying positive intentions unawares, but through inappropriate behaviour.

This part of NLP relates to inner rather than external 'communication'. You need to determine your own outcomes, whatever their origin. Self-knowledge of this sort requires no lesser skills than interpersonal communication. It demands that you understand how your rich, complex map of the world compares with other maps as valid and unique as your own. This calls for both intra- and interpersonal ('intra' – within; 'inter' – among or between) communication skills to achieve worthwhile outcomes consistently.

Intrapersonal communication involves introspection and self-knowledge. You cannot schedule it like a 'to do' list. 'Activist' business people often fall down sadly when it comes to doing mental 'business' with themselves to bring about internal change. Some individuals possess 'people' skills, to the envy of their more introverted colleagues, yet do not enjoy consistent achievement in their personal lives, and the sense of fulfilment that accompanies it. To use your mind purposely, you will need to learn a new set of skills not usually associated with material business and personal success. These include curiosity, patience and humility, as well as specific mental skills in accessing each representational system: visual, auditory and kinaesthetic.

Some people can quickly 'go inside', recall memories and imagine future scenarios in a realistic, lifelike way – as effortlessly as others get along socially in external relationships. These people often have clear purposes, and enjoy the benefits of intuition and creativity. Whilst maybe not renowned as either articulate or gregarious, they display sensitivity and empathy with other people. In other words, they possess intrapersonal skills, which compensate for the interpersonal skills they may lack.

Various outcome tests described in Chapter 4 add conscious, logical discipline to these intuitive characteristics. This means becoming familiar with your inner world of senses and unconscious intentions. It means using your whole brain – both the intuitive right side and the more logical, linguistic left. Holistic, whole-brain, multi-sensory thinking then forms the basis of goal-achieving behaviour.

NLP takes a simple, effective approach to achievement. It doesn't offer detailed formulae, but approaches human behaviour and achievement by way of models that will work in any goal-achieving situation. As well as knowing precisely what you want – a specific outcome

– the process demands action and flexibility. In terms of the cybernetic model, unless you do *something*, you will not make 'mistakes' or 'miss'. In consequence, you will not receive useful feedback. Unless you make mistakes, you will not learn. Responding to feedback requires a flexible attitude and willingness, if not a desire, for change. A simple model illustrates this. I have called this the Four-stage Achievement Model, as it seems to account for achievement in any sphere, and reflects the process that successful people from all walks of life follow. They usually don't realize they adopt such an approach, and do just what seems natural and right. The process consists of four stages, as shown in Figure 3.2.

In particular, did you do *whatever you had to* ('act flexibly') to achieve what you set out to? This comes close to the cybernetic, or goal-steering approach described earlier. It requires all the elements – a target, feedback and the ability to take corrective action. Miss out one, and you don't have a working system. Think back to where you have succeeded in the past, and notice how this process might have applied. In particular, did you do *whatever you had to* in order to achieve what you set out for? Think also about successful people you know, and notice how they behave:

✓ Do they set goals, rather than wait for events to happen?
✓ Do they change their behaviour to achieve a particular goal?
✓ Do they sometimes change their views, based on experience?
✓ Do they treat 'misses' as helpful feedback information?
✓ Do they learn from experience?
✓ Do they adapt to change?
✓ Do they allow for the feelings and opinions of others?
✓ Do they get up and start again if they fail?

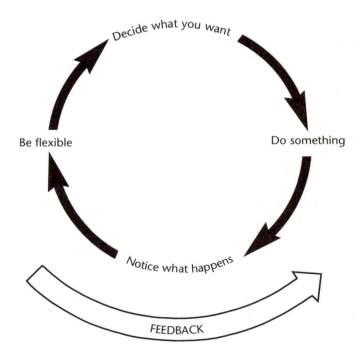

Figure 3.2 The Four-stage Achievement Model

This universal cycle of achievement seems to apply wherever we meet human success, however popularly attributed to genetics, hard work, enthusiasm, luck or fate.

The model applies to long-term life goals that span years, as well as to minute-by-minute effectiveness and productivity, so you can adopt it as a philosophy for success. Then, by applying several criteria discussed in the next chapter, you will add a whole goal-achieving technology to this simple pattern of achievement.

Change of State Model

Achieving a goal usually means more than material gain or an observable behaviour such as a skill. We want to know, do, have or get things because of the higher goal towards which they take us, such as happiness, contentment, or fulfilment. We usually express these life desires as states of mind. Achievement of any sort usually means *feeling* better than you did before you achieved the goal. In other words: goal-achievement involves a change of *state*.

'State' in this sense includes state of mind, but also values and beliefs, and behaviour, such as a habit. Ostensibly, your outcome concerns behaviour, including unconscious, habitual behaviour and its results, such as a possession, skill or capability. In NLP terms, 'state' includes your whole neurophysiology – mental and physiological: the mind-body system. All sorts of life situations involve emotional states we would like to change.

If you achieve a material outcome and it doesn't give you the satisfaction, happiness or state of mind you had hoped for, it follows that it did not rank as a sound or 'well-formed' outcome. It didn't change your state. It didn't have the *effect* you had hoped for.

We change state day by day, of course and indeed moment by moment, whether conscious or unconscious of what caused the change. However, we don't usually include state of mind, or even the state of our body in so far as it reflects this mental state, in any conscious goal-setting process, if we have one. By treating this as a key factor in every outcome, you will add a valuable dimension. Ask the questions:

✓   How do I want to feel and act when I get this, do that, or learn that?
✓   How does my outcome support my higher life goals – the quest for purpose and fulfilment?
✓   How does it conform to my values or what I hold most important in my life?

PRESENT STATE

The first step involves identifying your present situation, in terms of behaviour, thoughts and feelings, as Figure 3.3 shows. Change of any kind, whether achieving a goal, grasping an opportunity or solving a problem, means moving from A to B. From your position at A (your present state), you want to move to B (your goal, outcome, or desired state). You therefore need to identify A to know whether you have progressed to something better – B (if and when you arrive there).

Invariably, an outcome consists of a state of mind – not least to be happy, or happier, or less unhappy than at present. It follows that your present situation or 'state' might imply:

•   a state of mind (unsatisfactory in some way, or you wouldn't want to change)
•   material resources or 'things'

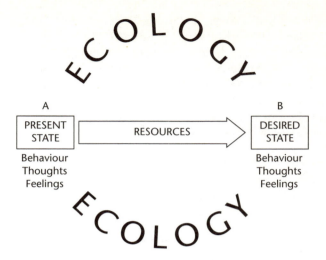

Figure 3.3   Change of State Model

- conscious behaviour (such as a lack of capability or unwanted behaviour)
- a relationship (not working)
- other more visible characteristics.

Identifying your total present state therefore plays a part in goal-setting. But the process also brings benefits in communication and self-knowledge, and plays a part in some of the techniques you will learn. It therefore makes sense to familiarize yourself with the process of determining your present state.

You can identify your present state by the sorts of words you use intuitively to describe a goal or outcome, such as 'I don't get on with my boss, I wish ...' 'I can't stand having to worry about money, I want ...'. You can also specifically identify the sights, sounds and feelings of your present state by 'going inside'. This happens naturally – but negatively – when we worry.

DESIRED STATE

You imagine a desired state – what you want to achieve – as you visualize your outcome, using all five senses. This happens naturally as we daydream about a pleasurable outcome. You will experience a desired state more realistically as you imagine the wider effects, spin-offs and longer-term consequences of your outcomes: for instance, the reactions of other people, and how you would feel if you experienced your goal in a part of your life that you hadn't considered. These feelings associated with an experience form part of the kinaesthetic or *K* sense which, in NLP, also includes tactile, proprioceptive and movement feelings. By becoming familiar with each sensory or 'representational' system (see Chapter 8) and its characteristics, or 'submodalities' (see Chapter 9), you will soon learn how to monitor and manage these states.

Most importantly, you can make like-for-like comparisons between aspects of your present state and aspects of your future state. You can also make changes in how you *perceive* things – again, in all the senses. What do you see in your mind? Does this take you nearer to the target you imagined? In this way, you will *test* for success or failure, not just in material or visible terms, but also in terms of change of state, and long-term life goals.

When setting outcomes, you can ask: 'What state of mind do I want?' This does not just mean transient feelings that come and go throughout the day, but longer-term attitudes, beliefs, values and mindsets – changes to your map of the world. In applying the state change process to your outcomes, as well as setting goals as to what you want to do, have or get, or know, you will ask the crucial question: 'What do I want to *be*?'

RESOURCES

To get from your present place to a desired place, you will need to call upon resources, whether internal or external (see Figure 3.3).

These resources include your past experience as well as the knowledge and skills you have acquired to help make changes. Your resources might include other people whose help you can enlist and on whose behaviour you can model yourself, or states you have known that would help you in the present, or latent skills you can develop and use, but now with the added experience and wisdom of years.

You can use the Change of State Model for personal change and achievement. By knowing your present state, the state you want, and the resources you can call upon – especially your empowering memories – you can start to apply this simple model in your life to achieve more.

Life Content Model

We differ in our personal characteristics and preference, and each of us sees their own world in different ways. This includes the way we pursue desires and outcomes. This pattern of 'experiencing' embraces such a large part of a person's life that NLP calls this next model the Life Content Model. It identifies some of the main differences in the way we experience life, and we can incorporate these distinctions in our goal-setting and decision-making processes. The model identifies five elements, or personal characteristics:

- doing
- knowing
- getting/having
- relating
- being.

Like sensory preferences, such as seeing or hearing, these features of how we each perceive experience tend to stay with us over a long period of our lives. In some cases, we refer to them as personality characteristics or traits. However, we can achieve much more if we identify and *consciously adopt* these basic outcome characteristics that apply to all our lives.

Unlike the mental 'strategies' we use for a specific skill or behaviour, these strategies operate at a higher or *meta* level, in the form of deeply ingrained thinking habits. They represent the macro level of our strategies for behaviour. That means that each of the five Life Content elements typically embraces many skills and activities: for instance, the many experiences we all have of *doing* to bring about some result or other. Any change at this level (say, in all our 'doing') will have a disproportionate effect on our total behaviour, and thus what we achieve or don't achieve. Let's see how these five tendencies appear in each of us.

DOING

Do you like action? Do you prefer to *do* things before learning much about them? Do you frequently use words like 'doing', 'action', 'moving', 'building' and so on? Do you tend to ask: 'What do we need to do around here?' Most models of personality and learning style identify this particular 'activist' characteristic. Most action-oriented, *doing* people will recognize this aspect of their personality, as will their friends and relatives:

- They always seem to get involved before others do.
- They don't need a second chance when called to the front of a training seminar or when given the opportunity to carry out even a daring activity.
- They provide most of the world's volunteers.
- They fill the ranks of top-flight business people and trouble-shooters – the movers and shakers.
- They love travel because of the new experiences it opens up.
- They don't want to live life second hand, but want to go out and do thing for themselves.

These characteristics will affect how someone approaches their outcomes. Simple awareness of the tendency can help you to set and achieve goals more successfully. Having control over it as a personality characteristic or 'meta program' will bring even greater success.

KNOWING

Some people consider it important to *understand* or *know* something. Typically, they will learn as much as they can about a new activity, skill or behaviour before they venture into *doing* anything. In some cases, the knowledge or understanding seems as important as the end product – the outcome itself. Such people gain satisfaction through knowing, sometimes without actually experiencing something in real life. A knowing person:

- values knowledge for its own sake
- will probably obtain all the information possible before making a commitment to do anything, and often gets no further than the knowing part of the process
- will probably read all the literature they can find about a car, computer or a holiday before committing to buying
- reads a large number of non-fiction books
- often uses the words 'know', 'understand', 'study', 'learn', 'find out' and similar
- asks questions, and listens well.

Although difficult for an action-oriented person to understand, knowing, to them, brings pleasure, a sense of power, a feeling of security or some other benefit. *Knowing* will also probably figure large in their approach to goals, as well as in their unconscious desires and intentions.

GETTING/HAVING

Another category of people has a particular interest in *things*. They need to *get* and to *have* for their main satisfaction. We might call them acquisitive or materialistic. They want to get and have more of the world's goods, and use words like 'getting', 'having', 'things', 'acquiring' and 'mine'. This may not always refer to material possessions or the tangible evidence of wealth and success. Sometimes, for instance, a person wants evidence of a personal achievement (of a 'doing' goal, for example) such as learning a language or acquiring a skill, in the form of a certificate, token reward or other evidence of recognition. In such cases, what a person *gets* may prove worthless in itself – especially in the longer term – but nevertheless symbolizes some activity or achievement. Such a person needs to *have* something to show what they have *done* or what they have grown to *know*.

People who concentrate on *getting* and having usually put knowing and understanding, and even doing in second place. If they can enjoy the end product without all the effort – fine. On buying a car or hi-fi, for instance, they will immediately enjoy the pleasure of having, and read the manuals later, if ever. You will easily recognize getting and having people, who opt for the latest gadget, and enjoy all the paraphernalia of a modern home and business. But you may notice more subtle evidence. The attraction of promotion at work might have as much to do with the prospect of a different chair, desk or room as with all the doing aspects of the new post, or the new relationships the job will open up. On a training course, some people will feel cheated if they do not leave the event with an armful of *things*.

RELATING

Some people rank *relating* to others as the most important part of their Life Content. We would probably call them a 'people person'. Such people concern themselves with other people's feelings, and what they might think. They don't do or learn things without outside recognition in mind. They ask of themselves, 'What will so-and-so think (of me)?' To identify them:

- Listen for words like 'relating', 'communication', 'in touch' and 'feeling'.
- Listen for people's names.
- Bear in mind that what people *think* or *feel* ranks high on their agenda. This sometimes includes deceased parents, rival siblings, bosses and subordinates.
- The kind of club they attend, car they buy, or sports they involve themselves in will reflect what they think somebody else thinks about them.

Relating people often seem to put someone else's interests before their own. They might well enjoy involvement in action and having or getting, but their real interest lies in the effect this will have on their reputation, popularity and important relationships. This need not imply altruism. Clearly, whatever our Life Content profile, we gain pleasure or benefit out of whatever strategy we adopt in our day-to-day behaviour – even if we pursue that pleasure unconsciously.

BEING

Others put *place* first, in both a physical and metaphysical sense. They use words like 'home' and 'being'. They will say 'I want to *be*' rather than 'I want to *know*' – or to *do*, to *get* or to *have*. For example, some people want *to be* settled or *to be* content or *to be* financially independent and this seems to dominate their lives.

This characteristic relates closely to personal identity, the person's position or role in the world, the community, or their place in history. Initially, this may seem like a semantic distinction. For example, one person might say 'I am a writer' (being), while another might say 'I write books' (doing), but each of these ways of experiencing and achieving outcomes will determine a person's behaviour in given situations. A person who *is* a writer, nurse, soldier, or comedian *acts* like that – but for reasons of identity, rather than the pleasure of *doing*. Life Content characteristics extend even beyond attitude, and affect our beliefs, values and identity, but none so much as *being*.

IDENTIFYING YOUR LIFE CONTENT PROFILE

Each of these Life Content types will probably seem familiar to you. To start with, you know people who exhibit these characteristics. But also, we all have some tendency to each, and thus can relate at least to some degree to the different behaviour of others. Nevertheless, we often have an intuitive preference, which dictates how we behave, especially in important decisions and life changes. Knowing your preference means knowing yourself at a very basic level, where excellence starts.

If you have not yet identified a dominant characteristic in your own life, think back to different occasions, such as major purchases or holidays, or pastimes and social involvement, to see whether any tendency comes first. By now, you may have identified some or all of these characteristics in your own life.

EXERCISE 3.1

LIFE CONTENT PROFILE

If you cannot readily identify which of the five characteristics comes first in your life, and the order in which the others appear, a simple exercise should make it clear. It will also identify the order in which you apply these criteria in your life:

1   Start by asking yourself, 'What is really important to me?', and write down your answer, expressing yourself *instinctively* rather than in carefully chosen words. Notice which Life Content area your answer lies in – doing, knowing, obtaining and having, relating, or being? You can usually tell by the words you use. If you want to 'sell more', this denotes a concern for doing. However, if you want to *be* a sales manager, or *be* salesperson of the month, that suggests a *being* preference. If you describe a goal as to 'have' or 'get' such and such, your answer will fall in the *getting/having* category. But you can usually allocate a goal to a category, whatever language you use, by its implication or meaning. For example, if you want to double your monthly sales commission or qualify for a better car, it would seem you fit the *getting/having* category. If you wish to provide for your family, do something for somebody

else's sake, create or strengthen an important relationship, or 'show' a particular person you can do it, your goal will fall into the *relating* category,

2   Then ask yourself: 'If I had that object of desire, fully and completely, then what?' Notice the answer that intuitively comes to mind, and write it down. This again will probably fall within one of the five Life Content areas. For instance, you might say that by selling more you would *have* more money, or *get* that new car or house. Therefore, *getting* follows doing. The words we use tell us how we think.

3   Then, based on your last answer, ask yourself again, 'If I had the object of that desire, fully and completely, then what?' Once again, write down your answer. For instance, you might decide that by getting more money or the house of your choice, you would find happiness or contentment. Here you have moved into the *being* category. 'If I had that, I would *be* happy.'

4   Ask the question once again, this time in response to your answer to step 3, and again write down the answer that comes to mind. Repeat this step until you have a combination of Life Content category cycles that brings you back to one you have already written down. You have now exhausted your own range of content areas, and you have arranged them in some order.

5   You now have a series of content areas for your life. For instance, *doing* to *getting* to *being* to *relating*.

6   Return to step 1, and ask yourself again, 'What's really important to me?' As you think about this, ask yourself, 'Is there anything I need to do, know, get or have or relate or be, in order to gain this?', and again notice the answer, if any. If something further comes to mind, it might well open up a different content area. For example, you might decide that in order to sell more, you need to *know* more, which would involve some sort of training. How you *express* this training outcome will further indicate your life content preference, so describe it in words you would use instinctively.

7   Now take a careful look at the combination of categories you have written down. This constitutes your personal Life Content pattern or profile. It should seem immediately familiar, because you have probably followed this pattern time and time again in the past in activities, work and family life. You may not have allocated your outcomes to all five categories, but that doesn't matter. And you may have more than one of each category – such as *have* this, *get* that and *get* so-and-so in order to *do* something then *do* something else. Or a repeated sequence like get–do–get–do–get–do. However many repetitions of a category or sequence, this indicates a *getting–doing* sequence somewhere in your profile.

Your preference, if you have one, will reveal itself simply as the category that appears in your list the most. You might reveal, or confirm, for example, a *doing* or a *getting* preference if either of those appeared most.

Whatever you identify in this exercise represents your unique profile, including the order in which the elements appear. You can now check the process once again, using different examples. You may surprise yourself by discovering that your cycle of Life Content reappears in the same order for different outcomes. This confirms the way you consistently experience these high-level, goal-achieving master strategies in your life.

The sequence you have identified has special significance. For example, a person might always seem to put *doing* or *getting* first to fulfil a more important *being* goal. This suggests that the *being* goal lies higher in their hierarchy of desires and life purposes. Maybe a person usually needs to acquire some knowledge (like a qualification) before proceeding to their *doing* goal (such as a new kind of job), in order to *get* a higher salary, in order to salvage a rocky marriage (*relating*) in order to be happy. That indicates a *knowing–doing–having–relating–being* Life Content profile. By carrying out this exercise, you will get to know yourself better. It explains some of the ways you have behaved in the past that have resulted in your present identity.

USING LIFE CONTENT KNOWLEDGE

Having considered your preference, and the weighting of your Life Content, you may then wish to change the order, or syntax, of some of them to correct an imbalance you feel in your life. This may particularly apply, for instance, to a very active, *doing* person, and a person who falls at the other extreme of having cerebral knowledge, but little experience. In the first case, you may decide to put knowing first – in importance as well as in sequence – and in the second case, get on and do things first.

You can also use this information in various specific ways. If you wish to embark on an important activity in the future, you might do well to follow a tried and tested pattern that has proved successful in the past. For instance, if in a past successful outcome you felt happier *knowing* about something before you committed to *doing* it, perhaps you should not shortcut the *knowing* stage in the future, even if not always as attractive as *having* and *getting*. Conversely, you may recall times when you missed out one stage and came to grief. Knowing your profile, and in hindsight, you acted, almost literally, *out of character*. It just happens that instinctively you need to know about things *before* you commit yourself either to doing or having. You have therefore learned, or at least confirmed, what seems comfortable and right for you.

CHANGING YOUR LIFE CONTENT WEIGHTING

You might also reconsider and maybe change the weighting and also order of your Life Content elements. You may, for instance, want to place less importance on getting and *having*, and more on *knowing*, including knowledge just for the pleasure of learning. Or you may feel that you need to balance your life by *doing* much more, getting more actively involved in things rather than just *knowing* or watching like a 'passenger'. Or you may recognize the *relating* part of your Life Content as rather weak, and consciously desire to weight it more strongly.

The *being* element frequently comes at the end of the sequence, and this illustrates a person's hierarchy of goals, which, for most individuals, culminates in outcomes like 'contentment', 'fulfilment' and 'personal happiness' – in other words, *being* what you want. You might determine that *being* will form the most important aspect of your life. In that case, using what you learn from NLP, you might well manage to by-pass some of the other Life Content categories and reach the *being* state of mind that you desire. You thus have discovered an effective, more direct route to reaching your desired state of *being*.

Acting upon such a discovery will mean some changes, of course. However, you will probably save yourself the years that many people invest in interim goals they think will give them the happiness they seek, only to meet disappointment and apparent failure. By focusing on *being* goals, you will learn to live in the present, and suffer fewer of the regrets even apparently successful people feel in later life.

Notice that the *being* category predominantly reflects a state of mind. One person, for example, feels financially secure in circumstances in which another would feel insecure. One person feels happy without the material possessions another person deems essential for happiness. You can use some of the techniques in the following chapter to test or 'future pace' your goals, in whatever category they fall. That means that once you have gained knowledge of yourself by identifying your Life Content traits, you have *choices* as regards your future. This, like any NLP model, helps us to create choices

DEVELOPING RAPPORT

An understanding of this pattern can also help you to understand other people, and develop the rapport that you need for effective communication. You can imagine, for instance, how these Life Content preferences affect learning and training. You will probably have met trainees who immediately want to become involved in action (*doing*) of any sort rather than go through the drudgery of learning and understanding things. You will also have met trainees (and indeed trainers) who put *relating* very high on their list, and always seem concerned about what others think in the learning process, and others, again, who only seem concerned with the eventual certificate, or salary increase, or other *getting* or *having* that will result from a training programme. You will find the same sort of knowledge useful in dealing with customers and clients, suppliers, scholars, work colleagues, family and friends.

Knowledge of this important aspect of a person will reveal more of their personal map of the world. Knowledge of your own Life Content profile will add significantly to your intrapersonal intelligence. You can bridge the gap between your map and theirs to communicate more effectively.

4 *Well-formed Outcomes*

A few common-sense criteria apply to what NLP calls 'a well-formed outcome'. This chapter describes the 'well-formedness' criteria, and explains how you can apply them to your goals in order to increase the chances of succeeding. You may have encountered some of them before in different forms, such as the popular SMART formula:

- **S**pecific
- **M**easurable
- **A**chievable
- **R**ealistic
- **T**imely.

With your knowledge of the NLP model and awareness of unconscious intentions, you can apply these sorts of goal criteria far more effectively. Rather than just willing yourself to succeed, or repeating positive 'affirmations', you can mirror processes that your brain already uses in achieving outcomes as a matter of routine.

Self-belief affects how we behave and achieve outcomes. A 'loser' self-belief, for instance, will not benefit a person's achievement record. Likewise, the way we approach goal achievement – such as through our Life Content profile – usually dictates ultimate success or failure. To state the obvious: it all *happens in the mind*.

I used to ask trainees to suspend belief. Although this appears a creative, flexible thing to do, I have since wondered what message we transmit to our unconscious mind when suspending belief. Which beliefs do you suspend? Obviously, beliefs that might hinder your options for acquiring new knowledge; beliefs you don't want, rather than beliefs you want. However, to know what you don't want to believe, you have to *think* about it. Then you have to think about it *more* in order to firmly establish your new belief and abandon the old one. As it happens, you may not have thought of that limiting belief for some time. Nor would you on this occasion if you did not have to suspend belief, or 'not believe' it. So, paradoxically, by 'suspending belief' you encounter negative thoughts unnecessarily.

In this case, leave well alone. Don't suspend anything. Simple, positive presuppositions of the sort discussed in Chapter 2 can slide into your unconscious mind, and form as good a basis as any for applying the outcome criteria in this chapter. Put another way, when considering your goals – what you want – don't believe, or suspend judgement; just pretend, or imagine – for a little while anyway.

Much conventional psychology involves digging up a negative, incriminating past before you ever get started. On the contrary, when considering goals NLP-style, you can leave old beliefs and goals behind. If they emerge as part of the processes you will meet – fine. Otherwise, like a track through a forest, they will soon become overgrown without any bother or attention. You don't need to put effort into blocking off old, redundant, neural networks when you have an almost infinite capacity to create new ones. Like an unused limb, any brain function soon stops functioning with disuse. So not only will redundant neural networks stop running your behaviour, you won't burn up oxygen and other fuels to keep these mental pathways in good repair.

The well-formed outcome criteria that follow will enable you to set clear, positive goals that have the best chance of success.

Positive

State your outcome in the positive. When asked what they want, many people start by recounting what they *don't* want. That works fine as a process of elimination, but it can have an unwanted, unpredictable effect, as your brain interprets such statements in a special way. The human brain doesn't seem to take account of negative injunctions like 'don't'. So 'Don't spill it!' – a common parental injunction to little children – records the central action word 'spill', and sure enough they spill it. You can produce the same magical effect with 'Don't trip!', 'Don't touch!', and so on. As we have just seen, 'suspend belief' can have the same counterproductive effect.

This means that we 'read' negative outcomes as positive. The brain pictures what it can picture (and hear and feel), rather than sensory-barren little words like 'don't'. Thus, by repeating what you don't want, you unwittingly signal your unconscious mind to quietly get on with its task. Failure results, or a sense of disappointment or puzzlement. Worst of all, you don't know *why*. You can make neither rhyme nor reason of why you habitually behave in a certain way and experience outcomes you didn't want.

You can check this positive criterion by examining the language you use, so it helps to make a list of your outcomes expressed as ordinary statements. Start by restating each goal in positive terms. To do this, you may have to adjust your desired outcome slightly, and think of new words that describe what you really want. You may require more than a mechanical reversal. In any event, your final, reconsidered, re-expressed outcome will finish up closer to what you really want. For example:

- **Negative:** I don't want to get into a dead-end job.
- **Positive:** I want a job with opportunities.

You might re-express this goal as:

- I want a job that will allow time off and sponsorship to study for qualifications.
- I want to work in a large company with plenty of room for promotion.

You could substitute whatever you mean by 'opportunities'. In short, make it positive but more specific and *useful* as a goal.

THE POWER OF POSITIVE QUESTIONS

Apposite questions help. You can hardly avoid accessing the appropriate part of your brain when posed a question. You may consider 'Was it sunny?' an irrelevant, illogical or plain stupid question. But in order to classify it as such, you would have to give it meaning – and that means doing a mental trawl of 'sunny', the perceived context of the question, your belief about the sanity of the questioner, and a hundred other sophisticated, parallel neural searches. So – like it or not – you have responded to the question, and in doing so have given it a thorough, unconscious once-over.

You can easily build up a checklist of probing questions that require you to use your inner senses. I have suggested a few questions for each of the 'well-formed goal' criteria shown in Figure 4.1. You will find these useful in many different outcome situations, along with other questions scattered throughout the book. For the moment, check your positive criteria by asking yourself questions such as:

- What do I want?
- What would I like to achieve?
- In what way do I wish to change?
- What will it look/sound/feel like?

These criteria build on the outcome models described in Chapter 3. They don't replace them. Keep those models in mind as you set positive, unambiguous targets for your inner goal-achieving system and clearly express your 'desired state'. I've included seven – eight if we include 'state in the positive'. Some of these overlap a bit, and some combine criteria sometimes listed separately.

Start by making a list of your wants, desires, hopes, and so on. Do this quickly and intuitively, rather than carefully thinking it out. Just as when in brainstorming mode, don't judge or evaluate. In this way, you will produce a comprehensive list that draws on your unconscious mind. With a well-rehearsed set of conscious goals, you will have plenty of material on which to practise the tests that follow. If you have less than a couple of dozen, keep writing – do some more hoping and dreaming. You've nothing to lose, and a whole future to win. Getting what you want starts with well-formed outcomes.

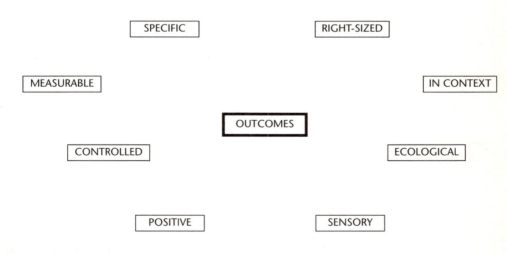

Figure 4.1   Criteria for well-formed goals

Specific

Express your goal specifically. At too high or abstract a level, the sincerest desire has no effect on the neural networks that ultimately produce all human achievement. 'I want to be happy' qualifies as a perfectly valid sentiment, but not as a well-formed outcome. Your internal goal-achieving mechanism – more sophisticated than any intercontinental missile system – depends on having a specific target. Otherwise, you could land anywhere in the 'world' you don't want, rather than within the specific target you want.

What do you mean when you say 'I want to be happy', 'I want to be in good health', 'I want to be financially independent', and so on? In turn, what does 'financially independent' *mean* (to you)? Try to express each outcome on your list specifically. Do you want to run a mile in ten minutes, climb the stairs without going dizzy, or weigh in at nine stone? What does 'good health' *mean*? What do you want *specifically*?

HIERARCHY OF GOALS

Being specific usually means descending your 'hierarchy' of goals (see Figure 3.1) from the long-term pinnacle of Happiness, Pleasure and Fulfilment to a short-term, more tangible goal. But that doesn't mean downgrading your objectives. In most cases, you will only reach higher goals by fulfilling the lower, or interim, goals on which they depend. What may seem like lowering your sights may prove the best goal-achievement strategy in the end.

For example, you may have to study to obtain qualifications in order to fulfil a job or career outcome, and in turn the goal of financial independence, then on to ultimate happiness and fulfilment. Probably several specific outcomes will combine to produce 'happiness', 'contentment', or whatever ultimate desire you had in mind. So a specific goal makes strategic sense when you want to move nearer to important life goals.

MAKING YOUR GOAL SPECIFIC

Making a goal specific may require more than making it positive. If you want to learn a particular language, for instance, you need to specify to what level – well enough to:

- get by on holiday?
- pass an exam?
- converse sufficiently in the language to take a job abroad?
- read novels in the original language?

If you want a better job:

- What kind of job?
- What salary and conditions?
- How far will you move away from home if you have to?

Specifying a new job doesn't create jobs that don't exist (say, in your neighbourhood), of course, or any other outcome. But without knowing specifically what you want, you don't have much chance of getting it anyway. Nor will you ever know whether you really achieved what you wanted or not. 'Outcome ambiguity' can sometimes provide a handy excuse, but at the same time signals low self-esteem. It will help little towards actual achievement.

Setting specific goals means you will sometimes have to face the fact that you didn't get what you wanted. On the other hand, when you do succeed you will have the special pleasure of knowing you got exactly what you set out to get. That will boost your self-esteem, and add ideal experience for proceeding to new and bigger specific achievements.

The more specific your goal, the less you can deceive yourself about what you need to do and your commitment to it. For example, people find that a specific dieting or weight goal works out better than just aspiring to 'better health'.

Go through your list of outcomes ruthlessly with a red pen and make them specific. If you can't put a goal into words, or better still, *see* it in mind pictures, it doesn't pass this test. So strike it off, or restate a specific *aspect* or *part* of the outcome you want. Better to give your attention to specific outcomes that have a good chance of success. That way, in the process, you will probably fulfil some 'unconscious intention' that you could not express in words. Remember the Positive rule, and also the presuppositions discussed in Chapter 2. Everything you have learnt so far remains valid as you learn new things.

EXERCISE 4.1

CHECKING FOR WELL-FORMED OUTCOMES

Making your goal specific doesn't guarantee success. To make your outcome well-formed, you need to apply all these criteria. But you have taken a real step towards changing your future, and your outcomes now have far more value than a list of wants and wishes.

In undertaking this exercise, you may need to completely rethink your desires. Some may disappear. New outcomes might occur to you. Moreover, as you make your outcomes more specific, you may find yourself wanting them more, just as you desire a holiday destination or dream car more as you learn more about it. The 'well-formedness' process reveals your motivation and commitment, and brings unconscious intentions to the surface. These important goal fundamentals will add to your chances of success.

Ask yourself these sorts of questions:

✓   What, specifically, do I want?
✓   How will I know without any doubt that I have achieved my goal?
✓   What evidence will I need to show others I have reached my goal?
✓   What, specifically, do I mean …?
✓   Can I specify size, shape, colour, texture and any other sensory characteristics or qualities?

A specific outcome has a better-than-average chance of success. In conjunction with the other 'well-formedness' criteria, you multiply your chances of finally getting and 'being' what you want in life.

Sensory

Express your outcome in sensory terms. What will you see, hear and feel when you have what you want? We represent 'real' experiences, like memories, in this sensory way, of course. A well-formed outcome will seem like a real life experience as you imagine it happening. Your mind then 'believes' that it has happened, and helps you to 're-run' it like a real-life memory.

Once you can visualize it clearly internally, an *imaginable* goal translates to a *realistic* goal for you, however big a hurdle it may have seemed rationally. If you say 'I can't imagine doing that', you probably won't. Conversely, when you say 'I can just see myself doing so-and-so', you have already started to make it happen.

This sensory part of the 'well-formedness' process serves several important functions:

- You automatically make your outcome more specific. You cannot easily express a nominal goal such as happiness in sensory terms unless you think of an experience that represents or *means* happiness. The sensory *image* of happiness, rather than the abstract concept, forms the specific outcome your goal-achieving system will pursue.

- You will test your outcome for realism and achievability. As we have seen, something that you cannot imagine, you probably cannot achieve. Behaviour and its consequences start in the mind. So unless you fix your outcome clearly in your mind (in sensory 'format', as the NLP model describes), you don't have a blueprint for success. Individual desires have lots of competition. Another desire will try to take its place. Like imagination, potential outcomes are unlimited, once you start to identify the unconscious ones and identify the self-beliefs that hinder you. So those that you envision in sensory terms rise to the top of the pile to translate into reality. They qualify as well-formed, not just in the specific way you state them, but also in the internal, sensory, neural networks that create them. Successful outcomes start in your inner world, and then translate into feelings, beliefs, behaviour and actual achievements in the outer world. Create them as you intend to experience them – in pleasurable, multi-sensory mode.

- In sensory outcomes, you imagine the *evidence* of success. You have something to 'show' for it – something you and others can see, hear and perhaps feel. This transforms an otherwise abstract wish into a tangible goal. Importantly, evidence can convince *other people* of our success, and for many people this forms part of their success.

- You experience a little of the real outcome as a sort of down payment, or trial, as when test-driving a new car. How often have you experienced more pleasure in dreaming about a coming holiday than from the actual event? Pre-experiencing, or future pacing, happens as we refine our sensory representation of the outcome to bring it close to reality. Of course, in 'inside mode' you don't have to imagine delayed flights, stolen credit cards, or any of the usual holiday anticlimaxes, so the inner experience captures the pleasure without the disadvantages. This natural process has its practical uses. If you don't like what you imagine, you will probably not enjoy the real thing. Put another way, you might do better without the holiday, visit to the in-laws, ten-mile walk, new car, and so on. By applying the sensory criterion, you will have the chance to eliminate or amend the outcomes you had listed. One seminar delegate imagined a particular kind of holiday in a remote location, of the sort he had never experienced but often dreamed about. On subjecting his outcome to the full 'sensory treatment', he found that after the third day he got bored and started arguing with his wife. So he changed his mind about this particular outcome, saving himself money, time and marital unrest.

Your mind knows best, from your lifetime database, how you will react to any sensory experience. To gain the most out of this well-formed outcome process, you will need to trust your own imagination and tap your unconscious mind. Ask yourself these sorts of questions:

✓   What will I see, hear or feel when I have fully achieved my outcome?
✓   What else will happen?
✓   How will I feel if I succeed in this goal?

In context

See your outcome in the context you desire it. When imagining an outcome, we usually picture ourselves in a certain situation, or setting. This happens automatically when you express an abstract desire, such as happiness, in sensory terms – you think of an occasion, situation or context. This reflects the different 'parts' of your life, such as work, social, home, weekends, holidays and so forth.

Nevertheless, an outcome that passes the 'well-formedness' tests in one context might not do so in another. This means making your outcome more specific, but in a particular way: to reflect the different contexts in which the outcome may apply. Ask, for instance, when, where and with whom do you want this to happen?

Usually, a goal applies to a particular context – the one you imagined when you intuitively formed the desire. The test here involves checking for undesirable effects of the outcome in other parts of your life. You can do this by carrying out the process consciously – perhaps following a simple checklist of the different areas of your life. Explore each possible effect, and notice how you feel about it. Use the same sensory process as in the previous test, but this time consider the context in particular.

CONTEXT-SPECIFIC CHECKS

To take an example, you might wish to improve your communication skills, but on applying the Context criterion you find that 'what you had in mind' related to a particular communication problem concerning one work colleague. It so happens you have no problems communicating at home, with friends and with other work colleagues. In this case, you will probably do better to leave well enough alone and tackle your problem *as a specific problem* (perhaps using some of the NLP communication skills you will learn shortly) rather than as one requiring a major life shift. You might revise your outcome, for example, to 'to get through to Jim', 'transfer to another department' or 'learn to be thick-skinned'. Make it context-specific. You may have noticed this in the Specific test, so each criterion acts as a double-check.

To check for context, imagine your goals in association with different places, at different times (the T in the SMART model), and involving different people. Build all these scenarios into your mental picture. Real-life situations happen in real contexts such as these. Rather than work and home life in general, for instance, you may imagine very specific contexts in which you would not want your outcome, as you start to notice some of the drawbacks ('I don't want to act in that way with Gary.').

Similarly, you may notice benefits of an outcome in specific contexts that you had not thought about: for instance, having confidence in an upcoming interview, or speech or presentation you had to give, or in a sport you take part in. In this case, you can create a specific, new outcome that conforms to the 'well-formedness' tests. By considering contexts, you can finish up with better-formed outcomes than you started out with.

A 'well-formedness' test may well change the *value* you place on the outcome itself, or its ranking. In this case, you can amend or abandon it. The tests have done their job. Better to give it some thought now, rather than face disappointment after exerting wasted effort, and sacrificing other goals you could have achieved instead. Ask yourself these sorts of questions:

✓ In what situations will I use/benefit from my new outcome?
✓ When do I want to do or use this?
✓ When or where might I not want this?
✓ In what situations will my outcome not benefit me?
✓ Will this outcome be appropriate in every situation?
✓ In what other contexts might my outcome prove useful?
✓ Where will I experience this outcome?
✓ Do I want this all the time in all areas of my life?

The Context criterion doesn't imply that you cannot achieve outcomes that affect your whole life, or have to make changes that apply just to certain situations. You can – but after carrying out the various 'well-formedness' checks, you may prefer not to. With a well-formed outcome, you avoid surprises – at least the unpleasant ones you can do without.

Measurable

Try to make your goal quantifiable. This usually means more specific, of course, but the Measurable test needs special attention. Not every objective has a measure, but with a bit of thought you can usually apply one. Aiming for a weight of 8 stone meets the test well. The more measurable a goal, the more specific you will usually have to make it. In the language-learning example earlier, an external certificate of some sort would provide a useful measurement of success. Some examinations go further with A, B and C ranking.

TIMESCALE

Otherwise, you can set yourself a time limit. Timescale provides a form of measurement, and may also enhance motivation if you respond well to the challenge of a deadline. Ask: 'How quickly can I do this?'; 'By when can I have this finished?' The time factor adds a significant aspect of specificity.

QUALITY

Some goals don't have a quantitative measure, but you can measure them in quality. For example, if you aim for a better job, you can include in your visualization not just a measurable salary level, but also a swivel chair, company car, people's compliments and greater respect for you, and the better quality of life you can expect after your advancement – in fact, any degree of qualitative detail. You can even give qualitative goals some sort of measure, like a *five*-pedestal chair, a *two*-litre engine, or a *three*-week holiday. Apply your innate creativity from the earliest stage in setting your goals. The actual process of imagining these qualitative features will help to create the clear, cybernetic target upon which a successful outcome depends.

REAL MEMORY RESOURCES

Sometimes, we don't commit to too much detail in our hopes, in order to avoid disappointment in the event of failure. But your unconscious mind needs a specific target to aim for, at least, and a multi-sensory one at that. Real objects have sensory detail that you can measure in the *quality of the pleasure they bring*. For this reason, real memories that you have already experienced before in another context, such as on holiday, at a friend's house, in the chairman's office and so on, provide a yardstick of success. You may not measure your outcome in numbers, percentages or letter grades, but you can measure it against X or Y occasion in the past. This makes memories important resources you can harness for a better present-day life.

YOUR OUTCOME SPECIFICATION

Neurologically, your cybernetic goal-achieving system needs to pursue a realistic image – the basis of most of these outcome criteria. This doesn't mean following logical steps, but purposely marshalling your unconscious mind to do for you what it does all the time on autopilot. Making your goal measurable simply reinforces its realism, and reduces your scope for kidding yourself about your commitment, or about eventual success or failure. You can hardly complain if you don't achieve what you want if you didn't include it in your 'outcome specification'. You do this by adding it to your outcome list, and then applying these 'well-formedness' criteria to make it specific in every possible respect. Ask yourself, for example:

✓ How will I measure the degree of success or failure of my outcome?
✓ How can I make my outcome a quality one?
✓ How might other people (name them) rate my competence or level of achievement in reaching this outcome?
✓ What will be the outward evidence of my success?
✓ What will this outcome compare with?
✓ Have I ever come close to such an outcome in the past?

Right-sized

Size matters. Set your goal at a realistic, achievable, but also a motivating level. If your goal seems too big, you may 'blank out' and not even begin. Your conscious mind invents plausible excuses, and usually wins. Your unconscious mind doesn't pursue the outcome anyway, because it does not form a credible, motivating, realistic, sensory target to aim for. On the other hand, if you perceive a task as too easy, you may lack the motivation to see it through to the end. We each have an optimum size or complexity of outcome that incorporates, among other factors:

• stress threshold
• experience

- capabilities
- resources
- motivation.

An outcome should present a challenge, and stretch you – but not too much, or it may induce panic. You can always make your next goal a little bigger – or smaller – depending on how you perceive it, and how it affects you. Figure 4.2 illustrates the relationship between perceived level of difficulty and perceived ability to achieve an outcome. Striking precisely the right balance, associated with personal mastery, will have a significant effect on results.

CHUNKING

Fortunately, with a little thought, you can easily fulfil this 'perceived size' criterion. For instance, you can usually 'chunk down' a big task into smaller components. 'Chunking' simply means breaking down – or building up – tasks to form 'chunks' of the appropriate size. Just look on each chunk as a separate outcome, and subject it to all these tests. You can make a task bigger, either by combining (chunking) it with another, or simply by giving yourself a shorter timescale. Notice that if a goal seems impossible – 'beyond' you – it will not normally help if you give yourself more time. You will just put off starting for longer. Choose achievable, motivating stages or chunks.

Goal stages

The first stage might cover gathering information, setting the ball rolling, checking feasibility and so on, or finding someone who's done it before and picking their brains. Most

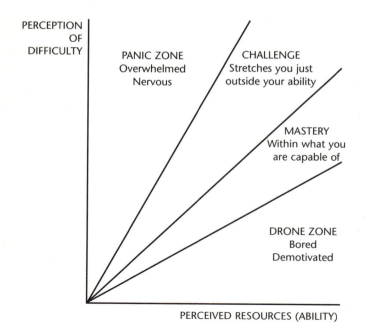

Figure 4.2   Perceived difficulty and ability

outcomes, in the form we conceive or present them, allow flexibility. You can change their *perceived* degree of difficulty in different ways and still get what you wanted. 'Perceived difficulty' concerns the way you feel personally about a task. It compares what you perceive about the task with what you perceive about your capability of achieving it. You can change how you think about both, which makes all manner of achievement *possible*. In your own 'real' world, that change may involve chunking down.

Chunking in context

As well as relating to your 'perceived capability', an outcome may seem bigger in the morning than in the evening, or when you arrive home compared with in the office, or when twisting and turning in bed in the middle of the night. Chunk size relates to context. More importantly, for present purposes, by subjecting an outcome to the well-formedness criteria, you will no doubt *perceive* the size differently anyway. So you may need to check on chunk size as you proceed – it changes.

This process happens inside, subjectively, regardless of your record of successes and failures in such outcomes. Thus, if you can clearly visualize yourself as having done something, it tends to create the belief that you can do it. In other words: it changes the perceived difficulty, or size.

Right-sized chunks

Don't opt for small or big chunks as such, but *right-sized chunks* – the right size for you. As you visualize your outcome according the 'sensory evidence' test, do you feel motivated, bored, scared – or numb? You may find that as you adjust your goal for other 'well-formedness' reasons – such as to make it more specific or measurable – its desirability and challenge will also change.

Likewise, as you apply each criterion, you will probably *feel* differently. Any outcome check may mean relegating a strong desire to further down your 'desirable' list. Or you may have to change an outcome out of all recognition and start your outcome process from scratch.

Typically, by spending time enjoying the final sensory rewards of success, you will increase your motivation to begin and gain the confidence to pull it off. It therefore makes sense to treat chunk size, including timescale, as an optional variable. Chunking forms such an important aspect of goal-achievement that it can operate as a philosophy of life. It concerns putting things in proportion, which has significance when attaining the ultimate human goals.

To apply the Right-sized outcome criterion, ask these sorts of questions:

- Is my goal too much for me to cope with?
- Will I be motivated right through to completion?
- How happy will I be if I achieve my goal?
- Will I be surprised at my own ability?
- Could I do this in less time?
- Would it be more realistic if I gave myself some extra time?
- Would this break down into two or three different outcomes that I would really enjoy doing?
- What could I do right now to make a start?

Controlled

Choose a goal you can achieve with your own resources. This concerns the extent to which your outcome lies within your personal control or influence. You need to assume throughout that you have responsibility for whether you achieve or don't achieve your outcomes. It then makes sense that you should have control over what you accept responsibility for. If you have something or somebody to blame (even if right at the back of your mind), your goal may not amount to much. Conversely, if you apply this criterion, the credit for success can only go to you, and that will improve your confidence and motivation in further outcomes.

'OTHER PEOPLE' GOALS

Two main categories of outcome apply here:

* Often, we adopt goals *on behalf* of other people, or with their welfare in mind. Unfortunately, fulfilling other people's goals, however worthy the motive, doesn't usually work. Parents know that their lofty ambitions for their children may not materialize, however specific, positive and sensory-based. People – including children – have goals of their own. Similarly, at work we adopt company or team goals. Again, you don't necessarily 'own' these goals, which in any case usually involve other people. Whatever your level of dedication, unless you have enough control, such as in the role of managing director or project manager, ultimate success lies outside your personal remit. Better in this case to gain control of the critical part of any project (see Chapter 23 on negotiation), or any specific part for which you can then safely accept responsibility.

* Your goals will often *involve* other people. For instance, you may depend on someone lending you money, acting as a partner, attending rehearsals, taking early retirement, and so forth. If you fail because somebody lets you down, you have wasted effort from the outset, in terms of well-formed outcomes. This doesn't mean that you can never rely on other people. You simply cannot set and undertake a well-formed outcome on that basis with a high probability of success. As a minimum, you will *perceive and value* your outcome differently from other people, so your motivation will differ, as will the effect of any conflicting goals that might have an impact on your present one.

Fortunately, you can usually find ways to circumvent control issues. For instance, you might restrict your outcome to part of a total goal (such as a corporate plan, or team project) within your personal control. This may require forethought and negotiation, but may save you a big disappointment. Other people involved in a bigger goal can set their outcomes, of course, but for present purposes, don't concern yourself with that. Only they can set well-formed outcomes for themselves or on behalf of a group or organization. You have no certainty of control over other people – managing your own unconscious mind will provide a big enough challenge.

According to this criterion, an objective 'to get on better with my boss' would not qualify as well-formed. You can't control their thoughts and behaviour. On the other hand, *how you react* to your boss does lie within your control, and you can learn NLP techniques for controlling your state of mind. In this case, you can adjust your outcome – to *understand* your boss better, maybe, or react differently, or have different feelings about it – to bring it within your personal control. Notice that 'to get on better with my boss' doesn't meet the Specific test, or the Measurable one. These tests usually go hand in hand.

START NEAR TO HOME

The Control criterion makes sense anyway. Usually, it pays to start with *yourself* when tackling any problem, and especially one involving people. A change of attitude, for instance, can sometimes eliminate a problem altogether. In addition, the ability to make changes of this sort will hold good in other situations. You may find that you solve several problems at once by concentrating on your inner feelings rather than a person's external behaviour (which you can't control). Chapter 19 on reframing will give you ideas about how to see things from different perspectives. That change of viewpoint – within your control – may alter both your attitude and your desires.

This criterion does not mean that you have to operate solo and refuse help. On the contrary. The benefits of NLP communication skills include influencing people to help you achieve your outcomes, in a win–win way. It just means that you don't depend on people and resources that you don't have and may not obtain. Nor do you blame people when they let you down – making 'people' judgements forms part of a successful outcome, and your responsibility. If you can use outside people resources *en route* to your outcome, treat it as a bonus, but don't bank on it.

INNER RESOURCES

Fulfilling an outcome independently may depend on whether you have the innate resources to achieve it. This concerns not so much outside material resources, but rather inner resources you can call upon. You can treat external resources such as money, tools, accommodation and the like as *separate outcomes*. In other words, organize your outcomes – including skills and other resources – into right-sized chunks. On the other hand, if you can cope with the size of your overall outcome, then you can treat gathering whatever resources you need as just another task (or series of tasks) among perhaps many that you will need to carry out on the road to final success.

Resources may include knowledge, skills and attitude. As well as adding to your knowledge, you can *acquire* skills, so you don't have to depend on innate talents (if you have them). As with any other resources you need, acquiring a skill can rank as an important outcome in its own right, such as learning to drive a car or use a computer. In this case, you will need to subject it to the 'well-formedness' tests, as with any goal.

Have you got what it takes?

'Resources' such as your age and physical build might also make a goal unrealistic. You can't regain lost years or 'add one cubit to your stature'. Aiming for the top in a physical sport may demand youth and physical build, for example – at least within certain margins. You will probably find yourself too old for some goals, and too young (for the moment) for others. These sorts of innate resources reflect whether 'you have it or you don't', *in relation to the outcome you want to achieve*.

This need not limit you much for most purposes. You probably know of people who have achieved similar outcomes at an older (or younger) age than you, and from a less advantageous starting point. According to the (paraphrased) presupposition 'If anyone can do it, I can', you can sometimes make a very ambitious outcome quite realistic. This test involves honesty with yourself, and perhaps seeking the advice of a close, equally honest friend.

However, all the other criteria still apply. Thus, sometimes a person may have the courage and stamina to achieve outstanding feats, but will not experience the pleasure they hoped for because of conflicting, unconscious intentions that pull them in other directions. We may achieve miracles, but if they don't take us to a desired state, we will know only hollow and short-lived success.

TEAM OUTCOMES

You can't treat Control as a black and white issue. It depends on the circumstances. A manager, for example, might reasonably treat a team or departmental project as their personal outcome. By virtue of role, position in the company hierarchy and ability to influence others, a leader will have enough control to assume responsibility and treat a team or corporate goal as a well-formed personal outcome. This would apply as much to a sports coach or manager or an orchestral conductor as to a business manager. On the other hand, a co-ordination or advisory role may not offer such influence over others. Similarly, an ordinary team member, or employee in a small company, even if influential, probably couldn't treat a team or company project as a well-formed personal outcome.

We usually have more than enough outcomes fighting for priority status. It therefore makes sense to abandon or amend a goal over which you don't have control. That might not work in an employment situation, but non-achievement at work due to lack of control will not do much for a person's career anyway. At best, you would have a lower chance of success than for an outcome that passed all the well-formed tests, including Control. For this reason, it pays to agree resources and responsibility at the outset, rather than when any excuse will seem lame.

Better, therefore, to set a well-formed goal that will *contribute* to team or organizational success. A soccer striker can aim for goal outcomes. A goalkeeper can aim for saves. But neither can take control of the target of promotion to the next division. Ask yourself questions such as:

✓ What will I do, personally, to achieve this goal?
✓ Have I done something similar to this before?
✓ Might anything or any person prevent me from achieving this fully?
✓ Can I implement any changes needed myself?
✓ How much of this lies within my control?
✓ Do I depend on anyone, or any resources, to achieve my goal?
✓ Do I need outside help?

Ecological

Think through all the indirect effects of your outcome. Ecology in the context of goals seems peculiar to NLP. It just means taking account of the wider, indirect effects of any outcome, such as on other people. You might liken this to the 'butterfly effect' mentioned in the Preface, in which a butterfly flapping its wings will ultimately affect the weather at the other side of the world. You need to make a goal right for you in your life as a whole.

This may involve other people, of course. Whilst you may not have responsibility for outcomes that *depend* on other people, you probably do take responsibility for the *effect* of your own outcomes on others. This becomes an 'ecological' issue in the event that you care about such people. In such cases, you will not really have achieved what you wanted if the negative effects on other people outweigh the pleasure you gain from the outcome in isolation. In fact, ecological effects can apply whether you care or not, or whether you know or not, as in the butterfly effect. The past has a habit of coming back to haunt us.

This criterion usually goes deeper than you might at first expect. We usually instinctively 'preview' a desire and imagine how it feels, just as we daydream about a coming holiday. However, we may not so instinctively put ourselves into other people's shoes and imagine how they will feel because of our behaviour or a changed situation. We can usually tolerate this in the case of strangers or people we don't want to take into account in this way. Well-formed outcome criteria don't imply moral judgements, but concern the effectiveness of achieving *any* goal. Once you identify ecological factors, you can *choose* whether to go ahead with your goal, amend it, or ignore the side effects you have identified. An ecological outcome means you have a better chance of achieving a final outcome that gives you the pleasure you wanted.

Ecology ranks as the main criterion in most outcomes, mainly because it will not usually surface in a conscious, logical appraisal of an outcome. And even the unconscious aspects of outcomes can vary greatly in the degree of indirect or marginal effects they have. You need to question your intentions from as many points of view as possible so that conflicting intentions will surface to your conscious mind. You thought earlier about the context or different areas of your life in which you will enjoy your goal. Ecological conflict – whether the effect on other people or on your other goals – may emerge in situations you had not considered.

Communicating with your unconscious mind to identify the ecology of an outcome will require a 'downtime' mode, perhaps more so than the previous, more logical tests. At the same time, self-questioning will help to explore as many aspects as possible. You can't logically *design* ideal questions of this sort, so you may need to resort to volume, just as when initially brainstorming for creative ideas. But even one naïve question can turn a would-be failure into success. For example:

✓   Who or what else might be affected if I achieve this goal?
✓   How will my life differ when this happens?
✓   What would *not* happen if I achieved this?
✓   In what way is this outcome important to me?
✓   Will this serve me well?
✓   Am I committed to this goal?
✓   Will this enhance my life?
✓   Is there anything else to bear in mind?
✓   Will this make me feel empowered?
✓   Is this really important to me?
✓   How will this fit my life at work/home/the club? (Specify)
✓   Am I prepared to pay the price?

✓   Does anything stop me from ...?
✓   Is there any part of me that would object to this outcome?
✓   Would I like to have achieved this in full by tomorrow morning?
✓   Am I sure this is what I really want?
✓   What might be the disadvantages?
✓   If I could change one aspect of my outcome, what would it be?
✓   How soon do I want to be able to use/have this?

Have the courage to amend or delete goals as these questions reveal ecological issues you had not considered.

By applying these criteria to anything you want to achieve, you will multiply your chances of success, and probably take more pleasure in your final outcome. The well-formedness testing process will soon seem intuitive, so not only will you no longer need to put in time and effort, but also it will happen unconsciously. In other words, you learn goal-achieving as an automatic skill – like riding a bike, swimming or peeling an orange. It means you have established the habit of success. Don't treat goal-setting as a one-off event. See it as a way of thinking, or a philosophy of life, rather than a checklist or formula.

Ecology lies at the centre of NLP methods and techniques. The emphasis reflects the systemic, holistic approach characteristic of NLP. Each outcome involves systems higher and lower in a total mind-body hierarchy, as well as outside systems with which you may interact, such as friends, family and community. The ecology check will usually identify systems mismatches – in effect, when they pull in different directions to achieve different outcomes. Because we usually take into consideration our conscious goals and desires, the search for congruity usually relates to unconscious intentions, such as the positive intentions that lie behind unwanted habitual behaviour.

Of course, ecology just provides another useful metaphor and a working model, rather than the last word in setting an outcome. For instance, in the case of a patently dysfunctional system (like a violent temper or irrationally low self-image in a certain area of life), we can only *expect* conflict with other systems – we don't change easily. You have to remove the bad apple, rather than addressing the relationship between other apples and the barrel. In that case, you simply *choose* to change or not change, and if necessary, accept the inevitable problems arising from dysfunctional behaviour as part of the 'desired state' package.

Finally, the Ecology check involves not just other competing systems that impinge on our different outcomes, but relates to your unique identity as a person – a different level of subjective experience. We will explore the concept of levels of experience in the form of the Neurological Levels Model in Chapter 10.

Keep in mind what you have already learnt about well-formed outcomes, as well as the main presuppositions that underlie NLP, as you proceed to consider in the following chapters your values, beliefs and unique identity.

5 *Values and Beliefs*

You have learnt the importance of developing clear, well-formed outcomes and how you can harness innate systems to achieve what you want. At the highest level in the hierarchy, outcomes usually reflect and confirm a person's values. For example, if security lies high up among your outcomes, it means you value security. Similarly, our outcomes reflect what we believe – for instance, 'I believe in honesty' – and this in turn often reflects these values, or what we consider important. Beliefs also include what you believe about yourself, such as 'I'm no good with numbers' or 'I'm a people person.' This chapter covers values and beliefs, including how you can change them, if you want to.

Values

A value governs whole areas of a person's life. We all invest time and energy in attaining values, such as freedom, independence or fun. This involves making comparisons and judgements about the extent to which we desire, esteem and attach worth to something – just as we attach a different value to different goals and desires. If everything had the same value, nothing would have value.

We make such value distinctions at every level – loyalty to family or colleagues, smoky bacon flavour, free speech, and so on. NLP usually refers to values as 'nominalizations' (in effect names, or words) such as honesty and fairness. Like outcomes and beliefs, values form a hierarchy. We each have a pecking order of importance in the principles, precepts or criteria we live by. Lower values need to align with higher ones, and at any level – like freedom and security – somehow reconcile with each other. These give some system to our lives that makes sense and keeps us sane. Without such a values hierarchy, a person could not make decisions or live with any kind of purpose.

VALUES, SELF-BELIEFS AND OUTCOMES

Values also reveal a person's self-image, or self-belief, especially higher up the hierarchy, where words like 'honesty' and 'faithfulness' appear. People will *see* themselves (self-image) as honest, fair-minded and so forth, and *believe* (self-belief) such about themselves. Such estimable values then combine to form self-esteem – another popular personality concept. A high or low self-esteem will reflect how we see ourselves in different areas of our life. Self-esteem, and the many self-beliefs that make it up, can empower or disempower us in achieving what we want. Each belief or value has an effect on the list of outcomes set out in Chapter 4.

On a day-to-day basis, we don't think about the values that drive us. Rather, we tend to think about immediate desires and short-term goals. These form the *objects* of our values, or the *means* of fulfilling them. But values also determine – at any level and in any guise – the whole direction of our lives, and the sorts of outcomes we aspire to in the first place. They provide the meaning and purpose without which, it seems, we humans cannot exist.

A person's hierarchy of goals reflects their values and self-image. For instance, people who see themselves as honest will tend towards honest goals, or goals that confirm and support their honesty. Values usually account for – or make sense of – our goals. Thus, a person who values material possessions will possess 'getting' and 'having' goals to match. Exercise 3.1 on Life Content profiling determined values, as expressed in the different elements such as knowing, doing or being, as well as our different approach to outcomes. At the top of a person's goal hierarchy, a value constitutes not just a framework in which outcomes fit, but the outcome itself. A value also reflects what we believe about something:

- I consider independence important. – *value*
- I want to be independent. – *goal or outcome*
- I believe in independence. – *belief*

What do you do?

A person might aspire to (desire the outcome of) 'fair-mindedness' or 'efficiency'. However, we can't actively pursue abstract concepts, or even define them, unlike tangible outcomes. What does 'fair-minded' mean, to you? What do you do or say? In fact, a person's everyday desires and behaviour will take them in the *direction* of 'fair-mindedness', 'efficiency' or whatever they consider important. Tasks and achievements that demand and display fair-mindedness and efficiency, if achieved, will provide *evidence* of success in living out these values or self-beliefs. The world, therefore, will say, not just that a person *did* this or *got* the other, but that the person *is* fair-minded. This reflects the 'being' element of the Life Content model described in Chapter 3. It comes close to a person's identity – 'I am a fair-minded person.' Such values therefore occupy a special place in a person's life, whatever knowledge, acquisitions, experiences and skills they have amassed.

Premium value

Even the smallest behaviour or outcome will support a person's values, but a 'being' outcome will also contribute to a person's *identity*. A 'being' goal therefore has a particular kind of value – a premium value – as true happiness, contentment and fulfilment happens in the 'now'. Put another way, a 'being' outcome, and the value that supports it, combines journey and destination.

A person will need to fulfil one or more lower-level, more tangible, 'stepping-stone' goals to achieve the ultimate, laudable, universal goals of 'fulfilment' or 'happiness', so it makes sense to consider values in conjunction with outcomes – of any kind, as we discussed in Chapter 4 – from the start. A value may take the form of an unconscious, 'positive intention' of the sort described in Chapters 2 and 3 – a tendency, if you like. Such an intention, operating unconsciously, will one way or another affect our conscious outcomes by taking us in another direction.

You can usually identify these forces through the 'well-formedness' testing process. This happens in particular when you consider the ecology, or wider implications of an outcome. The discovery of ecological conflict, or incongruence, might indicate the need to amend or abandon goals. Thinking in terms of values simply brings that unconscious process to the fore, and you can then *choose* to align your goals with your deepest values. That way, you get to know 'how you tick'. You have a better chance of discovering outcomes mismatches soon enough to do something about them. This means that you save yourself the time, energy and the pain of ultimately unsuccessful outcomes. In the long run, it pays to familiarize yourself with your values, but you need to keep them up to date by compiling an inventory from time to time.

In setting your goals, as we saw in Chapter 4, you may prefer to first identify your main values, and then apply a values check as part of your 'well-formed' outcome testing process. In other words, ask yourself, with respect to each outcome on your list:

✓   Which of my main values does this outcome support?
✓   Where does it fit?
✓   Would achieving this provide evidence of that value?

If a goal fails to pass the values test, you may decide to abandon it, rather than wasting time and effort and almost certainly meeting with disappointment.

Many people find this difficult. We can't define abstract value-type words easily. We might describe happiness or contentment, for example, as:

- **an outcome** – I want to be happy.
- **a value** – the importance of being happy or content.
- **a belief** – I believe it is important to be content with yourself/your life.
- **a personality trait** – a happy, contented sort of person.

As long as you know what you mean, you can use *words* such as the following to describe all your values:

✓   optimistic
✓   tactful
✓   responsible
✓   open-minded.

In other words, you can use them to describe aspects of yourself. Use these words as a checklist when setting outcomes for your hierarchy of goals, and when testing them for ecology.

COMPLEX EQUIVALENCES AND CRITERIA

Our operating values embody the *criteria* we apply to life. They take the form of so-called complex equivalences. Simply, something equates to, or means something else – usually a sensory experience, event, situation or behaviour as compared with an abstract quality or value: for example, 'Fruit is good', 'John was unfair.' They relate sensory experience like 'fruit' and 'John' to nominalizations or abstract qualities like 'good' and 'fair' or 'unfair'. (We'll discuss complex equivalences again later in this handbook.)

These have different significance depending on the context. For example:

- 'good' in moderation might mean 'bad' in excess
- 'good' for an adult might mean 'bad' for a child

- 'great' at the weekend might mean 'terrible' at work
- 'enjoyable' when seen behind bars might mean 'terrifying' on the loose.

Each of us unknowingly builds a complex mosaic of criteria, or equivalences, as we apply meaning to our daily bombardment of sensory stimuli. The more you can identify these in your life, the more control you will have over what you do and achieve.

VALUE LEVELS

Like outcomes, values occur at all levels. NLP usually applies the term to 'bigger-chunk' values such as honesty, integrity, faithfulness and such like. In fact, we value things and people, just as we pursue intentions, at every level of importance. These comprise characteristics or qualities, and simply reflect our personal 'hierarchy of importance'. For example, what do you rate important about a banana, a roller coaster, white socks, politics, organic food, humour and so on? In other words, what do you *value* about these things?

Even at a mundane level, values form abstractions, such as red(ness), flavour, portability, resilience, durability, temperature and so on – in fact, anything you can't tie up in a parcel but with which you might describe the importance or value of something to you. The most important ones, like honesty and love, just come higher up the hierarchy (for most people) – they have 'life' significance. As it happens, you may find 'red' and 'flavour' just as hard to define. In short, values don't come in sensory terms. You have to clothe them with tangible things, behaviour or metaphors (see Chapter 14) to make them amenable to the NLP model, and to change techniques.

Values reflect a person's expression of importance. What you value will always affect your outcomes, and permeate your thoughts and behaviour. You don't have to think about them all the time. On the contrary. You did that when you adopted them, probably a long while back, and as you repeatedly reconfirmed them from time to time as your life unfolded. Like checking the bookshelves in a person's home, you will form a good idea of a person's values simply by perusing their list of outcomes, whether in the form of dreams, wishes, desires or serious ambitions.

ASPIRATIONS

Sometimes, you cannot make a direct connection between an outcome and a value. For example, a goal of material success or a professional qualification might represent a stepping stone to a higher-level outcome, such as respect, fame, peace, contentment, security for your family and so on. This higher outcome, rather than the stepping-stone outcome, comes closer to revealing the *value* a person espouses. Put another way, our outcomes reflect values we *aspire* to as well as those we presently hold. We might even consider a short-term goal which conflicts with our true values as a valid means to an end.

THE PURPOSE OF LIFE

At the ultimate level, 'being' goals and desires, of the sort we considered earlier, equate to values that together form a person's identity. Indeed, the ultimate direction of a person's life usually reflects a handful of core values they have held over a long period. These provide purpose and meaning to life, as well as the *raison d'être* for all behaviour. Each outcome you pursue, therefore – even short-term tasks not usually associated with 'life' issues – demonstrates to the world, and to yourself, those core values.

Beliefs

Our beliefs, main life outcomes and values interweave to create a personal map of reality and unique identity. A person who values faithfulness or honesty, for instance, *believes* in these personal characteristics, for themselves and others.

Like outcomes, beliefs also appear in different guises and at different levels. At one level, a person can believe in the hereafter, and at another level that their computer doesn't move (although it does under a microscope). At the same time, a person's values might include love at one level and fluffiness at the other. In other words, a value and belief can sit much closer than values or beliefs respectively at different levels. For example, the *belief* 'I really think (believe) fluffy ones feel better' comes close to the *value* 'fluffy' than fluffy does to the values faith, hope or charity. As a word with no inherent sensory meaning, a nominalization like 'fluffiness' or 'faith' just provides us with a symbol – or model – of some sensorily perceived reality (like a fluffy bear, the touch of a baby's hand, or the sound of a cello).

SELF-BELIEFS

Most of our behaviour stems from *self*-beliefs – what we believe about ourselves. Self-beliefs often have far more impact on a person's behaviour than their belief about other people, the world, and worlds beyond.

EXERCISE 5.1

MEASURING YOUR SELF-ESTEEM

The list of traits below gives examples of common self-beliefs. We express them as 'I am ...' These examples suggest positive or empowering traits, but we could easily reverse them. We see ourselves, or *would like* to see ourselves, as holding these values, or believing in them. Self-beliefs or self-image, probably constitute the biggest single factor affecting a person's behaviour and achievement. They chart the course of a person's life. Consider, for example, the following traits:

- optimistic
- tactful
- responsible
- open-minded
- bright
- confident
- aware
- mature
- satisfied
- clear-thinking
- pleasant
- fair-minded

- presentable
- considerate
- sensible
- ambitious
- effective
- stable
- honest
- reasonable
- efficient
- purposeful
- warm-hearted
- normal
- understanding.

You can gauge your self-image's state of health by scoring each of these. Either answer 'yes' or 'no' (on balance), or, more accurately, score them on a scale of say 1 to 10. Apply the questions 'Am I an optimistic person?', 'Am I a tactful person?', and so on. A predominance of 'yes' answers or a score in the upper quartile indicates a positive overall self-esteem. Low scores in individual characteristics offer you important self-knowledge on which you can base changes using NLP skills. A couple of self-belief changes can change your life.

You can take it a stage further. This time, score on the basis of a different question: 'Would I *like to be* (an) optimistic (person)?', 'Would I *like to be* (a) tactful (person)?', and so on. You will probably arrive at a different score. Comparing your score with the previous exercise may reveal important gaps in your self-image. Large gaps between how you see yourself and how you would like to see yourself indicate opportunities for change.

The self-image gap closely represents the difference between present state and desired state in the model described in Chapter 3. Once aware of it, you can *choose* whether to change. You will find belief change exercises later in this chapter. The biggest gaps will indicate where you will gain most benefit from change techniques. Better still, you can start to identify the core values and beliefs that will best support you in achieving your present most important outcomes, and give these priority for making changes.

Disempowering self-beliefs

Whatever our philosophical or religious beliefs, most of us have a collection of working self-beliefs that account for perhaps 80 per cent of all our behaviour. These dictate the whole pattern of a person's life. Negative rather than positive self-beliefs seem to predominate, such as:

- I couldn't give a speech if you paid me.
- I'm hopeless at remembering names.
- I'm a slow reader.
- My mind easily goes blank.
- I'm always running late.
- People usually take things I say the wrong way.

Self-beliefs such as these act in a strikingly self-fulfilling way, and consequently follow a virtuous or vicious spiral of success or failure respectively. Once such beliefs find their way into a person's neurology, they will determine behaviour as much as education, good looks or willpower. The process starts out in an innocuous but insidious way. We start by *doing* something – maybe on a bad day or out of character – and finish up *being* something ('I'm stupid, 'I'm hopeless').

These working self-beliefs form a persons' identity. Change at the habitual behaviour level doesn't happen very readily for most people. At the level of identity, even greater forces of inertia operate. This confirms the need to make changes at a higher 'neurological level' – such as in beliefs and values – rather than just behaviour. (Chapter 10 explores the idea of neurological levels.)

By breaking down your values/beliefs in this way, you will identify inner resources you can bring to bear on your present outcomes – in other words, how you can make better use of your strengths. For instance, these could include how you might apply 'efficiency', 'fair-mindedness' and 'clear thinking' to specific goals. What new goals might you achieve, or what opportunities present themselves in the light of these valuable inner resources?

Hierarchy of values and self-beliefs

We each have a hierarchy of beliefs and values, in the same way that we have a hierarchy of outcomes or goals. Lower down the goals hierarchy lie the more specific and shorter-term ones. Similarly, some of our beliefs and values take the form of everyday operating rules or guidelines – the criteria by which we live.

For example, after a bad experience with a couple of bosses, you might devalue bosses generally. You now see (value) bosses as two-faced, hypocritical, looking after their own interests, and so on. Quite probably, your current goals list will reflect these operating rules anyway. You may have a hidden agenda to turn the tables on your bosses, bring about the downfall of one of them, impugn their character and so on, or simply to try for promotion to beat someone at their own game. With these new values, you may, for the first time, include the possibility of self-employment. Meanwhile, your short-term career goals now extend beyond your present company or industry. In any event, your beliefs (especially about bosses), values and current goals in life will realign themselves to accord with your changing identity. And your outcomes and behaviour will follow.

Higher values and beliefs will embrace perhaps several operating criteria. Although expressed in more abstract terms, they have even greater leverage over behaviour and achievement.

Self-belief and value sources

In most cases, we don't identify the origins of self-beliefs. If we can, it usually dates back to childhood. So-called 'imprinting' may stem from a chance remark made by a thoughtless parent, teacher or schoolfriend that we took too much to heart. We continue to create values in adult life, from the influence of higher education, professional training, overseas travel, major life events, serious illness and other trauma. These form almost indelible identity labels. But whatever their origins and whether or not we identify them, you can choose to change self-beliefs.

Other than as a hobby, you don't need to identify the source of your values and self-beliefs, but it may help to realise that you adopted them in a natural, unconscious way. They reflect your life experience as you grow to understand the world in your own unique way. However, as we meet new experiences, some of which demand new values and operating beliefs to 'make sense', old values tend to cling on to their place. Some, on the other hand, outlive their usefulness. Some may deserve a different position in your hierarchy of importance criteria. Some self-beliefs may prevent you from achieving the outcomes you consider most important today. By identifying the *typical* sources of values, you will remind yourself that they belong to you, to use, change, discard or reconfirm consciously from time to time as you choose. Think of general sources such as:

- family
- religion
- close friends
- school – a teacher, maybe
- a hero or heroine – a special person
- popular media – a million soundbites that bombarded your young mind
- peers to which you conformed
- profession or trade
- a book or fictional character that made a special impact
- a place
- your native culture, and other cultures you have experienced.

REAPPRAISING YOUR GOALS

When setting outcomes, you need to consider far more than the outward, visible goal or desire. To a large extent, you will have identified these factors during the well-formed outcome testing process, and especially when checking the ecology of each goal. However, by addressing your outcomes more specifically in terms of your beliefs and values, you will form congruent goals that have a better chance of success. Such goals will then give you the pleasure you intended they should.

The process works the other way. When identifying your self-beliefs and values, you may well create new desires – potential achievements that will better reflect the important values in your life. Often, a person pursues career goals at odds with their real values. Because we don't tend to think about life issues such as values and beliefs – at least on a month-to-month basis – sometimes years can go by before we realize that we headed in the wrong direction. A person then develops the feeling that they have wasted years of life – even with its material successes. Sometimes, this awareness dawns in time to make changes. All too often, however, by then the inner conflict of values has done its worst: broken relationships, abandonment of earlier pleasurable hobbies and interests, and general discontentment with life.

Hence the need to reconcile your values and outcomes – and better late than never. In any event, every morsel of experience and learning provides a potential resource you can apply to the future. Put another way, by treating failure as feedback, as we saw in Chapter 3, you can capitalize on even the most hurtful experiences. Paradoxically, having lost years through uncertain values and lack of direction, we tend to value the present and the uncertain future so much more.

Identifying your values and self-beliefs

Because of the relationship between outcomes and values, you can identify your values with reference to your list of outcomes, as described in Chapter 3. You will probably have identified some values when applying the 'well-formedness' criteria. This happens when you ask 'Why?' as well as 'What?' But now you can identify your values more specifically and comprehensively with a view to drawing up a definitive list, and a hierarchy or order, as you did for your outcomes.

EXERCISE 5.2

ESTABLISHING YOUR CRITERIA OF IMPORTANCE

Simply ask, in relation to each outcome, 'In what way is this important to me?', and write down your answer. This resembles Exercise 3.1 on Life Content. However, in this case, rather than categorizing outcomes into specific elements, you will relate them to any values you hold. Don't go to great lengths. A short phrase will usually suffice, or a single word may convey what you mean, but bear in mind that your values don't have to conform to stereotypes. Sometimes, you cannot easily define in words something important in your life. In this case, give it any name you wish – as long as you know what you mean. Usually, the process of identifying and writing down will help you to clarify and express values that you have hitherto adhered to unconsciously.

As we have just seen, some values and beliefs take the form of working rules and guidelines. These may reveal themselves in some of your outcomes, but not in others. More than likely, they will apply in certain parts of your life and not in others, such as between work and home. It therefore helps to consider your values using each of these different contexts as a checklist. That way you will identify values that you might have missed when thinking with a different role in mind, or in a different context. However, you will at the same time reconfirm your core values, as these will keep cropping up in every part of your life. You may find it helps to have a checklist of life areas to which you can apply the same question you have applied to your outcome list:

✓ family
✓ hobbies
✓ interests
✓ work and career
✓ personal development
✓ health and physical well-being
✓ social life and sports
✓ professional life.

For example, ask: 'What is important to me about my family?' Your answers might include:

• a feeling of security
• mutual honesty
• being needed
• close relationships
• continuity.

The same question applied to your job or career might elicit the response:

- meeting people
- making money
- having independence
- gaining respect from other people
- knowing I have value.

We saw earlier that outcomes at any level might suggest values. The ones nearer the top of your hierarchy of goals tend to reflect a few core or life values. Those applying to lower-level, short-term goals tend to take the form of operating values or rules of behaviour – sometimes called criteria. In the same way, our beliefs may occupy a high, cosmic or religious level, or at another level, relate specifically to a group of people or a particular kind of circumstance. Like outcomes, they form a hierarchy.

Consider values in different contexts. For example, you may give a different answer to the questions 'What is important to me about my career?' and 'What is important to me about working with so and so company (your present employer)?' Your present job has probably brought new experiences that might have changed your attitudes, beliefs and working values (for example, your attitude to bosses). We also have beliefs about places (for example, 'Walthamstow is a dump.') and things ('BMWs keep their value.'), at both a macro ('things don't last five minutes') and specific level. Similarly, what you deem important about your family can extend more specifically to your children, spouse, mother, and so on. You will understand yourself better by identifying these values.

This thorough 'What's important?' process will help you to identify your values quickly and comprehensively. At the same time, you may identify values and beliefs you realize you live by, but you now question or want to abandon. They may have outlasted their usefulness, and probably relate to earlier experiences and events that you learnt from, but you have since moved on in your life.

Blue-chip investment

Conduct this exercise thoroughly, and it will bring benefits you might not have imagined. In most cases, we cannot envision the benefits of self-knowledge without that self-knowledge. We change and grow as people, and our values change as we think about them from time to time. At a minimum, by identifying your beliefs and values you will make your outcomes better formed and aligned with a bigger, coherent life purpose. In terms of benefits, typically, by avoiding just one abortive outcome (say, an unnecessary failure, and its side effects, due to an unsatisfactory outcome) you will save more time and energy than you will ever need to spend on this self-awareness process. It yields a high return on investment. Most importantly, self-knowledge means an investment in yourself – blue-chip stock – and a future that, once lived through, you can never recover.

Changing beliefs

NLP has developed techniques to bring about changes in belief. Several patterns have evolved, the detailed features of which vary as trainers use them around the world. Thus, they rarely follow the precise language of the instigator. The examples that follow will give you an opportunity to try out a typical change process on a DIY basis. These belief-change exercises also affect your values, or what you believe has importance in your life.

Start with quite specific self-beliefs so that:

* You can draw on them soon in specific situations when you need such empowering beliefs.
* You can match beliefs to important outcomes you have already set.
* You can visualize your belief in action in a realistic, sensory way, rather than trying to imagine abstract concepts.
* You will build up your overall self-esteem by clocking up self-belief changes incrementally.

Bear in mind that when going 'inside', it helps to adopt a relaxed, downtime mode and follow the spirit of an exercise until you find the technique that works best for you.

EXERCISE 5.3

BELIEF CHANGE A

The following pattern, and some of the terms used, came from Robert Dilts. I have selected it (as with other exercises I describe) as a result of seeing it used successfully in practical training programmes and practice groups. It may seem long, but that's because I included some examples to illustrate the steps and make it easier to understand.

1 Identify a belief you now hold that limits you in some way: for instance, the belief 'I'm no good at public speaking', or 'I'm hopeless with numbers.' Choose a belief that, if changed, could open up real opportunities for you to achieve more in the next few weeks and months. You can call that your Present Belief.

2 Decide what you would *rather* believe – call that your Preferred Belief. State this in a positive form, just as you did in your list of outcomes. Complete an ecology check – ensure that any change will respect your family, friends and work colleagues, and that it will not conflict with other beliefs you want to maintain. Check back on the list of ecology questions in Chapter 4 if you need to.

3 Now, for each of six imaginary locations of belief change, create a label on a sheet of paper:

   a   present belief
   b   open to doubt
   c   belief archive
   d   preferred belief
   e   open to believing
   f   special beliefs.

4 Position these labels on the floor as if placed around an imaginary dinner table.

5 As you physically step from each one to the next in order, think of a vivid experience from your life that fits each description.

6 You should find it easy to identify your *current belief* – the one you would like to change – and imagine yourself in a situation that illustrates this.

7 Then think of a time in the past when you felt *open to doubt*, having a weak belief as doubts had crept in. The belief in doubt might relate to you and your abilities, another person, or even an ideology. It may have happened at a time of special change in your life, such as going to college, leaving home or going abroad.

8   For the *belief archive*, think back to something that you once held as a belief, but which no longer holds true for you. It exists somewhere in your mind, but as an old archive, filed away like a sentimental memento. You can probably think of several dating back to childhood, or from idealistic teenage years, but you may also have discarded some recently.

9   Assume your *preferred belief* as the one you would like to change to. So, for the moment, you need to imagine that you believe what you want to believe – or perhaps what it would feel like as a person whom you know holds the desired belief.

10   The *open to belief* position will represent some experience in the past when you felt open to believing – you had not yet formed a new belief, but your understanding and the facts of a situation made you open to changing what you then believed. Try to think of an actual situation when you experienced this particular state of mind. It probably preceded any belief you have since changed, but you can probably isolate an example to a specific time and place, such as a conversation, a holiday, a film, a book and so on.

11   For the *special belief*, think of a belief that you would never discard – something so important that you personally deem it almost a matter of life and death.

12   Having identified sensory representations of each belief, and the in-between stages, complete one circuit of the labels and, in each position, relive the events and states of mind, and associate them with the symbolic, physical locations. To start with, stand in the *current belief* location and experience again your limiting belief.

13   Taking this limiting belief with you, step from *current belief* into *open to doubt*, and, recalling the earlier *open to doubt* experience, notice how you now doubt that limiting belief.

14   Now take your doubted belief and step into the *belief archive*. Recollect your chosen discarded belief, and experience discarding your doubted belief and leaving it safely in the *belief archive*. Don't destroy it, it has probably served you well, and you can always choose to believe it again if you wish.

15   Having left that belief behind in the *belief archive*, step into your *preferred belief* location and experience again your *preferred belief*. Imagine yourself fully believing this new belief, and notice how it feels, and how differently things appear around you.

16   Now physically move on from *preferred belief* into the *open to belief* location, and feel yourself again completely open to believing it. Then take your *preferred belief* and step into the *special belief* place. Put your new belief alongside your current *special beliefs*, and make it very important to you.

17   Finish the exercise by experiencing your now very special and sacred *preferred belief* as you step back into the *current belief* location. You will now no longer hold the limiting belief as a *current belief*. You have transformed it, gently, step by step, into a new belief that will empower you in many situations.

You will need to use your imagination to make this technique work. Moving from one physical location to another – however silly it seems – helps you to make the transition into each state of mind. Physical location also helps to anchor each belief association in your mind, so that you can easily recall them to make the incremental changes.

EXERCISE 5.4

BELIEF CHANGE B

This belief change exercise adopts a different approach. I have added comments to remind you of some of the principles while carrying out the technique.

1   First, identify a belief you want to change. This belief will probably cause you to behave in a way you don't want to behave, such as a belief about whether you can or cannot do something, or a belief about another person, group or class of people. (Check back to the list of common negative or disempowering self-beliefs on page 64 if you need to.)

2   Then decide what you would like to believe instead. Always install a belief in place of one you discard, so that you don't have vacuums in your mind – just as you don't scrap old equipment until you know the new equipment works. Your new belief might simply reverse the old one, but you have the opportunity to design it to order, so you can enhance it as you wish, or perhaps make it specific so that you can use it in particular situations in future. For example, in place of 'I'm hopeless at public speaking' you might choose 'I can get a group to relax and put my message across in an enjoyable way', or 'I can rise to the occasion in front of a large audience and know I will leave a good impression.' You can say your new belief out loud, to help imprint it in your mind.

3   Subject your new belief to the ecology checks described in Chapter 4. Adapt the questions if you need to.

4   Visualize yourself in a future situation where you can put your new belief into practice. See things through your own eyes, so that you experience the feelings that accompany the situation, and that make it much more real.

5   Think of other situations that will demonstrate your new belief. The more you inwardly experience your new belief, the more you will believe that your behaviour reflects your true identity. You will align yourself with the empowering self-belief.

6   See a picture of yourself five years into the future. Look back and think about how the new beliefs have changed your life. How do you feel now? How did you and your life change? Go 10, 20, perhaps 30 years into future, and do the same.

Satir values

NLP, both as a discipline and a community, adheres to certain values itself, such as respecting an individual's beliefs and world view, and acting 'ecologically', as we saw in the goal-setting exercises. The renowned family therapist Virginia Satir has left us some statements that illustrate the sorts of values and rights people have:

✓   I do not have to feel guilty just because someone else does not like what I do, say, think, or feel.
✓   It is OK for me to feel angry and to express it in responsible ways.
✓   I do not have to assume the responsibility for making decisions, particularly where others share responsibility for making the decision.
✓   I have the right to say 'I don't know'.

✓ I have the right to say 'No' without feeling guilty.

✓ I have the right to say 'I don't understand' without feeling stupid.

✓ I do not have to apologize or give reasons when I say 'No.'

✓ I have the right to refuse requests that others make of me.

✓ I have the right to tell others when I think they are manipulating, conning or irritating me unfairly.

✓ I have the right to refuse additional responsibilities without feeling guilty.

✓ I have the right to tell others when their behaviour annoys me.

✓ I do not have to compromise my personal integrity.

✓ I have the right to make mistakes and to be responsible for them; I have the right to be wrong.

As well as aligning your outcomes according to the 'well-formedness' criteria in Chapter 4, you can now align them with your beliefs and values. Identifying beliefs and values – often two sides of the same coin – gives you important self-knowledge you can use in any sort of outcome, including those involving communication with other people. The knowledge and skill to change beliefs gives you extraordinary power over your behaviour, and will help you to achieve your goals more consistently.

6 *Communication Outcomes*

'Well-formedness' criteria apply to any outcome, including a communication. Communication forms a big part of NLP, and for many people offers a chance to try out the goal-achieving principles and processes described earlier. Many goals we set have communication implications, or form part of an outcome: for example, to maintain or enhance a relationship, to gain respect or attention, or to achieve a goal with the help of others, such as a team. This chapter looks specifically at outcomes. It gives you the opportunity to reinforce what you have learnt about outcomes and communication presuppositions and to apply it immediately in this important area of communication.

Expert non-communication

We all communicate expertly. Watch a group of pre-school children playing together, having had no formal training in the intricacies of language and interpersonal communication. From the earliest age, we detect the nuances of other people's feelings. A parent's tone of voice, or even the smallest facial muscle movements, betray anger, pleasure, surprise or disgust. Without attending drama school, we learn to display these clever voice, facial and body characteristics ourselves. We effortlessly acquire a sort of international human language that bridges people's minds. Whereas we can't convey detailed facts without language skills, we don't need spoken or written language to communicate how we feel, what we deem important, and what we want. When we combine a mother tongue (more or less self-taught) with a wide, natural repertoire of non-verbal communication skills, we start to exhibit the uniqueness of humanity, demonstrate the most complex social structures, and transmit our science and art to each succeeding generation.

Whilst most people will relate to this, at the same time it seems that most of the world's ills stem from poor communication or non-communication. This certainly applies in business, as hundreds of case studies have shown. It also rings true in family life and in our immediate social surroundings. The evidence shows up in escalating divorce rates and the breakdown of long-term relationships generally, with the attendant pain, especially affecting children. At a higher community, national and international level, the evidence grows even starker. Our televisions reveal wars, racial conflict and unspeakable evils between fellow human beings. The communication characteristics seem endemic:

- great difficulty in understanding people
- failing to put ourselves in their shoes
- seeing things from our own perspective, rather than that of others
- thinking we said something we didn't
- thinking we didn't say something we did

- not realizing the effect, or outcome, of our words and behaviour
- remaining doggedly convinced of our own world view of reality.

Change through communication

One of the main applications of NLP concerns promoting change through better communication. We have already met the presupposition 'communication is about the response we elicit' – in other words, the result or outcome rather than the process. It follows that we cannot rely solely on our sophisticated, inborn communication hardware, our extraordinary sensory acuity, and our human pedigree of language and higher understanding. However powerful the tools, all too often, in terms of outcome – or obtaining what you want – they don't work.

STANDARD HARDWARE

We can have little quarrel with our standard grey matter. We all embody more or less infinite potential for achievement, including through communicating with people. What we do with what we have counts most – in computer terminology, the software. Give or take a few per cent difference in neural electro-chemical capacity, which we hardly use anyway, every human comes endowed with a lump of brain hardware. How we run this mental hardware proves critical. Specifically, this concerns how we think, feel, and communicate to achieve outcomes. Rather than how many billion neural connections we can amass, it relates to the specific mental networks we create, and how these affect our behaviour.

THINK EFFECT

Although seemingly simplistic, you can join the upper ranks of communicator-achievers just by adopting and applying this presupposition. It just means thinking in terms of outcomes, or communication responses. That means focusing on effects, or outputs, rather than inputs, such as media, methods and words. It entails asking, simply: 'What effect will this have on this person?', or 'How can I bring about so-and-so effect on the person with whom I communicate? What do I need to do or say?' Questions like these, based on the above communication outcome presupposition, will usually produce insightful 'how to' answers. If they don't, you will quickly improve as you adapt your words and behaviour to correct for outcomes you didn't achieve. Refer back to the Four-stage Achievement Model in Chapter 3 if you need to. Communication follows the same ground rules as achieving any worthwhile outcome. However, because of the 'people factor', it requires its own chapter.

UNDERSTANDING COMMUNICATION OUTCOMES

The importance of goals and objectives does not just apply to communication, of course. Yet most goals seem to involve people in some way, and communicating with them. In a work context, we usually think more specifically about what we want, perhaps as part of a planning or budgetary process, or just to ensure we get it right. Personally, you may aim to achieve a certain skill, or a certain standard, say, in a sport or pastime, or to receive an accolade or some mark of recognition. A childhood dream to win an Olympic medal or become a pop star also forms a strong outcome, or target. In these cases, we know quite well what we want, and can usually express it. On the other hand, we communicate with others as an everyday, moment-by-moment activity mostly without thinking. In addition, we may not consciously know our true desires, even if we consider them. So we follow unconscious intentions. In this case, even if we pursue some outcome, usually our unconscious intentions will have an opposing effect on our behaviour, and will impede the outcomes. For this reason, we need to understand the nature of outcomes, and test the 'well-formedness' criteria described in Chapter 4. These apply even more in the case of communication, or 'people' outcomes.

Communication outcome ground rules

On the basis of the presupposition 'the meaning of a communication is the response it elicits', we can adopt a few valuable ground rules:

✓ Have an outcome. Know what you want.
✓ Identify your real, hitherto unconscious intentions.
✓ Say or do, or don't say or do, what you think you need in order to achieve your outcome.
✓ Notice the effect you have, and adjust your words or behaviour until you achieve your outcome.

You will find examples of this process throughout this book, and some specific applications in Part 2. This amounts to no more than common sense. You don't need to follow a rigid formula, still less to copy a specific example, as your circumstances will usually differ anyway. You will find all the principles and techniques you need as we cover each topic. The examples in Part 2 will give you a number of ideas about how to apply your communication skills in day-to-day situations.

Identifying your outcome

In everyday communication, just *thinking* about your outcome – even momentarily – will normally do the trick. We usually don't – or at least not in an effective way. What you then say and do intuitively will produce the response you want. However, a little thought about the nature of a communication outcome will greatly improve your success rate.

First, check that your outcome represents an output rather than an input. If you have to give a speech, for instance, your aim will probably include:

• prepare well
• know your subject
• rehearse
• research your audience, the venue, and so on
• say what you intend to say – no more and no less
• entertain as well as inform.

These consist of inputs rather than outputs. You can, of course, treat inputs as objectives, as you would any stepping-stone task leading to a bigger goal, as we have already discussed.

However, if you don't have an overall outcome for your speech, whether you do well or badly in these input activities will not necessarily influence success or failure in your overall communication outcome. The response, or result, rather than the process, matters most. If you don't achieve your *intended* response, you might as well have spared yourself the whole effort.

People often fail to apply this simple concept. For instance, the outcome, to many communicators, comprises the message they want to convey. They accept the above list of tasks as inputs, but see their aim, or output, through these, as transmitting a 'message' clearly. Unfortunately, human nature doesn't work like that. A dozen people might receive the clearest message, but *perceive* it differently. This means it will have a different effect on them. They will behave differently, change or not change, and so on. This reflects the NLP model – we see, hear and feel things according to our personal model of the world.

AXES TO GRIND

When giving a speech, each person in your audience will have unique beliefs, feelings and attitudes. They will find themselves in widely differing situations and life circumstances. Each will have different roles and 'axes to grind' regarding the subject of your speech. In short, each person has a different mental map. Each person will interpret a message differently. If word meaning doesn't create differences, then perceived body language ('The way she said it – I knew what she really meant.') surely will.

This requires congruency between the words you say and the way you say them, in every physiological respect. But it demands even more. Even a sincere, congruent message, if it doesn't bring the response you want, will not rank as an effective communication. You will need to do something different, as the above communication ground rules make clear: maybe a different message; maybe a different medium, environment, time or place. Change *anything* you have to in order to bring about change, or the purpose of your communication, as the Four-stage Achievement Model describes.

REAL EMOTIONS

Achieving *any* communication outcome, especially in a group, poses quite a task. None the less, you have a greater chance of success if you allow for real people with real emotions, and consider the effect that you may have on them through their different perceptions. This means humbly accepting that the simplest, clearest message, transmitted through the most professional speech or presentation, may not produce the effect that it would have had on *you* if you sat in the audience – a hard but vital lesson for any would-be-communicator.

Looked at in this way, communicating to more than one person seems impossible, or at least it seems far more daunting than dealing one-to-one. However, the basic presuppositions apply throughout. Nor does it follow that communicating effectively to an individual proves easy. Let's apply this to a person-to-person communication before tackling the seemingly more difficult group or mass communication situation. This might involve an interview, appraisal, passing on some news – good or bad – disciplining a staff member, presenting a report to your boss, getting to know someone at a social event, and so on – any person-to-person activity or relationship.

REAL RESPONSES

Adopting this approach, you will consider how a particular person will perceive your message. This represents the 'understanding' you need to convey. But, even with an individual, your outcome, and your responsibility as communicator, goes beyond that. What *effect* will what they perceive have? Clearly, different people react differently on receiving a given message, even though they all have a clear understanding of the *message* you communicate. This effect, which will influence their behaviour and possibly your relationship with them, forms part of your outcome, or response – perhaps unconsciously. After all, you can hardly claim success if, on transferring what you have in your mind to their mind, they 'take it the wrong way', 'get it all out of proportion', 'take it too personally' or misconstrue your intentions.

Given sincere intentions and the desire to maintain or enhance any relationship you already have with the person, producing the wrong effect means eliciting the wrong outcome. The emotional effect of a communication will probably affect a person's behaviour more than the message they receive and understand. In any case, whatever orthodox communication theory says, if you don't achieve the result you intended, you will have to do something different.

Thus, when considering your outcome, think in terms of effect. Think about the thoughts, feelings, likely beliefs and values, and probable reaction of the other person. Just keep your intention in mind, and expect your behaviour to take you there, in the cybernetic, goal-achieving way described in Chapter 3. With your goal always in view, you will at least head in the right direction. More than that, you will recognize when the actual response differs from your imagined (or *imaged*) response – so you will know you have to do something differently in the four-stage process of getting what you want.

Most communication failures happen not because we misjudge the effect we will have on the person, but because we don't consider it in the first place. That stage in the process doesn't take much time or effort, although, as we saw in the 'well-formedness' criteria in Chapter 4, you will not communicate effectively without it. Having mentally registered your intended effect, your inner cybernetic goal-achieving system does the clever work your conscious mind cannot cope with.

CHOOSE YOUR EFFECT

What effect do you want to have? If you don't want to have any effect on a person, or to cause any change in their understanding, beliefs, feelings or behaviour, then why communicate? Remember the communication presupposition in Chapter 2, which says that a communication equates to the response it elicits, and the Change of State Model in Chapter 3, which makes 'state' – including personal feelings in the case of a communication – central to your outcome. Consider the purpose of your communication, therefore, as with any outcome. Otherwise, you may as well pursue another outcome and the pleasure it will bring.

But it doesn't work quite as simply as that. In fact, you will probably have an effect on a person in any sort of interaction, *whatever your own intentions*. In other words – in the words of another of the communication presuppositions in Chapter 2 – 'you cannot not communicate'. So even a negative intention – say, not to upset, annoy, deceive or influence – works strangely just like an intention. We explored this negative outcome phenomenon in the 'well-formedness' criteria in Chapter 4. The NLP communication presuppositions writ large in your mind will achieve more than power or body language control. You cannot *not* communicate, so you may as well get it right, which you can do by applying these simple principles.

You cannot absolve yourself as communicator from the result of what you, knowingly or unknowingly, communicate to your fellow humans. You may recall another presupposition: 'The responsibility for a communication lies with the communicator.' This applies to us all in the role of communicators. And most communication happens as a two-way process, so we all have to bear that responsibility.

To summarize the implication of these communication facts of life: you may as well have a definite intention or outcome for any interpersonal communication (which means more or less any domestic, social or professional dealings or relationship), rather than create an unpredictable effect on the other person by default.

You can communicate one of any number of impressions to the other person, or create emotional and behavioural responses in them. You probably intended to do that anyway, but unconsciously. Figure 6.1 shows the many effects a communication can produce, whether intentionally or not. Communicating purposely avoids much of the unpredictability inherent in humans. Fortunately, as the illustration shows, when it comes to effect, or response, you have a wide choice.

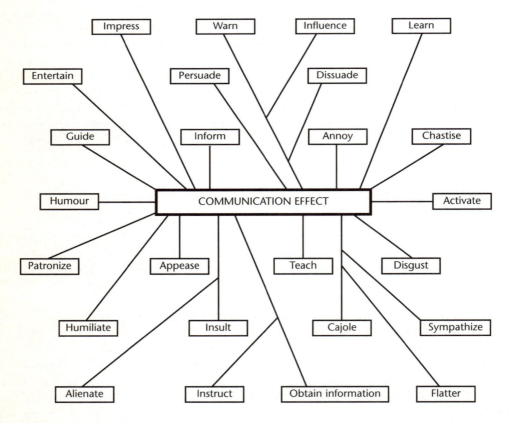

Figure 6.1   The possible effects of a communication

A few considerations follow from such a variety of effects:

- A communication intention does not have to qualify as 'good'. It implies no moral stance. For instance, if you intend to humiliate a person and you succeed in that aim, you will achieve your 'communication outcome'. You will need, of course, to check on the ecology or indirect side effects, of your 'success'.

- You may have to say and do different things to bring about each effect, such as varying your expressions and body language. For instance, certain behaviour may flatter one person but insult or hurt another. One person may accept, another reject, instruction given in good faith. One person may readily absorb information, while another person may find that it goes in one ear and out the other. You don't need a hidden agenda for the other person to assume that you have one.

- You need to develop some communication skills in order to achieve a precise outcome. You may need to differentiate, for example, between sympathizing and patronizing, or between warning and just informing. This doesn't mean you have to lower your achievement horizons. Rather, in addition to following the communication pre-suppositions and principles you have learnt, you will need to exercise some skill in applying them. This comes with practice, of course. For instance, you will start by learning how to achieve rapport with people generally, or break rapport, as your outcome requires. But I don't want to overstate the difficulty. After all, as we saw earlier, tiny children exhibit remarkable ability in recognizing some of these effects and naturally using the skills to achieve them.

Choosing your medium

Orthodox communication theory dwells at length on the medium. As we have seen, what lies between the two minds in the communication process matters less than the understanding you transmit, the effect it has, and whether or not you achieve what you intended. However, sometimes you don't have much choice of medium. For instance, you may not have the opportunities for face-to-face contact, and may have to make do with the telephone or a written communication. But any such restriction simply reinforces the importance of these presuppositions. It means you have to think more carefully about how you achieve what you want, given a particular medium. Clearly, a telephone call offers no opportunity for body language matching. But you still have a good deal of choice in language patterns, questioning, and some other techniques you will learn in this book.

You obtain less feedback on the telephone, so the feedback available takes on even greater importance. As it happens, tone of voice over the telephone can indicate a person's state better than visible physiology, which experienced communicators can fake.

In a well-formed communication, you will seek to have as many choices as possible, so look on what lies between the two minds in a communication as your opportunity for a well-formed outcome, and potential resources for you to make use of. Even broad categories of modern communication media offer plenty of choice, although, as we have seen, the most important skills lie at a more specific and personal level. Moreover, the logical choice of medium may not turn out to meet the NLP presuppositions, or give the best outcome.

For example, news of imminent redundancies or a corporate reorganization often reaches staff by way of a mass meeting addressed by the managing director. The MD wants to reassure staff that the change will bring long-term benefits and security for the staff who remain – a rosy future. Rather than reassurance, the reverse often results, and uncertainty and animosity follow. Whilst 'logical' in some respects (such as in timing the announcement, communicating to all staff the same way, and involving the MD personally), the 'medium' may prove inappropriate when considering the likely effects. Staff may well regard a personally signed letter, for example, as more personal, and this would avoid the typically polarized response of a mass audience. It would also communicate the benefits in a more permanent form, which the employee could read again and consider more carefully. This doesn't imply that a particular medium will always suit a particular kind of communication. It depends on all the circumstances, and in this case the culture and tradition of the company, the verbal communication skills of the MD, and the respect he or she commands. Thinking in terms of 'What *effect* do I want to produce?' (reassurance, say, or hope) and 'How will I best achieve this?' increases our chances of choosing the right medium and message to achieve the effect (the presupposition communication 'response') we want.

If you cannot use an appropriate medium, you may reduce your chances of success from the start. On the other hand, you may find more than one way to reach your goal once you set it clearly. Without such constraints, treat every conceivable medium as a choice. But make them *serve* – along with any *means* you consider – your communication *end*, or outcome. Some examples follow of media and typical communication types and roles that you might assume in bringing about a communication outcome:

- telephone call
- group presentation
- one-to-one personal meeting
- casual face-to-face meeting
- formal speech
- contributing to an informal discussion
- contributing to a meeting or debate
- training a group
- making inputs as a trainee
- coaching
- fax transmission
- word-processed or typed memo
- handwritten note
- formal letter
- chairing a meeting
- staff announcement
- formal warning letter
- formal face-to-face meeting, such as when disciplining
- written report
- written presentation
- stand-up presentation
- sales pitch
- making a case orally
- making a case in writing
- written proposal

- impromptu speech
- impromptu announcement.

In fact, a bewildering choice will usually present itself once you consider the nature and purpose of your communication. Let's say you have to communicate something to a member of your staff, colleague or boss. Having thought about the nature or content of the communication, the circumstances and your resources, you can then choose:

- a casual or apparently unplanned face-to-face meeting
- a more formal planned meeting
- a meeting on your 'territory', on the other person's, or in a neutral venue such as a meeting room or public reception area
- a light-hearted approach
- a humorous approach
- to delegate the communication
- a shake of the head, raising of the eyebrows, a grunt, a wave of the hand
- a scheduled lunch meeting, inside or outside the organization's premises
- an apparently unplanned lunch meeting
- an evening telephone call
- a weekend telephone call
- a social meeting
- a recorded telephone message (when you know of the person's absence)
- an e-mail message
- a written note left on the person's desk or chair
- a rumour
- a petition or group communication
- a Board resolution
- an invoice, to inform of a debt
- a thank you card
- a gift – for example, to express appreciation
- to sit on a chair or desk or wall outside
- to stand in the corridor, office or car park
- to walk to the canteen or station, or in the park.

Communicating to a group

Let's return to the group situation. The same process applies, as do the presuppositions, but you may need to take a more broad-brush approach. For example, ask yourself: do you want to entertain, inform or impress your audience (Refer to the range of possible effects in Figure 6.1), or what precisely? As we have seen, each person will react differently anyway. If you decide from the start that you don't want to entertain, but just inform, then you can at least avoid any half-baked attempts at humour and light-heartedness.

On the other hand, if you aim primarily to entertain, you can exclude from your content any controversial material that might have other unpredictable effects on your audience, or boring information that you can transmit in another way. Even when seeking to entertain – as a communication outcome – the group context demands that you take a middle-of-the-road approach. Thus, whilst you may not produce side-splitting laughter, neither will you cause offence and alienation. With this approach, although you may have to lower your sights in terms of the effect you will have on each individual, you raise your sights in terms of your overall communication aims – in this case, to give all or most of your audience an entertaining time.

Other considerations apply in small groups, such as training session or meeting, as distinct from a larger audience (when you cannot, for instance, achieve individual eye-to-eye contact). In a smallish group, you can communicate to individuals *as well as* to the group as a whole. In this case, you can achieve more with a group, as you may have influence on individuals (using one-to-one techniques) who in turn will help to influence the whole group. You can use peer pressure, team dynamics and group motivation when communicating to a group. You may have different, though complementary, outcomes for one or more individuals and the training objective for the group as a whole. As with any outcomes, these may form immediate, short-term aims, as well as longer-term goals.

REASSESSING YOUR INPUTS

Having established your intentions and considered the effects of your communication, you can then consider your inputs realistically. I listed some earlier, such as preparation, and knowing your subject. From what you have now learnt, 'preparation' includes getting to know more about the other persons, their background, beliefs and attitudes and the situation in which they find themselves – in short, how they might perceive your communication as individuals.

Similarly, 'knowing your subject' now means, as well as the content of what you want to communicate, knowing the human subjects, or persons, in your audience – or at least knowing that they have their own mental maps. Depending on this knowledge, you can decide how you will communicate your message and achieve your intention, and what you need to prepare.

In this light, information about your audience may well prove more useful than the factual or technical content of your message. You may find you simply do not need certain content to achieve your response, or 'change of state' outcome. Effective communication means an efficient use of your time and energy, as well as the pleasure of achieving what you set out to.

You may have intended to both entertain and inform, but by focusing on your ultimate outcome you may eliminate or play down one of these. An audience can usually obtain straightforward *information* in some written form or other. However, in a live communication, you may want:

- to help the group to understand the information they already have
- them to enjoy a topic they find heavy
- to motivate them (a different effect, requiring different inputs)
- a group to grow familiar with a subject in their own way and in their own time
- to warn them of the dangers of not having information (another effect or outcome)
- to make them aware of a few key aspects of a subject.
- to transmit an important message they will always remember.

Aim to achieve one main goal, and to do it well. When setting your outcomes, bear in mind that your group can probably derive better entertainment from five minutes' television than from your amateur speech-making efforts, or for that matter, more information from a good television documentary or a paperback book. Decide what you can *personally communicate effectively*, but in the context of a mixed audience.

Group and individual communication factors

Most of this chapter applies in both individual or group situations. The additional factors and skills you will need in each case include those listed below, most of which we will cover later in the book. For the moment, it will suffice to have an idea of the resources on which you can call for effective communication, and the nature of any preparation. Some of these topics have wider significance in NLP, and will appear in later chapters. For communication purposes, however, you need to appreciate just how much control you can wield in a communication.

One-to-one

✓   Identify sensory preference, such as visual or auditory (see Chapter 8).
✓   Identify meta programs, thinking strategies and personality characteristics (see Chapters 15 and 17).
✓   Get to know their background and personal interests.
✓   Gain personal rapport by 'pacing and leading' (see Chapter 7).

Group

✓   Establish an overall group outcome.
✓   Focus on 'influencers'.
✓   Create group rapport (see Chapter 7).
✓   Foster team spirit.
✓   Focus on the 'middle ground', or modal participant.

We have already addressed some of these, and we will deal with others, such as pacing and leading, and meta programs, later. A few additional implications apply to larger or mass groups, such as a conference of hundreds, in which the audience tends to react as one person. For instance:

✓   As part of your preparation, find out the modal profile of the audience, just as you would the background of an individual.
✓   Pitch your overall outcome in the middle ground, as with a smaller group. If in doubt, opt for 'zero knowledge', and simplicity rather than complexity.
✓   Use metaphorical, *sensory language* that incorporates all the main senses – seeing, hearing, and feeling.
✓   Use the *language patterns* we will explore in later chapters, whether to induce a mild trance state and inward awareness, or to make the audience alert and externally aware, depending on your desired outcome.

These large-group situations go beyond the traditional boundaries of NLP. However, you will see from the above factors that you can readily adapt much of what you have learnt. In particular, you can apply the same communication presuppositions in any communication context.

7 *Pacing, Leading and Rapport*

Pacing – matching a person's body language, voice and other characteristics – forms an important part of achieving rapport, and hence better communication. This chapter describes the principle of rapport, and different techniques to establish it and to change a person's behaviour, to achieve the communication outcomes covered in the last chapter.

Rapport

Rapport ranks high as an element in successful communication, and the word occurs frequently in NLP. It incorporates features not easy to define. But most people readily understand the concepts, and just as readily accept them as vital to successful communication. They include:

- a harmonious, understanding relationship
- empathy
- a 'spiritual connection'
- positive 'chemistry'
- a shared desire to transfer understanding
- a 'mind-to-mind' dimension of relationships, or meeting of minds.

You can witness rapport in the special, unspoken relationship between an orchestra and its conductor that produces harmony. Without it, all the skill in the world will seem inadequate.

Rapport has not figured large in orthodox communication theory, which has focused on the 'message', 'medium', 'channels', 'interference' and so on. This may have resulted from the difficulty of defining the term, or of incorporating it into the logical, predictable steps that management textbook writers prefer.

Sometimes, this special relationship just happens when you least expect it. Two people of very different temperaments and background instantly 'hit it off'. Conversely, it often doesn't occur, even when all the circumstances appear favourable for good communication. The 'chemistry' seems all wrong. In this case, communication in the way we defined it earlier will probably not happen, nor will any sort of longer-term relationship follow. Rapport therefore forms a fundamental requirement in interpersonal communication, and accordingly figures large in NLP.

You can't easily teach such a 'soft' aspect of communication. However, we all possess rapport as a natural skill to some degree, as evidenced by small children lost in their own communal world of play. But we can all learn rapport skills, even those people who have closed their hearts and minds to relationships for many years. We don't need to rely on genetic advantages for this fundamental component of good communication.

We sometimes describe this extraordinary interpersonal state as 'chemistry', or speak of a person as 'on the same wavelength'. It happens especially between people in love, close lifetime friends, and in long-standing work relationships. Rapport shows itself uncannily in domestic relationships that have matured over many years and through shared experience, including hardships. With rapport, communication needs few words, and may even benefit from silence.

You can also witness rapport between complete strangers striking up a conversation, who find immediate common interests and experience mutual 'likeness'. We express this in comments like 'He is my kind of person', or 'We hit it off immediately.'

Rapport does not imply a rare or mysterious quality. We literally see rapport all around us as we watch people engaged in deep conversation over a lunch table, chatting whilst hurrying along the street, or sharing commuter experiences at a bus stop. The seeing, or outward evidence of rapport, involves what we term *matching*, in which the parties adopt a mutual 'likeness'. Matching happens in several ways, as we will discover in this chapter.

RECOGNIZING AND ACHIEVING RAPPORT

NLP can help in achieving the following aims as regards rapport:

- to recognize rapport, and the lack of it
- to achieve, enhance and maintain rapport
- to break rapport.

Each of these requires an understanding of matching. In particular, they demand skills of observation and behaviour that enable you to match *purposefully* – with the specific aim of creating rapport in order to communicate more effectively. This builds on some of the communication presuppositions covered earlier:

- The presupposition 'you cannot not communicate' reinforces the fact that we communicate non-verbally continuously, even to the level of minuscule muscle movements and the nuances of voice pitch and timbre. Matching draws on this sort of unconscious communication when done effectively.

- The presupposition 'communication is about the response you elicit' highlights the need for more than words and formal processes when transferring understanding from your mind to somebody else's. We now know the power of rapport through matching, and its impact on the success of a communication.

- The presupposition 'the responsibility for a communication lies with the communicator' means that – in the light of what you have learnt – you may need to consciously match in order to create rapport and ensure *your* (the communicator's) outcome. Otherwise, you will probably communicate something by default, and pay for it in due course.

LOOKING FOR RAPPORT

Matching usually accompanies rapport and effective communication. To recognize rapport, look out for matching. When you take part in a communication, you will need to consciously notice whether the other person approximately matches your body and voice characteristics, for instance. An observer, such as a trainer, teacher or a third party at a negotiating meeting, can do this easily when not involved in the 'content', or subject as a party to the communication. Adopt the habit of watching for rapport as an outside observer first. When party to a communication, you will experience involvement in the content, and will need to acquire the skill to observe many aspects at once.

As a stranger, you can witness rapport all around you – in the street, on buses and trains, at the office. This provides a good training ground to understand the phenomenon and familiarize yourself with what to look for. Even as a third-party observer, however, we can hardly think about more than one or two things at once in learning mode, especially when we have previously not taken notice. For this reason, it will help if you concentrate on one aspect of matching at a time, such as voice speed and pitch, mannerisms, posture, and so on. Use these common matching characteristics as a checklist, but remain alert to matching *of any kind*. In this way, you will acquire the simple, basic observation skills you need at a pace you can cope with.

Different aspects of matching require different observation and listening skills. You may need to listen for a while before identifying a sensory pattern in a person's language, for example. On the other hand, you can spot a common posture and mannerism instantly, so you may wish to start with this feature when practising your skills. You will need different skills, at different levels, to intuitively recognize matching and rapport. You have unlimited scope for matching skills, and the true communicator never stops learning and doing.

ACHIEVING RAPPORT

To achieve rapport, you may need to match *purposely*. Do this in any of the ways described in this chapter. In the case of interests, values and so forth, it may involve discovering possible common areas. You can then use one of these as an icebreaker, a topic for examples and illustrations, or a subject for casual conversation. In other words, rather than trying to match out of your depth, identify where you might have common interests.

Even without knowledge of the other person's interests, once you identify them, you can take a genuine interest. Ask questions about what interests the other person, in a sincere way, and you will quickly gain rapport. People have the greatest interest in *themselves* and their work, hobbies and pastimes. The converse applies, of course. As the saying goes: 'People are not interested in other people's babies.'

You can bridge big gaps simply by accepting another person's mental map, and more so by showing genuine curiosity. Often, simple questions such as 'How does it work?', 'Tell me what you do in your spare time' or 'What do you like about (fishing, painting, Dickens, and so on?)' will put a person at their ease. You will confirm rapport as they start to match in the usual vocal and physical ways.

Pacing

Pacing, as in the phrase 'pacing and leading', refers to the concept of matching described earlier. It means, in effect, keeping pace with the other person, such as in body language and voice characteristics. In this case, we match or 'pace' with a view to *leading* – or bringing about change in the other person – rather than just to achieve and maintain rapport. Other than in that sense, NLP uses the terms interchangeably. This section covers the main categories of pacing/matching. Of course, we don't always want, or need, to lead, and as we have seen, simply achieving rapport produces great communication benefits. I have therefore mostly kept to the term 'matching'. You will learn about leading later in this chapter.

BODY LANGUAGE

You will notice one of the more obvious examples of matching when people in rapport seem to adopt similar body language. They tend to mirror each other's physical profiles, stance, posture and even gesticulations. Common examples of physical matching include folding arms, crossing legs, leaning back or forward, hand and arm movements, facial expressions, head-nodding and shaking, and any other visible activity. At a whole-body level, it produces, in effect, mirrored silhouettes.

At another level, an acute observer notices the tiniest muscular movements and nuances of expression. Although visible, we *sense* some of these body movements and characterize them subconsciously, perhaps using peripheral vision. Non-verbal communication (NVC) consists of two main types, *kinesics* and *proxemics*, each made up of several elements or characteristics.

Kinesics

Facial expressions include smiles, frowns, narrowed eyes and scores of subtle expressions that we learn to recognize from childhood. These transmit emotions such as friendliness, anger, disbelief and sympathy.

Gestures include finger-pointing, head-shaking, general arm and hand movements, and specific hand movements such as clasping with intertwining fingers, making a fist, facing one or both open palms upwards, and so on. Like facial expressions, these can convey:

- agreement or disagreement
- focus and attention
- a special point or emphasis
- openness and honesty
- congratulations
- acceptance
- resignation
- sincerity.

They can also communicate many more mind-to-mind messages. Each emotion can vary in intensity along a wide spectrum. For instance, a person can show:

- slight annoyance
- anger
- preoccupation
- non-interest
- passionate frenzy
- that they more or less accept your message
- that they agree enthusiastically.

This means that we can make hundreds of subtle communications without saying a word, or even without consciously communicating ('You cannot not communicate.'). With the support of appropriate language, we create synergy through non-verbal communication.

Kinesic movements that may form part of a communication include:

- pacing up and down
- strolling
- drumming fingers
- slapping thighs
- standing up
- sitting down
- clapping hands
- crossing legs
- folding and unfolding arms
- clasping hands behind the head
- laying a hand on one's head
- placing both hands palms down on a table
- pointing (for example, to nose or head).

Look around in a crowded office and you will observe dozens of examples of kinesics in a few minutes. Gestures typically enforce, or physically underline, a word or phrase, or point of issue. Changes of position often reflect the general tone of a communication. But these 'macro' body movements, as well as gestures, are graduated in speed and the amount of 'space' used. They vary from slight to wild and exaggerated movements that infringe the other person's own personal space. This means that physical movement can depict innumerable characteristics of the emotion and characteristics of the communication.

Proxemics

Proxemics involves physical contact, positioning and posture.

Physical contact includes:

- shaking hands
- slapping on the back
- prodding with the finger
- hugging
- patting
- touching the arm or shoulder
- 'holding' by the arms or shoulder with extended arms
- mimicked, gentle punching
- ruffling the hair
- holding hands.

Because of the way different people react to touching, and their need for personal 'space', physical contact can intensify a communication, both positively and negatively. It can transmit (often more powerfully than words):

- greetings
- friendship and warmth
- sympathy
- care and understanding
- insistence.

It can also convey many other sentiments.

Positioning includes:

- distance from the other person and encroaching on their space
- sitting close or at a distance
- the effect of physical barriers such as a desk
- orientation, including the direction of chairs.

The last option includes chairs facing the same direction (for example, when both occupy a settee or in 'theatre-style' seating), at 90 degrees (as when looking at a common document or object) or facing towards each other as in a more formal interview. To this we could add high or low level of seating and its well-known connotations of power and vulnerability respectively.

Posture includes:

- standing straight
- leaning (say, to the side against a wall or partition, with an elbow on a shelf or other support, or leaning forward with both hands on a desk)
- lounging
- sitting upright
- leaning forward or back, spread-eagled over a chair, and so on.

You will quickly realize how each of these postures suggests the kind of conversation and its tone, the level of formality or informality, and the general demeanour and emotion of the parties. Along with overlapping kinesics, these proxemic characteristics offer many NVC communication tools. At the same time, you need a good deal of sensory acuity to notice it all for the purpose of matching and to gain feedback. This presents a challenge when carrying on a normal conversation as one of the parties, needing to understand 'content' as well as the process.

This plethora of body language might explain why we rarely notice the matching process at the time, even when fully aware of matching as a phenomenon. Even when we do consciously think about the process, as with blinking, breathing and personal mannerisms, we soon lapse into unconscious matching behaviour when we become absorbed in a conversation. We cannot sustain conscious awareness for long, any more than the other person can. However, as with any skill you master, after a while you don't need to think about it. So the early, self-conscious learning period will repay the time and effort. Bear this in mind as you consider matching these kinesics and proxemics to gain rapport.

MATCHING VOICE AND WORDS

Evidence of rapport through matching extends beyond seeing. We also match voice tone and pitch, speed of conversation and other characteristics of spoken dialogue. For instance, we might describe voice characteristics as animated, grave, intense, and so forth. Such characteristics allow us to quickly deduce the kind of communication taking place by the general polyphony (for example, voice sounds heard in another room, or across the office) rather than distinguishable words.

Voice matching applies in telephone conversations, when you can quickly detect anxiety, annoyance and other feelings. As with visible matching, when in rapport we seem to sense vocal 'likeness' unconsciously. Indeed, as with physical body language, we could hardly concentrate on the complex mechanics of the voice when engrossed in the content of the communication and the relationship itself – in short, when in rapport.

Language matching

You will have noticed that young people, fellow professionals and people with the same background often seem to use the same sort of language. This includes words and phrases, and technical or special terms unique to their group. This illustrates likeness, or matching. More commonly, though, we tend to match words and phrases that reflect our preference for one or more senses – seeing, hearing or feeling. NLP calls these *sensory predicates*, and they cover hundreds of words and expressions that indicate the sense, or representational system, in which a person processes their thoughts: for instance, 'I see what you mean', 'That sounds fine', 'I know how you must feel' and such common remarks. People use sensory predicates to a degree you would never imagine without specifically listening for them. Chapter 8 deals in detail with representational systems.

OTHER KINDS OF MATCHING

Rapport can result from other kinds of non-verbal, non-physical matching, such as the following:

- *Common interests and experience* – for example, when you can't separate two railway-modelling enthusiasts at a party, or when nurses revel in their gory common experiences. You find the same common ties when lawyers or scientists speak with ease about familiar, comfortable spheres of knowledge and experience, sharing their own specialist terminology and in-jokes.

- *A common objective* – such as when people pull together in hardships such as war ('wartime spirit'), or undergo demanding business or outward-bound courses. Similarly, sportspeople often act in uncanny harmony in order to win, as in tennis doubles and rowing. We can witness this feature of rapport, paradoxically, when estranged parents share the same goal of doing the best for their children. The common goal 'match' overrides other differences.

- *Common values* – such as when people attach importance to the same sort of things, and in doing so have mutual respect for each other's integrity and wisdom. A common concern for the environment, for example, or a religious calling, can bridge differences between people of very different backgrounds.

- *Common background* – this forms an aspect of 'likeness', such as when people easily relate with 'their own type' in a working men's club, gentlemen's club, church or prison. Similar grounds for rapport exist when two people hail from a rural environment or inner city, share an expatriate or public school upbringing, and so on.

- *A common circumstance or situation* – 'We're all in this together', as when waiting for a delayed flight or train, stuck in a lift, bearing up in a local flood or heat wave, or enduring a particularly cold office. This reflects the 'common objective' characteristic above, and extraordinary 'wartime spirit', but in this case they share just the experience, rather than a definite objective. Positive as well as negative experiences and circumstances can bond people, as when people witness an outstanding sunset, spot a whale, or share ecstasy, wonder, fun or a special moment in history.

Such commonality doesn't guarantee rapport, by any means. Indeed, people in the same trade or profession sometimes feel threatened, and people from the same home town may feel vulnerable or embarrassed. In such cases, given similar basic values, we may relate better to a stranger.

In whatever disparate ways, matching does not confine itself to the physical matching we associate with body language, although no single instance of matching will always bring about rapport. However, when you want to deliberately match a person to gain rapport, you can choose from the many factors above. If one doesn't work, another might. NLP offers a more a flexible *way of thinking*, rather than a toolkit of techniques.

Matching helps to bring about rapport and effective communication. It offers a simple but extraordinarily powerful way of getting what you want out of any communication.

MATCHING GUIDELINES

No hard and fast rules exist for matching. Basically, you copy. Nevertheless, a few general ground rules may speed up the learning process and prevent embarrassment and failure.

✓ *Don't exaggerate* – You don't need to match identically, and in particular you shouldn't try to match what seem like extreme or unusual mannerisms or voice characteristics. Use your common sense. A person rarely notices conscious matching, and even more rarely unconscious matching, with both parties unaware of their behaviour. But it makes sense to avoid this possibility anyway.

✓ *Partial matching* – You can partially match, rather than reacting too precisely or over-reacting. In partial matching, you can match a *type* of behaviour but in a different way. For instance, you can clasp your hands rather than folding your arms, or play with your pen rather than picking at your nails, or cross your legs in a different but more comfortable way, or nod your head in time with the speed of a person's speech and level of animation. In this way, you will reflect the general mode – rhythm, or dance – of the communication, but without drawing undue attention to your matching behaviour.

✓ *Practise in a low-risk situation* – Don't try out your matching skills in an important interview or critical negotiation. Practise it with friends and family, or with strangers with whom you do not foresee or desire a longer-term relationship.

✓ *Respond paralinguistically* – We make feedback sounds all the time to indicate we understand what someone says: for instance, 'OK', 'Yes', 'Uhuh', 'I see', 'Whew', grunts and other sounds we understand colloquially. Such sounds can also indicate annoyance or impatience – in fact, a wide range of communication nuances. Known as *paralinguistics*, this universal vocal practice generally aids rapport by letting the person know you follow their communication. It usually acts as a kind of informal assent, and implies permission to carry on.

✓ *Timing, timing, timing* – Actors and comedians know the importance of timing, and this factor should feature high up on your list when matching for rapport. Precise timing does not mean instantly changing your behaviour to ape the other person. On the contrary, you will need a slight delay, and – as with the punch line of a joke ('It's the way you tell them.') – the timing of that interval requires skill and practice. Too long a delay and you will allow a temporary mismatch. Too short a delay and you may draw attention to your mimicking. An innocuous, well-timed change of behaviour will *flow* with the overall communication. Otherwise, delay can match the speed and manner of change in posture generally – which varies from person to person – along with mannerisms or voice as you join in the choreography of rapport.

✓ *Stay in character* – You will feel uncomfortable yourself when you behave uncharacteristically – another reason to avoid exaggerating. This self-awareness will communicate itself, and will not aid rapport. To some degree, self-awareness, or discomfort, forms part of the learning process, of course, as you move out of your familiar mental map and start to experience the other person's map of the world. Do this in small increments, and you will soon develop the skill of adaptability that top communicators use.

Avoid copying abnormal behaviour of any sort. You will usually suffer no embarrassment by matching normal behaviour, even if the other person notices it. This sometimes happens with fellow salespeople and trained communicators. The same will not apply when caught mimicking a facial tic, a myopic squint, a nasal flare, a one-sided curl of the lip, or mannerisms peculiar to the opposite sex.

Don't follow the common rule (that applies to many situations) to 'be yourself' if that means refusing to match different behaviour. You can keep your identity and stay in character while empathizing, or 'being somebody else', *for the purpose of rapport and a successful communication*. Effective matching relies on degree, common courtesy and – most importantly – common sense.

MISMATCHING

When you don't match, you mismatch. This can happen at any of the levels we have covered: for instance, if two persons' interests, values and beliefs happen to lie far apart. This doesn't mean you can never achieve rapport with a person of different interests. It just means you have to pace their values, in the sense of acknowledging and respecting rather than adopting them. Once again, you do this in the interest of a successful communication outcome, for which you will invariably need rapport. Matching at other levels, such as voice and body language, will also require that you leave aside your comfortable way of behaving, again with the purpose of a successful communication.

Negative chemistry

You will soon start to recognize mismatching, both as you observe people around you, and also as you practise matching in your own everyday communications. For instance, you will detect the absence of personal 'chemistry':

✓ Somehow you don't 'connect'.
✓ You don't 'hit it off'.
✓ You operate 'on different planes', in 'different dimensions'.
✓ The other person, you might say, 'comes from another planet'.
✓ It seems to go in one ear and out the other.
✓ I might as well talk to the wall.
✓ Conversation doesn't flow as easily as it does on other occasions.
✓ Whatever the content of the communication, the process doesn't give pleasure.

This often boils down to simple mismatching, but perhaps at a different, 'higher' level than more obvious physiology. Usually, when in a mismatched communication, we cannot genuinely profess to this 'meta', or higher, approach to matching. So-called negative chemistry probably has very real causes if we care to think and observe, so check back on the more or less unlimited range of matching behaviour, and especially state of mind, we can adopt.

So far, we have considered mismatching in a negative way, but in some situations you may wish to mismatch deliberately.

Perceived unlikeness

Before we address possible reasons for breaking rapport though mismatching, let's discuss what mismatching entails. It means reversing the matching process. *Perceived unlikeness* replaces perceived likeness. You can mismatch using all the matching devices discussed above, but in reverse: for instance, maintaining a slow, deliberate, quiet voice while the other person reaches high speeds and new peaks of emotion, will all but guarantee an icy, invisible barrier and resentment. Similarly, look away from the person to something or somebody else – just momentarily – and you will quash rapport more effectively than by ten minutes of thinly veiled rudeness in attempting to end a communication. Do it skilfully, and the person may not realize why the flow of conversation has suddenly dried up. We no more consciously notice mismatching *behaviour* than we do matching behaviour. Rather, we notice its *effect* on the way we feel.

Mismatching strategies

You have many mismatching strategies to choose from. For example:

- stand up abruptly from a sitting conversation
- sit down from a standing position
- stop in the middle of a walking conversation
- go silent for a few moments
- look into the far distance
- blow your nose
- sharpen a pencil.

The person might momentarily question your mental state, but will rarely detect your desire to break rapport.

Don't listen   Another option: simply don't listen. How do you do that? Don't put your fingers in your ears. Just think of something else altogether, such as the coming weekend, a sporting event or your bonus calculation. The other person can't prove anything (mindread), of course, and will rarely challenge you. Look in their approximate eye direction and nod from time to time. They merely sense something wrong, and *they* decide to end their monologue. You retain a friend, colleague or potential customer, and perhaps release the next period in your diary that might offer greater outcome potential.

Alternatively, go silent for a few moments for no reason (known to them). They think to themselves, 'Funny …', and usually lose some of their former interest in the content of the communication.

Importantly, with purposeful mismatching, any genuine relationship remains intact (close friends and relations make allowances for all sorts of idiosyncrasies), and you don't prejudice longer-term goals, or limit choices as yet unknown.

Mismatching on purpose

With simple devices such as these and a little practice, you can use mismatching to break rapport in various situations, for example when you wish to do the following:

- *Bring a communication to a close* – You may consider you have obtained your outcome (say, persuading, consoling, or informing) or you may decide to abort your outcome (you no longer want what you wanted, or no longer feel you have much chance of obtaining it). Some bosses know how to terminate interviews summarily without incurring personal resentment. Similarly, socially experienced hostesses can truncate a communication just as efficiently.

- *Redirect a conversation* – A fluid communication, especially with strong rapport, can take on any direction, pace or mode (such as serious, jocular, morbid or *laissez-faire*) that may not square with your intentions. A sudden mismatch can bring the communication to a temporary halt – like reaching a road junction – from which you can then lead to another direction, pace or mode more conducive to your communication outcome.

- *Attract attention* – Paradoxically, strong rapport can involve a light trance ('downtime') state. In this state, we enjoy the process ('Doesn't the time fly when you're enjoying yourself?'; 'We just talked and talked.') but may fail in pursuing the purpose or outcome of the communication. A sudden mismatch usually brings the other person into an alert, 'uptime' state in which you have their full attention. Use this device, for instance, when you want to make an important point. The surprise element creates an *emotional* response. The other person feels that something happened. This particularly helps to fix any associated message in their memory.

- *Temporarily interrupt a communication* – This often happens by default, of course, if a telephone rings or somebody barges into your office, but you may wish to interrupt a communication for your own purposes, such as:
  - to consider an important matter for few moments
  - to carry out an important brief task
  - to allow a communication to have an effect on the other person by allowing them time to reflect.

Declaring this tactical outcome overtly might prejudice your overall communication outcome by 'making an issue' of it or conveying a sense of lack of control on their part.

However, by achieving a mismatch as if at a 'natural juncture' in the communication, you maintain rapport, and can carry on your communication where you left off. You can even plan to have coffee served at a predetermined time or signal.

* *End a relationship* – Mismatching breaks rapport, and if done unthinkingly, spoils relationships, just as matching creates rapport and enhances relationships. The outcome of ending a relationship occurs from time to time in social settings, and sometimes in business. Fashionable 'relationship marketing' policies stress that you should identify and look after your best customers (according to loyalty and profitability), but that you should discard your worst. The same might apply to employees and teams. In this case, the 'weakest link' in a team may not relate to skills and task achievement, but to compatibility with the culture and mission of the organization or team. In such a case, the systemic impact of enhancing unrewarding relationships will not contribute to higher team or organizational goals. If you break rapport convincingly, *neither* party will wish to create or perpetuate the relationship. Given a clear outcome, you can use mismatching skills to bring about more beneficial outcomes without the acrimony that usually accompanies the ending of a relationship.

* *Save time* – Some of these purposes have the added benefits of serving as a time management device. People who accomplish much or occupy a leadership role seem to maintain relationships whilst frequently taking control of communications.

The matching habit

We have seen that matching happens all around us all the time. Unconscious, habitual behaviour accounts for almost all matching. Yet however familiar they seem, these habitual mind-body processes appear sophisticated in the extreme when we consider them as subjective processes. They work 'perfectly' inasmuch as we repeatedly achieve intentions we don't give a moment's conscious thought to, like drinking coffee, climbing the stairs or expressing surprise with our eyes. The significance of matching, as such an unconscious process, lies in its association with effective communication. NLP endeavours to apply this example of excellent human behaviour to more situations, and in a purposeful way, with a view to increasing our rate of effective interpersonal communication and change.

An 'unconscious' activity invariably loses its effectiveness when we do it consciously. For instance, try to demonstrate tying a necktie in public, or try folding your arms with your hands the opposite way to usual. Indeed, if you continually think about what you do while you do it when climbing stairs or running for a bus, you will soon break a limb. Such behaviour doesn't work that way. However, you can certainly create and change habits consciously, with practice. This applies when learning to drive, hitting a golf ball, knitting or tying shoelaces and in a thousand other instances of everyday activities we don't think about. Matching and mismatching behaviour fits this category.

Correcting a bad driving habit provides a good example of the change process. First, you need to know what you do wrongly (which you never think about). Then persevere in doing it correctly until one day, perhaps about three weeks later, you realize you have changed your bad habit. The realization suddenly comes that you did it differently without 'thinking'. Sooner or later, with enough practice, we all carry out even the most complex behaviours 'without thinking'.

NLP takes this approach with matching:

✓   You first need to notice matching in yourself and others. This requires observation skills you may have to develop.

✓   Then you need to introduce it consciously, a little at a time, so that you don't lose track of the content of your communication, and the reason for it.

✓   Next, you need to notice what happens when you use matching behaviour. Again, do this a little at a time, as it may stretch your limited conscious mind, just as when changing a bad driving habit.

✓   You will then proceed to change the other person's matched behaviour, while maintaining rapport, in order to further your communication outcomes.

As you continue to learn about how people think, you will increase your armoury both for matching and mismatching, especially at a higher, or meta, level. The meta programs described in Chapter 15 offer numerous opportunities for matching thinking style and personality traits. You can also draw on the Life Content Model covered in Chapter 3 to either match or mismatch a *doing, having, knowing, relating* or *being preference.*

Leading

Pacing means consciously matching the other person. This means keeping in pace in the many senses – physiological, voice, and so on – that we have considered. Leading, in the sense of 'pacing and leading', means having an effect on the other person's behaviour. Whereas matching *responds* to the behaviour of the other person, when you lead you become the agent of change, and *create* it. This gives you more control of the communication. Rapport, the immediate objective of matching or pacing, enables you to communicate effectively, or 'get through' to the person. Leading allows you greater scope in achieving communication outcomes for specific purposes.

LEADING ON PURPOSE

When might leading prove useful? Sometimes, whilst you can achieve matched behaviour, it may not help with a particular communication, such as when the other person adopts a negative state of mind, but your communication outcome requires a positive state. Likewise, some communication works better when seated than when standing. At other times, you need to adopt an animated rather than doleful tone of voice, or ordinary-volume speech rather than yelling and shrieking. Simply matching in these cases might make matters worse. You might achieve rapport (as can happen, paradoxically, in a heated debate), but the person's behaviour and temperament might not help you obtain what you want.

Top salespeople claim to know well the body language signals for a 'yes' and a 'no'. A person who leans back, with arms folded, legs crossed and head half turned away, for example, may not display the best posture to do a deal with. As we have just seen, rapport may follow when you simply match the body language. For instance, a customer feels more at ease with a salesperson who adopts their posture – however 'negative', inappropriate or otherwise – than if they lean forward with gesticulating open arms in a so-called 'positive' mode. Such 'pushy' behaviour tends to intimidate and annoy. This confirms the importance of matching for rapport as a general rule.

Such matched behaviour might work well in some communications, such as passing on information or discussing non-emotive matters. However, when you want to gain commitment and positive behaviour (like signing an order form), simply mirroring a customer's actions may not help towards a successful outcome. So, having paced to achieve rapport, you need to do some leading with a view to the *appropriate* mind-body state for the outcome you want – a sales order or other commitment, for instance. Bear in mind the presupposition that the responsibility for a communication lies with the communicator. That means that the communicator has to bring about the changes needed, whether in behaviour, attitude or feelings.

WHEN NOT TO KEEP COOL

Leading doesn't mean just doing it your way. As we saw earlier, rather than 'be yourself', we sometimes need to 'be the other person'. One school of thought says that when confronted with an irate customer you should speak slowly, quietly, and without excited body movements. This typifies orthodox communication theory before NLP presuppositions such as 'communication is the response you elicit' started to have their effect. But most of us know well that if you keep cool while the other person shakes with anger, it makes them worse! The cooler you seem to them, the more they think you don't care, act belligerently, have no feelings, and so on. Unless we intend such an effect (perhaps unconsciously), this illustrates matching inappropriate for the communication purpose.

Leading assumes that the other party, even if unconsciously, agrees to follow, or act like you. And that implies a measure of rapport, or mutual understanding to start with. Otherwise, the person will construe any behaviour – not to mention any words you say – negatively, and you will fail in your outcome.

Hence the need for pacing and leading. You cannot lead unless you first pace or match, and thus gain rapport. Go back to the earlier example of the customer adopting a 'closed' body language. Matching means just that – you match their behaviour, however unconducive it seems to your ultimate outcome. Leading then takes the form of an incremental process that depends on sensory acuity – the ability to monitor subtle feedback. In this example, you might uncross your legs while maintaining folded arms, perhaps leaning slightly forward in the movement. Then do nothing, until the person follows your lead in some way. They may well make the same change, or maybe uncross their arms. This happens entirely unconsciously on their part. It provides the signal that you have maintained the level of rapport you had before your lead. Carry on pacing and leading in small increments, always waiting for a match or 'crossover' match (an *equivalent* behaviour, or one that takes the *direction* you desire) before taking any further lead.

The same process would apply in the case of a highly irate customer, waving their arms and speaking in a loud, high-pitched voice. In this case, you need not match exactly, and that applies to any extreme situation. However, you need to 'go along' with the person in your level of excitement or concern ('I know just how you feel.') and the way it affects you in your body language, and in the speed, volume and pitch of your voice. In other words, act the way you would in the other person's shoes and feeling the way they do. By behaving congruently with those feelings, you will gain rapport more effectively than by precise matching, and certainly better than by pretending to keep cool.

MATCHING FEELINGS

Matching feelings offers a simple, winning tactic. To do this, you will have to use the body language that *for you* reflects those feelings. That way you will communicate likeness of feelings rather than just outward features. Hence, you may not match exactly, but you associate congruently with the person. In an extraordinary way, you can gain rapport even with the angriest person. This should come as no surprise, as your overall outcomes probably coincide: to reach a mutually satisfactory result. The customer perhaps wants fairness. You want to keep or enhance your reputation for caring customer service. You both finish up happy, or less unhappy, than without the communication.

Leading can then follow the same course as with the negative, unresponsive customer. Maybe drop your voice a little and wait for a response. Slightly slow down the pace of your speech and body movements, and again watch for any change. Otherwise, maintain whatever rapport you have gained, as you will certainly not succeed without it, even if you win the argument.

WHERE TO LEAD

As we saw from the checklist earlier, an important lead might involve persuading the person to take a seat, conducting them to a private room, and so on. You can achieve almost any change of behaviour from a position of rapport. Remember, though, that when in the role of communicator, you have to decide on 'appropriate' behaviour, seating arrangements and so forth. Thus, you will need to decide on the conditions conductive to a successful communication, or you will have no coherent strategy for leading.

In the last example, you will probably want the customer seated if you wish to come to a rational compromise or establish the facts. In another case, say involving an upset employee or colleague, you may decide to go for a stroll outside, or carry on a whispered conversation in an open-plan office. NLP doesn't lay down fixed rules about rapport strategy. Nevertheless, acting out the communication presuppositions – or even just believing them as 'true' – will keep you on the right course maybe 80 per cent of the time. Think about the response or outcome you want. That thought process will usually suggest the best environment, posture, message and tone for a successful communication.

Pacing and leading will test your communication skills. Matching alone demands special skills, of course, especially in observation and timing. However, when matching, you respond rather than taking the lead. In the case of leading, you first need to know where you want to lead the person, and what body-mind state and environment will best suit a successful communication. But you also need the 'sensory acuity' already referred to. In particular, you will need to notice subtle behaviour changes in response to your leads, and determine whether they follow the right direction for the outcome you want.

I don't want to overstate the difficulty of this special skill, though. You can achieve just about anything if you have well-formed outcomes and a flexible attitude, and practise till you get it right.

8 *Representational Systems*

The NLP model set out in Chapter 3 described the way we think in terms of our five senses. We also call these *modalities*, or representational systems. They determine how we *represent* the world around us. They comprise seeing, hearing, feeling, tasting and smelling. We all use our representational systems continuously. In combination, they heighten experience, motivate, or record an unforgettable memory just as in real, multi-sensory life. Chapter 8 deals with this central aspect of NLP.

The music of Beethoven or Bach can stir us powerfully as an auditory experience alone, of course. But coupled with the vivid spectacle of a concert and the movement of musicians in time with the music, with the deep, resonant, vibrating bass notes coming through the floor to your stomach – not to mention the occasional spinal tingles and other almost indescribable emotions – combining these senses equates to living and consciousness.

We then start to *experience*, rather than making mechanical 'sensory representations'. Add to this associations with earlier experiences of the same composition, the same venue, the same important person near you – all drawing on rich, multi-sensory memories, each with their own emotional impact. In such an experience, we carve out even deeper, wider canyons in our neural landscape. Or – more metaphors – we travel along busy mental motorways, made busier by yet more millions of synaptic firings. As we traverse old pathways again by way of new external experience, we unconsciously draw on special memory reservoirs. All this adds an extraordinarily rich dimension to the colourless, spiritless energy waves we originally sensed.

Not everyone uses all these sensory systems to the same extent, but a few minutes blindfold or deprived of any other sense soon confirms how much we depend on every possible representation to create the subjective reality we call experience – the mental map of the NLP model.

Seeing occupies the top representational system place, simply because we tend to use this sense most. It also takes up the biggest share of brain space, and according to experts, embodies the greatest complexity. In fact, what we term 'seeing' consists of various systems. We can 'represent' movement, distance, contrast or colour, for instance. In some cases, different visual functions happen in different parts of the brain, and work independently, as scientists have discovered from subjects with partial brain damage. In particular, the visual sense figures prominently in imagination, memory, and many aspects of the mind dealt with in NLP. For present purposes, we will consider seeing simply in terms of a primary sense, rather than addressing its awesome physiological processes.

Seeing

The process of seeing relies on a chain of events beginning with the optical recording of an outside object and finishing with what we believe we see, and what it means to us. NLP terms this our *understanding*, or how we represent an image in our personal map of reality.

Sometimes, the input at one end bears little relation to the output at the other end of the system. Moreover, the process involves more than sophisticated optics. Our final understanding takes into account *existing* mental patterns. These, in turn, depend on, among other things:

- what we have seen in the past
- how we classified or interpreted it
- how we recollected and changed it from time to time
- our attitude or feelings towards the experience
- what we expect to see on this occasion.

So seeing doesn't happen in the eyes alone, or even in the optical process. We see with our brain, or mind, rather than with our eyes. Put another way, the brain tells the eye what it sees, rather than the eye telling the brain. 'Visualizing', in the sense that we usually use the word, involves your whole mind, imagination, memory, beliefs and feelings.

With all these apparent obstacles and filters, visual representations reach the mind in no more distorted, generalized and incomplete a condition than any other representation. But how we 'visualize' something has a disproportionate effect on how we think, and in consequence behave. We often use the term 'visualize' to include imagining with all the senses. When it comes to changing how we think and behave, therefore – a major part of NLP – visual images form much of the raw material for change. As an NLP foundation skill, you need to learn how to access visual (V) memories, and how to change or manipulate them for your purposes. I know that readers and trainees on live programmes vary enormously in their ability to make clear internal representations, although this varies, as we shall see, from one modality to another. So, according to your 'sensory fitness', you may need to exercise mentally in one or more of the three main modalities. See a blue circle, a leaning building, an old friend, a pile of nuts. Familiarize yourself with the visual language of your mind.

Hearing

Hearing comes next in relative importance. Like seeing, we mirror this sense internally. We use sound – including the spoken voice – when storing and accessing memories, imagining the future, experiencing emotion, and in thinking generally. Some memories include a dominant auditory content. In this case, a sound will stimulate recall, and we can easily represent, or reproduce, it as we thought it happened. Not surprisingly, in view of the importance of other people in our lives, sounds in our memory usually include words, language and the human voice. We refer, for instance, to 'self-talk' and 'inner dialogue' – 'I said to myself …'. NLP refers to this aspect of the auditory representational system as *Auditory digital* (Ad), and for some purposes treats it as a separate modality. So-called 'left-brain' or abstract thinking, in words, numbers or symbols, utilizes this form of representation, rather than the five familiar senses.

The auditory representational system therefore comprises both analogue characteristics such as volume and tone, and the digital, or symbolic, aspects of language and speech (Ad)

– the words themselves. We access Ad, for example, when we 'rehearse' the words we will use in reply to a question, or 'talk' our way through a problem mentally. It provides another important part of the raw material for changing thought patterns and behaviour which you will become familiar with.

Feeling

The sense of touch or feeling comes third. This includes weight, temperature and texture, the sense of movement and position in space. For instance, you can 'feel' where you move your hand to, even with your eyes closed, and you can imagine yourself performing a physical movement such as riding a bike or making a tennis stroke. For NLP purposes, we usually include within the main 'kinaesthetic' (K) sense the sense of balance, known as the vestibular system. This sense covers more than not falling off a bike or the ability to walk across a plank. Feeling off balance, and the physical sense of disorientation, affects our whole body and visual perspective, as well as movement and position, and can influence our 'feelings' or state of mind. As it happens, the mechanics for the vestibular system occupy the inner ear, an indication of the proximity and interdependence of these representational systems.

Some experiments involved subjects harnessed into a mechanism that could turn their bodies through 360 degrees in any orientation. It transpired that a person's state of mind changes along with their physical orientation. In this case, people could not maintain previously induced states such as anger and rage after undergoing the other kinaesthetic changes. Similar results occur when you interfere with a person's balance, even marginally.

In NLP, the kinaesthetic sense includes 'feelings' of the emotional sort, which we cannot usually relate to a tactile, kinaesthetic or vestibular sense. In describing how you 'feel' about something, you usually mean more than the sense of touch and movement. Nevertheless, this involves more than a mental process, with different parts and functions of the body very much at work. Thus, we sometimes describe a feeling as 'in the stomach', 'down the spine' or in some physical way. Emotion involves *motion* – a pounding heart, a self-managing bowel, knocking knees, shaking hands – whether inside or outside, and whether visible or invisible to others. A *sensation* involves more than an abstract thought. For instance, it often contradicts what we think rationally. But human feelings also often beggar description in tactile terms.

Tasting and smelling

We use the final two representational systems, taste (gustatory) and smell (olfactory), very little in everyday human relationships. Whilst included as part of the VAKOG NLP model, for most purposes we use the three main systems (VAK), including the wider meaning of feeling in K. However, these senses do play a special part in memory and imagination, if not in normal communication. A taste or smell, for instance, may stimulate recall of a distant memory in a far more powerful, extraordinary way than a sight or sound. The childhood memories evoked by the taste of a madeleine cake in Proust's *Remembrance of Things Past* provide one of the best-known examples of this phenomenon.

Making mental maps

Representational systems process real, visible, audible, tactile stimuli in the real world. However, as representations of reality they have the same subjective, volatile features as feelings or distant memories. Each contributes to a person's mental map, but that map remains a map – no more than a perception or model of reality. It follows that we each see, hear and feel the same thing in a different way. Most people find it hard to accept that they don't 'see' tangible objects in front of their eyes. Yet we somehow can accept more easily that *other people's* views distort reality. This explains why we sometimes disagree with each other on seemingly 'black and white' issues.

We all tend to construe whatever we perceive through our senses as real, true and inviolable. Indeed, we could hardly cope moment by moment if we did not experience the world we inhabit as real. Yet, in times of reflection and introspection, a person will usually accept this humbling revelation more readily. Nevertheless, we may have to change our habitual perceptions *counter-intuitively* in the first instance. In effect, the real you – rather than a bundle of senses – takes responsibility for your thoughts and behaviour, and becomes the agent of change. Your clever representational systems *serve your purpose*, whether representing the outside world of your inner map of reality.

Sensory preference

As we have *seen*, we use the visual sense most, followed by hearing then feeling. This applies universally. However, within this modal tendency a person usually has an individual preference for which sense they use. You have probably heard people described as 'visual'. Similarly, we refer to 'good listeners', implying auditory skills, or 'touchy-feely' people, more at home with kinaesthetic sensations. We generally refer to this innate bias as *sensory preference*.

You can sometimes identify this preference from a person's interests, hobbies or occupation. Activities such as pottery and occupations like physiotherapy, for instance, require a special sense of touch. Architecture, art and design, and technical drawing demand strong visual skills. Some professions involve listening to people, and those that require musical skills obviously rely on the auditory sense.

AUDITORY DIGITAL

We saw in the section on the auditory sense that some people prefer to 'think' in dialogue or self-talk, and we classify this preference as *Auditory digital* (Ad). 'Digital' relates to the non-sensory symbols such as words or numbers we may use to think, rather than the analogue pictures, sounds and feelings of the three main representational systems. We usually associate this modality with logical, analytical, perhaps unimaginative thought, and with self-talk, in which we internally mull over a problem in words.

'Auditory digital' people often have a hearing preference, and we consider them good listeners – an example of inevitable overlap in thinking preference. Such people tend to use complicated sentences, and prefer abstractions rather than sensory, mental pictures or feelings. They feel more at home with logic, detail and what 'makes sense'. As we shall see later in this chapter, they tend to use neutral, non-sensory words like 'understand' and 'consider', rather than sensory words like 'see' and 'feel'.

DEVELOPING SENSORY SKILLS

Despite these considerations, it does not follow that you need to possess a natural sensory preference to do a job that seems to demand such a sense. People don't always have a choice anyway, and many consider their full-time work just a means to an end. They will none the less *acquire* and *develop* whatever sensory skills they need, whatever their natural inclination – simply by repeated practice. Having said that, what we refer to as a 'square peg in a round hole' might well result from a sensory preference mismatch: just because you *can* do something doesn't mean you *prefer* to do it.

In some cases, you can guess a person's sensory preference from the hobbies they have *chosen* to pursue, such as listening to music or birdwatching, rather than from their full-time job. We tend to do better in activities we enjoy, so more often than not we will use our natural talents and inclinations, including our preferred representational system. In turn, we become even better, and so strengthen a preference. Given a choice, a person will usually finish up in the sort of job or hobby in which they use their preferred sense most. At the same time, people at the top of their craft or profession will usually exhibit a dominant preferred sense that suits their skills – such as a highly tuned auditory sense in a musician.

CHANGING A PREFERENCE

We usually think of sensory preference as a natural or innate bias, and indeed it will usually originate in childhood. Yet in some cases our tendency changes depending on our exposure to work and life experience. Thus, a person in a 'listening' job may increase their 'natural' auditory aptitude out of necessity and practice, just as a manual worker develops physical strength and dexterity. Similarly, a graphic designer will increase their visual skills, as would anyone in a job requiring powers of observation. Practice in any modality will improve our proficiency in that sense, just as a blind or deaf person will tend to become more sensitive in the other senses on which they depend more than others. It remains open to debate whether our sensory preference results in our aptitude for certain skills and work, or whether our life experience and work create a sensory bias.

So far, we have considered sensory preference as an external sense, rather than as a 'thinking' or internal preference. A sensory preference will commonly apply to both external (real, outside things) and internal representations (thoughts and memories), although not necessarily so. A person who seems highly visual externally in their full-time job – a photographer, for example – may prefer another sense when recalling memories, imagining, and daydreaming.

PRIMARY AND LEAD PREFERENCE

A further distinction may apply to sensory preference. Our main, or primary, preference refers to the sense we normally use when we think and imagine, ponder or manipulate thoughts. We refer to this as the primary representational system (PRS). For instance, if you explore a future situation in your mind, you tend to use your primary sense most. However, when recalling memories, we tend to use the same sense to *access* them, but not necessarily the same as our PRS. Having recalled the memory, we will revert to our main preference to do the 'thinking'. For instance, if I ask you to remember the first football match (or pantomime, concert, wedding) you attended, what sensation comes first to mind in recalling it? Which sense formed the 'door' that unlocked the memory – a sight, sound or feeling?

Carry out the same exercise a few times and you will probably notice a recurring common, or dominant, sense that accesses the memory, no matter how you represent it from then on as your memory unfolds. This indicates your 'lead' sense. You may or may not use this sense as your primary sense for external representations and 'normal' thinking (such as thinking over a problem). In each case (primary and lead), however, you will probably use that sense consistently over the long term.

A person may not know either sensory preference until they carry out some introspection. In any case, you can easily confirm it with the exercises in this chapter. Armed with this knowledge and control, you can soon acquire further skills to handle your thoughts and senses in a more objective way: in other words, *you can choose how to think.*

A preference does not imply that we think one-dimensionally or act as if sensually deaf or blind. As we saw at the beginning of the chapter, we all think in a *multi*-sensory way, just as we experience 'real' life in all five senses. Moreover, we all share the simple statistical fact that we each have a dominant visual sense compared with the other main senses. A sensory 'preference' therefore means *relative* to the way other people generally think.

Most importantly, a preference or tendency does not imply an absolute disposition or genetic idiosyncrasy. Nor does it constitute an excuse for negative self-beliefs such as 'I can't draw a straight line' or 'I'm tone deaf.' We all function *perfectly* – preferences, mental maps and all. In any case, we can improve our sensory skills in one or all representational systems by application and practice.

Having described sensory preference, it remains to determine how you can identify it, in yourself and others, and also how you can put your knowledge and skill to use.

Identifying sensory preference

Identifying sensory preference, although not as easy as recognizing the colour of a person's eyes, will prove no more difficult than determining a person's preference for a certain type of food or sport, or a characteristic such as optimism or extraversion. In fact, although you know your likes and dislikes, you can only know the colour of your eyes by looking into a mirror. In the same way, you can't observe your own body language idiosyncrasies as you can another person's by simple observation. As we shall see, these help to determine PRS. So why not start with identifying somebody else's sensory preference?

Fortunately, clues abound, and we can divide these into different areas:

* words
* voice
* body language
* eye movements.

WORDS

The words and expressions we use may indicate a sensory preference. Consider these familiar expressions:

- I can see what you mean.
- That sounds fine.
- It doesn't feel right.

Each of these suggests a different representational system. We use such phrases all the time. In fact, some people tend to use one kind of sensory expression a great deal, whilst they may hardly ever use a word or expression that suggests another representational system. We don't usually notice casual language anyway, any more than our own mannerisms. In some cases, a person will deny that they use a particular sensory phrase, or will assert that they do use a word or phrase, against all the evidence of video recordings. By listening to a person over a period, you will soon determine recurring sensory words and phrases.

NLP calls such a word or expression a *sensory predicate*. Hundreds of common expressions occur, and these can indicate, or suggest, a sensory preference. Thousands of less familiar sensory words and metaphors appear in writing and speech more rarely, but still indicate a particular modality. In fact, less common and apparently illogical predicates usually betray more clearly the way a person thinks. Very common expressions, on the other hand, like the three examples above, might not tell us much once they enter into vernacular language in the way that a cliché or common metaphor does. Nevertheless, a range of sensory predicates recurring disproportionately in a person's speech or writing will indicate a preference, or primary representational system.

In some cases, an expression seems so illogical that we can only explain it in terms of a sensory bias, for instance:

- I can see what you are saying.
- Just focus on the volume.
- It looks very heavy.
- It sounds clearer now.
- Let's see whether the voice recording throws any light on it.

These examples may seem contrived, until you start to watch out for (listen out for, develop a feel for) such sensory expressions, which crop up in spoken and written language all the time. We don't give them much attention, even when used illogically. If you do, it probably indicates a sense you do *not* prefer, so it doesn't seem right.

Sensory predicates

The following lists will illustrate the ubiquity of sensory predicates. You may find that one of these lists makes more sense, or seems more familiar to you. That may well indicate your own preference. Conversely, if the phrases seem far-fetched, it might suggest a modality you use less than others.

Visual:

an eye to
in view of
see it (this way/like that)
cast your eye
get the green light

with a view to
see/don't see eye to eye
eying (her/him up)
watch out for

look at/into/out for/here

keep in sight

give the all-clear

spectacle/spectacular

shine, outshine

framed

eye for detail

evidence/evident

hazy (recollection)

window of opportunity

keep in sight/view/perspective

shed/throw light

in the dark

notice

see how (it goes, it works out, the land lies)

envisage

imagine

open ... eyes to

perspective

clear mind

keep your eyes open

blind to

observe

point of view

retrospectively

with regard to

overlook

circumspect

look at it (my/this way)

get the picture

keep/stop/start looking

enlighten/throw light on

run/pass ... eyes over

scan

vision

clear/unclear, clarify

reveal

mind's eye

on the lookout

spot (an opportunity/mistake, and so on)

eclipse

(have a) glance

see to

illuminate

see here

scope

image

review

focus on/in focus

inspect

watch out for

blinding(ly)

keep an eye on

reflect, reflection

hindsight

(in the) spotlight

dream up

eyeball to eyeball

see it (my/this way)

picture ...

big picture

Auditory:

hear me out

listen to this

lend an ear

ear to the ground

word in the ear

all ears

echo

sound out

amplify

rattle(d)

discuss

call the tune

(say it) out loud

sounds fine/OK/awful

listen in/out/here

bend his/her ear

in one ear ...

came to ... ears

reach ... ears

prick up ... ears

(take) soundings

(not a) murmur

in an uproar

orchestrate

fine-tune

beat your own drum

ring (a bell)
make/don't make a noise
say your piece
(same, right) wavelength
crash out
bark (as big as bite)
quietly (gets on with things)
call (on/for)
make a big (noise)
report
(not a) whisper
thunder(ed)
in tune
in/out of synch
sound off
take soundings
sound the all-clear
ear to the ground

chime in
ask
state (the facts)
tone (it down)
voice an opinion
keep quiet
harmony
(with a) bang/whimper
don't breathe a word
comment
speak up/out, for/against
tune in/out
rhyme (nor reason)
(not a) squeak
(seemed to) click
resounding
unheard of
speaks volumes

Kinaesthetic:

point out
attract
put ... finger on
dig up
impress (on him/her)
develop a feel for
empathize
struggle (to meet the deadline)
tie up (loose ends)
feel your way
lean/incline towards
push (on/ahead/it/him/her)
pull together
touch upon
take the plunge
touch base
firm
tangible
make an impression
feel the need
brush it off/have a brush with
run fingers over
rub (dirt in)
heavy
tackle
sting (take the sting out of)

point the finger
strikes me
wrapped up
tight (control, rein)
penetrate
move/moving
(not without a) struggle
feel the pulse
untouchable
shake (up/out/off)
at a stretch
pull it off
get a grip/hold/handle on
weigh/weight
stay in touch
(he/she's a bit) touchy

step on it
rub it in
shape up
groping (for example, in the dark)
(how she/he) feels
stroke
tangible
grapple with
throw/put out a feeler

get wind of

contact

beat about

(go/be) soft

not too hard on

shake (off/out/up)

cool it

tickle (fancy)

sympathize with

put my/your finger on

bumped (into)

leap in the dark

feel the pulse of

warmth, warm to

hard-hearted/headed/pushed/nosed

rough with the smooth

cooled off

thrash it out

itching (to go)

smooth out

poking around/one's nose in

feathers ruffled

Other modalities:

(hard to, can't) swallow

taste (his/her own medicine)

digest

get ... teeth into

tasteless/bad taste

soured relationships

eat your words

chew it over

swallow pride

(left a) sour taste

detect a whiff

keep his/her nose out

bitter experience

devour

smell a rat

keep (someone) sweet

Auditory digital:

sense

understand

learn

decide

consider

perceive

discuss

talk (it through)

question

experience

think (about it, things through)

process

motivate

change

theory

conceive

know

concept

Written language

We use terms such as those listed above in written as well as spoken language. We may express them a little more formally, just as we do in written language in general compared with the spoken word, but written sensory predicates indicate a sensory preference all the same. You can therefore identify a person's preference by examining documents they have written. Choose a relatively long passage, as you will need to establish a pattern in one or more sensory modalities. Also choose something that reflects the person's personal thinking and writing style, such as a letter or informal document, rather than something written in business or more formal prose. Letters or diaries work well.

Just listen

Otherwise, just listen, especially to a friend or close colleague whom you can easily monitor over a period. You can then confirm the person's preference in the other ways we address below. In the case of a casual acquaintance such as a client or supplier, if you don't determine their preference during your meeting, you may lose the opportunity and any benefit of using your knowledge to establish rapport. In fact, once you have acquired the knowledge and skill, you can usually identify a person's preference very quickly. You can then apply your attention to improving communication and relationships, and specific objectives like winning a sale or succeeding in a negotiation – your purpose or outcome.

Of course, stereotypes exaggerate these characteristics, and reflect only a distinct bias. In most people, even with a preference, any sensory bias will not usually appear so pronounced. Use voice clues in conjunction with other evidence of sensory preference (see below), as well as words. Once you can identify a dominant modality, language will start to seem more understandable and predictable.

VOICE

We can make some useful generalizations about the way sensory preference affects a person's tone, pitch and speed of voice. The 'visual person' (shorthand for a person with a visual sensory preference) usually sees images, and their speech, voice and mannerisms reflect that experience. If the mind-picture moves quickly, a person's words have to keep pace, and voice pitch rises at the same time. They breathe faster. So a visual person will tend to speak quickly at a higher than average pitch.

An auditory person tends to talk more slowly, with a rich, precise, rhythmic, pleasant voice tone. They appreciate sounds, in the voice as well as in music and nature. An 'auditory person' seems to like, in a simple, literal sense, the sound of their own voice – or any pleasant voice. They don't like discord and cacophony or unnecessarily high or low volume (which visual people would turn a blind eye to!). Sensitive auditory feedback produces a quality of resonance, and a level of order and accuracy in spoken language that doesn't happen when we simply narrate something we see in our mind.

A kinaesthetic person speaks slowly, intermittently or hesitantly, as they recognize their feelings and express them 'with feeling'. They prefer to 'think in feelings', rather than struggle to find apposite words that do their thoughts justice.

In each case, voice characteristics help to suggest or confirm a person's preferred representational system.

BODY LANGUAGE

When it comes to physiological clues, a visual person often uses more arm and hand gesticulations and head movements than a non-visual one. Thoughts take the form of pictures, and moving ones at that. These usually appear up ahead somewhere, a little above the visual horizon. Visual people will use their hands and body to help describe what they 'see'. Such people – you have probably met them – can hardly speak a word without using corresponding hand gestures, even when on the telephone.

An auditory person usually shows less physiological demonstrativeness. None the less, you might notice a significant head posture, turned to one side, characteristic of listening mode, as if on the telephone. Auditory people often enjoy rhythm, or any kind of repetitive, interesting sound, so expect some pen- and foot-tapping, head-nodding and other rhythmic behaviour. Remember also that they tend to think, when communicating at least, at 'listening speed', or the speed of (their) normal speech, so they don't tend to stumble over their words as happens when a visual person has to keep pace with their mental movie screen. They seem more measured and in control, and that affects their whole physiology, not just the correctness of their speech.

The typical kinaesthetic person also offers physiological clues. As we saw earlier, feelings affect the body as well as the brain, so they reveal themselves outwardly. A true touchy-feeler seems to communicate entirely by body. You can almost read such a person's mind. We say that they 'wear their heart on their sleeve'. Typically, they will look down, with a downward head, or even body posture, when in conversation. Remember that they have no movie screen to access, or mental telephone to listen to. Feelings come from deep inside, and their body movements reflect this. A kinaesthetic person may seem strangely still while accessing their feelings. During this time, they don't speak either, which explains sometimes embarrassing long gaps in dialogue. They communicate what they feel, just as a person with a different sensory preference communicates what they see or hear. Feelings translate even less readily into words than moving images. Nevertheless, expect to hear sensory predicates of the sort in the above list, just as with any preference.

EYE MOVEMENTS

We sometimes describe the eye as 'the window on the soul', and eye contact plays an important part in communication. We don't usually get on well with people who won't look us in the eye. We may label them 'shifty', and 'not to be trusted' – probably 'lying through their teeth'.

Folklore aside, important relationships exist between representational systems and unconscious eye movements. These movements include looking ahead, slightly upward or downward, and to the right or left. This relates to the fact that we access different parts of the brain as we recall memories, and imagine in pictures, sounds and feelings. In eye movements, this indicates sensory preference, just as physiology and voice offer us clues. It seems we can't fake these unconscious eye movements in the way that some people can fake the various mannerisms and – to a lesser extent – the voice characteristics described above. For this reason, they provide useful feedback in communication. For instance, if you ask a person to visualize something, you will confirm that they do it by their eye movements. Similarly, you can tell whether someone accesses a memory from internal recordings, or recounts it parrot fashion, as an amateur might in a well-rehearsed part in a play (characteristic of lying, and using a prepared story). In the former case, they have to go *inside*, and their eye movements reveal this neurological process.

Figure 8.1 provides a simple guide to what each eye movement means. Notice that the movements depicted reflect the way you see them in the other person, so when they look to their left, it appears as your right, and so on. Note that the eye access cues illustrated here apply to nearly all right-handed people, and to most left-handers. In a small minority of cases, the reverse applies.

As you begin to observe these eye movements you will encounter the usual exceptions and learning difficulties. In some cases, eye movements seem to happen much too rapidly to identify, but with practice, you will start to make sense of them. You may find this more difficult with a visual person, simply because they happen more quickly, but once you have established their visual preference, you need not occupy yourself with detailed eye movements.

In fact, you can exaggerate, and slow down, eye movements. Ask the person to think of

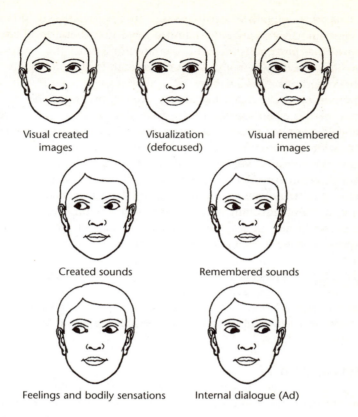

Figure 8.1   Eye access cues

a distant memory, or future event, for which they need a little mental effort. Because they don't do it every day of the week, it will take time and deliberation. With ingenuity, you can ask such questions in the course of your normal dealings with friends and colleagues without giving away your motives: for instance, 'Can you remember when you last used such and such file', or '... met such and such client' – anything they have to *think* about. This will usually produce a slower, more identifiable eye pattern than what you see in 'here and now' conversation. In this case, you will probably observe both the lead and primary representational systems.

Breaking rapport with eye movements

Eye movements also offer a neat method of mismatching that you can add to those described in Chapter 6. Use it to break or avoid rapport, or to bring a communication to a summary close. When in conversation, although few people have any knowledge of eye patterns, we unconsciously detect a lapse of attention, and know intuitively when a person wanders into their own inner world. This may result from the eye movements we unconsciously pick up, and may explain the rapport, or positive chemistry, we experience that does not seem to have any logical cause ('We had little in common, yet I felt as though I had known her all my life.'; 'We got on like a house on fire.').

Thus, when an eye movement does not conform to the nature of the communication – a probing question of the above sort, say – we intuitively know that their 'words and music' don't match. This breaks rapport in a painless way. In other words, you don't have to act in a rude or discourteous way and prejudice a future communication (on a better day) and any possible relationship – just go 'inside'. Think of anything other than the subject in hand, and your eyes will innocently betray you. Your partner in communication will simply sense a lack of response, without knowing why.

As a variation on the eye theme, you can look over the other person's shoulder, as people sometimes do at parties when somebody else takes their attention. However, such an eye movement (not part of the unconscious eye accessing cues) may annoy as well as break rapport, so it provides a less precise rapport-breaking strategy.

People sometimes think of eye movements as a key feature of NLP – perhaps because of their fascination – so much so that they tend to attach too much prominence and assume mystical qualities they do not deserve. From what you have learnt, you will realize that they provide a useful tool for identifying, or confirming, sensory preference, and help in the far more fundamental NLP aim of achieving rapport. But you will probably find much more success in rapport by matching simple physiology and voice characteristics.

No matter how useful these techniques prove, especially in trained hands, this model has not yet gained great scientific acceptance. Often, we have to accept with humility that we cannot predict people's behaviour in the way that we can inanimate objects. People don't act as compliantly as laboratory rodents. In conjunction with the other PRS identifiers, however, it provides a useful and sometimes remarkable confirmation.

Making sense of it all

Initially, some of these sensory preference indicators may seem like mumbo jumbo, but if you suspend your reaction for a while, they start to make sense. Notice, for instance, how these characteristics relate to one another. For example, if you think quickly because you see things quickly, you will tend to breathe and speak with greater speed, and at a higher pitch.

You can relate sensory preference to what you have learnt about the NLP model, especially with regard to our individual map of the world, and unique inner reality. On this basis, we should *expect* people to see, hear and feel things differently to ourselves, and to behave just as differently. Moreover, because we can't enter their heads to read their mental map, we should expect a few surprises in what people say and do. Interestingly, we tend to make allowances for foreigners, yet we expect people from closer to home to think and act as we do.

Notice these characteristics for yourself. Watch and listen. Preferably choose someone with whom you spend a lot of time, so that you can pick up their behaviour effortlessly and conveniently over a period. Obviously, the more you value a relationship or potential relationship, the more time and effort you will invest in achieving rapport, including through sensory matching. Start to notice a person's total behaviour, rather than just what they say, and the sort of mannerisms that you previously would have taken no notice of. In time, you will improve your skills of observation and enter a world of non-verbal language you never knew existed. This doesn't require special start-up skills or training, but simply the interest and willingness to learn and practise. You can achieve 'perceived likeness' by matching sensory predicates and other body language characteristics of sensory preference, and thus add a powerful tool to your interpersonal skills.

You can apply your knowledge of representational systems and sensory preference in different ways, especially to gain rapport and establish better relationships. For example, if you do not get on with a boss or colleague, you can identify their sensory preference and start to communicate in their 'language'. It probably differs from your own, which accounts for the lack of rapport. This means:

✓ using appropriate sensory predicates (in particular the ones they tend to use)
✓ using visual aids in the case of a visual person
✓ explaining things verbally to an auditory person
✓ respecting (by matching) a 'toucher' or 'non-toucher'
✓ 'pacing' the body language and voice characteristics associated with the other person's preference.

Better still, start to *adopt* their system – enter their 'map'. For instance, if something 'looks OK', look upward (as your visual colleague does) and start to *see* what it looks like. NLP practitioners report remarkable improvements in relationships as a result of simple sensory matching. As a bonus, by crossing sensory barriers you will extend and enrich your own map of the world.

9 *Submodalities*

The representational systems described in the previous chapter combine to form the main sensory 'modalities' of the thinking process. They each have special characteristics that we can recognize through a person's physiology, voice, eye movements and so on. As we saw, we can sometimes identify a preference, or primary representational system (PRS). However, each representational system has, in turn, its own neurological qualities or characteristics, known as submodalities, which we will cover in this chapter. These submodalities tell us more about the process of thinking, and in particular the nature of the unique mental maps and filters in the NLP model.

Fortunately, recognizing these submodal characteristics demands no special skills, just knowledge of the sort of things to look for. With a little familiarity and practice, most people come to understand and access them easily, just as we intuitively use the familiar five senses to describe how we perceive inwardly.

Submodalities reflect specific sensory characteristics of each of the three main representational systems. You can describe a visual image, for instance, by its colour, shape, movement, contrast, brightness and so on – just like a television picture. You can depict a sound as loud or soft, continuous or repetitive, high- or low-pitched, and so on. You can describe a feeling sensation as hot or cold, hard or soft, smooth or rough.

Sensory submodalities

Some of these characteristics emerged when examining the different clues to sensory preference. They make our experience in the real world rich and varied, and give it meaning. They have the same sort of effect on our inner world, which mirrors this reality. I list below some of the main modal characteristics, or submodalities.

Visual

associated or dissociated
location (for example, to the left or right, up or down)
brightness
blurred or focused
moving or still
size
hue, or colour balance
clarity
three-dimensional/flat

colour or black and white
distance
framed or panoramic
contrast
speed (faster or slower than real life)
saturation (vividness)
shape
perspective

Auditory

loud or soft

words or sounds

stereo or mono

speed (faster or slower than usual)

clear or muffled

soft or harsh

timbre or tonality

external/internal

distance from sound source

location of sound source

continuous or discontinuous

tempo

rhythm

pitch

digital (words)

Kinaesthetic (feeling)

temperature

intensity

duration (how long it lasts)

shape

movement

texture (rough or smooth)

pressure (hard or soft)

weight (light or heavy)

spatial position

speed/rhythm (for example, a heartbeat)

We can consider any sensory representation, such as a thought, image, idea, memory or sensation, in terms of its submodalities. These sensory qualities turn the inanimate energy of light and sound waves, and the molecules that trigger smell and taste, into unique 'experiences'. Your uniqueness as a person derives from the many qualities or perceptions your brain creates out of this external, 'real' world of energy waves and molecules. As humans, our mega-complex, super-efficient optical, auditory and other sensory organs make this soulless information accessible. More than that, our effectively infinite brain makes it *meaningful*. It turns cosmic energy into a baby's smile, a floating leaf in the wind, or the taste of bread and butter pudding.

We can barely contemplate the mysteries of 'consciousness', 'self' and such scientific enigmas of the brain machine. We therefore stick to nominalizations or metaphors when describing these familiar yet intangible human characteristics. Yet specific experiences, or feelings – emotions such as happiness, enthusiasm and confidence – correspond to different combinations of submodalities in a person's experience. A comprehensive description of each representational system, and its various submodalities at any moment, comes as close as we can to what we mean by 'conscious'. To use submodalities purposely requires some familiarity with this special language of thought, core skills in visualization or 'going inside', and the NLP model.

Reflecting on memories in a focused way brings an otherwise indescribable sense of personal identity and personal history into meaningful language. Submodalities, however metaphorical and subjective in terms of scientific method, help to bridge this gap, so we can begin to understand and express these vital aspects of human experience.

Submodalities and mental maps

One of the biggest contributions of NLP takes the form of the NLP model itself. This describes, in particular, the nature of the mental filters through which sensory data passes to form what we term subjective experience, or what each of us know as 'reality'.

As we saw, the filtration process involves generalization, deletion and distortion, which you will encounter in other NLP contexts. We usually describe the effects of this filtering process as feelings, beliefs, attitudes, meaning and suchlike. It creates 'actual' experience and 'real' memories – at least as they seem to us.

The filter analogy tells only part of the story, however. Outside the NLP model and its main presuppositions, submodalities don't make as much sense, so let's first revisit the model.

SENSORY SEARCHING

First, it seems we don't so much passively filter out unwanted experience, as positively *search out* experience with meaning. Sensory data resonates with our present store of experience, values and beliefs. Although perhaps a contradiction in terms in a more or less wholly unconscious process, we choose:

- what to notice
- what to ignore
- what we deem important
- what doesn't justify mental processing
- what something means, and what we believe about it.

As a survival instinct, we retain the best and dispose of the worst – just as when we filter used cooking oil. In fact, we delete, generalize and distort most of what our senses can technically process. The available data, in turn, represents just a small part of the outside world electro-magnetic spectrum, much of which we cannot assimilate with our senses (such as the infra-red and ultra-violet light frequencies). So, at best, we just have a little sample of reality anyway. Too voluminous by far to take on board neurally, we have little choice but to reduce even this humanly discernible sample to a few manageable billions of representations an hour. Hence our neo-cortical obsession with meticulous classification, meaning, purpose and – presumably – survival utility.

We accomplish this, among other means, by somehow designing, creating and maintaining – all unknowingly – our own 'filters' in the form of beliefs, feelings, values and the minutiae of sensory translation. In short, we do the best in the circumstances – hence the need for generalization, distortion and deletion.

The infinite complexity of the real 'territory' of the world brings with it some disadvantages. We cannot guarantee that we don't wrongly censor useful data while letting less useful information through by misinterpreting or wrongly classifying the raw data in terms of meaning and usefulness. We do this, in turn, by all manner of presupposition, complex equivalence (something equates to, or means, something else), attributing causes and effects, and mass violation of the very language of thought. To add cosmic insult to neural injury, we continuously remodel our filtration systems on the basis of these subjective end products of 'understanding', 'meaning' or 'reality' – in other words, according to what seems 'real', 'good' or 'right'.

All in all – amazingly – the system works. However, because most of it happens in the unconscious majority of the brain, we can hardly take the credit as rational thinkers. The wise policy therefore seems to be to learn about the systems and harness them more effectively in the light of our present needs and desires.

Changing the way you think

On reflection, we all admit to having certain mindsets, attitudes, prejudices, beliefs and feelings that we cannot always rationally account for. We might put them down to 'that's the way I am', but descriptions at this nominal level offer little room for intervention and change. In the first place, how do you change thinking by thinking? What do you *think*? Or what do you do to change unwanted behaviour if you keep doing it anyway?

By translating these universal human mind filters into modalities and submodalities, we have something to get our cerebral teeth into. We can understand just enough to bring about conscious change and exert the self-control that befits our rational *Homo sapiens* credentials.

The crude analogies of submodalities make change a feasible option. You don't have to wrestle with the philosophy of self and consciousness, nor study synaptic neuro-transmitters. In other words, you can leapfrog the Cartesian mind–brain dichotomy. You can *change* by painting sensory pictures and playing sensory tunes – in other words, by changing submodalities.

TUNING UP FOR BETTER PERFORMANCE

For instance, you can make a mental image brighter or larger, and a sound quieter or louder. This makes you feel and act differently. It can even change an attitude, such as to your sister-in-law, red meat or double-glazing salespeople. Imagine the salesperson in 1930s tennis garb, for instance, or wearing double-glazed spectacles.

This happens in our mental map, and involves perception, of course. But in another sense it happens in the *territory* of a real brain in a very physical way. It involves minute electrical impulses, chemical reactions and various happenings in the grey matter. In fact, we can make inner changes more predictably than outer changes (especially in fellow humans) because nobody, or no outside force, can interfere with the process:

* You can think what you like.
* You can imagine what you like.
* You can believe what you like.
* You can tune up your own thought patterns.
* You can start to manage your own future.

Submodality changes – like changing the picture or sound characteristics – when applied to a memory, will change its effect or meaning. It will influence, in particular, the emotional 'imprint' of the memory: how you *feel* about it. This will also affect, in consequence, your present behaviour, which invariably reflects your 'state'. You can thus translate states of mind such as confidence, or any specific remembered state, into 'manageable' sensory profiles or mental strategies you can use purposely. These include sights, sounds and feelings (modalities), their various qualities (submodalities), and the order in which they happen (syntax or strategy). This requires a little skill, starting with the basic core skill of accessing and changing, or manipulating, submodalities.

ACCESSING SUBMODALITIES

You can practise this skill using the lists of sensory characteristics given earlier in this chapter as a checklist – visual brightness, auditory volume, kinaesthetic texture, and so on. Access any memory, and concentrate on one modality at a time. Simply describe what you sense in as much detail as possible. You may find that the checklist helps by indicating what to look and listen for, thus deepening your experience and making it more realistic.

Some people find this process difficult, strange or even impossible, while others find it easy and pleasurable (in the case of a pleasurable memory). You will discover its effect by doing it.

I refer to this as a skill, in the sense that you never perfect it, and you will improve through training and practice. You can always discover rich, new thought qualities that bring memories alive and account for their unique effect.

I meet people who insist that when they close their eyes, they can only see the inside of their eyelids. Others have difficulty visualizing anything more than fleeting, unclear images. In most cases, our mental blind spots reflect a sensory bias or preference, and we may have special difficulty in accessing one system, just as a right-handed person cannot do much with their less-practised left hand. In this case, a person may easily visualize something, for example, but find difficulty eliciting sounds – or vice versa.

In any event, you can re-learn mental skills just as you can re-learn long-unused physical skills, or gradually start to use a limb months after an injury. You may need patience in your mental exploration, but it can provide one long adventure, and prove more than worth the effort in a completely life-changing way. Your entrance into this world of self-knowledge lies in submodalities.

SWITCHING SUBMODALITIES

We can associate certain submodalities with certain states: for example, a positive compared with a negative experience, an empowering experience versus a disempowering one, a helpful rather than an unhelpful state of mind. By inserting 'positive' submodalities (positive *for you*) into negative experience recordings, or strategies, we can replace negative associations – and their consequent behaviour – with positive, helpful ones. For example, make an upsetting or fearful memory with out-of-focus, dark-coloured images into bright, colourful scenes that have a different effect. The emotional effect of any memory, or imagined future, consists of the characteristics, or submodalities of the representational systems – the five senses – that created it. Not every modal characteristic has the same emotional effect, of course. Perhaps one or two submodalities will associate, for you, with the state of mind they evoke.

These submodality characteristics do not occur as standard patterns. For example, enlarging an image may not have the same effect on different people. Likewise, one person may associate relaxation with heaviness, and another with lightness. In general, though, big, bright, colourful images tend to associate more with empowering, pleasant representations, and vice versa. It pays to find out your own submodality characteristics, which will probably remain consistent in different roles, or 'parts', and in different areas of your life.

Whilst submodality awareness and skills may not affect your 'higher' values and beliefs directly – those, like honesty or faithfulness, that stem from a higher, non-sensory, neurological level – you can certainly start to take control at the level of your moment-by-moment state of mind. At the same time, by restructuring memories and imaginings at a submodal level, you will create new experience, and in this way you can *indirectly* change values and beliefs. Some of the belief change exercises in Chapter 5 illustrate this process.

Emotional intelligence

This aspect of self-knowledge, or self-awareness, figures large in the popular idea of emotional intelligence (EQ). NLP sometimes attributes less importance to self-knowledge than 'other-knowledge'. This applies in particular when applying change processes to other people, such as in therapy and other interpersonal communication, and this may reflect the background of the pioneers.

In fact, change doesn't just start *inside*, it starts inside *me*, rather than the other person. We know our own mental map well enough, but we know it simply as our 'reality'. The real insight comes when we understand its utter subjectivity and fickleness, and how we create our unique but distorted and incomplete world of experience, consciousness and personal identity.

Fortunately, the lifetime model of the world each of us sculpts in grey matter need not take a lifetime to change. We 'grow up' quickly when we begin to take responsibility for how we behave and the identity we express. The life-changing breakthrough then comes when you acquire the skills to make changes at source (to submodalities), and learn to take control of what was once unwanted, habitual behaviour. You then display what we now call *emotional intelligence*.

The concept of submodalities lies at the centre of much NLP thinking. It departs a long way from orthodox neurology, whether at the micro, synaptic level, the larger systemic dimension of neural networks and 'parallel processing', or the Cartesian idea of a metaphysical mind. Nor does it sit comfortably with mainstream cognitive psychology. The remarkable impact and growth of NLP has resulted from its effects rather than its theoretical basis or scientific credentials. Submodalities, and their extraordinary effect on behaviour and mental state, exemplify this. For most people, NLP works, and in most cases more effectively and quickly than conventional psychological processes. The idea of sub-modalities, in particular, usually registers quickly with NLP students, and soon becomes a dimension of their lives they can hardly manage without.

Sensory submodalities constitute an inner world ripe for exploration and further discovery. Using basic NLP skills, you can access these raw materials of thought and feeling, and 'transact' mental business at the level of beliefs, attitudes, and 'reality'. In other words: you can enrich your map of the world and convert it into purposeful behaviour and achievement.

10 *Levels and Parts*

Several popular models attempt to show how our behaviour depends on the level at which we do things: for instance, to carry out a task at work, to learn a skill, to express our individuality, to help a cause, and so on. This chapter examines these levels, and shows how they affect the way we perceive things, the decisions we make, and how we change our behaviour.

Hierarchies of needs, and experience

Most managers and human resources professionals will have encountered Maslow's hierarchy of needs – the one that uses the term 'self-actualization'.

MASLOW

Maslow's behavioural needs stages, or levels, appear in Figure 10.1. He described human beings as 'perpetually wanting animals' whose needs and expectations move upwards in a stepped hierarchy. Only when we have satisfied lower needs will we seek the next level of satisfaction. Lower needs, such as concern for our physical well-being and safety, he said, have greater motivational power than higher, inner needs.

The physiological level includes food and personal sustenance, and the next level, safety, includes shelter and physical protection. The lower levels concern the outside environment

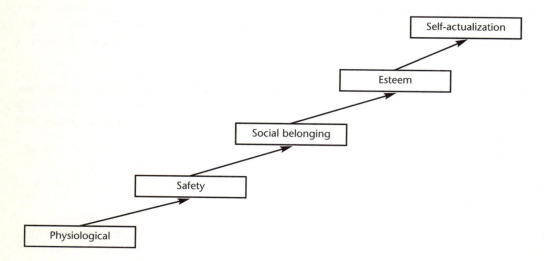

Figure 10.1   Maslow's hierarchy of needs

and people, while the higher levels relate to the person inside. The higher levels reflect long-term life goals such as we associate with the pursuit of happiness, fulfilment and a sense of purpose. The lower levels reflect the shorter-term goals that form stepping-stones to higher ones. Although we might aspire to higher goals, even in the face of lower-level needs, we will probably not achieve them without first gaining satisfaction at the more basic levels.

HERZBERG

Maslow provides us with just one example of this sort of hierarchy. In the late 1950s, Frederick Herzberg carried out studies into the motivation of people at work. He identified a number of factors under the two categories 'motivators' and 'hygiene factors':

- **Motivators** – the nature of the task, achievement, recognition, responsibility, and advancement
- **Hygiene factors** – salary, bonuses, commission, working conditions, acceptability of supervision, pleasantness of working environment, and job security.

He found that although hygiene factors helped to maintain a person's feeling about work, they did not themselves motivate. For example, staff soon accept a pay rise as the norm. However, the *absence* of hygiene factors will *de*motivate a person.

You will notice that these motivators reflect the higher levels of Maslow's hierarchy of needs, and the hygiene factors approximately reflect the lower ones. A person will give priority to the most pressing needs, which include a basic earnings level with which they can feed and clothe themselves. But that will not satisfy or motivate them – these belong with higher-level personal needs.

GRAVES

Graves worked on verifying Maslow's hierarchy of needs. He identified eight value systems that he asserted had emerged in human history to date (he died in 1970). Each value system arose in response to the needs and challenges existing in a certain period of history.

Starting with the equivalent of Maslow's physiological level, Graves specified the following values:

- **Survival** – If the world is a jungle, then I will act like other animals.
- **Safety** – If the world is uncertain and spirits rule, then I will ally with others, obey the spirits.
- **Power** – If the world is rugged, difficult and dangerous, then I will battle to live despite the dangers.
- **Obedience** – If the world is ordered as God ordained, then I will be obedient to rightful leaders and to God.
- **Success** – If the world is full of many options, then I will know that achievement is primary.
- **Friends** – If the world is the home of everyone, then I will unite with others.
- **Function** – If the world is in a state of upheaval, then I will develop personal harmony.
- **Global village** – If the world is an ecosystem, then I will work towards global harmony.

Graves emphasized that these were ways of thinking, rather than types of people. He used metaphorical descriptions related to the world to illustrate them. Although this model has a historical rather than psychological basis, you will notice the similarities to the motivation and needs models, and the neurological levels model in the next section that NLP has particularly embraced.

So a pattern emerges regarding human motivation and behaviour. This appears elsewhere, and NLP has also incorporated hierarchical models into its main methodology. Possibly by accident of the historical beginnings of NLP and the role of several eminent thinkers and therapists, one particular model, which we will now consider, has gained special status.

Neurological levels

Gregory Bateson originated the idea of logical levels, which Robert Dilts later developed. NLP uses the idea as a basis for understanding psychological states and for personal change. I have described these levels below, starting at the 'bottom' of the hierarchy. You will notice that the highest level, *spirituality*, corresponds with Maslow's self-actualization, and the lowest level, *environmental*, corresponds approximately to the two lowest levels of Maslow, physiological and safety. The higher and lower levels respectively also correlate to Herzberg's motivators and hygiene factors.

ENVIRONMENTAL

Environmental factors concern your place or location, and the surroundings or context in which you do things. It includes the constraints that affect your behaviour, the physical environment in which you try to fulfil your outcomes, and any people involved. At this level, you will probably face the questions:

- When do I do it?
- Where do I do it?
- With whom do I do it?

BEHAVIOUR

The behaviour level concerns what you actually do to achieve something, in the environment of the home, office, factory, a social event or whatever. 'Behaviour' might include thinking as well as speaking, listening and acting. It includes whatever *happens* in the environment. To elicit behaviour, ask the question:

- What do I do?

CAPABILITIES

The capabilities level concerns a person's resources and capabilities. Competence in any sort of skill or profession depends on a person's *belief* about their competence. Capability consists of more than behaviour, or even a collection of behaviours. It goes beyond sensory representations to include such aspects as skills, talents, gifts, resources, strategies and internal states. These, in turn, depend on further cognitive abstractions, such as beliefs and values. Your present behaviour resulted from earlier learning and experience, for example, that resulted in your capability. A person's belief about their capabilities might affect their actual behaviour, of course, just as a person's higher beliefs about themself *as a person* will invariably affect their capabilities in the familiar self-fulfilling way. Each level draws upon a higher logical level or levels. The idea of capability poses the simple question:

- How do I do it?

BELIEFS AND VALUES

Change at this level will affect the person's motivation, and concerns our *reasons* for doing something. Our beliefs and values subsume our capabilities, just as our capabilities stem from the behaviour that goes to make them up. You may have suffered stress and frustration and undergone sacrifice in the process of acquiring a capability, for instance. You did that because of its importance in your life – how it fits in with your values, and what you believed about it. Your motivation and commitment to acquire and sustain a capability – and indeed to do anything (behave) – comes from this level.

These (Life Content) beliefs and values will largely determine the sort of *having*, *doing*, *relating* goals and so on that you pursue in your life, and the criteria, or operating rules, that you instinctively apply to whatever you do. The sorts of questions that will elicit these beliefs and values include:

- Why do I do it?
- What is important to me about …?' (for example, work, family, a goal, a special task and so on).

IDENTITY

At this level, a person attempts to express or change their self-image and purpose in life. Life has to have meaning. We all need a reason for living. You need to know who you 'are'. From this understanding of yourself, your values and beliefs emerge as the unique reflection of your identity. Your identity forms the aegis of the 'levels' of your experience, and unifies the 'parts' of your personality. Some questions to ask at this level of identity include:

- Who am I?
- What is my purpose?
- Why am I here?

SPIRITUALITY AND HIGHER PURPOSE

At the level of spirituality, a person attempts to communicate or change their experience within part of a 'world', community or bigger system. We might describe the identity aspect as a mission, or higher purpose, while a spiritual level might represent a level of experience beyond social and political systems. We all live within systems, and these in turn serve larger systems. If your life serves something bigger than yourself, it gives you higher purpose and meaning. Your higher purpose includes how you use the gifts that you bring to the world. So it concerns not just what you want to *obtain* (results, outcomes), but also what you can uniquely *contribute* to the world. This level poses questions such as:

- Who else does this serve?
- What is my greater vision?
- What is my *raison d'être*?
- Why am I doing what I'm doing?
- What is my contribution to the group, the organization, and the world at large?
- What is my destiny?

Applying the model

You can easily apply a skill or aptitude to this model. Think of something you do well. It will probably lie at the behaviour or capability level – let's say listening skills. If you classify this as behaviour, it might take the form 'I listen carefully', 'I always pay attention to whoever I am with', and so forth. You express actual behaviour, or what you *do*. This will, in turn, form part of a capability such as 'getting on with people', 'communication skills' or suchlike, that will usually form a *group* of behaviours.

At the lowest environmental level, you might notice that you:

- close your door when talking to colleagues, to keep down noise and distractions
- move comfortable chairs to face a colleague, rather than remaining at your desk
- meet Joan in the canteen at a quiet time to discuss an important matter.

Each aspect of context, surroundings and environment will affect your behaviour.

Notice that you will probably find it easy to make changes at this level. Sometimes, it just requires attention to the place and time. However, you will have to *do* something (behaviour), and you may need the knowledge and organizing skills (capability) to do it, as well as a little motivation (based on your beliefs and values).

If you then go up the neurological levels from capability, where you started, you will probably identify beliefs such as:

- Every person is important.
- The Golden Rule, 'Do unto others ...'.
- You learn something new every time you communicate.
- Life is short.

You will usually preface this description with 'I believe', 'I feel', 'I think', 'as I see it', and so on.

Then, going up a further level, you might *identify* yourself as a 'people person'. Here, we usually speak in terms of 'I am ...'. Rather than what you do or think, you *are* your identity. You express your uniqueness.

Change forces for a behavioural skill might end there, unless you have a higher motive for what you do: an ideal, cause, religious precept, professional rule of conduct and suchlike.

You can apply the model just as easily to something you do badly, of course. In this case, probably a *negative* 'identity' will appear, a *lack* of capability, inappropriate behaviour, an *absence* of higher purpose, and so on.

The self-knowledge you gain from this multi-level perspective on your experience may help in solving a personal problem at any level, such as a habitual behaviour you want to stop, a negative self-belief, or a feeling that you should find a different type of work. At whatever level you enter the model, by extending up and down, you will gain perspective on your experience, desires and motives.

CHUNKING

The process involves chunking up (to the big picture, general, abstract) and chunking down to the small level (parts, detail, specifics, material, sensory world). Starting at a small-chunk level, you will start to find out why, for example:

- **Environment** – My desk is untidy.
- **Behaviour** – I don't put things away.
- **Capability** – I don't understand the filing system.
- **Belief** – We need creativity, rather than too much order.
- **Identity** – I'm a disorganized person.

Alternatively you could have entered at a higher level, with the 'presented' problem as one of low self-esteem as a 'disorganized person'. In this case, experience at lower logical levels would furnish *examples* of the problem.

Using the levels, you can understand the problem better. In particular, it gives perspective, a different viewpoint, and allows objectivity. This especially helps in deciding on the 'real' or 'root' problem, but also the best level at which to intervene – in other words, the level at which you have the best chance of achieving lasting change.

LEARNING FROM LEVELS

You can apply just about any experience and you will probably gain insight and perspective from the chunking process and the metaphor of levels. Use the suggested questions to make headway if necessary. Even from this simple example you can gain some insight into the principles behind personal change from the neurological level model, for example:

- The levels interconnect, interrelate, and probably overlap systemically. (When does behaviour become a capability? When does a self-belief become a matter of identity?)

- The levels interact in both directions, sometimes in chicken-and-egg fashion. For example, do I see myself as a disorganized person because my desk is untidy, or is my desk untidy because I see myself as a disorganized person?

- Higher-level experience has a greater effect on your life. For example, you can soon tidy your desk (environment) by putting things away (behaviour – next higher level), but you may not succeed at this if you don't understand the filing system – you don't have the *capability* (next higher level).

- Similarly, you will probably not change if your belief system or identity condones, or even applauds, untidiness – say, for the sake of creativity, individuality, rebellion, and so forth.

- You will probably revert to old habits if you continue to identify yourself as a disorganized person. That probably entails questioning your capability, and making excuses for counter-examples (denying the evidence of actual behaviour) – in other words, self-fulfilling your 'disorganized' self-belief and identity.

Although not evident from the model itself, the example (and other examples you may care to think of) suggests that any change will have to happen at a *higher* level. In this case, a new *value* such as 'tidy desk, tidy mind' will probably solve the lower problems. For instance, with such a value-belief, you will readily go to the effort of learning the filing system. After a few weeks of tidy desks and some praise from your colleagues, your 'disorganized' identity will probably evaporate.

However, the *symptom* of an untidy desk may just represent a disorganized way of life that includes the garage, bedroom, kitchen, garden, car, computer hard disk and everything you touch. In that case, change may not happen so easily. You might know the office filing system inside out, but your home life remains the same. You haven't solved the real problem. Furthermore, other beliefs may contribute to the identity problem. For example:

- I'm like my mother (who can't organize a knife and fork).
- I never have enough time.
- I'm overworked and underpaid.
- I deserve to have a secretary.
- There's far too much paperwork in our company.

Beliefs may concern yourself, your work, your family, the government, human kind, the stars or whatever. They serve as important factors in your life, and any or all may affect your identity as a person, how you rank your capability, your behaviour, and the environment in which you find yourself.

EXERCISE 10.1

IDENTIFYING THE APPROPRIATE LEVEL FOR CHANGE

You can test for yourself the useful rule that change will need to happen at a higher logical level (even perhaps two or more):

- Think back to what you do badly.
- Extend it up and down the hierarchy.
- Consider where change will need to take place, and what that might entail.
- Consider changes you made in the past, and what finally unblocked the problem or ensured the change would last.

Later, we will consider NLP change techniques that apply at different levels.

OTHER APPLICATIONS

Congruency

Another use of this model concerns congruency, which becomes more of an issue as we understand a person's experience at different levels. Each 'part' of us needs to 'sing from the same songsheet' if we want to achieve worthwhile purposes.

Ecology

We have already emphasized the importance of ecology in NLP. The Neurological Levels Model offers a useful *aide-mémoire* and checklist, and helps to add new perspectives to behaviour and outcomes. The higher abstractions of experience lift your mind beyond the immediate effects of your outcomes. You can *reframe* an experience using this model.

Problem-solving

The model can help with problems generally, for instance regarding another person or persons, such as: 'John's desk is always untidy.' You can apply the same multi-level thinking as in the personal example above. The model can also apply to an organization with a little change in the definition of the levels. Essentially the same chunking and reframing process will apply.

Model-mixing

You can use the language models described in Chapter 12 in conjunction with neurological levels. One will help with chunking up, and another will help with chunking down. In the latter case, gathering specifics may focus the problem within the environment level. You can ask, for example:

- How specifically?
- Compared with what? (Who sets the standard for 'tidy'?)
- According to whom? (One particular colleague, an important client?)
- Always? Was there ever an occasion …?

This questioning might reveal a lack of storage space, for instance – an environmental matter. John might leave his desk perfect every Friday night, so the problem has an important 'when' aspect. Who sees his desk anyway (environmental)? The problem takes on a different complexion in a reception area compared to a backroom office customers never see.

In the case of an organization such as a company, you may face the 'presented' problem: 'The drawing office (reception area, accounts section or wherever) is always untidy' – in other words, non-personal problems of the sort you might face in your job. The levels in this case need some amendment to refect an organization, for example:

- identity, mission, vision, corporate personality
- beliefs, philosophy and culture
- capabilities, skills, knowledge, intellectual capital
- behaviour, customs and practices
- environment, equipment, surroundings and location.

In some cases, you may stretch the model to an equivalent spiritual level, or higher purpose. An organization sometimes espouses a higher cause, such as women's issues in the case of Avon, or the global environment in the case of Body Shop. As you consider real examples, you will quickly see that similar interdependencies apply, whether in organizations or individuals.

Yet the NLP model does not in itself relate to inanimate organizations, but to the human kind and human behaviour. So, although we can use the model to help diagnose a problem and create options for change, actual change will no doubt require other organizational models. In the case where we need change at a personal level (to solve a corporate or departmental problem) – such as in some customer service programmes or executive coaching – the usual NLP application of the model will work.

The fact that you can apply the model to organizations, even partially, as well as individuals, illustrates the versatility of a simple model.

Parts

A human being boasts a complex bundle of systems. We incorporate many different facets and functions that sometimes seem to operate in conflict with each other. It seems we run our lives as if made up of different personalities, thinking and doing things in one way at one moment, and the next moment acting 'out of character'.

The idea of *parts* poses a philosophical enigma. We often attribute various personality types, whether classical (phlegmatic, melancholic, introvert, extrovert) or contemporary (swinger, techno buff, and hundreds more) to different people. But we also observe different characteristics within the same person in the form of changing temperament and moods, opposing beliefs expressed as doubts, and the many roles that modern life imposes on us.

PARTS AND PERSONALITIES

Areas of a person's life, such as work or family, seem to take on their own characteristics as parts. Some people assume different traits, or parts, depending on the day or week, such as on weekdays and at the weekend ('She's a different person in the office.'). Similarly, our disposition will vary according to the situation in which we find ourselves, the role we assume, the person or persons we happen to be with, our present state of health, and so on. In any of these cases, a person may appear to think and act very differently, giving the impression that we personify different parts from time to time.

This idea features commonly in conventional psychology. It also occurs as a feature of the greater awareness of the unconscious mind that Freud introduced to cognitive fashion. No surprise, then, that the concept of parts figures large in NLP.

The idea of different 'personalities' has little basis in neurology, other than in pathological or abnormal cases such as schizophrenia. However, it offers a useful metaphor. For example, when exploring our unconscious mind to identify positive intentions and to ensure ecological outcomes, we assume different personae, or *think of ourselves* as different people. From childhood, we can all think from the perspective of a particular aspect of our personality – or play out a role. This dominant human feature – the parts we act out – assumes particular importance as self-knowledge, an aspect of intrapersonal intelligence and one of the seminal topics of NLP. Usually, insights into our parts will reveal hidden intentions, beliefs and values, and maybe incongruence in our behaviour. Parts figure in our understanding of the 'subjective experience' and 'perceptual maps' we encountered at the beginning of this book.

CONGRUENCY AND ALIGNMENT

The idea of congruency – another NLP watchword – also borrows heavily on the parts idea. As a source of incongruence, we try to *reconcile* parts, and identify and resolve conflicting intentions. We covered this in the 'well-formedness' criteria in Chapter 4. A specific, positive goal forms the basis for a cybernetic process that largely runs unconsciously, but the system might become confused with conflicting targets and feedback. Alignment, another popular NLP theme, involves persuading all the parts to go in the same direction and act as one, and to communicate 'with one voice'.

These invisible parts, on the face of it, seem no more than innocuous, idiosyncratic features of any individual mental map. Looked at in this way, the massive filtration process depicted in the NLP model surely lends itself to a few internal aberrations. We usually afford these parts no more significance and attention than the average in-law, or many a 'real' person. Nevertheless, the parts reveal themselves in our behaviour – most often when things don't go just as we expected or wished. So, however benevolent these cerebral tenants, they seem to spell conflict, and act like spanners in the familiar works of life.

When set in the context of the more popular systemic approach to human change and the NLP New Code mentioned in Chapter 1, the parts model seems dated. Indeed, motley elements, interrelationships and sub-systems come as standard in any systemic hierarchy. Rather than parts, the systemic model takes the whole as its foundation.

Despite this, the parts metaphor can operate harmlessly alongside other systems perspectives, provided we don't assume that a recalcitrant part implies a 'broken' person (a presupposition in much orthodox psychology, but anathema in NLP circles), or that a harmless skeleton in the cupboard takes on a life of its own just because it once seems to have had one. Unfortunately, in seeking to identify parts, usually dating back to childhood, we tend to focus on *why*, rather than *how* to change in the present.

'I AM' STATUS

Fortunately, the Neurological Levels Model provides a perspective on the apparent conflicts inherent in subjective experience. The symptoms of these different perspectives, or opposing intentions, often surface at the level of behaviour. But they also emerge at the level of beliefs and values – often when using NLP methods as part of a conscious ecology health check, as we did in Chapter 4. However, the lofty quasi-person status we accord these parts surely ranks at the Identity rung of the neurological ladder. Parts take on 'I am' status. Paradoxically, we aim, when chunking up to higher neurological levels, to reach a simple, more unified model, rather than to introduce new players, especially of the malevolent sort, which role somehow these parts adopt. Sadly, *anthropomorphic* parts – as distinct from simple metaphors for traits or attributes – can cause a great deal of bother.

The identity metaphor itself reflects the unifying aegis in all these unruly infants. Identity alone subsumes and outlives all the other mental paraphernalia. In Cartesian terms, this transcends even the physical, neural bundle itself. In latter-day neurophysiological terms, 'parts' constitute no more than neural trunk roads in a rich, extensive, neo-cerebral landscape. However idiosyncratic or equivocal a person, they have one map of the world, one defined identity, and no one to blame when the buck stops.

Once we chunk up to a high level, unified 'identity', incongruencies and misalignments appear as no more than a feature of the NLP model itself. We expect it. Specifically, we expect deletions, distortions, generalizations, misunderstandings, ambiguities, mysteries and such like. In other words, whatever the 'parts' metaphor stems from, it characterizes a rich, multi-faceted, dynamic map of reality.

CHOOSING PARTS

In one sense, conflict between 'parts' reinforces our freedom to choose, unique individualism, and true personality. We can rise above these personalities and see ourselves as if from outside. This simply reinforces the notion of identity, consciousness and existence ('*Cogito ergo sum* – I think, therefore I am.'). In any event, it amounts to no more than a very realistic illusion – a mental map. At worst, none of us can ever affect the territory of 'external reality', whatever thoughts we harbour or dreams we dream. Put another way: you can change a map more easily than you can a real landscape. Paradoxically, by identifying conflicting parts, we create choices that may bring benefits: for example, to change our outcomes, beliefs, values and feelings; to give more attention to a part that we have neglected; to think and act differently.

MAKING EXCUSES

We interpret, or attribute a meaning to, every behaviour. Cognitive psychologists sometimes refer to these as 'excuses', although they pervade our lives even more than the excuses we make in the usual sense of the word. Sometimes, our intuitive excuses defy logic. Roger Sperry, joint Nobel Prize winner in neurophysiology, demonstrated this dramatically in his so-called 'split-brain' experiments in the 1960s.

Subjects' right and left brains were effectively separated by excising the joining corpus callosum. The patients suffered from major brain seizures, and the surgery offered some hope of confining the seizure to just one side of the brain. Extraordinary effects followed. Each side of the brain acted like a different person, but the left side could articulate its behaviour and give reasons (excuses), while the right side (associated with the unconscious aspects of our behaviour) remained mute, although quite efficient at all the tasks it could accomplish, such as spatial tasks. The left-brain 'person' remained unaware of what the right-brain 'person' did in the laboratory exercises, but once made aware of the resulting behaviour, rationalized or *invented* a reason for it. To serve the human compulsion for meaning and reason, it made any old 'excuse'.

The dual-brain phenomenon gives us the most obvious examples of the 'parts' analogy in operation. But it seems the metaphor holds good deep inside the hemispheres where identity resides. This has numerous implications for NLP. It certainly fits the status of the unconscious mind as the prime mover in just about all our behaviour. This extends to unconscious outcomes (positive intentions) which surface in the form of incongruent behaviour. For present purposes, parts have further implications: by adding more personalities to our already dual, or bicameral, identity, we multiply the scope for excuses and render rational behaviour almost out of human reach. The NLP 'filters' model seems neat and manageable in comparison.

Roles

The roles we play also have the effect of psychological parts. We assume different behaviour and attitudes depending on which role we occupy. We often assume different personae, for instance, in a home, work or social setting. Roles play a big part in a person's life, and relate closely to their desired outcomes, beliefs, values and behaviour. We don't usually assume them formally, or even consciously. Like beliefs and values, roles operate somewhere below the surface of our day-to-day conscious lives.

For example, in the role of a mother, you will exercise your *values* in so far as they affect being a mother, and any *self-beliefs* you may have in that role (check back on empowering and disempowering self-beliefs in Chapter 5 if you need to). When you assume the role as an *identity* (which, as it happens, a non-mother might, and a mother might not), it comes naturally.

Fulfilling a role equates to the 'being' category in the Life Content Model described in Chapter 3. An outcome 'to write a book' – a behaviour – need not involve a new role. However, an outcome 'to be a writer' will affect a person's identity as they 'live out' the role. In the same way, compared with *doing* some DIY building work, *being* a builder will probably involve new self-beliefs and the sorts of values espoused by a builder, as well as new behaviour as you 'play the part'.

Roles pervade our lives more than we might imagine, and influence all our behaviour. In addition to obvious roles such as mother-in-law, student or bookkeeper, we occupy roles quite unconsciously, such as victim, follower, confidant or scapegoat. These will nevertheless affect our thinking and behaviour in one way or another. 'Role parts' may well relate to the unconscious 'positive intentions' we have already discussed. Roles fall high up the neurological levels, and affect everything around and below. I will give some examples of roles we adopt, whether consciously or unconsciously:

artist	associate	customer
stepmother	sage	leader
entrepreneur	intermediary	doctor
messenger	mentor	father
motivator	sympathizer	stepfather
helper	pacifier	follower
teacher	boss	confidant
visionary	bully	son
supporter	mother	writer
clown	hero/heroine	uncle
speaker	cousin	tycoon
worker	ally	reader
scapegoat	daughter	in-law
colleague	competitor	nephew
close friend	subordinate	decisionmaker

Use this as a checklist, identify yourself in them, and add other roles you think of. Awareness of your roles can add much to your self-knowledge and control in your life. The same benefits apply to conscious awareness of your values and desired outcomes. For a simple test for a role, prefix an identity type statement with 'I am': 'I am a brother, entrepreneur, tycoon', and so on. As in the earlier self-esteem exercise, don't expect cut-and-dried answers. Mark yourself out of ten on a continuum – some roles play a bigger part than others.

Roles form an aspect of our complex identity as people. They fall high up the hierarchy of neurological levels, so they can have a large effect on our capabilities and behaviour – the lower levels. Having identified your de facto roles, you may consciously decide to dispense with some and acquire others. They relate closely to outcomes, so your goals lists will give plenty of clues about the roles they 'service' or infer.

ROLE ASPIRATION

We saw earlier the difference between 'building' and 'builder' as an activity or a role respectively. In the same way, in setting an outcome to learn watercolour painting or do some rock climbing, you may wish to decide whether your true intentions lie in *being* a painter or rock climber. If you need to, check back on the 'doing' and 'being' categories in the Life Content Model in Chapter 3. Usually, this 'being evolution', or sense of purpose, will follow anyway as we take interest in a particular activity and start to clock up achievements.

In some cases, we might not intuitively label ourselves in such a way, but nevertheless *aspire* to such a role ('I want to be ...'), or simply live out the role unknowingly – although close friends and family will probably readily associate you with the changing role. For example, your nephew might see you as hero, or your drama club friends might see you as an unpaid counsellor.

By aspiring to what you ultimately want to 'be' you can often dispense with the interim outcomes that do not give the satisfaction and sense of achievement that arriving at the ultimate 'being' outcome provides. For example, if you can achieve contentment (*being* content) without acquiring the knowledge, undertaking the activities, and gaining the possessions that you associate with contentment, you may save yourself time, energy and disappointment. But bear in mind that being content doesn't preclude you from any 'doing' or 'having' goals. It simply means that you enjoy the benefits of contentment *during the journey*, as well as on reaching the destination. The trick lies in recognizing that you have a positive choice, to get where you want to, or to stop and smell the roses and learn some lessons on the way.

Moreover, by identifying and *aligning* with a role-part, you may acquire skills more readily – your new self-beliefs will support your behaviour. For example, by seeing yourself as a musician, you will probably make better music – more as a musician would. Self-development trainers often apply the same principle to prosperity and wealth-creation. The person who thinks themself rich rather than poor has a better chance of acquiring material riches. We saw in Chapter 5 the powerful, self-fulfilling effect of such self-beliefs.

Roles sometimes emerge as we consider our goals. Conversely, you can use the roles you identify as a checklist in identifying your outcomes, self-beliefs and values. Ask:

- What do I want in my role as ...?
- What do I believe about myself in my role as ...?
- What is important to me (my values) as ...?

This helps to ensure ecological systems in your life.

Identifying and reconciling parts

When we looked at clarifying goals in Chapter 4, we saw the importance of ecology and the many indirect effects of outcomes. These perspectives sometimes involved 'parts'. We also saw that behind every behaviour lies a positive intention. We don't always consciously recognize our intentions, of course, any more than the parts of us that own them. Desires and intentions may conflict with each other, so we need to reconcile them in order to pursue clear, unambiguous outcomes.

In effect, each of us is made up of not just one person, but many parts – different inclinations, personalities, however we describe them – each vying for its own outcomes. We even use phrases like 'One part of me wants to do it, and another doesn't.' You need to somehow persuade this inner 'team' in your life to work together, pulling in the direction 'you' (the conscious you, or the real you to whom all the parts belong) decide upon.

ALIGNING YOUR INNER TEAM

I will describe an NLP process for building congruence in your 'inner team'. You may wish to amend the technique to make it more appropriate to you, but you will again have to call upon all your powers of imagination, so try to free yourself from all interruptions and suspend judgement while you undertake the exercise.

You will bring to awareness different parts of yourself. One part, for example, you might think of as the supreme diplomat, always correct socially, and courteous; another part might act bluntly, and perhaps a little rudely. One part might seem to have endless patience, say with children or in a hobby; another part might appear short-tempered, and so on. We each have many parts to our character, even though most of the time we don't think about them. You can usually trace each of these parts to memories in which you see yourself acting out the part. They reflect different 'positive intentions', and may account for the conflicts of ecology in behaviour we addressed in Exercise 4.1 on 'well-formedness'.

EXERCISE 10.2

ALIGNING YOUR INNER TEAM

Think first about these different parts of you – helpful and unhelpful, public face and private face, empowering and disempowering, and so forth. Each, according to the presupposition, pursues some positive, beneficial intention on your behalf. You can use the earlier list of typical roles as a checklist if you need to, but usually you just need to think about different areas of your life, such as work and home, for these parts to emerge:

1   Close your eyes and imagine going to somewhere you feel very relaxed and comfortable – maybe a place in nature, a favourite room, or a completely imaginary, safe, pleasant place. Then imagine a table with six chairs round it.

2   Ask your unconscious mind for two parts of yourself that you really *enjoy* to come forward. When they arrive, welcome them as they take their seats at the table.

3   Now ask your unconscious mind for two parts of yourself that you find *useful* or *practical* to come forward. When they arrive, welcome them as they take their seats at the table, and introduce everyone.

4   Ask your unconscious mind for two parts of yourself that you particularly *dislike* and which usually spell unhappiness for you, and similarly welcome them as they join.

5   Now say to all your guests, 'Please tell me, who here feels the most misunderstood?', and ask the one who responds: 'What is your positive purpose, your positive intention for me, a gift you want to bring me?' Listen carefully to the answer. Notice that the others hear, understand and appreciate the importance of this particular guest's gift. For example, a blunt, rude part might consider it only truthful to 'call a spade a spade', and it 'cannot stand hypocrisy'. A 'short-tempered' part might feel it expresses itself frankly and openly, without any social graces, and doesn't think we should suppress our feelings. This part of you might want to attract attention, to appear strong, or just to 'get things off my chest'. Listen carefully to each interpretation or purpose.

6   Then ask of the remaining five parts: 'Who among you feels the most misunderstood?' Ask the one who responds: 'What is your positive purpose and the gift you want to bring to me?' Again, listen to the answer, and notice that the rest of the guests understand and appreciate the importance of this guest's gift.

7   Repeat the process with the remaining four, then three, parts of your team.

8   When only two parts remain, say 'I welcomed the other parts to this table. Please tell me the gift that you bring me', and listen carefully to each of their answers. Notice that the others understand and appreciate the importance of the gifts that these parts bring.

9   Finally, watch as the six parts create a circle of gifts by holding hands, allowing the inner team to gradually merge inside you.

Some people have great difficulty in imagining highly subjective inner happenings, much less 'real' personalities. However, when you have had some practice at manipulating modalities and submodalities, you will find it much easier to recognize even the subtlest inner senses. You will be able to communicate with yourself in a way that perhaps you had not imagined possible.

This particular pattern allows you to identify the many parts within you. More particularly, it seeks to reconcile different desires and intentions, and may help explain unwanted behaviour. Most people find that after carrying out the exercise – and you can do this several times as you become familiar with the pattern – they experience a sense of wholeness and confidence. You will realize that these inner parts of you are on your side. They *are* you, and want to promote your welfare.

Your Inner Interpreter

This simple process will help you to change your attitude about any behaviour, such as an unwanted habit, a mistake in the past that haunts you, or some recurring, unhelpful behaviour in your work life.

Our interpretations of experience usually depart from reality in three ways:

1   We interpret something as *permanent*, rather than a one-off occurrence, or covering a specific period. This closely reflects the 'being' aspect of roles and personality. Instead of

saying 'I did' something, we say 'I am' something, implying permanence. We use absolute terms such as 'always', 'ever', 'never', and 'every'.

2   We interpret something as *all-pervasive* in our lives. For instance, something that happened in a particular situation – say at work – we infer reflects every aspect of our life – 'It's hopeless.'

3   We put a *personal* interpretation on things. For example, we say 'I messed things up' rather than 'Things went all wrong.' Instead of 'My desk is untidy', we say 'I'm an untidy person.' Instead of 'The interest rate went up', we say 'I didn't foresee a rise in interest rates.'

These interpretations usually betray a pessimistic bias, rather than an optimistic one, and a subjective rather than objective perspective. The exercise helps to correct this imbalance. Usually, an optimistic outlook has a better effect on outcomes than a pessimistic one. In other words: what we *believe* will influence our success.

EXERCISE 10.3

ENLISTING YOUR INNER INTERPRETER

By following this pattern, you will encourage what we shall call your *Inner Interpreter* to work for you, rather than against you. For this exercise, once again use your imagination in a simple, childlike way. Remember, you will get in touch with subconscious parts of your thinking, so addressing (or listening to) the logical, rational side of the brain – with the most plausible criticism – will have no useful effect. You need to open yourself up to parts of you that usually go unknown and unhindered.

1   Think of a specific time when something didn't turn out the way you wanted.

2   Ask yourself how you explain the way it happened. Listen carefully to your Inner Interpreter as an interpretation emerges, and write down what you hear. If you can, note where (which direction, in space or inside you) the 'voice' comes from.

3   Repeat the first two steps using two more events that have emotional importance to you.

4   Now look at the three interpretations you've written down, checking them for permanence, pervasiveness, and personality. Assess the similarities between them.

5   Rewrite the explanations to make them more optimistic, making them specific to a time or occasion, and to the place they happened. Then make them impersonal, in effect separating yourself from your behaviour.

6   Try to detect where in space these different explanations came from. You may have to go back and experience them again. Did they all come from the same direction?

7   Realize that this vital Inner Interpreter helps to explain the world, and start to appreciate its concern for your welfare. Thank it for bringing you safety to the present.

8   Now you have established communication, use your Inner Interpreter to produce even more positive reasons for your three experiences or behaviours. New interpretations may well come to mind. You may gain insights into your true self that will give a new perspective and make some change inevitable.

9   Imagine the voice moves to your elbow, and it becomes like a familiar TV newscaster. Try moving the source of the voice down to your little finger, and change the tone of voice again – make it friendly and familiar – maybe like a ten-year-old child, or a cartoon character. Then listen as your Inner Interpreter voices the new excuses you thought of and other optimistic ones. Check how you now feel about your three emotionally important experiences with these new explanations. Savour your enjoyment for a while.

10   Let your Inner Interpreter go back to where it started, or where it feels best. Give it the voice you find most reassuring, compelling and motivating.

Let your interpretations come to you instinctively – don't force them. Some might arise easily from conscious analysis, or plain common sense. Others might just occur to you. Or if you become stuck, why not imagine how you would interpret an event or behaviour if such an interpretation existed!

The unconscious mind sometimes responds amazingly to the silliest games and 'pretend' devices, but as an example, I will suggest the sorts of interpretations, or 'excuses', that might occur in a business application – let's say losing a big contract to a rival firm after you have given the final presentation to the client:

*   We always seem to lose out on price (quality/response time/after sales service).
*   That's the worst I've done.
*   It's all we could have hoped for in the circumstances.
*   I went on too long.
*   That's the last chance we'll have with them.
*   Well, you win some, you lose some!
*   I knew it was slipping away from us.
*   Maybe we weren't meant to win it.

We cannot live for long in disequilibrium, so we will not do well with a number of conflicting interpretations. Usually, one or two suffice to give meaning to an experience. An interpretation or 'truth' then stays quietly in its mental pigeonhole doing its negative work on us, producing emotional effects out of all proportion to something that happened maybe long ago. By allowing your less vocal parts to have their say, you will gain new insights into the behaviour or experience. At the least, this will give it a new meaning or perspective ('reframe' it) and bring it into a more objective place in your life. In some cases, you will identify a positive intention behind your behaviour that had not occurred to you. You can then think about ways to fulfil that intention in a better way. It will probably not present any great problem or involve a great change – you just hadn't taken account of it.

11 *Timelines*

We use the term 'timeline' in NLP to mean the way we mentally store pictures, sounds and feelings of our past, present and future. It sets 'subjective experience', at the centre of NLP, in the dimension of time. Tad James and Wyatt Woodsmall popularized the subject in their 1988 book *Timeline Therapy and the Basis of Personality*. This chapter shows you how you can identify your own and someone else's timeline. It includes an exercise designed to remove the effect of disempowering memories.

The concept of timelines goes back to Aristotle, Jung, Freud, William James, Milton Erickson and others. Greek and other languages have verb forms that reflect the concept of past, present and future. Time and temporality have concerned philosophers for millennia. But a therapeutic approach to the timeline idea developed much more recently. The late Milton Erickson used a hypnotic technique similar to the ideas of Tad James and Wyatt Woodsmall in their book.

Time and subjective experience

We build up experiences over time – a lifetime – and these determine how we relate to the world. They affect our beliefs, attitudes, values, feelings and perceptions. We wrap these elusive concepts of personality and consciousness in memory. 'Identity' seems to amount to a collection of memories, spanning time. We *identify* with a past and a future.

MEMORIES

In the sense in which we use the term 'timeline', 'memories' can lie anywhere in time – past, present or future. Neurologically, they seem to amount to the same thing, except that they lie in different positions along a metaphorical timeline and in relationship to our ever-moving 'present'. Therefore, you will sometimes encounter the term 'memory' applied to the future as well as the past.

All our thinking, including imagining, worry, deliberating and so on, concerns the present, the past and the future, of course. You can think about a person, thing or event at the other side of the world right now. You can recall what you did one day last week. And you can likewise imagine in detail an occasion in the future. In each case, you use the same sensory representational systems of sights, sounds and feelings.

However, somehow we know whether something happened in the past, happens now, or will happen in the future, even though in each case we have a vivid mental experience. For example, you might imagine next Monday's staff meeting (a predictable affair at best) in far more realistic detail than a hazy memory. Or you might imagine having supper tonight far more easily than the familiar room next door at this moment.

LINEAR TIME CODING

Everything happens, in effect, along a timeline. The present moves inexorably along that line, but we always have a past, present and future. Clearly, we have a way of coding experience in a linear fashion so that it fits somewhere on our personal timeline and the order of events doesn't become mixed up. With such a finely tuned skill, we can place the minutest happenings in strict order during an hour or day, or differentiate experiences ten years ago by weeks, days and hours. Perhaps this remarkable human ability accounts for consciousness, a sense of identity, and our unique place in history. Whatever this clever neurological process of time cognition, it forms a vital part in all of our lives.

The language of time

Just like the sensory predicates discussed earlier, the time factor reflects itself in our language: for instance, 'You'll look back on this one day ...' suggests that the experience will then lie behind us. When we put something 'behind us', we usually mean it takes its place as past and gone and will not unduly affect our present. We can forget it and treat it as history. Similarly, we 'look ahead' to the future and speak about time as 'on my side'. We express the relentless passage of time in phrases like 'Time waits for no man.'

Whether we treat such language as metaphorical or as reflecting distinct neural patterns, it provides a useful model for understanding subjective experience and personal change. We can also apply it to personal communication. Just as with sensory predicates, a method of storing time indicates a preference, and perhaps a different way of thinking from what we know, so it gives us an insight into another person's map of the world.

Like the language of sensory preference, time predicates can seem strange to a person with different internal strategies or preferences. Although we all have a timeline (or we can usually presuppose it anyway), it may differ from another person's. We may store and recall memories in a very different way, for instance, and thus change the very meaning of time.

Timeline types

Traditionally, we refer to two broad types of time awareness and timelines.

ANGLO-EUROPEAN TIME

In this sort of time, events happen one after another in strict sequence. If you haven't finished a task by the time of your next appointment, you have to drop it and move to your appointment. Time will not wait. If a task occupies you fully for ten minutes, you can't do something else during that period. Anglo-European time relates especially to business, organizations, mass production systems, bureaucracy, and people working in teams who depend on each other. The tendency probably dates from the Industrial Revolution, when – perhaps for the first time – punctuality and an ordered way of life became essential for progress.

ARABIC TIME

Countries with warmer climates generally have a different notion of time. Time happens in the present. If you have an appointment at three o'clock, your present task, even if it runs on to half past, takes precedence. Anything else has to wait. Anything in the present receives priority. Fortunately, in a culture of Arabic time, the person waiting to see you probably thinks and acts in the same way, so no one suffers.

In some countries, a businessperson may hold several meetings simultaneously – all squeezed into the present. Somehow, the work gets done anyway, although as a visitor you don't receive the attention you feel you deserved. In such a culture, things happen eventually, but invariably 'tomorrow'. If they don't, in Arabic time terms they can't have had much importance anyway.

In such a culture, you may need to visit a government official on several successive days before eventually securing a face-to-face meeting. A feeling of strangeness, discourtesy, inefficiency or impatience might arise, but this applies *mutually*. Each system of time seems foreign to the other party. None of us copes well with too much difference or apparent lack of meaning. We generally construe our 'map' as the 'territory'.

According to this notion of time, things happen all at once and now. That, of course, removes the whole notion of a future, as many of us perceive it. Indeed, we see evidence of this. For instance, people may act fatalistically, looking ahead no more than a few weeks, oblivious of the concept of long-term planning, time scheduling and rigid appointment systems. It even seems to impinge on a person's value of life itself.

TIMELINE STEREOTYPES

These examples just stereotype us, of course, and reflect extremes. But differences exist all the same. This applies to how people relate to time in the same country. People living in the southern USA seem more biased towards Arabic time, for example, and this also applies in other countries. But this north–south or east–west sort of divide also applies to country residents compared with city people in many countries as a rural–urban phenomenon. In this sense, time awareness seems more like a feature of modern industrialized society.

Child time

As we have seen, children also typify Arabic time almost universally in the way they live in the permanent present. A small child can just about cope with three or four bedtimes ahead, but thereafter the future doesn't exist. Nor indeed does the past of a few minutes ago when she howled in anger at her little brother – now the best of friends. A telephone call interrupts you when playing with your little child. As an Anglo-European time person, you try to remember where you left off – the point at which something interrupted time. Too late. Your child has no inkling of your problem. She has now entered deeply into something else – her own world of reality. Another game. Another present-moment experience.

So whilst we can see these differences starkly from country to country and at different ages, they in fact represent different methods of time storage between one person, of any culture, and another. Thus, in a single family or office, people will identify these two types. People express themselves, and we describe them, in familiar ways:

- How's the time going?
- He has no idea of time.
- She's always there on the dot.
- I've never known him to be late for an appointment.
- We're running out of time.
- Where's the time gone?
- Keep an eye on the time.

Timeline as a model of experience

The time factor features in other models of subjective experience:

- You will remember that the 'being' person in the Life Content model seems concerned about the present, and the importance of gaining pleasure and fulfilment in any situation, rather than waiting for a future that may never happen.

- Anglo-European time associates more with left-brain (logical, sequential) thinking, whereas Arabic time associates more closely with what we know about holistic, sensory right-brain thinking (see Chapter 15).

- The Change of State Model (Chapter 3) incorporates the idea of change *over time*, to affect the *future*.

- We also saw that we can use time as a useful trade-off in the size criterion in Exercise 4.1 on 'well-formedness'. People act differently depending on the way they think about time, such as in their approach to outcomes (see Chapter 3). Although an abstract concept, time can motivate and demotivate, and thus affect a person's behaviour and achievements.

- The cybernetic feedback idea (see Chapter 3) involves *growing better over time*. Time – like so-called 'failure' – represents an important feature of achievement.

Another major distinction concerns the difference between people who dwell in the past, and those who dwell in the future. Some people's lives seem ruled by what has happened in the past – regrets, failures or pinnacles of achievement from which they don't seem to want to move on. Others seem to live their lives in the past, unwilling to 'put things behind them' ('That's all in the past and you can't do anything about it.') and 'get on with their lives'.

Others dwell in the future, always hoping for this, looking forward to that, or dreaming about a rosy future that never seems to happen. They plan, organize and visualize, but don't seem to find the motivation to *do* things. Putting the past *out of mind*, they perhaps don't learn very much from it.

These two types have in common the fact that they don't accomplish as much as people who have a more balanced perception of time, with a past, present and future that take a proper place in their lives. With such a notion of time, we can learn from the past, plan for the future and yet value the present in which we can find the truest sense of personal fulfilment – the 'being' element in the Life Content Model.

Some of these differences may reflect a person's upbringing, education, the sort of work they do, the odd gene and suchlike. But whatever their origin, in essence they represent a different method of processing time – no more unusual than a preference for visual or auditory senses, or a bias towards left-brain rather than right-brain thinking. We will explore these sorts of high-level, ingrained, habitual thinking 'strategies' in Chapter 15.

Timeline characteristics

Often, as we have seen from some of the language expressions we use, the past lies behind us and the future in front. But for some people, the past goes out to the left, and the future goes out to the right – two familiar timelines.

Figure 11.1 illustrates these different sorts of timelines. The first, A to B, goes in a straight line behind, through, and out in front of the person concerned. This exemplifies the Arabic time mentioned earlier, and in this case part of the timeline lies *inside* the person, who will typically look or point behind to denote where the past lies, and ahead for the future. The other – the typical Anglo-European timeline – goes in a line from somewhere to the left to somewhere to the right, but always lies in front (of the person's eyes). The line extending left and right towards C and D illustrate such a timeline. In this case, no part of the timeline lies inside the person.

This provides no more than a simplistic, metaphorical model of a remarkably complex neurological process. However, it offers a useful way to understand how we each store time differently. It also helps to explain some of the differences between the two main time stereotypes we have met.

For instance, a 'through time' person will always have an image, or awareness of time, past, present and future. The timeline stays somewhere in view. In fact, the line may form a U or V shape, or go up and down, or zig-zag, rather than a straight line from left to right. But 'through time' never lies inside. Because they can always 'see' time, a 'through time' person will have an *awareness* of time, as in the case of the Anglo-European stereotype described above. They will 'look towards' and plan for the future, and look to the past to draw lessons and savour memories. The present sits in between, and constantly blends into the future–past line along which time – and life – relentlessly travels.

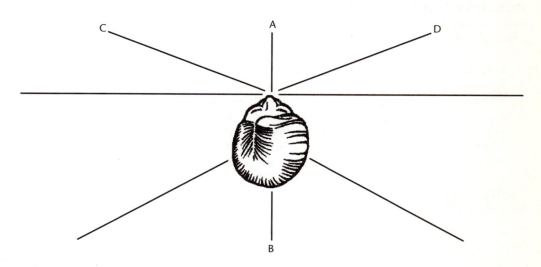

Figure 11.1   Timeline directions

An 'in time' person has their future extending out ahead. If you think of this graphically, what lies immediately ahead *hides* the near future, which in turn hides the distant future. Tomorrow and the next few days may constitute the 'future'. This again typifies the short horizon characteristic of Arabic time. The present, using the 'in time' metaphor, doesn't just form part of a line, but goes inside the person, and so has a different meaning. With this time strategy, the present exists as an all-important part of you. Similarly, the past lies outside, and you can't see it. It stretches out behind you, and 'out of mind'.

When you identify your own timeline, you will understand better how you 'code' time. This will influence the way you set and achieve your outcomes, and will explain much of your behaviour. When you identify the timelines of other people, you will start to understand how they see *their* world, and create their own map or reality. Just like knowing a person's sensory preference or characteristics and interests, this provides valuable information when it comes to communicating. Rapport, as we have seen, depends on perceived likeness. By seeing time as the other person does, you will think like them. Thus, we can start to bridge the universal mind gap between each other that causes so much misunderstanding and pain. A person's timeline means more than just a snippet of information about them – their chronology. It reveals part of the structure of their mental map, and the process by which they program their lives.

Identifying a timeline

If asked 'Could you point to the past and future?', where would you point? If you respond instinctively, without analysing the question, you will probably point or look in directions that denote where you 'see' your past and future. You may already have an idea of where your own timeline lies, after reading about the different kinds of time awareness above. By asking a few questions, you can make this more specific.

EXERCISE 11.1

IDENTIFYING YOUR TIMELINE

Once you enter a relaxed, 'downtime' state, you can easily address these questions to yourself and record intuitive responses. Use the following process:

1   Think about something specific that happened a week ago.
2   Notice where it seems to come from, or where the memory sits now in space.
3   Do the same for events that happened a month ago, a year ago, and ten years ago.
4   Repeat the whole process, but this time thinking about something that will happen in the future. Preferably choose something you expect will happen – maybe a regular occurrence that has happened before, such as a birthday or Christmas function.
5   Notice whether these directions suggest a line, with the past going off in one direction and the future in another.

Unless you have given your own timeline thought in the past, you will probably find it easier to identify another person's timeline than your own. As with sensory preference, a person's largely unconscious, non-verbal body language helps us to identify this and other personal characteristics. Sometimes, for instance, a person will refer to events in the past while gesticulating, and perhaps looking, to the left. When referring to the future, however, they seem to focus on the right. Others might suggest by their gesticulations that the past lies behind them.

Don't worry if you don't obtain immediate answers. The logical mind usually considers all this nonsense, and will try to rationalize out of even thinking about it. Ask, for instance, 'If this memory *did* have a location, where might it lie?' Try not to expect a timeline of any particular kind to emerge. Everybody 'positions' time in some way, or we could not distinguish between when things happened – and even what has yet to happen. This timeline presupposition, or belief, seems rational, so it will probably satisfy your left brain and allow your unconscious mind to communicate. The idea of a timeline just provides us with a metaphor in any case, as with the map metaphor, so by imagining a timeline, you simply use the powers of imagination you have possessed from childhood in the same way you might imagine a map when thinking about a real landscape, or a dragon when thinking about an in-law. You can even imagine different timelines and notice which one feels right and comfortable, or what new perspectives you gain.

USING TIMELINE SKILLS

Along with identifying and changing submodalities, identifying and managing timelines affords you a very valuable NLP foundation skill. It will help in different specialized techniques and change methods. So give it explicit attention. You will acquire the habit of using it just as you might intuitively use visualization or future pacing, or manage your state through submodalities. Timeline methods offer several benefits:

- You can focus on the past or future, as you wish. You can create choices. For instance, as a worrier you can decide to think less about the future, and start to appreciate the present more.

- If you dwell too much on the past, you can switch your thoughts to the future part of your timeline. That way, you will avoid unhelpful regrets and self-recrimination.

- You will start to appreciate how other people handle time, and gain special rapport with them. Depending on your roles and relationships, you may influence other people in all sorts of ways. Better communication helps in bringing about your own outcomes.

- You can gain another perspective on anything just by changing its time context. This will change how you feel, so you have a resource to use in the present. In this sense, your timeline becomes a treasure trail of rich, valuable, empowering experience.

- The additional perspectives will also help in solving problems in a more creative way. A manager or entrepreneur can apply the concept to a company or organization, to set more realistic plans.

- You will understand yourself better, and set outcomes for the future that reflect your true identity and purposes.

- You will – in an almost literal sense – start to create your own future. The power of this tool lies in the way it can affect the present, by changing our outlook, feelings, beliefs and behaviour. Our future consists of no more than a succession of these presents, over which we have more control than we usually admit – especially when we have the knowledge and skills to make changes.

Once you have a working knowledge of your timeline, you can start to apply some of the techniques you have already learnt, but this time in a more specific time context. In particular, you can identify and change submodalities in any memory along the whole timeline.

EXERCISE 11.2

EXPLORING YOUR TIMELINE

I will suggest a simple timeline exercise as an introduction, of the sort you might find at an NLP seminar anywhere in the world. Apart from the skill you acquire, the exercise itself can uplift and bring a person's present life with its problems into a new perspective. For this particular exercise, allow yourself plenty of time. Try it after first roughly identifying your timeline as above, but before you undertake specific timeline techniques that involve switching submodalities and 'removing' memories:

1 Enter a relaxed, 'downtime' state and try to avoid any interruptions.

2 Notice your feelings. Think about your hands, head, where your body touches the chair or the floor, your feet, and so on. Think about where the real 'you' resides – in your head, somewhere near your heart, or down in your stomach, for instance.

3 Float out of your body upwards, and imagine seeing yourself from above. Notice everything you can about yourself from your position on the ceiling, and then rise out of the building to look down on your house and neighbourhood.

4 Keep rising, and as you start to enjoy the experience, you can speed up so that soon you will see the Earth as a map, countries, then continents and eventually the world itself, as you have seen it in satellite photographs. You can still imagine yourself as a dot somewhere down there. How do your problems feel from this distant vantage point? What now seems most important? Learn something new from this privileged viewpoint – something you can take back with you and use in the future.

5 Come back all the way down, enjoying your homeward journey, and notice any emotions as you grow nearer to your familiar environment and the body in which you reside. Finally, come to rest just above yourself.

6 Now imagine your timeline going out in one direction to your past, and another to your future. Start to travel again, but this time along your future timeline, passing over the days, weeks and months that lie ahead. Notice the goals you previously set now happening in the present, and the desires and dreams realized. Enjoy especially the feelings and sense of purpose and fulfilment in having attained what you set out to achieve.

7 Move further into the future. Experience having achieved your key longer-term goals. Think of new desires and outcomes that from your future perspective now seem possible – things you may not have dared to even imagine. Now you have the experience and wisdom to create an even better future.

8 If you wish, you can carry on to explore the end of the line. You may find a door, a tunnel of light, a new country landscape, or whatever. Once again, as you did from outside the

Earth, remember what you learn from this privileged position. You can learn much from your future older, wiser self. Take back with you a special message from your future self that might help you as you make the actual journey.

9   Look back along your timeline and see how your whole life has progressed – the many experiences, pleasures and pains, the mistakes you made and lessons you learnt. Did you intend this life? Or would you like to change things now you can review how you have lived?

10   As you return along your timeline towards the present, notice again each experience. If you wish, you can descend into an experience and make changes – whatever you want to change now that you know the consequences.

11   Come back to the present and into your body. Savour for a while the sensations, and review what you have learnt. Look back into your past and see how you arrived at the present. Look out again to the future and see what you can achieve, and what you need to do now to ensure that your life will follow the course you want to take. Take time to notice things around you. You can now ponder what you have learnt from a conscious, here-and-now perspective. Write down anything worth remembering, to make your journey truly unforgettable.

I will now give an example of a timeline technique to remove a negative or disempowering memory.

EXERCISE 11.3

USING TIMELINES TO OVERCOME NEGATIVE MEMORIES

This exercise will provide you with more experience, and will give you confidence as you prove for yourself the effectiveness of the process:

1   Identify a belief or behaviour you want to change.

2   Float above your timeline at the present position, and move backwards towards the past.

3   Try to find the earliest experience associated with the belief. To test this earliest experience, go further back to a time before the experience. You should then feel different because the imprint has not yet affected you. If not, you may need to search for an earlier example of the feeling or behaviour.

4   Dissociate from the experience – see it from outside yourself – and explore the situation. Notice the effects this experience had on you. You may see the thread running through your life, beginning at the time of the imprint and connecting all the painful experiences that link to it.

5   Identify other people in the memory, and take 'second-person' position, seeing things through their eyes. Look for the positive intentions behind the actions of any people involved in your experience.

6   Now move away from the timeline and look at the person from a dissociated point of view – as an outside observer – and do the same again. For each of these persons, try to find the resources that they would have needed to make it a positive experience.

7   Do this for each person involved in the imprint.

8   Now associate into your own position at a time before the imprint happened. Notice the resources you identified to succeed in the imprint-scene, and take these with you into your younger self.

9   Come right up to the present, and experience the changes.

Timeline theory has grown in its relative importance within NLP, and in particular appears in therapeutic applications. Many of the NLP topics in this book link well with the concepts, and including the timeline idea makes some techniques more effective. For example, you can make the submodality changes we covered in Chapter 9 within the context of a person's timeline. Similarly, you will easily relate some of the macro behavioural strategies, or meta programs, that we will consider in Chapter 15 to the timeline metaphor. It also adds another important new perspective on any situation, such as we need in problem-solving (see Chapter 19 on frames and reframing).

CHAPTER

12 *Making Sense of Language*

Language plays a crucial part in communication, but usually unconsciously. Depending on the sort of language we use, we can communicate with a person in different ways and achieve different effects. Vague, imprecise or even illogical language, for instance, can bypass the conscious mind and thus have a greater effect on a person, especially emotionally. On the other hand, well-structured questioning can elicit the specific information missing from most communication.

This chapter covers both kinds of language: 'artfully vague' language, encapsulated in the so-called Milton Model; and the Meta Model, which helps to elicit specific meaning from a communication. It also introduces a language device known as E-Prime.

Vague language

Some kinds of words have a greater effect than others, and some seem to slip through unnoticed. For instance we seem not to register negatives. We saw, for instance, when we considered well-formed outcomes, the paradox of 'don't spill'-type injunctions. In different ways, you can make a communication more effective by deliberately choosing language to bypass a person's conscious, rational mind, where objections and resistance take place. If you want to make lasting changes to long-standing habits, the unconscious part of your mind controls such behaviour in any case.

We usually associate language with the left side of the brain, so why bypass the left, logical side of the brain? This side, in fact, applies mainly to conscious, or 'uptime' understanding, and reflects only part of the communication story. It concerns the symbolic, logical aspects of language. As we have seen, we associate the right brain with imagery and emotion, and – speaking of language – metaphors, hidden meanings, humour and other rich language we find in poetry and the best of prose. With such language, we can often make a communication effective by speaking to the emotional rather than logical part of a person's mind. In this chapter, we will first consider vague, irrational language you can use for better communication and other purposes.

In fact, we use vague language all the time. Primarily, this happens because we filter out much of the deeper meaning of a communication, and dispense with the language that we would need to communicate it fully. As we saw, this filtration process, a feature of the NLP model, involves deletion, generalization and distortion. The Meta Model described in this chapter helps to make the resulting non-specific language specific, and to recover the 'deep structure' of the meaning.

We aim for specificity, and small chunks, for a purpose, of course – not least to arrive at a rational, or 'true', meaning. But all manner of vague, non-sensory or abstract language has its place in everyday communication. Without it, we would have difficulty communicating the full meaning, or deep structure, of everything we need to convey.

THE DEEP STRUCTURE OF LANGUAGE

Take 'Linda Callum broke her leg' as a common enough sort of communication. The statement doesn't tell us everything that the communicator probably knew – the deeper, fuller meaning. As it happens, Linda Callum 'is' a 32-year-old single mother born in Welshpool, a part-time care assistant and the daughter of so-and-so ... she broke her left femur, the main bone that links the knee and the pelvis, close to the lower end, when she fell while playing hockey on Sunday 3 March 2001 for the Fleet senior team, when she ran into the opposition winger, Mary Stringer, a 23-year-old ... and so on and on.

Rather than the longer, 'truer' statement, we would invariably use the short but far less informative communication 'Linda broke her leg', maybe adding 'on Sunday' or 'playing hockey', but probably not much more. Even the verbose fuller version reflects just a tiny fraction of the deep structure that we might have communicated.

Our 'purpose', or the content of the communication, usually determines the level of detail required: for instance, a medical communication in the hospital, a communication from the hockey coach, or a fellow player, or Linda's little girl (not even mentioned in the long version) or a report in the parish newsletter. In each case, we make do – without guilt or even awareness – with no more than a rough caricature of a communication: in other words, with vague language.

From your knowledge of the NLP model, you will realize that this involves a double filtration process:

1   in *representing* the real world, or what we code and store as deep structure data
2   in what we withhold or further generalize, delete and distort in *communicating* our understanding to others.

Put another way, we lose meaning:

*   between the territory and our mental map
*   between our map and somebody else's.

Withholding masses of deep structure data does not imply, therefore, that the communicator knows everything about Linda's accident, or about Linda herself. But, almost certainly, they know *much more* than they would ever communicate in the course of a normal conversation.

CLOSING THE UNDERSTANDING GAP

This raises some possible communication problems:

*   The communicator may make a faulty assumption about what the hearer, or communicatee, knows already – for instance, about Linda and her personality, appearance, roles, values and so on; the meaning of a 'femur'; the fact of her hockey

pastime, her height of six feet one (I didn't mention that?), and so on. This happens by virtue of our endemic tendency to presuppose. In some situations, the hearer will fill the knowledge gaps by asking questions such as 'When did it happen?' or 'How does she feel now?' But you don't know what to ask if you don't know what you don't know. And worse, you may think you understand the communication when you don't. In that case, the speaker will assume that you do.

• A communication gap arises partly because of the different mental maps we each have of the world. These, in turn, result from our unique life experience, beliefs and attitudes. That means we see things differently. What one person construes as significant (and therefore includes in a communication), another deems of little or no importance (and would therefore not even think of mentioning). This results in generalization, distortion and omission of information sufficient to render a communication meaningless. At best, we fail to achieve our communication outcome. More likely, we transmit a meaning that produces entirely the wrong response – such as pain, enmity, mirth or a blow to the head.

In this case, the simple, practical necessity of abbreviating a communication adds to the risk of omitting important, perhaps crucial information. Most of our everyday communication involves a (largely unconscious) complex compromise between the time and effort it takes to communicate, and the perceived need to tell the full story. This probably aids survival.

Communicating for quick results

Let's assume I require information concerning a brick heading towards me at speed. I can probably do without data as to its nature, shape, size and weight, its early trajectory, its thrower, and the possible pain and structural damage that such a missile could cause to a human skull. But I need to know *it has started its journey*, or part way through communication of the 'deeper language structure', the missile may summarily floor me with a cracked skull. The injunction 'Watch out!' – though grossly generalized and begging so many rational questions – for my part would have served as a more effective communication. The communicator's meaning or intended outcome (to save my head, I guess) revealed itself in an appropriate response. In other words, 'Watch out!' did the trick. An overly precise neural transfer would probably have not done so, had I lived to consider it. The presupposition 'the meaning of a communication is the response it elicits' again makes sense. Moreover, vague language certainly has its place.

Hence the practical need for a compromise in most communications. Common sense will suggest such a compromise when we apply the communication presuppositions. For example, we would ask ourselves (quickly, in this case) how we might best stop that fellow suffering a blow from that brick. Answer: shout a contextually appropriate warning. 'Appropriate' might mean fast, loud, unambiguous, credible, congruent and so on – whatever will do the communication trick of giving rise to a successful outcome.

LANGUAGE AND COMMUNICATION PRESUPPOSITIONS

Similarly, the presupposition 'The responsibility for a communication lies with the communicator' suggests that if for any reason the message doesn't get across, the communicator will not receive any thanks (when I regain consciousness) for imparting complete, precise information with precise language and diction. In short, they will suffer the blame, and rightly so, according to a would-be victim. In so far as the communicator intended to prevent me suffering harm, they failed. More precisely, the communicator learnt through feedback that a certain communication produces a certain outcome or response. Given time, you can change your message, medium or behaviour (in accordance with the Four-stage Achievement Model in Chapter 3). Otherwise, you will know better next time.

Apply these simply presuppositions, and the 'well-formedness' criteria described in Chapter 4, and the sort of message and behaviour that will achieve your desired outcome will seem quite obvious. We can make complex communication decisions in split seconds. Remember, we all possessed interpersonal expertise from earliest childhood. Just yelling 'Harry!' may constitute vague, ambiguous language, but on some occasions you need such language, as well as congruent behaviour, to accomplish the special communication job in hand.

THE ROLE OF IRRATIONAL LANGUAGE

Sometimes, language seems not just vague, but illogical or stupid as well. Yet, amazingly, it has the effect you want. We describe a question like 'Have you got the time?' as a 'closed' question. That means (when referring to the time of day, rather than time to spare) it should produce a 'yes' or 'no' answer. Invariably, we don't answer such a question at all, but respond 'twenty to' or whatever. In other words, we read the other person's mind, decide they want to *know* the time, not just whether *we* know it, and act on that mind-reading judgement by telling them the time. This illustration does not seem so banal when people speak in other than their mother tongue, and use language more literally. Within a culture, we can manage with the silliest language.

Likewise, a photographer uses a closed question when they ask 'Can you move to the left a little?' Again, they don't really want an 'answer' to this question, and they certainly don't receive the logical 'yes' or 'no'. Instead, we act on our assumption of *their* communication outcome (we presuppose 'the meaning of a communication is the response it elicits') and move a little to the left. In this case, an *unanswered* question (not vague, but a little strange linguistically on examination) provides a very effective communication.

By using language that did not sound like an injunction (injunctions, or too thinly veiled commands, sometimes irritate people), the photographer also fulfilled the 'state of mind' aspect of their communication outcome (refer to the Change of State Model in Chapter 3). They produced the right *effect*. They didn't risk giving offence, and kept the wedding guests happy.

We use language in this vague yet economical, effective and sometimes unwittingly ingenious way in our day-to-day lives. In fact, we can become too clever. 'Can you move to the left a little?' seems like a grammatically logical question. It seemed so to the people at the end of the wedding group, cramped against a low balustrade that the others could not see but which the photographer had noticed. Those at the end shouted 'No!' – an acceptable reply to a simple closed question. The rest of the bunch, however, moved to the left, and half a dozen tumbled over the balustrade in a heap onto muddy grass. So intuitive skills, including vague surface language communications, just like harmless habits, can let us down.

For one thing, we don't know what the other person already knows. In other words, we don't know the content of their mental 'black box'. Yet we readily assume they *should* know certain things. But worse, in communicating with people (unlike with dogs and computers), we confront ubiquitous 'subjective experience' – each person has a unique way of understanding the world. Hence the common communication retorts:

- Why on earth did you assume that?
- What was going through your mind?
- Wasn't it obvious?
- You could surely have asked.
- I'm not a mindreader.
- How could I have known you meant that?

Even our innate skills may not apply to every context of our lives, such as work and family, so we don't always show them in their best light. We don't do justice to these intuitive communication skills that date back to early childhood and have served us so well from a survival point of view. For instance, we may not take as much care when communicating with our closest loved ones as we do in our professional capacity. Nor may we adopt intuitive skills when making an important communication we consider too daunting, and for which we received too much prior notice. In this case, the left brain becomes too closely involved and we don't use the holistic skills we have developed bicamerally (using both sides of the brain).

Hence the importance, as we have seen, of focusing on outcomes – and doing so in a sensory rather than intellectual way. Instead, we emphasize the external process or content of the communication, in a left-brain, conscious, 'in control' way. By prioritizing sensory outcomes, our senses drive the process, so the left brain doesn't have the exclusive right – or the chance – to impede progress.

DUAL-BRAIN LANGUAGE PROCESSING

We usually try to make language clearer and more specific in order to improve our communication skills. Language used in other ways departs from such a convention. The 'proper language' function seems to occur mainly in the left side of the brain, as neuroscientists have shown from research following pathology and trauma in left-brain regions. Strokes provide a far more common example, though, as speech normally suffers when these affect the left side of the brain.

In fact, language calls upon both sides of the brain. When engrossed in an exciting novel, for instance, we enter the sensory world of the story and use visualization processes associated with the right side. 'Once upon a time' can create an instant mild trance as we go inwards to experience, or 'live out', the story. Metaphors and analogies derive their power from this brain feature. The logical, structured, symbolic aspects of language, on the other hand, require left-brain processing. These very different aspects, when combined, give language its power, and humans their unique place in the world. By purposely and artfully employing vague language, we can redress the imbalance towards 'correct' but ineffective communication.

The Milton Model

The eminent hypnotherapist Milton H. Erickson used particular language patterns that bypassed the conscious, rational mind and thus had a greater effect on his clients in bringing about change. These language patterns later formed the basis of the Milton Model, one of the first NLP models.

ARTFULLY VAGUE

What some call 'artfully vague' language can have a hypnotic effect, and Erickson's use of language in this way added to his reputation as the leading hypnotherapist of his time. Most right-brain language processing happens unconsciously. We have already seen that we use sensory predicates (like 'I see what you mean.') without realizing it. In the same way, we pepper our conversation with metaphors, similes, anecdotes and suchlike. However, NLP uses 'Milton' (so named to avoid confusion with another Erickson) language patterns in a conscious or purposeful way. This gives the communicator special influence, as communication bypasses the usual resistance and logical arguments.

People new to NLP find most of these language patterns familiar as grammatical constructs and figures of speech. The novelty usually concerns their *deliberate* use, and the paradox that vague language can add to rather than detract from the effectiveness of communication.

The Milton language patterns I describe below may relate to anything and anybody, and may appear in many formats, so they go unnoticed in most of our conversation. In any case, we would find it difficult to question every nuance of language whilst attending to what we actually talk about. Consequently, we may unthinkingly accept irrational 'equivalences'.

SUGGESTIVE LANGUAGE POWER

Individually, these occur as 'throwaway' statements, and don't usually provoke resistance or objection, even if we mentally question them momentarily. Cumulatively, on the other hand, they can exert a powerful suggestive effect on the listener, and fulfil communication outcomes (responses, or communication meaning) on the part of the communicator. Even when used purposely, these language patterns need not imply devious or harmful intentions, or manipulation – an indictment that NLP practitioners have borne over the years. Along with many other generalizations, distortions and deletions, they provide 'neutral' language tools for which the communicator must take responsibility as to their use.

The Milton Model simply consists of language patterns, with examples. When applied in therapy, the 'artful' use of these vague language patterns depends on the skill of the therapist. The sorts of questions that restore proper meaning (deep structure) from the generalization, distortions and deletion that the language has borne, form the Meta Model, which we will consider later in the chapter.

INDUCING TRANCE

The Milton Model stands alone as a trance-induction model, but here I want to show it for its more general usefulness in communication, change and problem-solving. It has far wider applications than its therapeutic origins, and in this wider context both models can happily work together, depending on our communication outcomes.

I have therefore prematurely suggested some Meta Model questions in this section. These help to describe the nature of the language violation, and suggest how skills in both models will improve communication. It will also help to explain the Milton Model more effectively, and we can address the Meta Model more briefly later.

Milton language patterns

Don't let the strange titles bother you. You will easily remember the familiar patterns themselves, and the sorts of words used to illustrate them.

UNIVERSAL QUANTIFIERS

A 'universal quantifier' means a set of words that have a universal or absolute character: 'And *all* the employees ...' or 'You will *never* ...'. Other telltale words include 'always', 'all', 'every'. Many other words, like 'continuous', 'constant', or 'unending' imply absolutes that can easily bypass rational questioning.

COMPLEX EQUIVALENCE

'Complex equivalence' refers to a situation where two statements have equivalent meanings: for example, 'You are old – you can't relate to young children', or 'You've been going for hours – you must be tired.' One thing means something else. Complex equivalences lie at the root of NLP. We equate a sensory input with something we know within our perceptual map. This underlies the importance of meaning to humans. We unconsciously seek to classify everything, and in allocating items to mental categories, we assume equivalence, or likeness. The complexity of these equivalences lies not least in the subjective filtration of sensory inputs. Further complexity lies in our unique repertoire of beliefs and values, based in turn on a lifetime of random experience, all of which we *equate* to every phenomenon we experience.

PRESUPPOSITIONS

We have already set out some of the presuppositions that form the basis of NLP teaching. In fact, these seminal presuppositions receive our attention because we present them *as presuppositions*. We usually unthinkingly accept hundreds of presuppositions that occur more or less implicitly in our everyday language. If we happen to notice a presupposition that seems strange or too all-embracing, we may reject it, or hesitate in accepting it. But we have difficulty in coping with the volume of presupposition we meet anyway. We operate on presupposition just as we do on complex equivalence, and all this happens largely below the level of consciousness. Like the omissions of surface language mentioned earlier in the chapter, it seems to form an essential part of the way we communicate, relate and survive as a species.

In fact, we all presuppose all manner of things as a matter of course in most of our everyday conversation and written language. Think of them as the linguistic equivalent of assumptions. We accept presuppositions, and think and behave 'as if they were true'. This gives them their special suggestive and persuasive influence as language devices.

The simplest statement may include several presuppositions. For example, we might presuppose:

- **existence** – that somebody or something exists
- **feasibility** – that somebody or something can do something
- **complex equivalence** – that something equates to or means something else.

We make such presuppositions in all these language 'violations', so here we have an example of perceptual filtering or 'meaning making', just as universal as complex equivalence. No surprise, then, that these Milton language patterns overlap and several may co-exist even in the simplest statement. A single harmless statement might include several linguistic violations.

UTILIZATION

Utilization involves using spoken words or happenings around you: for example, 'And the sound of the traffic in the distance …' or 'As the sound of footsteps grows quieter …'. We can utilize what may seem like distractions or interruptions to help induce a mild trance state that makes change easier. You can sometimes weave these into a communication, in the same way as a metaphor or anecdote. Because the 'interruption' comes from outside, however, a particular coincidental sensory occurrence may have a more credible and timely impact on the listener than the eloquence of the communicator.

The power of utilization illustrates the fact that a communication does not need a sterile environment or medium. Rather, its effectiveness lies in the response or outcome. Two people can hold a mutually riveting conversation in a noisy railway carriage or at a crowded dinner party. As we have already seen, the secret lies in rapport, which, paradoxically, a 'shared' environment or outside happening can actually enhance. In *utilizing* the environment, we harness it purposely as a communication resource.

MINDREADING

The familiar pattern of mindreading involves claiming to know the thoughts or feelings of another person without specifying the process by which you came to know the information: for example, 'I know that you are wondering …', or 'You think I don't know …'. In this case, 'you are wondering' may reach a person's unconscious mind and make them do just that. This acts like the 'slip' in the negative injunction 'Don't slip!', in which 'slip' becomes the implicit cybernetic command for the unconscious mind. With the right words and congruency, you can make a person accept a statement as an unconscious command they should act on immediately. Mindreading affords just one example: 'Now you must be thinking …'.

NLP doesn't do mindreading, but you can go one better. Using this sort of vague language, you don't need to know what a person thinks: you can transfer what you have in *your* mind to theirs, bypassing rational resistance to achieve your communication outcome.

LOST PERFORMATIVE

Lost performative patterns take the form of value judgements, omitting the performer or holder of the value judgement: for example, 'it's good to remember ...' – Who says so? On what basis have you made your opinion or judgement? Or take the statement, 'Valerie can't manage a large typing pool' – in whose opinion or judgement, based on what criteria, or with what authority?

Watch out for telltale words that imply judgements: '*Obviously*, she has more experience'; '*Clearly* the situation ...' – clear or obvious to whom? More often than not, we take the implied value judgement as a universally accepted truth. Repetition reinforces the process. We don't need to hear 'It's good to remember' or 'It pays to take your time' very often before we assume that it's good to remember and it pays to take your time.

CAUSE AND EFFECT

A cause-and-effect pattern implies that one occurrence causes another. We commonly use implied cause-and-effect patterns such as 'If ... then ...', 'As you ... then you ...'. Other cause and effect words include 'because' and 'make' (as in 'Two and two make four' or 'It makes me ...'). We often accept cause-and-effect statements without questioning the actual causal relationship. In real life, events don't happen in a neat cause-and-effect way. More than one cause may exist, or a string of causes, in which case you may never know the original cause.

We live in a rational, linear-thinking, cause-and-effect society, and tend to ascribe causes and effects to everything. Paradoxically, we don't act so rationally when it comes to checking whether such a relationship actually exists. The ubiquity of these language violations, rather than their complexity or ingenuity, gives them their suggestive power.

UNSPECIFIED VERBS

In this case, the process word (verb) lacks a complete description. What, how or when, for instance, often remains unspecified. 'He upset me.' – in what way did he upset you? 'She hurt her foot.' – in what way? We think of verbs as 'doing' words, but some verbs do less than others. Words like 'travelled', 'helped' or 'worked' do not tell us *how*, so we have to guess or ask. More likely, we unquestioningly assume.

Many of these verbs have long since turned into nouns, and this gives a clue as to what to watch out for, for instance:

- educate = education
- fulfil = fulfilment
- understand = understanding
- train = training(s).

You cannot wrap education or fulfilment in brown paper and weigh it at the post office. You cannot represent it in a sensory way as a 'thing'. Consequently, we all give nominalized words like 'respect' (a verb and noun) our own meaning – who respects whom, for instance, and based on what, goes unquestioned. We therefore need to ask: 'What do *you* mean by respect?'

Bureaucrats thrive on unspecified verbs, or any kind of abstractions. To recover the missing information, you have to find out who does what to whom or what, and how they do it. Conversely, the tendency to make nouns into verbs (such as 'tasked') doesn't help, as the abstract quality of the noun often endures, and we remain ignorant of the real 'action' meaning.

MODAL OPERATORS

Modal operators imply possibility or necessity, and we include them in our rules for life or criteria: for example, 'You *can* learn...' (possibility); 'You *must* come' (necessity); 'You *should* take care...' (implied necessity). Parental or educational conditioning tends to reinforce modal operators of necessity: for example, 'You must try', 'You need to work harder', 'You will have to', and so on.

Some people accept the suggestion of possibility or necessity respectively more readily than others, so in that sense the tendency operates like any other personality trait. In this case, modal operators then have double power, as they already comply with a person's filters or mental map at a higher, or meta level as a meta program, as we shall see in Chapter 15. They exist ready classified in familiar mental criteria or belief pigeonholes. This means that Milton language patterns will have a greater effect if you first identify the 'can' or 'should' disposition of the other person. Pacing and leading to change a person's thinking either way can then take a strange course: 'We must always have free choice.', 'You must achieve whatever you care to...', or 'You can follow the obligatory rules as you like.'

You can communicate modal operators without using specific words like 'should': for example, 'You have to give her a ring' will convey necessity as well as a 'must', 'ought' or 'behoves', so don't rely on just a few key words. Think about the suggested injunction and your intended result. This gives the communicator more vague language tools, and renders the language pattern even less vulnerable to logical resistance.

NOMINALIZATIONS

Nominalizations largely consist of 'process' words that have frozen in time, thus turning into nouns: for example, '... provide you with new *understandings*' – meaning 'You will understand (verb)'. Credible, respectable words like 'education', 'independence', 'respect', 'relationship' and 'insight' fall into this common category. Attempting to define nominalizations using a dictionary soon indicates their potential for vague, if not meaningless, communication.

TAG QUESTION

Sometimes, a question added after a statement can displace resistance: for example, 'Can you not?', 'Isn't it?', 'Shouldn't he?' This implies that the communicatee makes the real judgement or decision, when in fact the reverse may apply, as tag questions exercise a strong suggestive power – don't they?

LACK OF REFERENTIAL INDEX

Sometimes, a phrase does not identify who or what the speaker refers to, as in the case of 'One should ...'. An unspecified verb, as we have seen, excludes the 'doing'. Lack of referential index excludes who or what does the doing: for example, 'They've done it again.', 'Someone needs to sort this out.' Often, both parties know whom they refer to (for example, management, Susan, the government), but in some cases a depersonalized, unattributed communication will invoke less resistance. These sorts of language violation occur so commonly that we rarely stop to question them. Examples include: 'They are out to get me.' – who 'are' they? 'Things are getting out of hand.' – what things?

COMPARATIVE DELETIONS (UNSPECIFIED COMPARISON)

With comparative deletions, the *comparison* has no attribution – you do not know to what or to whom it relates: for example, 'It's more or less right.', 'That's not so bad.', 'He's getting better.' 'She's the worst kind of friend'. Invariably, the comparison has no basis. The comment 'You could have done better', for instance, raises the question 'Better than whom, or what?' – compared with a top professional, an enthusiastic amateur or a four-year-old, or with yourself at another time and in different circumstances?

As well as omitting the standard of comparison, the pattern may also omit the nature of the comparison. For example, in what sense can we take 'worst kind of friend'? – worst at what, and in what respect? Similarly, better in what way? In what way could you have done better (even knowing the yardstick)? 'Better' can imply 'good', and 'worse' can imply 'bad' on no literal basis whatsoever. At the same time, 'getting worse' implies a situation or person quite bad to start with, so this can make the language pattern very suggestive. You will notice that in many cases these language violations involve a presupposition.

PACING CURRENT EXPERIENCE

Pacing current experience involves describing a person's experience in an undeniable, verifiable or 'uptime' way: for example, 'You are sitting here, listening to me, looking at me.' This simple device can help to create a sense of togetherness, or likeness and rapport. 'We are sharing this experience – together.' You can start a communication, such as a meeting, speech or training session, using this device. The more 'yes' answers you can elicit, the less chance of a 'no' next time. Pacing current experience produces easy agreement. It need not qualify as true, as in 'You are listening to me.' So, although apparently describing reality and calling upon an uptime, 'here and now' state, this language may bypass rationale, and provides a powerful trance-induction tool.

DOUBLE BINDS

Double bind patterns create the 'illusion of choice': for example, 'Would you prefer to make that change now, or simply let it happen as we talk?', or 'Your unconscious mind is learning something else, and I don't know whether you'll discover just what you've learnt now, in a few moments from now, or some time later …'. In the first illustration, the attention focuses on the presupposed *choice* (now or later), not questioning the presupposition (to change). In the second illustration, the attention focuses on *when* you will discover what you have learnt, not questioning the presupposition that you will learn something else (at any time).

Salespeople use this device when setting up sales meetings: 'Can we meet on Thursday at four, or would you prefer to fix a date for next week?' The pattern weights the communication in favour of the communicator, but the *perceived choice* usually means the other person feels they have control, so they will tend not to resist.

CONVERSATIONAL POSTULATE

The conversational postulate takes the form of a question, inviting either a 'yes' or a 'no' response – technically, a 'closed' question, as discussed earlier in this chapter when introducing the idea of vague language. It allows you to choose whether to respond or not, and avoids authoritarianism. For example, in response to 'Could you just look up for a moment?', we tend to look up, rather than answer 'yes' or 'no'. These occur all the time in everyday conversation, and have become part of language culture. Their very ubiquity makes us more vulnerable to the pattern.

For example, 'Have you got the case notes?' will either result in the person producing the case notes or otherwise an answer of the sort 'Yes, but I'm not sure whether I can release them.' (meaning 'You know as well as I do that you have no right to see them.'). A 'yes' or 'no' answer would have placed the responsibility on the communicator to specifically request sight of the case notes. A simple 'Yes' , or even 'Yes, they came across last week.' would then have negated the inbuilt suggestion, but mostly we don't reply to such a closed question in a 'yes' or 'no' way. We often reply with action – in this case, handing over the notes. If the communicator intended to obtain sight of the case notes 'by fair means or foul', this illustrates how Milton language could help to bring the outcome about. Remember the effective communication has no moral, or right and wrong implications.

EXTENDED QUOTES

'Last week I talked to Tony, who told me about the exhibition in Birmingham where he talked to someone who said ...' – this involves 'chaining' a series of contexts, which tends to overload the conscious mind and dissociate the speaker from what they say. As well as depersonalizing a communication, a quote can have an impact out of all proportion to its 'pedigree', as public speakers and other influencers know well. Extended quotes and anecdotes can enhance this effect. We might react to a person who 'goes on and on' with 'I just agree with her – it's less bother' or 'In the end I just give in.' More likely, though, the seeming volume of supporting anecdotes, however irrelevant, may unconsciously affect our rational judgement.

SELECTIONAL RESTRICTION VIOLATION

A selectional restriction violation serves as a complex label for a badly conceived sentence that does not make sense, such as: 'You've hurt the chair leg.' (Only humans and animals can have feelings such as hurt.) It seems that we no more question a literal impossibility than we do a grammatical illogicality.

AMBIGUITIES

Phonological

Juxtaposing *homonyms* (for example 'hear' and 'here') can cause confusion and direct attention unconsciously to the out-of-context meaning (as in 'Hear, hear', used after a speech). In our continuous mental filtering, anything that doesn't readily self-classify sticks out and attracts our notice, taking our limited attention away from something else in the communication.

Syntactic

With syntactic ambiguity, you cannot determine the function (syntactic) of the word from the immediate context: for example, 'They are visiting relatives.' ('visiting' – a verb or an adjective?), or 'They are training consultants.' ('training' – a verb or an adjective?). These mostly occur as a result of poor grammar, of course, but you can use them positively to create ambiguity and bypass conscious objection.

Scope

In the case of a scope ambiguity, you cannot determine by linguistic context how much one portion of a sentence applies to another portion: for example, 'Speaking to you as a child ...' (who does 'as a child' refer to – The speaker or hearer?), or 'The disturbing noises and thoughts ...' (to which does 'disturbing' relate?). The same comments apply as to syntactic ambiguities.

Punctuation

We can identify three types of punctuation ambiguities:

1 **Run-on sentences** – I want you to notice your hand me the glass.; Notice your watch what you are doing.
2 **Pauses** – So you are feeling ... better now?
3 **Incomplete sentences** – So you are ...; If you can change that, then perhaps ....

You will find some of these Milton patterns self-explanatory. Others need further explanation and examples. Some do not constitute 'proper grammar', but this usually goes unnoticed in speech, more so than in writing. Vagueness in itself rarely reduces the effectiveness of a communication, and depending on the outcome and the likelihood of resistance, it may even improve it. In the light of the presuppositions you have learnt, you can now choose from among more tools the communication that will best bring you the outcome or the response you want.

Meta Model responses

Once you identify vague language patterns, you have choices. For example, you can decide:

- not to presuppose something
- not to accept an implied obligation
- not to equate two things without good reason
- not to assume a cause-and-effect relationship
- not to accept absolutes.

You still may not have understood the meaning of a communication – the deep structure of the vague surface language used. You can choose to clarify a communication by asking questions.

In fact, we usually ask ourselves the sort of questions mentioned earlier in this chapter inwardly when confronted with uncertainty or ambiguity: for instance, 'Who says so?', 'How do you know?' 'Always? – surely not'. By asking such questions you can recover the deeper meaning of a communication, discover the intent of the person, fill in missing information, and so on. The Meta Model fulfils this requirement, representing the other side of the Milton vague language patterns coin. It suggests lines of response and questioning to make vague language more specific and expose any language violations.

The model directly relates to the NLP model itself that describes how we filter incoming sensory messages. The Meta Model, which covers many of the Milton language violation patterns, applies specifically to language communication. It attempts to restore what we have filtered out of the full meaning. It may not bring us into the territory of reality, but it gives us a fuller understanding of another person's map of that reality. The Meta Model recovers the deep structure or meaning behind shorthand language, with all its vagueness. It comprises tests, or angles of questioning, that explore the three types of language violation: generalization, distortion, and deletion. Most writers classify these into these three categories, but often arbitrarily, and in any case with overlap. I have omitted the classification, but you can easily detect a deletion, distortion or generalization of the language.

Fairly standard responses apply to any use of each particular language pattern. However, concentrate on the *reasoning* behind the questions, so that you can:

- phrase them in a way that best communicates with the particular person
- reflect your own style of language (rather than sounding contrived)
- maintain rapport
- devise different forms of questioning to serve the purpose.

With your understanding of the Milton Model, the questions I have used for this model will simply reinforce your understanding and jog your memory of the many different patterns you need to watch out for. So think 'meta'. Rather than using the Meta Model as a formula, ask questions with the specific purpose of:

- making a generalization specific
- revealing the real meaning behind a distorted statement
- restoring deletions or omissions from the communication.

In other words, use the patterns as a checklist, but stay flexible in the way you clarify, specify and recover meaning. In particular, make your response with a view to maintaining rapport – much more of a skill when you make an implied challenge to the other person. You will probably think of other responses as you become familiar with the process. The more specifics you can elicit, the more 'deep structure' meaning you will reveal. You may need to ask several questions, or the same question in slightly different ways. Several oblique, 'soft' challenges may have a better communication result than one ingenious, more direct question.

Although clearly related to the Milton Model, the Meta Model list of questions does not cover all the Milton patterns. We usually classify Meta Model questions into the familiar generalization, distortion and deletion categories of the NLP model. However, as with the Milton language patterns, these overlap a good deal, and NLP trainers do not apply them consistently anyway. Nor does the order have any significance when applying the model to everyday communication. So I have just listed here typical statements and responses – more than enough for you to start identifying them and using them for better communication.

Mindreading:

- She doesn't like me.

    – How do you know she doesn't like you?

Lost performative:

- It's wrong to criticize.

    – How do you know it's wrong?
    – Who says it's wrong?

Cause and effect:

- You make me angry.

    – How does what I'm doing cause you to choose to feel angry?

Complex equivalence:

- You're always shouting at me – you don't care about me!

    – How does shouting at you mean I don't care?
    – Have you ever shouted at someone you care about?

Presuppositions:

- If my boss knew how overworked I was, he wouldn't ask me.

    – How do you know he doesn't know?
    – How do you know you're overworked?

Universal quantifiers:

- She never listens to me.

    – Never?
    – Has she ever listened to you?

Modal operators of necessity:

Words to watch for include: 'should', 'shouldn't', 'must', 'must not', 'have to', 'need to', 'it's necessary'.

- I have to finish this tonight.

    – What would happen if you didn't?

Modal operators of possibility:

Words to watch for include: 'can', 'can't', 'will', 'won't', 'may', 'may not', 'possible', 'impossible'.

- I will not pass this exam.
    - What will prevent you passing it?
    - What would happen if you did pass?

Nominalizations:

- Communication around here is non-existent.
    - Who fails to communicate with whom?
    - What do you want to communicate?

Unspecified verbs:

- He hurt me.
    - How, specifically, did he hurt you?

Simple deletions:

- I'm fed up.
    - With whom?
    - About what?

Lack of referential index:

- They don't care.
    - Who, specifically, doesn't care?

Comparative deletions:

Words to watch for include: 'good', 'better', 'more', 'less', 'most', 'least', 'worse', 'worst'.

- He's the worst boyfriend.
    - Compared to whom?

Applying these sorts of questions usually has the effect of:

- chunking down an issue
- restoring the deep structure of a communication
- reaching the core or root of a problem
- changing the other person's point of view and state

- bring a person into here-and-now 'uptime'
- removing the problem altogether, the other person remaining unaware of any intervention on your part
- identifying outcomes and intentions.

Soft front ends

Meta Model questions can seem challenging and abrupt, and you can easily lose rapport if the other person perceives them in this way. You can acquire the skill of asking questions in a non-threatening way, and thus bypass any resistance. I will give some examples of such language prefixes, or 'soft front ends':

- I'd like to understand this, so what exactly do you mean by ...?
- I'm just wondering how is it that 'x' means/causes you 'y' (relate the words or phrases used).
- This is new to me. Is this always the case?
- Can you imagine, just for a moment, what would happen if ...?
- I'm slow today. Can you just spell out, how specifically ...?
- Did I hear that right – you have never ...?
- Let me just double-check on this – you always ...?
- But let's imagine, what if you *could* ...?
- OK, have I got this right? You can't ... Does that mean that something is stopping you?
- That's new to me. Do you know who said so, or where your assumption came from?
- I think I know what you mean, but can you say who, specifically, doesn't ...?
- I think I know how you feel, but is there anything specific ...?

You will notice the difference in the other person's reaction as you start to use soft front ends. Remember your communication outcome and you will instinctively make allowances for antagonism and negative responses. You can use these questioning patterns in any communication, not just applying Meta Model questioning.

This technique will make the above Meta Model effects more effective and consistent. Most important, you can maintain rapport for the purpose of your communication outcome.

E-Prime

With a few exceptions, I have written this book in a form of English called E-Prime. Developed by Harvard business graduate David Bourland and based on earlier ideas of the founder of general semantics, Alfred Korzybski, and others, E-Prime simply excludes all forms of the verb 'to be'. That includes the many forms of the verb, such as 'be', 'been', 'were', 'was', 'will be', 'am', 'are', 'is', 'being', as well as those concealed by apostrophes (for example, 'it's', 'they're').

The verb ranks as the most frequently used in the English language, occurring in most sentences, and often several times. However, it can lead to unclear meaning and poor grammar, not least in the overuse of the passive tense ('It was understood', 'It is estimated') that has long bothered plain English promoters. It has created interest among NLP practitioners as it accounts for much of the generalization, deletion and distortion at the centre of the NLP model itself.

IDENTITY AND PREDICATION

Alfred Korzybski identified two particularly misleading uses of the verb 'to be'. The first he called the 'is' of identity ('Joan is a nurse.'), and the second the 'is' of predication ('Joe is stupid.' or 'That leaf is green.'). In both cases, the use of the verb implies an absolute truth or quality – something either *is* or it *isn't*. In practice, things come in many shades. Often, what purports to represent truth just conveys a subjective reality, and when offered in 'is' terms, unquestioned opinion. Joan, for instance, *is* also a wife, daughter, student, squash player, a gifted seamstress – not to mention her one day a week as a teacher helper at her daughter's school when her shifts as a part-time nurse allow. Whatever Joan *is*, she 'is' (fulfils the role of) more than a nurse. Omitting what Joan isn't grossly distorts any description of her. Even 'Joan works as a part-time nurse.' would suffice – it recovers some of the deletion of meaning, lets us know more about her, and costs just a couple of words.

The 'to be' of predication, such as 'Jim is boring.' happens just as frequently, and probably with even greater violation of meaning. Again, a moment's thought usually identifies the illogicality of 'is'- type predication:

- The qualification or description originates from a person, although the 'is' allows us to skip this information (useful if you happen to hold the opinion, but unfair to Jim). Once we know the speaker or opiner, it puts the statement into its proper, low value context. We encountered this lost performative language violation in the Milton Model earlier.

- Whatever or whoever the source of the description, such a statement can never constitute 'reality', or even a semblance of truth. In other words, somebody's identity doesn't hinge on the status or intelligence of the person using the 'is'.

- It assumes Jim doesn't change, when in fact we all do, all the time. To start with, Jim didn't come into the world a bore. Moreover, he doesn't present as a bore on every occasion.

When used in everyday conversation, such phrases as 'He's stupid' or 'She's a stick-in-the-mud' can rarely contribute to effective communication. Yet, even without credibility, 'is' descriptors can create emotion and spoil relationships, especially when comment reaches the object of the predication secondhand.

Given a moment's thought about our communication purpose, and the response we want, we can easily replace such language. 'Jim came across to me as boring at the last meeting' might come nearer to a rational communication of understanding, or even 'Jim seems boring to me almost every time I hear him.' In either case, Jim doesn't receive his 'is' identity label. Better still, we now have – more obviously – just somebody's opinion. And the truth of any description has no more credibility than a person's ranking of the speaker's own opinion of Jim.

In addition to the passive tense, these language patterns allow easy shortcuts that do little for such a rich language. These occur in just about any communication context, in spoken as well as written English. Of course, we can't communicate more than surface language, as we have seen. However, without the convenient 'is' label, we would at least have to choose *what we actually want to say* about a person. We soon realize, of course, that we don't have to use a complex equivalence at all. For example, we don't have to say 'Bill is a farmer.' Instead, we can say something meaningful, such as what Bill says, does, looks like, and so on (depending on the outcome, or purpose, of our communication). Alternatively, don't generalize, distort and delete in the first place, risking a communication response you didn't bargain for. We can usually say what we need to say easily – even at a surface language level – given a moment's thought about what we want to communicate, and the response we want.

RESTORING IDENTITY

Bill's identity will consist of a wide range of factors:

* Bill farms two acres.
* Bill owns and operates a 1000 acre farm.
* Bill receives £10 000 a year European subsidy for not growing anything on his farm.
* Bill, an accountant aged 56, has just bought a farm.
* Bill grew up on a farm, and has farmed all his life.

These examples expose the untruth of a blanket identity such as 'farmer'. However, *any* 'is-type' complex equivalence of Bill as a person would equally mislead. For example, Bill:

* leads the local scout group
* ran in the mile for the country in his twenties
* has four grandchildren
* holds several non-executive directorships
* often goes rambling in Cumbria
* chairs a regional chapter of a management association
* suffers from asthma.

This illustrates the illogicality, untruth and ubiquity of the 'is' of identification. It packs the three main kinds of language violation into the one little word. Bill takes on a number of roles – the simple concept we addressed in Chapter 10. But no simple role – let alone characteristic or behaviour – equates Bill to anyone but himself.

LANGUAGE SHORTCUTS

How can such a popular word create such ambiguity and encourage shortcuts in language? The little word 'is' creates absolutes such as 'This is true.', 'He is a bad man.' and so on. It assumes everything *is* black or white, when real life proves otherwise. It 'labels' people and things so conveniently that we no longer need to make our language precise. Perhaps worst of all, it doesn't inform us of the speaker or source of an opinion (which any such statement represents, of course). Strangely, people rarely question even the most blatant unsupported statements that the verb invites. So meaning becomes lost, communication breaks down, and relationships suffer.

We take all sorts of shortcuts in everyday spoken language or in tabloid writing. Having to replace 'is' and other 'to be' words will make you think about the actual meaning you want to communicate. Almost invariably, you will find a better, clearer way to express something, often by using active 'doing' verbs and specifying who carries out the action. Fortunately, with a couple of million words to choose from, the English language provides a wealth of alternatives.

E-Prime restores more direct meaning to language, especially the *doing* part, identifying who does or says what, and who has responsibility for an assertion. Most instances of the passive voice simply disappear when you apply E-Prime. In this way, abstract terms – the bane of creative writers and those campaigning for plain language in official documents – become concrete, sensory things you can easily understand.

BETTER THINKING

E-Prime goes much further than missing out 'to be' words. Usually, you have to rethink precisely *what you mean*, so it forces you to *think* clearly as well as communicate clearly – in other words, to use your brain. For this reason, it can have an impact not just on your thinking, but also on your behaviour, relationships and life in general, to an extraordinary degree. Our conscious thought patterns rely on language, and each affects the other, continuously and fundamentally, so E-Prime serves as a personal change agent, problem-solving tool, stimulus to creativity and much more.

You don't have to go the whole way. A less purist version of E-Prime will provide enough benefits to make the initial effort worthwhile. For instance, you could restrict E-Priming to identity, predication and the passive voice.

Most people find it frustratingly difficult to put E-Prime into practice, mainly because the 'to be' verb occurs everywhere, and has worked its way into so many figures of speech. Speaking E-Prime colloquially presents greater problems than any form of writing, yet can speed up learning if you want to abandon written sloppy language. At the same time, whereas we may tend to write normally then correct to E-Prime (which doesn't help the unlearning process), by applying it to everyday speech we gain all the clear thinking benefits as well as the faster learning. At worst, thinking in E-Prime offers numerous communication choices, and acts as a sort of perpetual reframing device. The links with NLP therefore *seem to me* obvious.

E-PRIME IN THE HANDBOOK OF NLP

E-Prime comes in many degrees and types. This book retains the verb 'to be' in a number of special circumstances:

- quotations – these usually appear in quotation marks
- well-known sayings and specific descriptions, such as NLP presuppositions (for example, 'The map is not the territory')
- indirect references to other text or speech (for example, 'She claimed she was …')
- references to E-Prime and the use of the verb 'to be' (like this reference)
- references to 'being' as a topic.

Eliminating the most common verb has resulted in thousands of changes. Fortunately, with all the English words available, E-Prime has many alternative ways to say things. This involves careful consideration of the intended meaning and the clearest way to express it. To that end, the book makes use of some of the language devices such as metaphor, presupposition and the models in this chapter – all with the intention of achieving better communication within the constraints of a book. This aspect of E-Prime makes it valuable as a NLP language device for communicating 'deep structure' or meaning.

13 *Trance Without Trying*

Many people experience their first exposure to hypnotism through seeing a televised stage performance. This often produces feelings of mystery and danger, the loss of one's liberty, mind control and suchlike. In fact, this represents a poor caricature of the far less mysterious techniques mainly used in therapy. This chapter covers the trance, self-hypnotism and relaxation techniques that form the basis of many NLP behaviour changes.

Trance states

The most common misunderstanding concerns the popular concept of hypnotism as a 'special' state. In fact, we undergo trance every day in perfectly normal situations. We put others and ourselves in trance, and depend on this human ability to carry on a normal life, if not to actually survive.

Even in the case of stage and television hypnotism, however, people won't normally do anything contrary to their beliefs and values – and you can talk most people into doing silly things easily enough when you get them in the mood.

We use other words for 'self-hypnotism' and 'trance' that seem relatively un-controversial. For instance, we all daydream and enter a private world of thought. Most of us have experienced driving for a longish period, unconscious of the actual driving, or doing anything in the external word. Suddenly, you arrive at your destination, amazed at the gap in your conscious life. Sometimes, a child running near the road or a police siren sounding in the distance shakes us out of trance during the journey, but we can just as quickly re-enter our hypnotic state soon afterwards.

'UPTIME' AND 'DOWNTIME'

During these periods, we go 'inside', or into mild trance, sometimes referred to as 'downtime'. This contrasts with 'uptime' – the conscious, alert, 'here and now' state of experience. Most people underestimate the percentage of their time spent in downtime. Unconscious of events happening in time, time stands still as we span one conscious period to the next. Similarly, time ceases between going to sleep and waking up, or when in conversation with someone and what they say 'goes in one ear and out the other'. For the moment, you inhabit a world of your own. In fact, in an extraordinary way, you inhabit your inner world of *reality* – no less real to you than the here and now. How often have you come to the end of a well-deserved holiday and found it hard to believe how quickly the days have gone by? Read an absorbing book or article, and the same happens. You live the story or the subject your mind thinks about. We can happily daydream in an undirected way, or contemplate in a more purposeful way – both characteristics of downtime states.

When we enjoy our work, time passes quickly, as we 'use our minds' and go inside (to consider a problem, a pertinent recollection, or a future scenario). Even when contemplating a problem at work, you may need to spend long periods inside, going over pros and cons, different scenarios, how you might convey it to your boss, how so-and-so might react, and so on. You cannot carry out this function in uptime, such as in the middle of a conversation with a colleague or when presenting a report to a group on your findings.

Clock-watching happens in uptime – a watched kettle never boils, and you can barely believe that the time can pass so slowly on a Friday afternoon waiting for the weekend to start. 'Consciousness' – at least of the 'here and now' – confines itself to the limited world of awareness. We live most of our lives in a downtime, trancelike state, but don't realize it. No wonder we underestimate this important dimension of our lives.

Given a little more thought, it becomes obvious that this inner state accounts for the majority of a person's life, not just in time, but in values, beliefs, decisions, emotions, pleasure and pain, hope and despair, and our unique identity.

SELF-HYPNOTISM

Nothing particularly marvellous or strange happens in hypnotism or trance-induction. We focus on other than the things immediately around us. We go into downtime. It just seems strange because we especially *notice* a phenomenon usually beyond our awareness, and because it happens in a different context to our usual daily downtime periods. We also tend to devote a great deal of attention to the person doing the hypnotizing, like magicians who can control a person's behaviour. Most professional hypnotists work as therapists rather than on the stage, and most of these agree that hypnotism implies *self*-hypnotism. In other words, you can't force a person to think or do anything against their will. Often, a person doesn't believe they have succumbed to hypnosis, at least on the first few occasions. They don't associate it with the 'special' state of mind they expected.

In George du Maurier's novel *Trilby*, a bearded madman hypnotizes women to do his bidding and commit crimes for him. Called the 'Svengali effect', this image still pervades the public's understanding of hypnotism. More recent films and television drama perpetuate the image, as does the popular press.

Sleep exemplifies downtime behaviour, but trance does *not* constitute a form of sleep. In fact, the brain stays active and alert when in waking trance. Rather than closing your mind, in this state you adopt a highly focused state. In this case, you direct your focus inwards, on something other than your immediate surroundings. This characterizes the period before dropping off to sleep, when the brain ticks over at a fairly slow 'alpha' rate, but the mind works as actively as ever, 'putting the world right'.

TRANCE WITH A PURPOSE

We have plenty of evidence that when people move from an everyday waking state into other levels of awareness, they gain benefits and find useful new perspectives on their life. This applies in mediation, contemplation, prayer and in simply winding down and relaxing at the weekend or on holiday. We often make important changes in behaviour and thinking during these downtime periods. It seems that we get in touch with our true identity, and gain an honest picture of ourselves, our strengths and weaknesses, values and purposes. With most people, such periods happen too rarely. Or when they do, they happen haphazardly, so that we don't take full advantage of the potential for change. Purposeful trance can fill this gap in the lives of busy achievers.

Trance has not played a major role in NLP training, although the Milton Model in the previous chapter has always occupied an important position. However, the models and techniques of NLP concern the unconscious mind, and share the same sort of processes that apply in the state of trance. In any case, trance provides us with a powerful tool for personal change. Many NLP practitioners practise therapy of different persuasions, and in some cases traditional hypnotherapy. Some new adherents undergo specialized hypnotism training in conjunction with the main practitioner syllabus.

Suggestion power

We can't adequately describe the human mind, let alone explain it. The unconscious mind, for all practical purposes, presents no less an enigma than a galactic black hole. No surprise, therefore, that people have difficulty defining hypnotic states. We make do with illustrating them as they apply in everyday life, and describing their effects, or results. Given such limitations, we might define hypnotism as:

> a state of mind in which we act on suggestions more readily than under normal conditions.

This makes sense in so far as we know that trance seems to bypass the conscious, critical, rational part of our brain, where objections and resistance happen. It follows that by going straight to the control centre of behaviour, and the beliefs and attitudes that support it, you can develop greater power of suggestion, and therefore change.

Focus and awareness

Despite popular belief, trance involves greater rather than less focus or attention, in that the potentially millions of sensory stimuli that bombard our uptime senses have less distracting effect. Of course we may experience an equal bombardment internally, such as when magnifying problems (known as 'worrying'), or letting our imaginations run riot on some exciting issue. Trance used in therapy and self-development, however, involves directing and focusing these thoughts according to some purpose or outcome. The skill, whether of the person in trance or the hypnotist – or both – involves inducing downtime *consciously*.

This contrasts with the unconscious, haphazard way that we usually alternate between the material and our inner world. Again, paradoxically, we have greater *awareness* than when trying to solve a problem in alert, uptime mode. In the latter problem-solving mode, you tend to 'bang your head against a brick wall', 'go round in circles', your mind goes blank, and suchlike. When your brain 'hurts', you probably refer to the limited, conscious part.

Looked at in this way, consciousness or unconsciousness may not matter. The question concerns the *object* of our consciousness. In a dream, we retain consciousness of the bizarre happenings. Similarly, on a car journey, consciousness means whatever occupies your thinking mind while on 'autopilot'. You may *drive* unconsciously, but remain perfectly conscious of whatever occupies your mind – hence the useful distinction between inner and outer, downtime and uptime. *Quality of experience* does not differ between internal and 'external' representations. Ultimately, they all happen inside.

Neurological change

The state of trance has special qualities. In particular, you can reach parts of the mind that at normal times you cannot access. This means that, given effective techniques, you can make changes to behaviour not otherwise possible. Behavioural change almost invariably involves habits, or more precisely, mental habits that we refer to as 'mindsets', 'beliefs', 'values' or 'attitudes'. In NLP terms, change involves changing the way we filter, or interpret, reality – more specifically, the way we generalize, delete and distort sensory inputs and stored memories. It means changing mental patterns or programmes.

Neurologically, this means changing neural connections, and involves synaptic, chemical processes. In a state of trance, all this becomes possible, and in some cases quick and easy. The ability to enter a state of trance, or to self-hypnotize, provides a resource for people who want to change for the better and achieve their desired outcomes.

We mostly accept the powerful effects of hypnotism. One of the most extraordinary examples concerns its efficacy as an anaesthetic in surgery. Victor Rausch, a dental surgeon, used hypnosis and self-hypnosis in his practice, and chose to use self-hypnosis as his only anaesthetic when he had to undergo gall bladder surgery himself. The successful surgery went without pain. Hypnosis has also helped to control fears, to secure relief from allergies, and to improve self-confidence, among many other applications.

By using trance skills, along with a few other NLP skills, you need not depend on professional therapists. You can use trance in everyday personal life, such as to enter an appropriate state to prepare for achieving difficult outcomes. Importantly, self-hypnosis gives you more rather than less control. You may need some level of trance to take control over the thoughts and behaviour that control you at an unconscious level, out of the reach of rationale and willpower.

Relaxing at will

Unlike some techniques involving other people, in which we especially need to apply special sensory acuity, you don't need special skills for self-hypnosis. Anybody can do it, given practice. Like any skill, the more you do it, the easier it becomes. The skill involves relaxing at will. In fact, most self-development processes such as visualization and various NLP change techniques, start from this downtime basis. As it happens, most people have their own methods for relaxing, even though they don't necessarily use them for self-development of this sort, but perhaps just to wind down after a hard day.

In any case, you can find plenty of books on the subject. The main aspect of the technique involves slow, deep breathing, and progressively relaxing each part of your body. It usually helps to imagine each limb growing progressively heavier (although some people like to imagine becoming lighter, and floating) and perhaps to imagine your limbs disconnected from your body. Once physically relaxed, you need to empty your mind of 'busy' thoughts so that you can think about what you want to, rather than letting your mind take control.

MENTAL RELAXATION

The usual technique for *mental* relaxation involves visualizing a pleasant, comfortable scene or 'secure' place – any sensory association with the state of mind you want. In practice, this will induce slow, 'tickover' alpha brainwaves. We associate this alpha state with the feeling of calmness but at the same time mental alertness, rather like just before falling asleep. Obviously, an appropriate environment will help, especially if you have not yet practised much 'conscious' or purposeful downtime. You need to avoid interruptions or any discomfort or disturbance that might stop you entering a downtime mode for a reasonable period. Soon, you will learn to ignore noises and other distractions, just like commuters on a noisy train, lost in their newspapers or dream world.

ENTERING ALPHA STATE

The mind visualizes best when you can stimulate a relaxed, alpha state of mind, without the pressure of the objective world around you. In this state, while relaxing your body, your mind remains alert and open to suggestion. I will suggest a useful technique based on visualizing descending numbers.

EXERCISE 13.1

STIMULATING THE ALPHA STATE

Find a comfortable place, and make sure you will not have interruptions. Go through a basic relaxation exercise, feeling each limb growing heavier, and then including your neck, face and eyes. Now count downwards from 100 to 1 slowly as you progressively relax (start from 50 or 30 if already fairly relaxed). Keep your breathing slow and deep. When you reach them, repeat and visualize the final numbers 3, 2 and 1 several times. Make them memorable in some way. For instance, use a particular colour or typeface, or even a bizarre representation of the number. Also, try to make the numbers dynamic – for instance, picture yourself writing the numbers with a special pen, maybe on your bedroom wall, or keying them onto an imaginary computer screen. Try to incorporate sights, sounds and feelings.

You will now always associate those numbers, portrayed in your special way, with the state of deep relaxation you achieve during these exercises:

- Let 3 represent full *physical* relaxation, so don't visualize the number 3 until you feel you have reached that state.
- Number 2 will represent *mental* relaxation, when you have eliminated 'busy thoughts' and awareness of your surroundings.
- Number 1 represents the deepest state you can achieve, from which you can create subjective outcomes.

This simple descending sequence of numbers opens the door to a whole new inner, subjective world, and effort put into this practice will repay itself many times over. Once in a dreamy, trance-like yet highly aware alpha state of mind, you can easily practise the submodality and other exercises described in earlier chapters.

SELF-TALK

Talking to yourself usually helps. After all, we usually run an internal dialogue of some sort, so we may as well use the process for positive purposes. You can incorporate your outcomes into the dialogue, or personal mantra. This may take the form of, for example, an underlying outcome to learn as much as you can in every situation, and to stay relaxed and confident. So repeat to yourself 'relaxed, confident and learning all the time', or words to that effect. Or link the words with the physical process, such as 'breathe and let go, breathe and let go'. You may need to repeat these at length. You usually only need to tell your conscious mind once to remember something (not that it necessarily will, of course), but your unconscious mind doesn't work like that, so you may have to suspend rational, sensible criticism and resort to rote learning methods.

This will become easier each time, but it helps to reinforce your learning by incorporating positive intentions and beliefs into your inner dialogue, especially when about to come out of trance. For instance, 'I can easily return to this place whenever I wish, just by taking three slow breaths', or such words.

Post-hypnotic suggestion

You can incorporate useful post-hypnotic suggestion while in trance, to take effect after you come out of trance. This can relate to any change you like, whether in behaviour or the feelings you experience in certain situations and with particular people. For example, you may want to suggest that you will feel calm and resourceful whenever your boss telephones or calls you to their office.

At first, choose something that you will genuinely use and that you will have the chance of checking soon in a real-life situation – such as in a weekly staff meeting, or at the weekend with your family. This compares with visualizing your desired outcome, and the feelings that would accompany it, as part of a well-formed outcome. You can now add trance or self-hypnotism to the methods described in Chapter 4. You will now realize that 'going inside' to create goals in a sensory, cybernetic way involved a trance-like state, or self-hypnotism.

ANCHORING A TRANCE STATE

It may also help to link your post-hypnotic suggestion with a cue, or trigger. When in trance state, you can explore different triggers, or anchors (these terms mean much the same, but the different metaphors help to make their purpose clear) that help you to associate with the state you want. For example, you may have noticed a photograph of your little daughter on your desk as the boss's internal telephone rang, and found that it helped you to feel the confidence you needed. Sometimes, a little child helps to place your values in perspective, or any special relationship that you value more than your job, or even career. Looking at that picture can serve as your cue: 'Any time I look at Sarah's picture, I feel confident and resourceful, looking forward to responding to my boss in a professional, efficient manner.' A mental picture of Sarah provides an anchor. We will consider anchors in more detail in Chapter 16.

NLP doesn't split hairs. Once you adopt the few key presuppositions and understand the concepts, you just need common sense to apply the technique to your own situation. Incidentally, you don't have to 'obey' post-hypnotic suggestions. Whilst the cue may remind you of a word, picture or state of mind that you fixed under self-hypnosis, you can always choose to behave any way you like. So, if you want to, you can sit there and tell your boss what to do with their job when they come storming in. On the other hand, you can change a cue using the same process under trance.

We use post-hypnotic cues without knowing it, just as we spend much of our time unaware of trance. Whenever you worry and dwell on matters in downtime, the most innocuous anchor will connect you with an unwanted experience. Anxiety about flying on a business trip in a couple of weeks' time may respond to specific cues or triggers, such as the sound of the engines roaring, or a particular sight or smell. So when you experience the trigger in two weeks' time, it produces the very experience you underwent 'under trance', and all the negative feelings that went with it. In this case, the cue produced a negative, or limiting, rather than resourceful state, but it can also work positively.

We risk such random associations every time we let our unconscious mind take control. Better to learn how it works, then intervene purposely. This explains the effect that the boss's telephone ringing had on you before you simply replaced it with another cue, or superimposed another meaning on it. Most people's lives abound with the power of unconscious suggestion, and automatically triggered feelings and behaviour.

Sometimes, negative feelings connect to our private and social lives, rather than work. A person may dread going home after work to face arguments with a partner over money problems, difficulties with a teenage child, and so on. By dwelling on this during the day and while driving home, they will intuitively comply with that post-hypnotic suggestion. Any innocuous sound, sight or feeling could produce the trigger that creates the feeling. For instance, they may associate closing the garage door before going into the house with all that painful emotion, as if a real cause-and-effect connection existed. This means that at the very time you need a resourceful state, to avoid the same old arguments, resentment and pain, you find yourself locked into the feelings and behaviour.

These ubiquitous, negative self-suggestions seem all the worse when we make a conscious effort to change. For instance, you determine that *this* time you will behave differently. Nevertheless, without knowing why, you close the garage door and suddenly the old 'you' takes over again. However, by noticing the point at which this change happened, you gain important information for a positive post-hypnotic cue. In this case, on creating an appropriate empowering state – calmness, assertiveness, or whatever state you think appropriate to the circumstances – you can use the sight of the garage door, its sound as you slam it shut, or the cool feel of the chrome handle, as your empowering anchor. That neutral little sensory package (closing a garage door) will then have a different, more useful meaning. Most importantly, you have timed the cue just right – at the very point when you would otherwise have entered a negative state.

TECHNOLOGY FOR REAL LIFE

Make your suggestions specific, and your cues unique to whatever situation or behaviour you want to influence. This amounts to a technology for real life, and it works best in real-life situations. The more specific you make them, the more both the states of mind you experience under trance and the cues you choose will fit the bill. Choose *designer anchors* – they don't cost any more. If a certain golf club member has a negative emotional effect on you, then treat it – or him or her – as a *special case*. This involves programming *in a context* – an outcome criterion described in Chapter 4. You then avoid the risk of triggering that state and behaviour in another inappropriate context. After all, you probably don't want to change your whole personality, simply to develop a better relationship with certain people in certain situations.

You need not limit the number of post-hypnotic suggestions and cues you can set up.

The system works all the time, and you may as well make use of it. Usually, you don't need the cue after a short time. It has done its job. By then, your re-patterned neural networks will automatically produce the behaviour you prefer. You have changed the structure of your experience. Thereafter, leave empowering, self-reinforcing habits well alone.

CHAPTER 14 *Metaphors*

NLP uses the term 'metaphor' to include similes, analogies, allegories, stories, parables, jokes and so on. You can describe them as either simple or complex. A simple metaphor may consist of a word or two, like 'Val's an open book', or a simple simile such as 'It's like ice'. Complex metaphors extend to parables, analogies, anecdotes and whole stories. This spans a wide range of literary structures and devices. The singular term 'metaphor' often embraces all this.

For our purposes, we don't need to give metaphors special literary significance. Their significance lies in the fact that they convey *sensory thoughts and feelings* (associated with the right brain), rather than reasoning and abstract concepts (associated with the left brain). In other words, they communicate to heart, rather than mind. They call on your imagination. Along with other sensory representations in the NLP model, we represent metaphors by seeing, hearing and feeling.

A metaphor consists in *something else* which has a *different* meaning, but one that we know, and that familiar meaning may help us to understand another word or concept. It makes things easier to understand. For example, you don't know Val well, but you know the meaning and characteristics of an open book – anyone can read it, for instance. A simple metaphor like 'an open book' adds instant, rich, picturable meaning about Val. We might therefore describe her as 'an open book'. Similarly with the simile 'It's like ice'. You know about ice, so you convey understanding about anything 'like' ice. You just need to picture the metaphor in order to picture it or feel the metaphor to feel it. A metaphor draws on your vast lifetime reservoir of sensory experience to help give something clearer meaning, quickly and effectively.

We associate metaphors with mind pictures, imagination, the 'holistic' right brain and the unconscious mind. A metaphor can stimulate creative thinking, reveal new perspectives on old topics, and create 'insightful', ingenious combinations of ideas. This combination produces a synergy of 'picturable' meaning, more real and credible to a person's picture-loving mind than abstract words. A gripping novel includes the linguistic devices that make up 'metaphor' in NLP. A captivating public speaker will use metaphors freely and with great effect. In this chapter, we will consider metaphors mainly used in communication, and in particular interpersonal, one-to-one communication. This includes both inner (self-communication) and outer communication.

Right-brain communication

Metaphor provides us with a powerful communication device. One word that has meaning will immediately confer meaning on something that doesn't, and save a large number of words. A picture paints a thousand words, and a metaphor provides a linguistic picture. Like the Milton language patterns described earlier, metaphors can do what nominal or abstract words, however carefully chosen, cannot do. For instance, sometimes you can communicate in an inoffensive way a matter that might otherwise have caused embarrassment, resistance or resentment. 'I once heard of a ...' tells a story, but can convey a very real message. Importantly, metaphors help to create and maintain rapport. People listen to your story. 'My topic for today ...' somehow does not produce the same degree of attention and rapport as 'I once met a ...'.

NLP uses complex metaphors, such as stories, in particular, but we all use metaphors most of the time. For the most part, we don't realize the part they play in our language and everyday lives. However, we can all consciously adopt metaphors in new ways, and in other parts of our lives, to achieve more worthwhile outcomes, including when communicating. They can penetrate deep into a person's heart and mind and produce extraordinary changes in behaviour, feelings and attitude. We have already encountered the presupposition: 'Communication is the response you elicit.' Metaphors as used in NLP create effects on people to bring about change for the better. We need to value any help we can obtain to put our message across in the difficult area of human communication.

A metaphor can evoke feelings and motivate people to action and change. Motivational speakers and self-help motivational books rely on compelling metaphors, and the more sensory and memorable the metaphor, the greater the motivation of the listener or reader. The secret lies in the way the metaphor goes to the heart of a meaning by linking it with something that already has meaning, bypassing left-brain resistance and gaining direct access to the 'heart' (or unconscious mind) of the person. Whatever the logic or linguistic merits of the metaphor, its significance lies in this unconscious resonance. A well-chosen metaphor will make most types of communication more effective, and thus help bring about the communicator's desired outcome.

SENSORY REPRESENTATION

NLP focuses on the senses. We create reality through our five sensory modalities, or representational systems. You will remember that in setting well-formed outcomes, you needed to translate your desires into sights, sounds and feelings as sensory evidence of an outcome. This creates the essential reality for your inner goal-achieving system. Strong sensory images usually associate with strong emotion – which makes them memorable. A memory associated with strong emotion may well remain for life. Thus, we can remember incidents going back to early childhood, especially strongly emotional ones (to us at the time). Strong emotion, in turn, incorporates memorable sensory characteristics, in the form of the submodalities. Imbued with emotion, we can usually recall them easily – all too easily if they cause unpleasant feelings. Vivid sensory images also help to create futures. Making a goal 'real' by strong sensory representation gives it a better chance of happening. We describe it as 'well-formed', or more effective.

These vivid representations usually involve behaviour, happenings and people that we understand through experience, rather than inanimate concepts, or things we don't understand. Metaphors have the same sensory power as any sensory memory, so can act as a bridge enabling us to understand anything we cannot readily represent in sights, sounds and feelings. An 'open book' can bridge an understanding gap about Val. 'Like a bowl of cherries' can bridge the understanding about what life means to somebody to whom we apply the simile.

Metaphorical language uses easily imaginable sensory images, and provides an effective tool for communication and creative thinking. By using a metaphor, you can convey an idea that you could not express in rational, abstract language. This applies especially when describing a novel concept or creative idea that you could not otherwise communicate well.

METAPHORICAL EFFICIENCY

Metaphor can make communication not just effective, but also efficient. Even when communicating a seemingly simple message, you can make the job much quicker and simpler. 'She's a dragon' exemplifies not just her, but also the economy of language – efficiency – characteristic of metaphor. 'It came like lightning' expresses speed and suddenness without all the superlatives for the sensory emotion embodied in lightning we would otherwise have to employ. This doesn't just save words, but makes for richer language that produces instant mind pictures – efficiency. Effectiveness, in turn, results from the sensory power of the metaphor that drives meaning right into the other person's mind, creating the response you want.

You would probably get your message across one way or another if you had a well-formed outcome. But paradoxically, we take greater communication risks when using precise, realistic language than resorting as metaphor does, to the ludicrous or impossible (as a human being, Linda *cannot* be a dragon, nor can Charles be 'wooden'). All this presupposes a common culture, of course, in which we don't need to spell out even subtle metaphorical allusions. The learning and display of metaphorical skill starts long before school years ('You pig!').

'Efficient' doesn't necessarily mean in the sense that one word tells its own story because of its association – although it often does. Sometimes, we use a whole story, parable, or analogy in narrative form, requiring many words. For example, a process – like a growing tree, mining iron ore, or running a cross-country race – may provide the apposite analogy, and only in describing the process will you unfold meaning. In other words: the quality rather than quantity matters – or, in NLP presupposition terms, the response. Efficiency involves transferring maximum understanding, or output, with minimum effort, or communication input.

METAPHORICAL EFFECTIVENESS

As we have seen in the communication presuppositions, the response, effect or meaning transferred (from map to map) forms the essence of a communication. So communication doesn't lie just in the appositeness, richness or ingenuity of the analogy or simile, but rather in the effect it creates – however logically apposite or even relevant.

'Once upon a time ...' can have a magical effect on children. More to the point, a story, anecdote or real-life example will multiply the effectiveness of any communication, at any age, and to any kind of audience. How often have you heard, 'I don't remember the subject he talked about, but I remember the story about so-and-so.' We rarely remember the structure or logical sequence of a presentation after a few days, but some image or other can spring to mind after decades. Invariably, the image will have derived from a metaphor or sensory illustration. We understand them at the time, learn more, relate better to the speaker, and remember them longer. This makes metaphors our most effective communication tools.

In view of the 'response' presupposition, however, your success will depend on:

- the choice of analogy or story
- the skill with which you make the comparison.

You will need skill and know-how to make the best use of metaphorical language. For many, this will mean a new kind of learning. Appropriate metaphors usually arise *intuitively*, rather than as a result of a logical search. As we have seen, this requires communication with your own unconscious mind, rather than technical skills for communicating with other people – in other words, *intra*- rather than *inter*personal intelligence. Part of the skill therefore involves managing your uptime/downtime state, and other inner resources that will help towards your communication purpose – skills not usually associated with communication theory. Focusing on the response you want, rather than the detailed mechanics of how you will achieve it, will usually produce the intuitive analogies you need to achieve the purpose.

KEEPING IT SIMPLE

Sometimes, you need to simplify a complicated idea, situation or process. Einstein's cosmic ride on a beam of light was, for him, the breakthrough in simplifying a concept in a way that he had never entertained. We usually associate this classical role of metaphor in creative thinking with artists, scientists and original thinkers who change the course of history. In fact, whatever mystery we ascribe to eureka-type intuitions, they reveal another aspect of communication: communicating between the unconscious and conscious mind. Looked at in this way, we can start to envisage the role of the unconscious mind and its world of metaphor in ordinary person-to-person communication.

If you can simplify a complex thought by thinking in metaphor or analogy, as Einstein and so many other great scientists and inventors have done, you can use the same metaphor or analogy to convey it to somebody else. The mark of a great thinker lies in their ability to communicate the most complex ideas in the simplest way. In this case, simplicity makes the communication effective, and increases your chances of gaining the response (such as to inform or enthuse) you wanted – your communication outcome.

The idea of the human mind as a map illustrates the use of metaphor in this way. We don't just resort to metaphor for linguistic 'colour', as perhaps in fictional or journalistic writing, or for its efficiency in encapsulating an idea in one word. In this case, something we know well (a map) helps to *bridge the gap* (more metaphors) to something we don't know – a new or weighty concept. The first NLP presupposition uses the 'territory' metaphor in the same way. In this case, the *combination* of metaphors adds further synergy and elucidation. A simple analogy, or relationship, makes the picture clearer (between a map and the mind, and territory and the material world).

Metaphors and such figures of speech don't require 'teaching'. We learn them and use them and don't realize it, just as we all use our mother tongue perfectly well and master many other language patterns from the earliest age.

Figures of speech

I will now give some examples of simple metaphor in everyday language. I evolved this list over a few weeks for an earlier book, *NLP in 21 Days*, and reproduce it here (slightly more evolved) with permission from the publishers. These illustrate just how much we draw upon these in everyday conversation, but also in the way they evoke sensory images that take the mind into whole worlds of discovery and meaning:

put down your roots	branch out
turn over a new leaf	in the mire
plain sailing	lay the foundations
an uphill climb	all downhill from here
she's a star	he's a wily old fox
a whipping boy	reap what you sow
water under the bridge	get your wires crossed
blaze a trail	change gear
spare tyre	peter out
under a cloud	silver lining
which side your bread's buttered on	in the soup
on the back burner	have your cake and eat it
make mincemeat of	a taste of your own medicine
career ladder	glass ceiling
up against a brick wall	paint yourself into a corner
open door	blind alley
easy road	put the brakes on
counting the pennies	back to the wall
on the carpet	spanner in the works
nuts and bolts	loose screw
baby with the bath water	milk them for all they're worth
odds-on	hedge your bets
on your high horse	rein in
nest egg	ring fence
switched on	switched off
burnt out	frozen out
eye to eye	neck and neck
feet under the table	hand in the till
tongue in cheek	knuckle under
Achilles heel	take it on the chin
heart on his sleeve	heart in my mouth
wool over his eyes	put her foot in it
put your heart into it	let your hair down
splitting hairs	hand in glove
finger in the pie	head in a noose
head over heels	toe in the water
gloves off	no holds barred
game, set and match	long shot
own-goal	level playing field
sticky wicket	on the back foot
on your toes	back to base
through the roof	through the back door

up in smoke

sabre-rattling

tighten your belt

no stone unturned

countdown

cobbled together

one more hurdle

in at the deep end

head in the sand

cast-iron case

tin-pot

weakest link

two-edge sword

big guns

shoot from the hip

down and out

all sewn up

for the high jump

carry the torch

eye on the ball

watertight argument

gold-plated engineering

battleaxe

Effective stories

Everything in life – if not life itself – seems to translate into stories. We all possess unconscious competence in constructing and telling 'life narratives'. NLP takes this instance of unconscious competence – in this case, in using language for effective communication – as a source of modelling *conscious* change and effective outcomes. This means that you can start to do what you do in a different way to achieve even better results, according to the Four-stage Achievement Model described in Chapter 3. Even better, you can apply your skills in areas you have not previously used them, consciously and with a view to achieving goals or outcomes. You already possess these basic skills. A better understanding of the power of metaphor adds to your communication toolbox and increases your success rate. A simple simile or an apposite analogy can carve out a neural pattern that a couple of well-written textbooks would have difficulty achieving.

MANAGING BY METAPHOR

Let's say that as manager, you have to communicate something sensitive or unpleasant to a junior colleague. Whilst we all have natural language skills as a resource when facing new situations and new people, we can't always draw on our own successful experience to simply 're-run' it. We meet new situations that our experience cannot match. However, we saw in earlier chapters that by consciously deciding on your communication outcome – say, to console, warn, encourage, motivate or suchlike – you will harness your natural goal-achieving system.

In this case, make sure you have a clear target. For instance, do you want to communicate information? What effect do you expect this to have, and what effect do you want to produce? With a clear outcome in mind, you will watch and listen for feedback, and have the flexibility to change in order to obtain the response you want.

With a well-formed outcome, you can harness your natural metaphorical language skills to help bring it about. Ask yourself how best you can communicate in this particular case, for this specific purpose, to this particular person, in this context, and so on. You might draw on a 'story' from your own experience, of course: 'I know just how you feel. In my last job …'. Or you might recount a case you have heard of, or that your junior colleague knows of but perhaps has not made the personal connection, that might help.

Top communicators sometimes describe how metaphors and simple illustrations just come to them 'from nowhere'. However, top communicators rose to the top because they know the power of metaphor, and have acquired unconscious competence in using them. And, most importantly, they recognize the vast reservoir of experience we all have in our unconscious mind, ready for use. With truly intuitive behaviour of this sort, you don't risk the danger of what you say sounding contrived.

Nevertheless, unconscious competence starts with conscious thought, effort, practice and many mistakes along the way, so in this case it makes sense to ask yourself by way of preparation whether some analogy or story will help you to achieve the effect (say, consolation, encouragement) you want. Expect intuitive guidance and insights anyway, but treat them as a bonus.

GRABBING ATTENTION

Public speakers, professional trainers and salespeople know well the power of anecdote and metaphor. They use these to grab an audience's attention and to keep it all the way through, then to conclude in a memorable way. We use submodalities in a similar way to create 'compelling futures' – strong sensory evidence – as part of a well-formed outcome. Memorable images play an even more important role in memory processes. In this case, a bizarre, humorous or impossible outcome will stay in the memory for a long time. By exaggerating whatever you want to remember, such as a person's face, you will carve out for it a special, unforgettable place in your memory. The same process can link the face to the name, and so help as a social skill. My book *Remembering Names and Faces* goes into more detail on this subject.

Attention-grabbing has even greater importance where we don't have a visual element, such as in radio or literature. Many people remember radio drama, in particular, after many years. Television doesn't have quite the same effect, as we call less on our own imagination to fill the sensory gaps. When listening to the radio or reading a novel, we create our own visual reality, so we can create life without boundaries. This happens intensely when children sit mesmerized by a simple story told by a teacher or parent.

Lovers of good literature will also remember the metaphorical descriptions of people and places so typical of storytellers such as Dickens, Hardy and Shakespeare. Interestingly, this skill requires not so much literary excellence and an extensive vocabulary, but rather storytelling skills, in which metaphor forms the indispensable ingredient. The late Catherine Cookson boasted no great literary skills, other than the ability to tell a good story. Other best-selling contemporary novelists fall into the same category. We have evidence of their success as communicators from book sales and ardent fans.

DEPERSONALIZING

Metaphors have other uses in communication. You can depersonalize an issue by expressing it through metaphor. Remember: 'The meaning of a communication is the response you elicit.' So you don't need a special style or structure for the process of 'good communication'. Moreover, because you bridge very different maps of the world, it pays to do anything, or not do anything, to avoid offence, embarrassment or unnecessary objection – unless you *intend* to provoke it. Keep your outcome in mind. Do everything within your knowledge and skill to avoid eliciting the wrong response because a critical, sensitive or disbelieving left brain blocked your message. Talk to the 'child' in the person – the unconscious mind – through stories and mind-pictures.

'I heard of a person …' can often impart a message without an over-personal reaction. People function like that. Interestingly, even though the person knows, or guesses, that you simply want to 'make a point', they will not react as negativily as they might have done had you made the remark directly, even in courteous terms. In other words, if the cap fits, they will wear it, provided they do not perceive any personal indictment or slur on their integrity and intentions.

Try to stay detached from the issue, or 'content', of the communication, as would a messenger, using the language devices we encountered in the Milton Model. Sometimes, the messenger gets shot, of course. However, with a little skill in the choice and use of metaphor, a messenger will come off better than the unprepared principal.

IDENTITY AND OWNERSHIP

As communicator, aim to persuade the other person to identify with the metaphor before you deliver the 'message' – in metaphorical terms, before the story ends. By the time the story has ended, they have already accepted the metaphor as representing them or their situation in some way. Remember that the person you communicate with makes the association themselves, and forms any meaning. You cannot know their map, and cannot begin to know the mental associations they will make with a particular metaphor. The metaphor has no meaning in itself. Each person will understand a story differently. But they also *interpret* the same story in different ways. Try to choose a metaphor that points them gently in the *direction* you want them to go (your communication outcome). The continuous uncertainty in 'right-brain' communication means that you need to exercise all your observation powers to pick up feedback, stay in rapport, remain flexible enough to change, and focus on the response or outcome you want.

In bringing about change, using metaphors will usually produce longer-term solutions to a person's problems, because the solution comes from inside the person themself. They, and only they, can make the neural 'connection' that will ultimately bring about change. Most importantly, therefore, they *own* the problem. Even with hindsight, they 'thought of' the answer. In other words, they add their own ending to the story.

Any business manager will confirm that this element of personal ownership constitutes a vital factor in successful planning, team working, problem-solving and general effectiveness. It overcomes the common communication tendency for a person to dislike somebody telling them what to do, offering sympathy, or even giving advice. A person generally likes to feel in control of their life, and not dependent, at least with regard to important issues and decisions.

By using metaphor, the *idea* provides the insight. The client or problem-holder probably takes the credit, plus the benefits of a solution. The communicator makes do with having achieved a communication outcome – by whatever means, and whoever receives the credit.

CHOOSING YOUR STORY

Looked at in this light, you will realize the sort of skills you need, whether in choosing a metaphor, delivering it, and staying focused on your outcome or response. You aim for somewhere in the middle – between an obviously connected anecdote and a loose metaphor that has no logical link at all. On the one hand, you don't want your metaphor to connect easily with the issue in the conscious mind of the person, otherwise you lose all the advantages of direct, unconscious communication. On the other hand, you need to weave your metaphor seamlessly into the message to create a vivid mind picture that the other person will positively relate their problem to. You can add to your skills the various Milton language patterns, to suggest a successful outcome. To this, add sensory acuity to detect non-verbal responses, and the flexibility to introduce new metaphors that come to your mind if you need to re-focus on the target.

Remember that in skilled hands, the process of communicating with 'unconscious competence' can happen as unconsciously as the process of receiving the message. As explained right at the beginning of this book, rapport will underlie this and any sort of communication. It sometimes accounts for maybe 80 per cent of success. Using meta-phorical language will add to your success rate, but will also allow you to succeed in far more important communication outcomes, and change people's lives for the better.

To some, this smacks of undue indirectness and deviousness, but in terms of the NLP model, the reverse may have more truth. The real power of metaphor lies in bypassing the conscious, analytical, critical, logical, literal mind – the more limited part of the mind when it comes to creative problem-solving. The message goes *directly* to the unconscious mind, where the main resources lie. However, with proper use of vague language, going direct doesn't provoke the usual left-brain resistance and inappropriate interpretations or excuses.

As we see in young children, who well exemplify this aspect of the mind – and love stories – the unconscious brain deals in sensory, literal interpretations, and the present moment. All this can result in extraordinary consequences if a well-formed communication uses metaphor as a resource. You will recognize a successful outcome by the effect on the person – a safer test than their verbal acknowledgement of understanding or acquiescence. But they will usually not see themselves as having responded to, or even as a party to, a communication of any consequence. They just start to *behave differently*, and maybe show some emotional effect as well. In other words, if you make an appropriate metaphorical 'hit', they fulfil *your purpose* in the communication.

Metaphors for rapport

When communicating, by putting yourself in the other person's shoes you will go a long way towards an effective communication before you ever start to use these powerful tools. Two other presuppositions mentioned earlier reinforce the message for the 'metaphorical messenger':

1   **You cannot not communicate** – Whatever you didn't say or didn't do or didn't intend forms part of the communication in so far as it affects the other person's understanding and feelings.
2   **The responsibility for a communication lies with the communicator** – This doesn't impose a social rule. It simply means that we behave according to intentions, or outcomes, and a communication outcome – like any other outcome – needs to follow the 'well-formedness' criteria set out in Chapter 4. In particular, you need to keep the outcome under your control.

In turn, using metaphor involves more than adding richness to your language. It means using the best tools for the job.

NLP doesn't set rules, but it comes quite close to it in this matter of requiring rapport for effective communication. This need for rapport adds more to the communicator's responsibility. We can't define rapport easily, nor easily establish and maintain it with people with whom we don't seem to have a natural affinity. Unfortunately, we can't always choose whom we communicate with – we have too much communicating to do just to survive. Apart from its obvious application in a work situation, and family with whom you don't have a choice, this follows from the simple presupposition that you cannot not communicate. That means you can even have an effect, or create an unintentional outcome, on complete strangers.

'DESIGNER' METAPHORS

We identified matching as a key to rapport, including matching the interests and experience of the other person. A whole world of metaphor opens up here. A home-loving person with young children may respond to family metaphors, whereas a military person may respond better to win–lose expressions, as may a competitive sporting person. An investor, similarly, will relate to 'bulls' and 'bears', and a businessperson to 'bottom lines'. Choose designer metaphors when you know a person's interests.

Our language displays our values and interests, and metaphors do this in a way that communicates naturally, without having to spell things out. Most importantly, as metaphor forms a large part of everyday communication, like expressive body language, we don't notice it amidst the content of a communication.

Metaphoric motivation

Metaphors evoke emotions in a way that no other kind of language can. They can bring an audience to laughter, then tears, then back to laughter again. They can instruct, correct and reprimand without leaving any hard feelings. They reach deep into each person's mind and trigger images and sensations dating back to the earliest days of their life. They help a person to draw on their own resources.

Emotions also form the main ingredient of motivation. How many times has a story, such as of bravery, hardship, single-mindedness or sacrifice, touched the emotions in a way that the most carefully argued case can never do. It can produce enthusiasm, commitment, action and change. Often, even crucial decisions hinge on an emotional experience. Many professional communicators, such as counsellors, therapists, trainers and consultants – and their clients – could benefit more from metaphorical communication.

Change of any kind, especially change that disturbs long-established habits, tends to provoke resistance. As we have seen, metaphors short-circuit the logical left brain, and thus avoid resistance. A story can access the unconscious mind so that even a person's outward behaviour changes unconsciously. The person simply feels different. New conscious intentions then arise as hidden desires surface, and the behaviour that will bring them about. Change requires commitment of heart as well as mind, and metaphors offer communicators a direct route to a person's heart.

Metaphor and memory

Metaphors and analogy play a central part in the mind and memory. Somehow, they outlive wisdom couched in more sophisticated, objective language. We often hear these sorts of statement:

- I'll never forget what so-and-so said to me many years ago. He said it's like …
- I'll never forget the story of that young girl …
- What she said changed the picture completely …
- The only thing I can remember …
- She had a way of explaining things easily.
- It's the first time I understood just what that meant.

In each case, metaphor probably played a part in the success of the communication. Metaphor has also established a place in memory training systems. Many systems enjoy proven results, but they all have a major visual element, and most focus on metaphors.

PEG SYSTEMS

Various 'peg' systems associate numbers with easily remembered objects, and those things bring numbers to life. For example:

- one – bun
- two – shoe
- three – tree
- four – door
- five – hive
- six – sticks
- seven – heaven
- eight – gate
- nine – wine
- ten – hen.

Anyone can easily remember a peg list, and can then use it for life to represent numbers. It helps if, as in this case, the metaphors rhyme, or have some other intrinsic association with the number. But the main power of metaphors lies in their amenability to sensory representation. To use a metaphor, you can place sensory things in a wheelbarrow – or at least see, hear and feel them. Using the power of imagination, they allow exaggeration by adding unforgettable characteristics in content, as well as ingenuity in the manipulation of structural and process qualities by way of submodalities – such as size and brightness – as we saw earlier in the book. For instance, you can make a shoe house-sized, an apple tree can rise through the clouds, and you can adorn a humble hen with spots like a leopard.

Remembering follows a simple process:

- Associate a chain of events or objects (classically, items to buy at the supermarket) with a number metaphor.
- Link the number metaphor with a 'storyline'.

- Simply recall the story (a skill we all possess, going right back to early childhood), and you can recall whatever chain of events or items you want.

For instance, take the first item you want to remember as sugar. You might associate it with a one-metre diameter bun sandwiching, or coated in, sugar. For your next item, tomato sauce, you could imagine it in a large, shoe-shaped container, or a training shoe filled with sauce. Take your pick. Whatever comes to your mind first when *establishing* the memory will probably come to you first in the future when *recalling* it. Just keep your visualization as stupid and bizarre as your fertile imagination can make it.

Memory storylines

Memory systems draw on stories, or complex metaphors, to extend the potential for remembering almost indefinitely. You can remember any list of random items by incorporating them into a memorable storyline. For instance:

- cathedral
- banana
- pony.

The story might run: 'The cathedral fills up with ripe bananas, and along comes a hungry pony …'.

The extent of what you can remember using such metaphorical systems has no limit other than the length of the story and your unlimited (for all practical purposes) imagination. Even a person with a 'memory like a sieve' self-image can remember a dozen random objects after a few minutes' story-setting. Serious memory specialists can advance to recalling hundreds of guests at a conference, or a telephone directory or two. For most of us, using these innate memory powers to recall the names of clients, guests at a party, delegates at a training course or meeting, or facts for an exam will repay the small time investment manyfold. In any event, you possess the tools to remember anything you need to as part of your work and life, if you care to use them. Like inner resources of confidence, persistence and various self-beliefs, you can draw on memory resources as tools for achieving all kinds of personal outcomes.

NLP has not addressed memory processes as much as some other topics, but it has certainly contributed much to our understanding of metaphors and the management of submodalities – both at the heart of the memory process. My earlier books *The Right Brain Manager* and *Remembering Names and Faces* cover memory and memory systems in more detail. In this book, I emphasize the scope and power of metaphor.

Intrapersonal intelligence

Emotional intelligence (EQ) emphasizes interpersonal intelligence and the wide meaning of communication that NLP also deems important. EQ also emphasizes intrapersonal intelligence, more concerned with inner self-communication, or self-awareness. As well as the interpersonal communication that we have mainly concentrated on so far, metaphor also has a part to play in self-communication, especially in describing identity. Uncharacteristically, this seems to have applied more in a corporate context than in personal development.

IMAGE AND IDENTITY

Companies and other organizations have used metaphors and visual symbols to establish an identity, or personality, in the minds of their employees, customers and the general public. Whilst their mission statements correctly encapsulates their aims, these documents tend to seem bland and not particularly memorable. However, by introducing a metaphor, people can relate more easily to a company, product or person. Esso ran a promotional campaign a few decades ago that became a classic: 'Put a tiger in your tank.' The Esso tiger soon established almost cult status as motorists dangled furry tiger tails out of their filler caps. Esso, until then just another oil company, left the competition behind. Suddenly, it had an identity of its own, and the secret lay in a metaphor that anybody could see, hear and feel. A product can assume a personality of its own, which attracts personal emotions. Love it or hate it, you can't just ignore a (VW) Beetle.

Companies have used the metaphor idea to enhance their image or to create a new personality, sometimes in conjunction with outside consultants who facilitate the process. Initially, staff members contribute appropriate metaphors to reflect the collective identity of the firm. For instance:

If our company were a car, what make and model would it be?

You can apply the same metaphorical brainstorming to just about anything. For example, what if our company were:

- an animal?
- a brand of clothing?
- a book?
- a film star?
- a place to live?
- a holiday destination?
- a type of food?
- a fictional character?

Clearly, Marks and Spencer would have a different identity to Primark, as Jaguar has a different identity to Fiat. However, each identity will resonate with a large potential customer base once a company establishes it clearly and streamlines all its policies, promotion and behaviour to conform to that identity. You can't easily get mad or glad about a faceless corporate entity. But a person can become excited about something they can see, hear and feel – something real. The metaphor bridges this mental gap to capture the right-brain, visual, story-loving tendency in us all.

The potential of metaphor also applies in individual situations, such as therapy, self-development and goal-achievement. A similar process applies, as the metaphor helps to focus or consolidate an identity. We each have a picture of ourselves, however difficult to define in words, and this reveals itself – like so many other aspects of a person – in self-talk ('You clown!', 'You nuthead!'), although we don't consciously resort to metaphors.

MODAL METAPHORS

In establishing a personality, a company – even the largest multi-national – tries to identify with actual (or at least modal) people, who fit a specific profile. Therefore, the two identities – supplier and customer – match, and matching produces the affinity. For example, we might see a company or organization in personified terms, such as:

- a friendly and reliable person who prefers family life and old-fashioned values
- a young, ambitious and contemporary person who loves freedom and fun
- a visionary, innovative and intellectual person who takes pride in their state-of-the-art knowledge.

Which companies would match such a specification? Which metaphors, in the categories suggested above, could one apply to both a company and its customers? Who do you know among your friends, relations and work colleagues who fits these descriptions? Would they describe themselves the same way? The last question reveals an important aspect of intrapersonal intelligence: the question of identity can cause problems in a person's life. A person's self-image may differ radically from how others see them, especially people who don't know them well. Similarly, somebody may have a work persona, and a home and family persona. You can imagine how a confused identity can mix up a person's values and outcomes, and the behaviour that follows from these.

The various unconscious aspects of well-formed outcomes dealt with in Chapter 4 go to the root of these important individual characteristics. The value-identification process described in Chapter 5 will go a long way towards creating a true, comfortable identity you can live with. Metaphor provides a powerful tool in this process. Once chosen and established in a person's psyche, it acts as a convenient template for a shorthand check on behaviour, outcomes, relationships and so on: 'Does this (behaviour, outcome, value) fit my identity as a greyhound, oak tree, mediaeval castle or whatever?' Just choosing a personal identity metaphor will help a person to place their values and outcomes hierarchies in order.

Therapists use stories to some degree. For example, a counsellor might start a story and ask the person to finish it off in their own way. In choosing the storyline, whether a well-known parable or story or a purpose-designed one, the counsellor will try to incorporate one or more of the issues requiring resolution in a metaphorical or analogous way. We unconsciously identify ourselves with characters or morals in a story, so finishing off the story can reveal insights into a person's identity that would otherwise have remained below the surface. As we have already seen, you need skill in choosing the story, but also in only *partially* telling it. You need to stop after the person has had time to associate with it, but not so soon that the person cannot create their own ending. Trainers have used similar processes in group settings, but the power of metaphor still remains untapped.

15 *Meta Programs*

We all sort sensory information in our own, unique way. This means that we think and behave differently, even given identical situations and inputs. This reveals itself in our personality characteristics or dispositions, such as introversion and extroversion, thinking and feeling, and so on. Neurologically, these long-standing patterns of mind and behaviour reflect well-established brain patterns. We create neural pathways, or routings, much as a river becomes deeper and wider as more and more water flows into it from smaller streams. Well-entrenched personality traits act like great river canyons, or busy highways that seem to attract more traffic the wider they grow. Change becomes harder the longer we live.

We sometimes experience surprise at how people react so differently to different situations, words, people or places. However, in view of our different life experiences, we hold beliefs, values and ways of thinking that make every one of us unique. And while we can rarely identify their origins, we can imagine how attitudes and beliefs grow as our interpretation of experience takes on a self-fulfilling life of its own. This chapter explains the mental 'programs' that affect our personality, values, attitudes and behaviour. You will soon begin to recognize them in yourself and in others, and to use them both to communicate more effectively and to take control of your life.

Personality programs

As individuals, different things motivate us, and we make decisions according to different criteria. We feel strongly about certain things, and prefer behaving in a certain way in given circumstances. In short: people use their own minds.

We don't understand this complex process, and it doesn't feature consciously in how we live our lives on a day-to-day basis, whether communicating with people or trying to achieve our desires. We know that people act in a certain way when we do or say certain things, but we have little to work on when we want to persuade them to do something or let them know how we think and feel. Everybody acts differently, and with different motives. Much of the time, we act inconsistently, and often without reason, at least as seen by others. In fact, we don't know what happens inside the black box of our own mind, let alone somebody else's.

Fortunately, you don't need to understand the human mind fully to use it or encourage somebody else to use it, any more than you need to understand electricity to enjoy its many benefits. How a person thinks determines how they behave, so knowing what happens in a person's mind – even without knowing why or even how – can give us enormous benefits. This applies in selling and marketing, influencing and persuading, therapeutic change work and communication in general.

Through NLP, we can identify the higher-level mindsets, or 'meta programs', that give rise to behaviour. These programs translate the material world around us into the thoughts and behaviour that give each of us our unique personality and identity. We sometimes refer to them as traits, personality, disposition or identity – 'That's just the way she is.'

For all our uniqueness, in another sense we seem much alike. 'Human nature' repeats itself from person to person, and indeed from culture to culture and nation to nation. We exhibit a range of standard thinking characteristics. For instance:

- We do what we think will give us pleasure rather than pain.
- We interpret the environment around us consistently, according to our view of the world and the values we have acquired throughout life – what we deem important.
- We live and act for some purpose or meaning.
- We have values we hold to and expect others to respect.
- We aspire to happiness and contentment.
- We think with language.
- We aspire to self-actualization, or a higher expression of our personal identity.
- We need to communicate with people and have satisfying relationships.

So, however different the content of our thoughts (or application software), we all perceive with the same basic structure of thought and the same process of sensory representation (operating software), using a standard brain (hardware).

On the other hand, the sensory data we select and reject, and the meta programs to which our behavioural strategies conform, vary. This meta level (*meta*, from the Greek meaning 'over and beyond', in NLP, used in the sense of a higher logical, systemic or experiential level) relates to our personality traits. Jung and others have identified a manageable number of traits, or psychological 'types'. These had their own predecessors in the form of temperament, and the classical elements of wind, fire, water and earth. The Jungian and later derivations have loosely found their way into NLP as meta programs.

No canon of meta programs exists. On the contrary, well-published lists vary from half a dozen or so to more than a hundred. Fortunately, for practical purposes we can reduce these to a couple of dozen rather than hundreds, depending on the precise definition we adopt. I have included enough to illustrate them, and show how they affect us all, especially in interpersonal communication. However, I have not included so many examples that they lose their meaning, or so few that you miss their significance and ubiquity. Importantly, we need to understand the neurological principles that underlie disparate kinds of behaviour and human change.

PERSONALITY PROFILES

As well-known thinking characteristics, or 'personality features', you will probably find NLP meta programs all too familiar. From their pre-Jungian origins, they are found in various psychometric instruments, such as Myers Briggs, and the '16 PF', and in various learning instruments, such as Honey and Mumford's Learning Style Questionnaire and the Margerison McCann Learning Wheel, both based on Kolb's learning styles, which in turn trace back to Jung.

The Myers Briggs types consist of the 'preferences' shown in Figure 15.1, and you will notice similarities to the descriptions of the meta programs in this chapter. These types constitute analogue scales, or continua, rather than either/or criteria as some personality

Extroversion	⟺	Introversion
Sensing	⟺	Intuition
Thinking	⟺	Feeling
Judging	⟺	Perceiving

Figure 15.1   The Myers Briggs types

constructs do. Statistically, few people fall at the extremes, although the descriptors of extreme stereotypes help us to understand the traits.

Leslie Cameron Bandler classified some types in the early days of NLP, most of which serve as the examples I give in this chapter. These have gained popularity in the NLP community. Others, like Myers Briggs, appear more in management and corporate training environments. The NLP contribution, apart from the 'meta' description, mainly consists of:

* setting meta programs into the structure of the larger NLP model that describes how we filter sensory inputs by generalizing, deleting and distorting sensory data; they illustrate different perceptual maps
* showing how we can purposely identify and change these neurological patterns or meta habits
* showing how we can use these behavioural models in interpersonal communication by matching, to gain rapport and communicate more effectively.

I have chosen to include in these 'thinking styles' or 'personality types' (from now on, I will use the NLP jargon term 'meta programs') right-left brain dominance, along with those typically quoted in NLP, but I have omitted sensory preference (see Chapter 3). Brain dominance, or 'hemispherical polarization' (non-NLP jargon this time) does not figure explicitly in the main NLP meta program 'lists', but it influences many neurophysiological models, including, to different degrees, the NLP meta programs usually listed. The split-brain research of the 1960s and developments in scanning technology in more recent years have given us a body of knowledge about hemispherical brain polarization that serves NLP well. Importantly, we can view this particular meta system from a physical brain rather than a metaphysical mind perspective.

I also include the elements of what we call the Life Content Model (see Chapter 3). Usually, NLP doesn't classify this as a meta program, but like the bicameral brain model, it has proven popular and useful outside NLP, for example in business and training. It proves its worth in outcome-setting, and provides several matching factors for rapport in communication. Like any mind model, it overlaps with other meta programs.

Whilst these programmes reveal themselves essentially as behaviour, we usually associate them with personality types, or traits. For this reason, here I have described kinds of *people*, although (for the NLP purists) this certainly doesn't imply either a role, an immutable disposition or an identity. Nevertheless, they tend to apply in the long term, and influence the whole or a major area of a person's life. In ordinary parlance, they reflect – at any point in time – a true personality or character trait. In terms of the NLP model, each represents a *program that runs programs*, or meta program. We can view these in several ways:

- In neurophysiological terms, each relates, to some degree at least, to a part of the brain, such as a hemisphere, region, or main 'sensory highway', and any corresponding part of the body 'affected' emotionally.

- At the neural or synaptic level, each characteristic consists of a dynamic network of interactive electro-chemical connections.

- Metaphorically, each forms a brain pattern or system, with smaller patterns inside, and forming part of a bigger pattern. Or each forms part of a map that helps us to make sense of the territory of reality. The programming metaphor reminds us that these traits follow syntax or sequence, and we can change them just as we can change a computer program using the same hardware.

Meta programs

LEFT OR RIGHT BRAIN

The logical (left-brain) thinker contrasts with the intuitive (right-brain) thinker. The well-researched subject of brain dominance plays a major part in learning, self-development, creativity, and other fields. It appears explicitly in marketing in the form of advertisements that appeal to 'heart' as well as 'mind', and less directly in psychographic market segmentation. I have suggested mainstream marketing applications in my book *Mind to Mind Marketing*.

Various questionnaire-based instruments can identify this basic personality differentiator, sometimes termed 'hemispherical polarization'. My book *The Right Brain Manager* includes one such questionnaire, but they abound on the Internet, and you can download some. Other research has resulted in four-quadrant brain classification, but still based on the different brain locations associated with different thinking functions. The respective left- and right-brain characteristics usually cited include the following:

Left brain:

- **Verbal** – This side controls most speech, reading and wiring functions. It remembers facts, recalls names, and knows how to spell. Left-brain stroke victims may suffer from speech and language defects.
- **Analytical** – We associate this side with logic, rationale and analysis. It evaluates factual material in an organized, logical way. This applies to many aspects of scientific method.
- **Literal** – It only understands words in the most literal sense. Thus we *don't* associate it with metaphor, puns, innuendo, imaginative literary devices, 'reading between the lines', punchlines, and humour in general. It may experience difficulty with poetry.
- **Linear** – It processes information sequentially, in a line, one step at a time. It follows classical 'if … then' logical processes. It arrives at one solution only, and stalls if one logical stage doesn't fit.
- **Mathematical** – It handles numbers and other symbols well, and can cope with advanced mathematical concepts. It acts like a digital computer, although not as quickly.
- **Conscious mind** – It often equates with characteristics of the conscious mind, as well as attention, alertness to the here and now, and so-called 'uptime'.

- It also controls movements on the right side of the body, and processes images seen through the right eye.

Right brain:

- **Non-verbal** – This side works in images, rather than words. Outstanding artistic talent in autistic children sometimes links to the right brain.
- **Holistic (or non-linear)** – It can process many kinds of information at the same time, or in parallel. It sees problems holistically – the 'big picture' – and can make intuitive leaps. It can evaluate the whole problem or issue at once. It remembers faces, even from incomplete data, seeing the features 'as a whole'.
- **Spatial** – It handles perceptions of space and location. It enjoys jigsaw puzzles, and stops you losing your way in town, or even in your own home, as can happen to right-brain stroke victims.
- **Musical** – It has innate musical talent and appreciation, although much of the routine work of music theory happens in the left side.
- **Imaginative** – It can fantasize, make up stories, knows how to play, and sees the funny side of things. It can ask 'What if?' in a creative way. It harbours creativity and inventive talents, and produces the occasional 'eureka' type of insight, as well as everyday intuition, hunches and gut feelings.
- **Spiritual** – It understands worship, prayer, pictorial symbolism, and mysticism.
- **Unconscious mind** – It often equates with characteristics of the unconscious mind, or Jung's 'collective unconscious', trance and so-called 'downtime'. It deals with feelings not easy to articulate.
- It also controls the left side of the body, and processes images through the left eye. Left-brain stroke victims often have the right-side body paralysis, and vice versa.

Some of these well-known characteristics appear in other meta programs. Although brain polarization applies on a continuum, even a small bias will produce recognizable characteristics that we can measure with psychometric instruments. But as a rule, treat all meta program descriptions as stereotypes. For example:

- Even strongly left- or right-brain-dominant people do not usually exhibit all the characteristics.
- Most people fall somewhere between the two extremes on the continuum.
- The two sides of the brain connect together with about 200 million nerve fibres (via the corpus callosum), and we all use both sides all the time anyway. Almost every function, like maths, music, reading, science and art, involves *both* kinds of functioning.
- A fair proportion of left-handers do not exhibit any bias.

Most importantly, the significance of brain polarization lies not in *what the brain does* (such as maths or poetry), but *how it does it* – in a linear/sequential or holistic/parallel way respectively.

TOWARDS OR AWAY FROM

We describe this meta program type as the 'towards' (pleasure) rather than 'away from' (pain) person, and vice versa. You will notice the similarity between this meta program and positive and negative goal-orientation (see Chapter 4) – focusing on what we want or what we don't want respectively. In fact, normal, healthy people prefer pleasure to pain. But our orientation – the direction in which we *look*, or focus, if you like – may tend towards pleasure (what we want) or pain (what we don't want). Sometimes, trainers refer to this program as 'direction'. In fact, in each case we pursue or move towards happiness, even when that happens as an unconscious 'positive intention'. In that case, we may seem to veer further away from our conscious or stated goals.

Marketers use the universal pain/pleasure motivators in selling and promotion. Negotiators, educators and other influencers also use this feature. Together, these two motivation orientations closely reflect the needs hierarchy of Maslow and similar models, so a very large population might respond to meta program matching. In the case of the Needs and Hygiene Model, one 'ladder' applies to us all – reflecting the universal pain–pleasure continuum. In practice, a person may respond disproportionately to the pain and pleasure poles.

For example, which do we more readily respond to – the pleasure of buying, or the pain of not buying? In the case of an insurance policy, do we respond to the peace of mind and security for our children, or the pain of poverty and dependency? In other words: whilst always wanting pleasure and eschewing pain, do we look forward, or behind our backs? In well-formed outcome parlance (see Chapter 4), a 'towards' person will readily imagine the goal as already achieved. The pleasure of perceived success then motivates the person to action. An 'away from' person might become locked into their present state. This inherent *orientation* difference operates as a mindset much like the powerful optimism/pessimism, half full/half empty divide.

Harnessing direction

'Towards' people usually make good planners and managers, but will probably depend on 'away from' people for checks and balances, such as on cash flow and risk assessment. 'Away from' people will usually focus on the disadvantages of a situation or proposition, having an instinct for what might go wrong. This provides a valuable balance in a team, and an important check on any major decision. Such a person may also respond well to pressure, and a 'doing' person (see Chapter 3) will no doubt enjoy the action as a trouble-shooter. On the other hand, an 'away from' person can easily get diverted to attend to complications and obstacles and lose focus on the objective of a job, and its priorities. Therefore, each personal tendency will assume different utility in different contexts.

The fear of pain, according to much research, does not motivate as well as a positive reward (or perceived pleasure) in a work context. However, the threat of redundancy can motivate even the most positive people, although this usually applies just for a short time. A long-term career goal – not subject to any single employer – will usually act as a positive, motivating (although maybe unconscious) cybernetic target. In other cases, such as in a penal institution like a prison, or in the military, averting pain (and worse) will act as a strong motivator.

The once popular idea of Situational Leadership makes a similar distinction regarding leadership style and context. Consensus management and positive affirmations may not help when we need soldiers to go 'over the top' in the heat of battle. In peacetime, however, authoritarian leadership may not work. Similarly, in some life-threatening contexts, only fear (of perceived pain) will motivate quickly enough for the purpose. That way, at least we live to tell the story. But even here, a positive overriding cause, and values such as patriotism or courage, may sustain motivation more consistently in the longer term.

INTERNAL–EXTERNAL

The internal–external dichotomy concerns the *source* of a person's motivation. The internally rather than externally motivated person:

- does not need outside recognition
- can exercise self-motivation
- can measure success or failure against their own self-set standards
- may not take feedback very well, however constructive
- doesn't care about what others think
- has an internal 'frame of reference'
- knows when they have done a good job – they can feel it.

The popular advertising copy that runs 'imagine what they will think …' has little effect on these people, and may even prove counterproductive. They don't care what 'they' think. They set their own standards, or frame of reference, and measure against them. You can find their 'hot button' with expressions such as:

- It's up to you.
- Only you can decide.
- I'll leave you to decide/get on with the job.
- Let me know what you think. (They usually have an opinion.)
- Carry on with so-and-so when you think that's finished.
- Just let me know if you get stuck.
- You'll work something out, I'm sure.

With this description, you can easily imagine a person with the reverse meta program. The externally motivated person:

- looks for external guidance and recognition
- requires a yardstick or standard, and procedures to follow
- likes to have a colleague near by to call upon from time to time to bounce ideas off
- needs a 'thank you' or 'well done' now and again
- needs interim approval or guidance – 'Is that what you meant?'
- will offer unsolicited progress reports
- might circulate copies widely so that people know their contribution, and so that they avoid stepping on anyone's toes inadvertently
- will value a monetary bonus disproportionately if it offers recognition and approval, even without a human face.

Broadly speaking, an external frame of reference will suit junior or untrained staff who need supervision. At a management level, however, we expect accountability and initiative. In both cases, this may conflict with a person's natural inclination, and so can cause emotional problems as well as misunderstanding and ineffectiveness in the job. It works in other ways. A young, self-motivated member of staff will soon become frustrated if oversupervised.

THE RISK-TAKER VERSUS THE CAUTIOUS, CONSERVATIVE PERSON

The pioneer leader in contrast to more sheep-like follower also describes this sort of person – the 'I'll try anything new' person versus the 'Is it tried and tested?' person. Again, the relative value of these personal characteristics depends on the context, the task or job, the nature of the organization, and the seniority and responsibilities of the person. However, even at a high level, a professional salaried manager may not have to take the same risks as an entrepreneur in a small firm or a self-employed person. Some kinds of work demand one type or the other. For example, we expect an auditor, financial accountant, quality controller, surgeon or airline pilot to display a tendency towards caution.

SPECIFIC OR GENERAL

The 'specific' versus 'general' distinction involves the importance of detail (small chunk) compared to the big picture (large chunk). A 'specific' person:

- works with parts, and specifics
- prefers to take small, logical steps
- reads the 'small print'
- focuses on product components and detailed specification rather than the overall product
- considers features rather than benefits
- places matters in focus rather than taking an overview
- dots i's and crosses t's
- ties up all the loose ends
- prefers the coalface rather than a head office
- chunks down.

This person tends not to see the forest for the trees.

At the other end of this spectrum, a 'general' person:

- emphasizes the whole
- takes a 'broad-brush' approach
- sees the 'big picture'
- stands back and tries to gain perspective on a subject
- likes ideas, concepts, hypotheses, systems and abstractions
- concentrates on purpose, overall direction and 'bottom line'
- prefers ratios to absolute numbers
- prefers relationships to specific elements
- prefers concepts to the nitty gritty
- chunks up.

As you consider people you know with these different traits, you will probably think of the sorts of words and expressions they use, as well as those in the lists here, that will help to identify their meta program. From what we have seen about the importance of chunking, in various contexts, both these viewpoints clearly have value. Emotional intelligence depends on the skill with which we can take a flexible approach and create choices. In this case, that means chunking both up and down to gain multiple perspectives. In terms of communication and rapport, we will not have much trouble with long-standing meta programs if we can identify them and make allowances.

Identifying people's meta programs will help in matching for rapport. You can 'pace' the characteristics of the meta program, such as chunk size: for example, 'If you look at this closely ...' or 'The overall impression I get ...'.

SAMENESS OR DIFFERENCE

The 'sameness' or 'difference' personality distinction refers to people who notice and sort by difference, rather than sameness, and vice versa. It applies, for instance, when a person sorts information, assesses a problem or interprets (represents) an experience, event or situation. It applies in learning and decision-making, and can determine whether a person will accept change and grasp opportunities. 'Sameness' people tend to exhibit or prefer:

- conservatism
- difficulty in adapting to change
- loyalty to a supplier or employer
- routine and continuity
- safety and comfort
- predictability and dependability
- noticing associations and relationships.

'Difference' people tend to emphasize:

- focusing on exceptions
- amenability to change
- preference to variety and choice
- identifying irregularity, incongruence and mismatching
- novelty and challenge
- creative problem-solving.

You will find a good deal of overlap between 'sameness' people and the cautious, conservative type described earlier. Similarly, you will notice many similarities between the 'difference' person and the risk-taker. Both the latter more or less invite surprises, uncertainty and change. 'Sameness' people guard the status quo. Paradoxically, a risk-taker or 'difference' person will feel no less 'comfortable' in a changeable, unpredictable lifestyle than when life doesn't change. The frustration and boredom of routine can cause much anxiety for such a person. Each person feels at home with their particular preferred meta programs. Within these familiar neurological boundaries lies perceived pleasure; outside lies perceived pain. In terms of communication, a different meta program seems like a different world and a different language. Nevertheless, consider meta programs as an *opportunity* for matching and rapport.

PROACTIVE OR REACTIVE

'Proactive' versus 'reactive' describes the extent to which a person will lead or follow, take the initiative or wait for guidance and instruction. Typically, proactive people tend to:

* act first and think later (if at all)
* provide the world's volunteers
* arrive first
* speak first
* have an opinion
* jump in at the deep end
* try anything once
* organize situations and people
* persuade people
* start things off
* come up with practical ideas
* show impatience
* assume control
* give directions.

They typify the hands-on activist. Reactive people, on the other hand, will:

* wait and follow
* weigh up a situation
* act cautiously
* find it difficult to begin anything
* succumb to suggestion, persuasion and forceful personalities
* comply with rules and procedures
* behave passively and loyally
* live and let live
* make good team members and back-up staff
* generally conform.

Such a person often makes a good number two. They will not threaten the number one, and will carry out instructions well, provided the number one doesn't go off on a long vacation.

KNOWING

Some people want to *know* – the specification, how it works, the small print, the features. This and the following four types form the so-called Life Content Model described in Chapter 3. This trait has significance in the 'knowledge worker' concept and the 'information society'. Increasingly, knowledge has value, rather than material objects. Instant telecommunication means that the popular travelling, press-the-flesh executive 'doer' must concede power to the 'knowledge' person.

DOING

Some people want to *do* – 'When do we start?', 'Just let me try it.', 'What do I have to do?' Others may call them 'activists', or a similar description, according to various personality psychometric instruments. Many managers fit this type. It does tend to favour short-termism and requires the balancing effect of a number two or a team with other qualities.

HAVING AND GETTING

Some people want to *have* or *get*. When assessing their outcomes, this person will want to know what they will actually gain, possess and own. This has marketing implications for customers of this type. A hotel, travel operator, catering provider, trainer or insurance company will need to address the questions: 'What will the customer "take home"? What tangible residue of the invisible service will they retain?' It has a great effect on motivation, such as in education, training and sales performance, so it should form part of a reward or incentive policy. People who like *things* will go to great lengths to get them.

RELATING

Some people want to *relate* – 'What will so-and-so think? Will they be happy? Will they like me, respect me more? Will this purchase impress them?' This may reveal the stereotypical extrovert, but also the person who has an external frame of reference for recognition and motivation. Such a person emphasizes relationships, whether colleagues at work or friends and family. They may need people to motivate them – perhaps more importantly, to give them a sense of belonging and the continuity of a relationship. They ostensibly value people for their own sake, but in fact gain pleasure themselves in security, comradeship and other relating benefits.

BEING

Some people want to be – 'What will this make me? How will I feel differently? Will this make me a golfer, writer, or good mother? Will I be content, happy, fulfilled?' At one level, this equates to identity and the timeless 'Who am I?' question. At another level, it indicates a person who lives for the moment and can enjoy present circumstances without regrets for the past and apprehension about the future. It characterizes a person with an 'in time' timeline (see Chapter 11), and often applies to long-term ultimate goals that we covered in Chapters 3 and 4, such as 'to be happy'.

Implications and applications

We usually find people who lie somewhere within these continuums of personal traits. But more than that, at some times we all behave in ways characteristic of running such a meta program, even when seen by others to act 'out of character'. In particular, people will act differently:

- in different contexts (such as work and play, home and training course)
- when adopting different roles (such as boss, daughter or club secretary)
- when in different moods (such as angry, confident or depressed)
- depending on their current outcome (such as a friend to help, a job to do, or competition to overcome)
- according to their motivation (such as an important principle to adhere to, to save face, to gain peer recognition)
- according to the rewards anticipated (such as money, fame or a quiet life)
- according to life's present circumstances, such as when sick or in hospital, or on holiday.

These meta program descriptions illustrate important differences in the way we think. You will probably identify other characteristics that make us different, and far longer lists than the above often appear. Nevertheless, the implications of how we each experience at this neurological level extend deep and wide. For instance:

- People act as much on emotion as logic, and in any event according to their meta programs and strategies – their perceptions, rather than 'reality'.
- They have implications for learning, whether in education or professional training or sports coaching. They affect the methods and language of teaching.
- Each represents a potential market segment, simply because many millions of customers fall into each category.
- They give rise to a range of matching opportunities for better communication, especially with work colleagues, family and close friends with whom we can invest time in the relationship and understand longer-term thinking patterns.
- They have implications for employee recruitment and managing teams. We can avoid placing 'square pegs in round holes'.
- They can form the basis of rewards and incentive policies.

Ways of thinking at this level change very slowly, and remain remarkably consistent. Many, affecting beliefs and attitudes, have formed wide, deep and fast-flowing rivers in our mental landscape that seem impossible to divert by virtue of the power they have assumed over time. It will usually take something special for us to act and think differently at a level close to our identity – in a way that affects us at the core of our being, where pride, respect and individuality reside. NLP technology extends to changing these meta programs, mainly through the various behavioural strategies that typify them. However, simply identifying and understanding these meta programs, in yourself and others, will create choices and promote your personal development.

PROGRAMMED VALUES

People's values also tend to form meta programs in directing their decisions and behaviour. Identifying the main values, like integrity, and faithfulness, may not help much practically because of their level of abstraction, just as happiness does not usually qualify as a well-formed outcome because it lacks precision and sensory evidence. Nevertheless, some of the values or criteria that emerged when completing the values elicitation exercise in Chapter 5 will suggest meta programs that you can add, or that will provide further examples of the above common programs. These values will usually answer the question: 'What is important about so-and-so?' Applying the same question to each successive answer will confirm how these meta programs run most of our lives. Criteria such as 'meeting people', 'solitude' or 'time to think', for instance, tell us about a person's meta programs, and will usually slot into one of the common ones I have described.

These programmes tell us a great deal about a person – for those not too keen on introspection and deep thinking, sometimes more than they understand themselves. By using the words and phrases in communication that echo their programmes, you will enhance rapport at a deeper level than simple behavioural matching. As part of the person's reality map, your words and responses will 'make sense' – something we all look for in other people.

NLP adopts the term 'criteria' when dealing with the lower-level or 'operating values' set out in Chapter 5 that don't seem as important as 'honesty'-type values. These criteria influence many of our behavioural strategies or chunks, and form meta thought programmes. They occur in Life Content elements and syntax, left-right brain characteristics, sensory preference, and the various meta program types described in this chapter.

HIERARCHY OF PROGRAMS

You can identify a hierarchy of meta programs just as you did outcomes, values and beliefs. You might see yourself as a dyed-in-the-wool archetype in one or two cases, whereas others will have far less significance in your life. This will reveal the important pecking order of importance, and you will understand yourself and your motives much better. Bear in mind that just like outcomes and values, these behavioural programmes sometimes work in conflict with each other. You may therefore wish to consider how they affect the main outcomes in your life and whether, on balance, a trait empowers or disempowers you in securing the most important things. You may wish to check where meta programs run counter to each other and you need to do some reconciling of parts (see Chapter 10). The more we come to terms with these programs that run other programs, the closer we will come to our true identity and purpose in life.

Once identified and understood for what they represent, meta programs involve conscious, chosen behaviour rather than hidden, mysterious symbolism that inhabits our dreams and runs amok in the collective unconscious. These will reveal an overall picture of the person that should include different contexts in which the criteria will apply.

Identifying meta programs in another person will give a very valuable insight into their mental maps, and will explain behaviour that might otherwise have seemed useless or counterproductive. An 'away from', detail-loving, self-measuring, 'doing' person may seem like a thorn in the flesh to a positive-thinking manager, but will no doubt make a good ally as an accountant or quality controller, or as part of a project team. Such people have saved companies from liquidation.

On the other hand, an 'away from', 'big picture', 'knowing' person may scupper potential. Instead of identifying and tackling problems, they will probably throw up their hands and want to call the whole thing off – 'We're getting nowhere.', 'Let's abort.', 'It's not worth the trouble.', 'The figures don't stack up.' These represent the stereotypical negative thinker.

Meta programs offer us important models of subjective experience, and examples of the networks of mental filters that govern all our thinking and behaviour. They have different values depending on the context and the outcomes you have in mind. In humans, *purpose* reigns, and these master programs can either help or hinder those purposes. Therefore, it pays to identify, understand and control them in your own life, and to allow for them in others.

CHAPTER **16** *Anchors and Anchoring*

Sometimes, a sound, smell or taste takes us instantly back to a long-forgotten memory – maybe the smell of soap at school, or a tune that has romantic associations. Perhaps you don't know what triggered the memory – a sight, sound, feeling, smell or taste – or any combination of these. By associating with a past sensory experience, you recall – literally re-experience – the feelings embodied in a memory, as well as the sights, sounds and tactile sensations. We refer to the trigger, or memory stimulus, as an *anchor*.

This chapter introduces the concept of anchoring, and describes related techniques that you can apply in many useful ways.

Understanding anchors

A word can act as an anchor, reminding of you of the meaning you have given it in your mental map and any emotional associations. Words can have as much impact as the smell of a special perfume or the sound of roaring jet engines. A person's name, for instance, takes on special meaning when you associate it with an actual person with whom you had either a very pleasurable or traumatic experience. From that point on, you cannot hear the name without recalling the emotions wrapped up in the name. A work colleague unfortunate enough to have such a name may remind you of a schoolfriend decades after you last met the person, and long after you would ever have expected them to have any significance in your life. Conversely, a name in a special relationship will often create a new anchor. It now has new meaning, and its own long-term place in your map of the world.

An anchor may produce a positive, empowering state, or a negative, disempowering one, depending on the original experience it triggers in your mind. To have its consistent effect, a phobia requires a highly efficient negative anchor. The reassuring sound of a certain voice, a motivating word or phrase, or some little idiosyncratic behaviour of a sportsperson before they enter a contest, provide examples of positive, or enabling anchors.

Sometimes, we feel on a high, or unusually down, for no apparent reason. In this case, we have probably experienced an emotional memory, unaware of the anchor that triggered it. The most mundane stimulus can set in motion this powerful, automatic anchoring system. If we could only harness it, it would empower us to achieve all sorts of outcomes.

Anchors abound, and vary as much as the many submodalities we have already considered. They may take the form of a:

- facial expression
- tone of voice
- colour
- texture

- musical instrument
- word or expression
- advertisement jingle
- company logo
- door (for example, the boss's)
- piece of furniture or utensil from childhood
- house or room
- street or building
- taste
- smell
- a person's gesture or mannerism.

MULTI-SENSORY

The list above shows that anchors occur in all five representational systems. The examples occur so commonly that we treat many as stereotypical – a romantic song or tune, a food that reminds us of school dinners, and so on. In practice, anchors keep emerging and surprising us. The strangest, innocuous nuance of a sensation can instantly open the whole multi-sensory panorama of a long-forgotten memory. It *transports* us to the world it opens up.

At the same time, memories often comply with the domino effect: one triggers another, which in turn triggers others. These may switch from one sense to another. For instance, the colour of gentian violet may trigger the smell, then the tactile feel of the antiseptic brushed on your cut hand as a young child. Proust's madeleine cake in *Remembrance of Things Past*, referred to in Chapter 8, exemplifies a powerful taste anchor.

PLACES

A place, such as a town, village or country, can act as an anchor. Rather than the name, or an abstract idea about the place, the anchor may involve a specific sensory experience; for instance, seeing the town name sign as you cross its boundary when driving back to your hometown after many years, or seeing a photograph of a person you link with the place. Just about any place can have this effect. You may pass through a village that prompts distant, hazy recollections that you can hardly place, and that almost seem to come from another life. Landing at an overseas airport in a country with special memories can have its own special effect. The smell and balmy heat of landing in a particular African capital has a special place in my emotions. In other cases, a smell may remind you of a familiar industrial town, to which it will instantly transport you in spirit.

TRACING ANCHORS

Anchors have their origin some time in your past, and you can usually trace them back to a strongly emotional experience, not necessarily one that has life importance. For instance, a fear of water may originate from when somebody pushed you into a swimming pool as a child and you thought you would drown. In this case, water, despite its many positive associations for many people, triggers the state of fear – and behaviour to match.

Although we usually trace an anchor a long way back, you can't blame 'anchored behaviour', such as a phobia or an irrational association of a person's name, on your parents' genes. Nor need you retain any habitual behaviour if you decide to do without it. The trick involves achieving the 'positive intention' behind any anchored behaviour in a way that doesn't have the disadvantages. You can choose to change your intention once you identify it. Either way, you can understand the effect of anchors on your life, and acquire the skills to change them if you so choose. We often identify this important characteristic of identifying, understanding and handling negative anchors with people who seem satisfied and fulfilled in their life.

However, you can't always trace the origin of irrational, 'triggered' reactions. Typically, this doesn't bother NLP practitioners, who concern themselves more with the present than delving into the past, as in more conventional psychology. Once your past loses its power over your present, it starts to assume secondary importance. It takes care of itself. The timeline techniques in Chapter 11 can identify a first occurrence of an emotional memory or imprint, and will usually reveal the origin of an anchor.

ANCHORING BY DEFAULT

So far, we have considered anchors that happen unexpectedly, or by default, rather than purposefully. In these cases, a thought or feeling suddenly takes precedence over your present external situation and state. But anchors come in different shapes and sizes, and have different characteristics and effects:

- Usually, we cannot account for a particular behaviour or feeling, nor control it.

- In many cases, we know quite well the association, especially if it happens frequently, such as the sound of your boss's voice on the telephone, your little child whimpering in the night, or the sound of mail dropping on the carpet when heavily in debt. Nevertheless, the suddenness and intensity can still take us by surprise, and we may experience a sense of loss of control.

- In some cases, you can identify the anchor after a little thought, such as when hearing a tune on the sound system in a department store that evokes some memory.

- In other cases, you may experience an unexpected, sudden change of state that you cannot explain. Even a passing advertisement hoarding, or a fleeting image on the television, or the silhouette of a stranger in the distance can act as an anchor such as you have not experienced for years.

We can have little doubt about the strange power of anchors. We need to learn to use them in a positive, purposeful way.

ANCHORING BY DESIGN

You can create a purposeful anchor that will apply to yourself, or to someone else. The principles remain much the same, and only the techniques differ. Once you become adept at accessing memories in each representational system – a fundamental NLP skill explored in earlier exercises – you can apply anchors to yourself easily and with extraordinary effect. Anchoring another person's behaviour may apply in therapy, coaching, or a similar context. In this case, you will need to call upon some of the communication and observation skills described earlier, especially what NLP terms 'sensory acuity'. This involves making finer and more useful distinctions about the sense information we gather from the world. We use the term most frequently in the context of person-to-person communication, matching, rapport and using skills such as anchoring.

ANCHORING EMPOWERING STATES

You can use an anchor personally to achieve a particular empowering state of mind quickly. For instance, we all experience circumstances in which we could benefit from a dose of confidence, patience, assertiveness, calmness or suchlike. Better still if we could evoke such a state quickly and to order. First, you will need to identify:

- a situation in which you could use a better state
- the state you prefer
- an anchor that will recall it.

The 'situation' you want to change will no doubt mean a negative, disempowering one: a state of mind or behaviour – usually a habit, or recurring situation – that hinders you from achieving your outcomes. For instance:

- You feel unnecessarily nervous, and you stumble during a sales presentation.
- You lack confidence when meeting new people, so you fail in an important client negotiation.
- A certain person annoys you, you lose your temper, and forfeit the respect of other colleagues.

Accessing an undesired state
Choose a real-life, preferably recurring, situation so that you will have:

- a personal application for your anchor – NLP doesn't deal with hypothetical cases
- a mental scenario in which to practise your anchor, to test it
- a chance to apply your anchor in that specific, live situation in the not too distant future.

Try to choose a situation, fresh in your mind, that you experienced quite recently. Otherwise, a *vivid* older memory will do, provided you can re-experience in detail the characteristics, or submodalities, in each representational system, and all of them together (as in real life). By re-experiencing the situation in as realistic a mode as possible, you will also recall the emotional (non-tactile) feelings that accompanied your experience, and that no doubt account for the disempowering state you want to overcome.

You will need to access this state to test your anchor. This means you don't need to wait for it to happen – next week, next month, or whenever – to discover whether your anchor works. You have all the imagination required to run a realistic 'dress rehearsal'.

Accessing your desired state
Follow the same process for your desired state. You may well have experienced that state at some time in the past, or in a different context in your life. For instance, often a person had

supreme confidence as a child that they have long since lost. As an adult, a person may have much more confidence in a particular sport or hobby they enjoy than in the situation that causes the negative reaction, or 'problem state' – in other words, in a different context in their life. Sometimes, we overlook resources we already possess, but 'somewhere else'. Maybe you feel calm when with a certain person, or acted more assertively in a previous job, or assume a different state when with your own family or in a more familiar environment. We explored these parts, which can help as well as hinder, in Chapter 10.

We have all experienced a whole range of emotions, both positive and negative. The problem arises when one or two unhelpful ones dominate our lives and quash our hopes. However, every state you have experienced will serve as a *potential* resource that you can call on for specific purposes. By developing self-awareness, you will learn to do consciously what you sometimes do, very effectively, unconsciously. Anchoring provides a tool to practise this long enough for your new behaviour to become as strong a habit as the old behaviour.

Give your desired state a name, so that you can always associate it with a particular anchor. You need not use a standard term like 'confidence'. You can call it the 'X factor', 'Friday afternoon feeling' or whatever you like.

Anchoring criteria

Before choosing an appropriate anchor, keep in mind three important criteria for effective anchors:

- Choose an anchor that you can always trigger – anywhere, any time. Otherwise, you may not manager to trigger it at the precise moment you need it. We might describe this anchor feature as *portable*, as you need to carry the ability to trigger it with you always.

- Choose an anchor *unique* to the state you desire, so it will not have a confused, uncertain effect. You can have a different anchor for any number of states, of course.

- Choose a *discreet* anchor. You don't want to attract undue attention, simply to adopt the right state of mind for the situation instinctively.

Which modality?

We saw earlier that an anchor can draw on any of the five modalities. NLP uses the first three – sight, hearing and touch – for most purposes, including anchoring, as a matter of practicality rather than theory. What about tastes and smells? These account for some of the strangest and most powerful examples of anchored states and behaviour. A whiff of a smell can span decades in a moment, and you find yourself re-living an experience that you can hardly believe has lodged in your memory. The same applies to a taste: 'That reminds me of something …' – your mind starts exploring your early experience database for the connection. Nevertheless, the practicalities soon become apparent when you apply the anchoring criteria above. Smell and taste anchors don't allow much portability, unless you can bottle one and use it discreetly, like a nasal spray. A certain contrary law says that the very time you really need to use your anchor, you will have left it at home. So aim for practicality – which probably means using sights, sounds and tactile sensations that meet the three criteria above.

Within the three main modalities, your anchor can borrow any sight, sound or tactile experience that complies with the above simple rules of practicality. The kinaesthetic sense (the tactile part) seems to provide the main source for purposeful anchors, such as the hackneyed examples of touching wood and crossing your fingers. At some time in the dim past, these may well have produced a sense of hope and expectancy – a positive, helpful state for certain situations. However, once an anchor loses its uniqueness, it degenerates into a physiological cliché and will have no unique application.

Touching your thumb and little finger, however, may fit the bill, provided it doesn't have any other associations (for you). For a sound, you could use a voice, and a word or words, or music, a clicking thumb-and-finger sound, and so on. Check back on the criteria above, and you will see how each of these measures up.

For example, your favourite song or a piece of music may do marvels for your state of mind, but unless it passes the 'portable' test, it will not provide a reliable anchor. Fortunately, you can apply sensory anchors internally or externally. Internal ones meet the criteria of portability and discreetness, so inwardly hearing a person's voice saying a particular word or phrase in a particular tone will work well. Similarly, you might choose for a sight anchor a special scene you can recall that has memories that will promote the state you want. Alternatively choose the face of a person who has a similar effect. In this case, you can link this with the sound of the person's voice. Just make sure that you choose either a neutral anchor (such as clicking your fingers, clenching your toes, and so on) or one that only associates with the state you want – and will probably continue to do so (people change, of course, as does the effect they have on us).

Usually, a kinaesthetic anchor will suffice. In the following procedure, I will use three anchors simultaneously – one from each representation system. This will give some extra insurance of success, and will also give you extra practice.

EXERCISE 16.1

ANCHORING A BETTER STATE OF MIND

1   Identify the resource you want.

2   Think back to a specific occasion in your life when you felt this resource – for instance, confidence or calmness – and give it a name.

3   Now identify a specific anchor in each of the three main representation systems:

   - *K (Kinaesthetic)* – Think of a physical gesture, such as a clenched fist, squeezed fingers – anything unique and discreet that you can easily remember and associate with the particular resource.
   - *A (Auditory)* – You can use a word or phrase that evokes the feeling you require. Choose a phrase with a suitable tone that you can say to yourself, such as 'no problem', or the word you chose to describe the state, such as 'confidence' or 'calm'.
   - *V (Visual)* – Think of a visual image that evokes the feeling you want: for example, the actual scene that recalls the confident state, a specific object or person in that empowering scene, or even some visual metaphor or natural phenomenon that, to you, symbolizes confidence.

4   In your imagination, take yourself right back into the experience of, in this case, being confident or calm. Remember the place, what you did, and what you could see, hear and feel around you. Allow yourself to re-live and enjoy the experience as fully as possible.

5   Just as the feeling of confidence reaches its peak, apply all three anchors you have decided on. To reinforce this, repeat steps 4 and 5 a few times.

6   You can test your success by 'firing' the anchors and checking that they immediately access the state you desire. You will probably also find the kinaesthetic anchor on its own works well enough. None the less, you may wish to try firing all three when you meet your first real test in the outside world – you've nothing to lose either way.

7   Identify the first thing you might see, hear or feel in a forthcoming situation in which you would like to respond with greater confidence or calmness: for example, the voice of a person who tends to crush your confidence or ruffle your feathers, or the room in which you have to conduct a regular meeting, or even the feel of sitting in a particular chair. By identifying this negative trigger, you will associate it instantly with the new anchor, and thus the new state, so your anchor will *pre-empt* the negative state of mind by catching it at the incipient point. You need not limit your new anchor to this specific scenario, of course. Fire your anchors the moment you feel you need the resource. At worst, you will only experience a fleeting negative state.

Soon, you will find that you don't need even the kinaesthetic anchor. You will have created the habit of associating the new state with certain types of situation. In some cases, the same experience or phenomenon changes its meaning and has an empowering rather than disempowering effect. For instance, seeing your boss's door may now bring a pleasurable adrenaline rush and a sense of challenge. You have re-routed a neuronal network in your brain, and changed the meaning or representation of an experience.

You can apply the process to any state you can recall and anchor. Choose different anchors for each state, so that each has a unique association. If you have difficulty recalling times when you enjoyed a desired state, you can imagine how *someone else* would feel. Choose a person you associate particularly with the state (for example, extremely confident, cool and calm).

Stacking anchors

You can anchor a few different states with the same anchor by 'stacking' anchors. For example, you may want to feel calm but at the same time assertive, or confident and also empathetic and caring. In this case, use the same process, but keep to the same anchor, to induce the states simultaneously rather than consecutively.

You can also apply the above process to several different memories of the same state, such as different occasions, going back to childhood, in which you experienced the confidence – or other attribute – you want to have instant access to. This simply exploits your valuable resources more fully, as well as reinforcing the process.

You can also acquire the habit of anchoring an empowering state whenever it happens to arise. This might apply to a surprise meeting with an old friend that really did you good, or completing a really difficult task and experiencing a 'can do anything' high. Each of these offers a resource you can use in the future, and you can anchor them all. For example, you could set up the same anchor every time you feel happy. After a while, the anchor will have a very strong effect and you will increasingly turn happiness into an unconscious habit.

You may encounter other kinds of anchors, and different versions of those I have listed. However, once you understand the simple principle and process, you can experiment and find what works best for you.

Anchoring has numerous applications beyond personal change and development. For example, trainers can anchor behaviours and states in a group using the same principles. Even the colour of a marker pen, where you stand in the room, the words and gestures you use, and any specific behaviour or mannerism, can have associations for a group once you establish the anchor. Many of us associate feelings with a teacher or lecturer's idiosyncrasy, the smell or squeak of chalk on a board, a finishing bell, or a particularly enjoyable residential training course will have left us with one or two triggers that bring it all back. The NLP approach simply makes as much of this natural process as possible *purposeful*. It will happen anyway, but unreliably. Anchors improve memory, and remembering assists learning. We will consider some specific training applications in Part 2.

17 *Strategies*

We achieve outcomes by doing certain things in the right way and in the right order. This applies to baking a cake, picking your teeth or running a company. We call this sequence of thoughts and activities a *strategy*. NLP emphasizes the mental program, although strategy includes the physical activities, which, in any case, your brain masterminds. This reflects the fact that most of our behaviour, once learnt, happens unconsciously, or by habit. It also stems from the fact that success depends not just on manual skills, or even observable actions of any kind, but on a person's state of mind, beliefs, attitude and so on – in other words, on mental programs or strategies.

In this chapter, you will learn about strategies, the ubiquitous part they play in our lives, and how you can identify or 'elicit' them in order to understand yourself and others better, and make changes if you decide to do so.

Strategies for living

You need a strategy to fail, just as you need one to succeed. You need a strategy to swallow meat, pump blood round your body and carry out scores of such critical life functions. Thankfully, these operate cybernetically as 'hard-wired' systems – you can forget about them and live to talk about it. You need a strategy for climbing stairs, making a tennis stroke or getting dressed. Once learnt, or 'installed', these also happen automatically. At the same time, you need a strategy when you do something deliberately, such as catching a train or gaining the attention of a group of trainees.

If you want to do what somebody else does, you need to identify their strategy. You need to choose somebody as a subject who exhibits the behaviours you want to emulate. In every case, you require a strategy: a mental model, pattern, recipe or blueprint for real actions that have an impact on your external world.

STRATEGIES AND SYNTAX

The recipe consists of the same constituents, or raw materials, as any other thought process. We can call these *elements*. They consist of our representations of sights, sounds and feelings and the many characteristics or submodalities of these systems. A large number of elements may make up what seems like a simple activity, such as using an electric kettle or polishing a shoe. In this, as in most cases, you have to place items in the right order, or syntax – just as words make up a meaningful sentence – for it to work, for example:

- positioning the kettle before you turn the tap on, so that you avoid drenching yourself with water

- placing water in the kettle before you switch the power on, so that you don't burn out the element
- putting your leg forward before you move your weight towards the sink, so that you don't collapse onto the floor.

For even the simplest activity, we rely on multiple muscles and other organs. These perform physiological processes, including pumping, filtering, electrical firing, contracting, expanding, reacting chemically, sensing and measuring. Much of this, and more, figures in the most basic activities.

The mind does more than mastermind these complex processes at the level of behaviour. We don't even start a task unless we feel sufficiently motivated to do so. Nor do we finish it unless we have commitment and some incentive. In other words, we don't achieve anything unless we have 'a mind' to do so. For instance, a certain goal might never enter your mind in the first place if you don't believe you can do such a thing, if you think you don't deserve such an outcome, or if you just don't feel like it. Nor will you give a goal the necessary commitment if it conflicts with your basic values, even if this happens unconsciously.

These thought processes assume importance because they determine whether we do something well or badly, quickly or slowly, efficiently or inefficiently. But more than this, they determine whether we start, keep going, and finish. As well as organizing and overseeing behaviour, they determine the cybernetic outputs, or outcomes, we can achieve.

CYBERNETIC STRATEGIES

From the cybernetic goal-achieving model in Chapter 3, we saw that you need a target or outcome in order to harness the innate motivation to achieve – and indeed, to live. That target, to which you applied well-formedness criteria, forms part of any strategy. It serves as the intention, whether conscious or unconscious, inherent in any behaviour.

Both the four stages of the success cycle and the Change of State Model (also covered in Chapter 3) involve basic life strategies. A strategy takes you from your present state, using any resources you possess, to your desired state. Events don't happen by accident in these goal-achieving processes, whether for good or ill. Sophisticated controls apply. In other words: *people work perfectly*. The crucial skill involves taking *conscious* control to align these powerful systems with your present desired outcomes. By understanding and identifying strategies, you can start to take control of what might otherwise have happened by default, such as:

- an underlying 'positive intention'
- an outcome badly formed in negative terms (what you didn't want), which therefore brought disappointment
- a self-fulfilling negative self-belief
- habits you considered just an immutable part of your 'make-up' as a person.

NLP provides you with the skills to harness these mechanisms for specific purposes, or conscious outcomes, on a day-to-day basis. You don't override the sophisticated cybernetic mechanisms, nor could you, however hard you tried. Rather, you co-opt them to work *for* you rather than *against* you, as habitual, automatic behaviours sometimes do.

NEURAL STRATEGIES

In terms of neurology, or what happens in your brain, these strategies 'run' in the form of networks of neurons and synaptic interconnections. These may span large areas of your brain, and seem to act like several computers working in parallel. As you receive sensory messages, the system makes decisions by searching your database of past experience, beliefs and values, triggers whatever functions required for the job, and 'instructs' your body to what seems like instant action. Because they involve electrical transmission, we sometimes liken the process to an electronic computer, but the analogy soon breaks down. In fact, the human brain (hardware) *creates*, as well as executes, its own programs. In effect, the human brain comes with its own dedicated programmer. The computer analogy then becomes even less useful. The process also involves chemical reactions and fluidity, and analogue rather than digital changes, quite the opposite of a fixed printed circuit board. In this light, the human brain works more like a bowl of boiling soup, with many ingredients interacting. The synthesis of these disparate electro-chemical processes creates the marvels of thought and mind – what we humbly try to represent as 'strategies'.

The body forms part of the same mind-body system. In response to a program, it matches this dependable, more or less perfect, cerebral system. All this helps to confirm the strange cybernetic life-supplying systems that relentlessly pursue our personal targets with extraordinary flexibility and adaptability. We can certainly trust their ability to run consistently successful strategies, once installed.

Importantly, even a crude appreciation of the capacity of your mind will help you to trust a system you cannot consciously control, yet on which you none the less depend every moment of your life.

All our strategies conform to the four-stage cybernetic model described in Chapter 3:

1   Decide what you want.
2   Do something.
3   Notice what happens.
4   Change what you do until you get what you want.

The inputs to this grand system consist of:

• a target (outcome)
• the ability to move towards it (through a body)
• feedback (through the senses)
• flexibility to change behaviour in order to come nearer to the target.

We need strategies for each part of these processes, such as:

• setting outcomes and desires
• motivation and the perceived pleasure of rewards
• exercising, or outliving, values and beliefs
• pre-testing outcomes (future pacing)
• carrying out physical behaviour
• sensing inputs through representational systems
• deciding and choosing alternatives
• adjusting your behaviour in response to what happens.

Each of these strategies has a number of elements, such as seeing something, hearing something, feeling something, saying something or doing something. These may happen internally (seeing in your mind; feeling right or wrong, true or false; speaking to yourself inside), or externally.

Strategic purposes

You can elicit a person's strategies in order to discover how they achieve their outcomes, and to replicate their success. You do this by modelling, which we cover in greater detail in the next chapter. You might wish to elicit a strategy for different reasons, such as the following:

- **Modelling internal representations, or 'unseen' behaviour** – Because strategies include internal representations, we cannot simply mimic external movements – in whatever detail – and hope to achieve the same results. In one sense, only what happens externally matters. Every thought must first convert into behaviour before it can have any effect in the real world. You need more than dreams, imagination, or even tremendous creativity – you must do something. However, this demands strategies for what happens inside and outside. You may need a strategy, for instance, that:

  - keeps you going when others have given up
  - you use out of pleasure, rather than drudgery
  - you believe can and will happen
  - gives you constant feedback
  - allows you to do something else at the same time (as when driving)
  - assumes that you deserve success.

  Adopting an appropriate, or empowering, state of mind will give you a better chance of acting like a person in that state, or at least you will learn their behaviour more quickly and easily. If you can discover and model a person's inner representations (sights, sounds and feelings), you have identified the 'control centre' of their strategy, and the source of their success. Modelling a successful strategy means you need to elicit the critical inner states, working beliefs, and special sequence of elements, rather than emulating outward behaviour alone.

- **Bringing about change in others** – For example, if you can identify the strategy behind a behaviour a person wishes to change, you can 'scramble' or disrupt the strategy. Alternatively, you can help the person to adjust their strategy to achieve the desired change. NLP phobia cures, for instance, 'scramble' powerful but unhelpful strategies.

- **Gaining rapport by matching** – Once you identify a person's strategy, you can, in effect, play it back to them to gain rapport, motivate them, stimulate a decision, create an empowering state of mind, and so on. These skills help particularly in selling and negotiation, but will also increase your influence in any communication.

- **Supplementing your own strategic repertoire** – You can adopt all or part of a person's strategy to enhance your own effectiveness. People often emulate their mentors and heroes by adopting their physical behaviour, mannerisms and way of life. Many successful people owe much to early role models that they unashamedly aped. By adopting the mental programmes, or strategies, of such people, you can emulate their success more effectively and consistently. But no matter whose strategies you borrow and try yourself, you will extend and enrich your map of the world by learning from others.

The TOTE Model

NLP applies the TOTE Model to strategies and strategy-elicitation. Engineers have long used this model, similar to the four-stage cybernetic model set out earlier. TOTE stands for:

- **T**est/**T**rigger
- **O**perate
- **T**est
- **E**xit.

The Test or Trigger starts off the sequence for the strategy, such as making a decision. For instance, you may see something (V), hear something (A), or feel something (K) that stimulates you to action – say, to buy something.

The Operate stage accesses internal and external information regarding the outcome – in this case the article purchased. A great deal happens in a short time. You will represent a 'total product', including intangible aspects of the product such as value for money, convenience of purchase, and so on. This may involve looking at the product (V), feeling it (K), weighing up pros and cons as you talk to yourself (Ad – auditory digital) and perhaps the pleasant feelings and associations (K) the product evokes. We usually suffix *internal* representations with 'i' (Vi, Ai, Ki), and *external* representations with 'e' (Ve, Ae, Ke).

The second Test compares the information you have represented with the initial trigger or test that introduced you to considering the purchase. For instance, you might compare what you have accessed about a particular holiday with the feeling of needing a relaxing break that triggered the strategy, or you might compare new sports equipment with what you saw somebody using to great effect and which stimulated your interest. This will involve more VAK representations. You will typically make a comparison in the same representational system – Vi (your picture of well-deserved relaxation) with Ve (glossy photographs) or more Vi's (sunsets, sea and sand, people's faces), and so on. This second Test stage will usually include a Ki feeling, whether positive or negative.

As a result of this test, you will either decide to buy or not, and thus either Exit the strategy or do some more testing. If your trigger and test match – your perception of the product complies with your need or desired outcome – you will exit the decision strategy. If they don't match, you will exit in the same way, in both cases having made a decision.

Imagine, for instance, that you consider buying hi-fi equipment to help you wind down after work with your favourite music, rather than taking an expensive holiday with nothing to show for it afterwards. In this case, after exiting, you start another strategy sequence with different content. You may recycle a strategy in this way by:

- changing your outcome ('I don't want a relaxing break, I want to work in another section.')
- changing your strategy for a relaxing break ('I'll buy a comfortable chair, or take up yoga.')

- adjusting your strategy ('I'll save up for a longer holiday next year.')
- extending or re-entering your Operate stage ('I'll wait a few weeks and shop around.')

Each of these may involve:

- chunking up (say, to develop a more easy-going attitude)
- chunking laterally (as in the chair purchase)
- chunking down (take a couple of pills).

Notwithstanding loops and recycling, the TOTE Model seems to apply to any strategy.

Beryl Heather, who co-authored *NLP in 21 Days*, used two very simple illustrations about making a cake and weeding the garden which we included in that book. These illustrate the TOTE principles in a very simple way, so I will reproduce the examples here, with kind permission from the publishers.

MAKING A CAKE FOR TEA

Test:

- I decide I want a cake for tea – the trigger.
- I visualize the finished cake – a chocolate one – and this becomes the test to feed forward to later in the strategy.

Operate:

- I go through questions and answers in my head: 'Do I have the ingredients I need to make a chocolate cake?' I see in my fridge or cupboard eggs, margarine, sugar, chocolate and so on.

(Second) Test:

- The ingredients fulfil the requirements to make the visualized cake.

Exit:

- I exit the thinking strategy, and begin the behaviour of making the cake.

WEEDING THE GARDEN

Test:

- My garden needs weeding.

Operate:

- I run through my schedule for the week, and conclude that I have no time to do the weeding.

(Second) Test:

- My garden still needs weeding. At this point, instead of exiting, I recycle, as the second test did not turn out satisfactorily. I have not achieved my outcome.

Operate:

- I decide to telephone a gardener in the neighbourhood, to ask if he can help me with the weeding.

(Third) test:

- If he agrees, the weeding will get done.

Exit:

- I exit the thinking strategy, and make a telephone call.

A strategy will always incorporate internal VAKOG elements, for the simple reason that we cannot do anything except as masterminded in the brain, and we cannot 'think' except in VAKOG representations. Sometimes, the *initial* trigger happens internally, such as when you remember you have to speak to someone, buy something, or carry out an overdue task. Then we have choices – for example, in time, place and method. We appraise any options internally, and in doing so will usually call on more than one representational system, although usually *including* our primary representational system. The K feeling of rightness, appropriateness, pleasure and suchlike that forms part of a decision also involves inner processes. We might apply tests in other representational systems (V, A and K tactile, as well as K emotional).

A decision to buy might take weeks and also involve many external representations, such as poring over magazines, window-shopping, and talking to friends. Whilst the TOTE Model provides a useful theoretical model for any of these cases, it may prove impractical to model an extended or high-level strategy – simply because of its size and complexity. We therefore need to reduce a strategy to low-level components. It doesn't matter how short and simple a strategy, as you can always link successful strategies together to achieve a bigger outcome.

You may find that sometimes the TOTE Model doesn't seem appropriate. A model, by its very nature, doesn't always fit the real world it tries to represent, so don't expect too much from this or any other simple tool. If you understand strategies enough to know that a certain strategy doesn't fit the TOTE Model, then the model has probably served its purpose. Use it as a guide to learning, and as a checklist for eliciting and modelling.

Eliciting strategies

You can identify a person's strategy by observation and questioning. However, for the purpose of elicitation, you need to aim for the right chunk size. Running a company demands far too big a chunk, although even at this level you can break down behaviour into a number of skills and activities that you can more easily identify, and if necessary copy. At this macro level, setting a strategy compares more to conventional project management, such as when planning a conference, a wedding or any complex group of activities. NLP doesn't become involved much at this level, which extends beyond the individual to bigger systems to which the NLP model may not apply. The smaller the chunk, the greater the likelihood of eliciting the important elements of a strategy, and the order in which they happen, or syntax. It goes without saying that once you master these lower-level strategies, you can then link them together to fulfil any size of project or achievement. As an analogy, we incorporate numerous individual skills and activities when driving a car or playing golf.

Some strategies do not relate to behaviour or specific activities. For instance, confidence and perseverance may contribute to the success of many tasks, and may indeed spell the difference between such success and failure, whatever the technical skills of the person. These nonetheless lend themselves to strategy-elicitation:

- They consist of mental skills, rather than outward, visible behaviour. We often overlook these inner traits, although, as we have seen, state of mind accounts for much of a person's success. Timothy Gallway wrote books called *The Inner Game of Tennis* and *The Inner Game of Golf.* Professional sportspeople often attribute 80 to 90 per cent of their success to 'mental attitude'. My book *Masterstroke* addresses the mental side of golf.

- We can usually reduce them to fairly small chunks. For instance, a person will usually adopt the appropriate state of mind very quickly, usually through the action of some sort of anchor or personal triggering mechanism such as a visual image or a few words of inner dialogue. Even a small activity may comprise many such internal 'events' or elements.

- We can apply strategies such as confidence to all manner of situations, so eliciting such a characteristic represents a sound investment of time and effort. You develop a resource you can call upon repeatedly.

I will list a few examples of strategies at the sort of chunk level amenable to strategy-elicitation:

- self-motivation
- producing creative ideas
- spelling
- remembering facts for exams
- mental arithmetic
- making a buying decision
- persuading
- putting, in golf
- serving, in tennis
- rifle shooting.

You can choose from hundreds more, but these illustrate the degree of size and complexity that suits strategy modelling. When eliciting strategies, it makes sense to choose something you can use in different ways and in different situations. For instance, we can all use the ability to remain calm and unperturbed in many different contexts. This gives such a strategy extra value, as it can lead to greater benefits and life changes. Similarly, although we look on spelling as a specific skill, it has such fundamental importance that it offers an ideal candidate for strategy-elicitation. It goes without saying that you will need to model a very confident person, a superb speller and so on to arrive at the best model, bearing in mind that you will not surpass the skill of your subject – at least in the short term. So avoid mediocrity, even if you rank yourself less than mediocre in the area you want to model.

MADE-TO-MEASURE STRATEGIES

People may run a different strategy for the same state in different situations: for example, a strategy for feeling confident in front of a group, and a strategy for feeling confident in a one-to-one interview, such as for a new job. You would identify the differences if you elicited each mental strategy. Even more important, perhaps, you will encounter very different strategies for doing apparently the same thing well. This may result from the fact that we have different primary representational systems, or sensory preferences. One person may use words and phrases, hearing them inwardly, perhaps in a particular voice. Others prefer to see images in their mind. Either strategy will work in creating a sense of confidence, peace, assertiveness, or whatever. You than have a choice. You may find that a strategy that uses your PRS works best.

On the other hand, you will enrich your mind more in the longer term by experiencing in different ways, which means getting to know different mental maps. From that point, you will need to try different strategies in accordance with the four-stage 'flexible' model, to discover what works best for you.

CONTENT-FREE STRATEGIES

In many cases, you can elicit a strategy without reference to the 'content' of an activity. This might apply, for instance, to a strategy for confidence. However, as we have seen, a buying strategy may differ, depending on what you buy, the medium (such as online), or a key factor such as whether you will spend your own money or somebody else's. Similarly, a different strategy may apply to speaking to a small group, depending on whether you wish to train, chair a meeting, communicate a company policy, motivate a brainstorming group, and so on.

In the case of some specific skills, therefore, it helps to know the content. Take rhythm. Whilst a strategy for rhythm can apply to a wide variety of content (such as playing drums or a banjo, or dancing), the skill of playing drums – or, even more so, producing a drum roll – will involve the specific content of the drum, the kind of drum and the kind of roll. Similarly, whilst we might treat dancing as content-free, it takes on content in a specific dance routine.

ASSOCIATION

You will find that many of the concepts and techniques described in this book will help when identifying and changing strategies. To understand and copy a strategy, we need to *associate* with the model – to experience behaviour from their viewpoint. Usually, we mimic just by watching, as an outside observer. However, to fully replicate their competence, you need to know what happens inside the person. This means finding out what they see, hear and feel *inside*, as well as outside. So when eliciting a strategy from another person by questioning, encourage them to associate with the experience (first position). Similarly, in replicating the behaviour, you will associate with the strategy, just as if you had got inside the skin of your model (second-person), before finally doing it yourself (first-person).

By associating, we tend to think in the present, just as in the original experience. When eliciting a strategy, it helps if you choose the appropriate language and keep to the present tense: for instance, 'You're in the restaurant, you ask for the menu ... then what?' Ask what *happens* next, rather than what *happened* next. We live our intuitive, unconscious lives in the present, so by adopting present-tense language you will communicate in the same mode. Even when a person recounts something in the past tense, they will usually switch to the present on being posed a question in present tense.

ANCHORING STRATEGIES

As we saw in the previous chapter, anchoring has many uses, including anchoring states when modelling strategies. Often, you don't elicit a complete strategy, so you will need to revisit it to finish the job. By anchoring a subject's state, you can immediately recall it to make further enquiry. Sometimes, a person will only run a strategy occasionally, such as a creative, 'flow' state, or when in a critical, competitive situation that the person only faces once in a while. In such cases, you will need to recall the true state, and you will save time and effort by anchoring the state ready for quick recall. The modelled subject will probably also assume value, as they usually don't adopt the state consciously, and may want to use it other life contexts.

STRATEGY CHUNKS

Successful strategy modelling depends on chunk size. It will determine, for example, the approximate number of elements in a strategy. This means formulating the right 'package' of thoughts to produce a discrete event, such as a 'decision' or a specific process like remembering how to spell a word or calculate a sum in your head. This means deciding where the strategy starts and finishes.

For example, a buying strategy may start with the moment the person becomes aware of needing or wanting something, and finish with a definite decision to buy. Bear in mind that a person may have a different strategy for buying a burger compared to buying a house, car, or insurance policy. For this reason, you would need a strategy for each if you cared to replicate the behaviour, unlike, say, a single spelling strategy that can apply in any spelling context. But this simply underlines the importance of:

- deciding exactly what you want
- considering possible contexts and applications
- setting chunk size, and strategy start and finish points.

Usually, you will identify about half a dozen elements that form a discrete strategy. Identify just one or two, and you may have missed some, or may have chosen too small a chunk that does not constitute a discrete strategy that you can replicate.

Don't expect the subject to do your job for you. By limiting the number of elements in a strategy sequence, you can establish more depth and precision. Bear in mind that the strategy starts at some trigger point, which will usually *precede* what you might expect to start the strategy, or what you might deduce from just observing. This acts as an anchor, as described earlier, although the subject will probably not know that, so this gives you a chance to apply questioning skills. A McDonald's 'big arches' sign in the distance might serve as the anchor, although the person may think the decision to buy took place immediately before purchasing. Persevere when identifying this critical start point. For instance, say 'Go back to before you drove in. You are driving ... what happens next?' If it turns out the person made a conscious decision at home before setting out, you will need to go right back there to find a strategy start point. What triggered it? However, in the case of a pure 'impulse' buy, you may need to do some detective questioning to locate the trigger. We can base the existence of some trigger or other on the reasonable presupposition that we have a purpose, or meaning, in doing whatever we do – whether rational or otherwise.

STRATEGY LOOPS

We considered the idea of strategy loops earlier in the TOTE Model, and you will probably encounter them again when eliciting a strategy. A feeling (K) may create an inner dialogue (auditory digital – Ad), which in turn recaptures that feeling (K, Ad, K). This loop can operate instantaneously. Where this happens, the modalities may apply 'synaesthetically' – one automatically triggers another, and they all seemingly work concurrently and inter-dependently, rather than consecutively. If you don't identify this loop through questioning, you may detect it from successive left and right downward eye movements (refer to the eye accessing cues in Chapter 7). Practise observing sensory cues. You cannot rely on what people say they do, as so many of our strategies operate unconsciously. In other words, you may understand more than the person about what happens in their (unconscious) mind.

TOTE QUESTIONING

Usually, you can identify a strategy by asking simple questions. I will give some examples based on the TOTE Model.

Test:

- How do you know when to do something?
- When did you begin?
- What made you feel the time had come to do something?
- What triggered that idea in the first place?

Operate:

- How do you do it?
- How do you identify alternatives?
- How do you get information?

(Second) Test:

- How do you know whether you have succeeded?

- How do you become satisfied?
- How do you choose between alternatives?

Exit:

- If any question remains, you will keep testing, go back to the Operate stage, or start a new strategy.

EXERCISE 17.1

SPELLING STRATEGY

Spelling provides a good example of a strategy. Good spellers tend to adopt a similar strategy, so, once elicited, we can adopt it universally. In addition, NLP practitioners have conducted detailed work in this area, including with dyslexic people.

Most of us initially learn to spell by speaking letters and words out loud, with the emphasis on sounds, so you would expect people with a strong auditory sense to do well. This does not reflect what actually happens, however. Spelling relies mainly on visual skills. Conversely poor spellers generally try to rely on the sound of the word, or phonetics. Whilst detailed strategies vary, the best spellers report seeing an image of the word that 'feels' familiar, or right. So we now have a well-proven strategy, which can make anyone a good or better speller. Whilst spelling strategies vary in detail, the dominant visual element remains an important constant:

1   Look at the word you want to remember how to spell for a few moments (Ve).

2   Look away from the word, then, moving your eyes up and to the left, visualize the spelling (Vi).

3   Look back at the original image on the page (Ve) to fill in any missing letters and correct any errors, repeating the process until you can easily visualize the proper spelling in your mind. It may help to place the image up and to your left, a little away from you. You may want to imagine the word written in felt pen on a flipchart, or on a blackboard in chalk, or maybe in big plastic sign letters – choose a system that has impact and makes it easy to remember. You can include further representations in addition, such as sounds and feelings (Ai, Ki)

4   Look away again. Then look up at your mental image (Ve), and write the word down. If incorrect, go back to step 1, and carry out the process again.

5   Try looking at your mental image and reading the spelling backwards (something almost impossible to do phonetically). This provides a good test, and will boost your spelling confidence.

Let me suggest a few more tips for an effective spelling strategy:

- Break down longer words into convenient parts, so that you only spell, in effect, two or three short words. You can cope with even the longest word – as you can an international telephone number – in this way. Make sure you then see the whole word together.

- As well as imagining real writing, such as on a whiteboard, blackboard or flipchart, you can make the image a movie, and imagine *writing* the words. See and feel yourself writing with the marker pen, perhaps, and even hearing the noise of the pen on paper, or chalk on the blackboard. This brings the activity to life, and makes it more memorable. Imagine using a favourite colour.

- Imagine doing your learning in an environment that boosts your confidence – perhaps on the kitchen wall, or drawing the words in the wet sand at a favourite beach – rather than risking negative connotations of school from your visualization.

- You can go a stage further and try to match the actual submodalities of memories from other areas of personal competence – perhaps learning a game, or sport, or remembering cooking ingredients. In this case, go back to the submodalities checklist to see the sort of characteristics that apply to your empowering memory, then switch them one by one to the spelling situation. What sort of visual image attracts you most? Even without employing all the winning submodalities, changing to the basic visual strategy usually transforms a poor speller immediately.

EXERCISE 17.2

CONVINCER STRATEGY

Unlike the spelling strategy when applied to the best spellers, decision strategies vary widely from person to person even though we rate the same people competent or incompetent at making decisions. However, the majority fall into a few patterns. These largely relate to the number of times a person runs through the decision-making process, how long they need to make a decision, and so on. What seems like a 'no' decision to a salesperson or negotiator may simply reflect a person's strategy – 'Yes – but not now'. In time, or with enough attempts, a successful sale may follow. But personal change of any sort involves decisions, not just in buying, so what NLP terms a person's *Convincer* strategy provides valuable information in any communication.

Convincer strategies fall into four types:

1 **Automatic** – The person sees or hears about something, and makes a decision straight away.

2 **Number of times** – The person has to appraise a situation or subject a number of times before making a decision. For example, they will compare a number of products, visit several stores, and try on different clothes before deciding to buy. These people buy just as much as the 'automatic' person, but they need to convince themselves in this repetitive way. A salesperson who understands this and has patience will do well, as most of their competitors will have given up after a couple of attempts. Most of us – not just salespeople – can only cope with a couple of 'no's – or *perceived* 'no's. It feels like rejection.

3 **Consistent** – The person undertakes a full decision appraisal on each occasion. They will usually obtain any information available, consult with others, and generally leave no stone unturned in their desire to make a wise decision, so they check the magazines, compare competitive product features, watch television consumer programmes, find people who have made the same purchase, and so on. You will need to demonstrate equal or superior background knowledge to make a sale.

4 **Period of time** – The person needs time to make a decision. They will sleep on it, think it over, and perhaps think about it again in a few days. Just give them time.

You can add Convincer strategies to the list of meta programs given in Chapter 15. Notice how these fit the TOTE Model described earlier. All you have learnt about strategies applies to modelling, which we will cover in the next chapter.

18 *Modelling*

NLP had its origin in modelling well-known therapists who demonstrated remarkable communication skills. Using NLP, you can identify many of these skills, use them in various ways, and teach them to others. Through practical modelling, therefore, we can all share the benefits of skills possessed by the sort of people we can usually only admire or envy. Better still, you can understand the structures and processes at work, to do some modelling of your own. We have already dealt with strategies, upon which we base modelling. Modelling addresses the question 'How to do it?', as opposed to the question 'What to do?' This chapter adds some special criteria, and further background to this more extensive topic of modelling.

The fact that you can copy somebody's behaviour should not seem remarkable. We watch children and performers do it, and most of us can do a bit of mimicry if we overcome our inhibitions. Modelling, as we use the term here, means more than copying a skill or behaviour. It means making a model, or *simplified construct*, of a very complex system. We need to do this in order to:

- understand a skill
- replicate it in another person or context
- predict what will happen when somebody else applies the model.

Artificial intelligence tries to do this using machines. NLP seeks to replicate human excellence not in machines, but in other merely competent people.

Modelling factors

In modelling a person's behaviour, you need to take account of several factors:

- Visible *external behaviour*, such as we associate with movements in a sports stroke, manual dexterity in a manufacturing process, a craft, and so on – this compares in behavioural complexity with everyday tasks such as dressing in a hurry or eating and drinking while standing and chatting at a buffet lunch. However, we usually model *valued* skills we only witness in very skilled people, rather than common behaviours that – although equally remarkable in their processes – most people acquire through normal life experiences.

- A person's total physiology, which includes breathing, expressions, gestures and so on – the movements we seem to have no control over but which reflect our mood or feelings and help us to express what we mean when communicating. Breathing sometimes plays a big part, such as in rifle shooting or any skill where we need to relax.

- Thinking strategies that involve sequences of VAKOG representations – at this level, we can identify submodalities at work, and consciously (initially) apply them ourselves to create the thought characteristics, or qualities, of the subject we model. This level of modelling probably offers most opportunities, as we already have a fairly robust NLP model of sensory perception to start with. The limits therefore lie as much in the skills of eliciting detailed modalities and submodalities as in the need for theoretical models. A good model based on a less than excellent subject will therefore produce better results than an inaccurate model of the world's best practitioner.

- A subject's beliefs and values, or map of the world – these will also contribute to a person's overall effectiveness in carrying out a task or skill. This includes, not least, their motivation to make a start, keep going and bring about a successful conclusion. These operate above (or 'meta' to) the sensory VAK level of behaviour. However, in so far as we associate behaviour memories with beliefs and values, we can change VAK representations of those behaviours. You can thus create or 'tune up' inner 'experience' – the submodalities of behaviour strategies – that supports the values and beliefs you wish to strengthen. Alternatively, you can *reduce* the sensory power of experiences that support beliefs and values you would prefer to 'tune down'. You can do this by changing or switching submodalities, as we saw in Chapter 9.

Modelling processes

Following these simple criteria, we can carry out different modelling processes:

- You can model external behaviour by observation and taking 'second position' – or seeing things as if through the eyes of your subject (in a communication, the other party). This applies to any simple operation, such as a discrete physical movement in a sport, a simple office or factory routine as we have to learn in a new job, making up a bed in hospital style, and so on. This applies to countless simple skills that anyone can add to their personal armoury of ability. Simple skills can have a disproportionate effect when integrated with more ambitious goals as interim or stepping-stone outcomes of a 'doing' rather than 'knowing' or 'getting' kind. Taking second position means, in effect, getting inside the skin of the other person. This demands sensory acuity, and also 'downtime' skills of visualization, but you can develop these with practice. Many NLP techniques involve 'going inside', and this provides a foundation for modelling skills, among others.

- You can test the effectiveness of a model by taking 'first perceptual position' – doing it yourself (also termed *association*). Do this both internally, through future pacing or visualization, and also externally – trying it out in practice. Doing it 'internally' means fewer risks, if indeed any risks exist in the behaviour itself. 'Externally' provides a more robust test of a successful model, of course, and does wonders for your confidence.

- You can model thinking strategies by questioning, with a view to identifying VAKOG syntax – the modalities and submodalities pattern associated with any behaviour. You can confirm this using sensory acuity, noting sensory cues (such as eye accessing), language clues such as sensory predicates, and physiological cues in breathing, expressions and micro-movements.

- You can identify the meta programs (see Chapter 15) that underlie beliefs and values by means of various questioning processes. Sometimes, in ordinary conversation we elicit a person's interests and values. However, you cannot always model the detail required to replicate this logical level of experience, produced over a lifetime of experience in response to billions of random stimuli – even if you could access it in the person's unconscious mind. In short, we don't have the technology to model a *person*, or even a *capability* at the level of, say, artist, comedian, musician, and so on. Nevertheless, linked with lower-level behavioural modelling, an *appreciation* of a person's non-sensory values and criteria will help to make strategies more effective. And, as we saw in Chapter 5, we can *change* specific self-beliefs in more than one way.

Modelling opportunities

Despite these reservations, enormous opportunities exist in the specific skills areas that many people want to improve. Useful behavioural strategies need not impinge on self-beliefs, identity and higher values (although sometimes they do). These may include techniques for playing a musical instrument, putting in golf, spelling, remembering names and faces, and suchlike. By successful modelling *groups* of useful, related strategies (behaviours), we start to acquire the thinking strategies associated with capabilities and self-belief in these areas of skill and expertise. We create internal sensory 'experience' through repeated visualization. This tends to establish self-belief and values, just as external sensory experience changes our characters over the years. But, as with ordinary life, the process takes time. The advantages of modelling lie in:

- **Consciously** directing thinking strategy changes – we can direct our activities, and *choose* the most appropriate resources. This overcomes what seems like a genetic lottery for so-called innate talents. Conscious harnessing of unconscious systems means greater access to human potential, so much of which lies at the unconscious level.

- **Concentrating** experience by mental rehearsal and intensifying submodalities – this speeds up the process, like fast forwarding and reversing a video recorder. Learning by experience can take a very long time, and ten years' experience may represent no more than one year's experience ten times over. We can practise mentally much more efficiently. For a start, we don't (or needn't) 'miss', so we avoid amassing numerous negative memories for our fragile self-esteem to cope with. By intensifying submodalities, we can improve a strategy in quality rather than speed of learning. In each case, we start from the already high level of competence of a successful subject.

- Acting **purposefully** to bring about (longer-term) outcomes under our conscious control – we can match resources to a hierarchy of goals and values to move from a present to a desired state. Begging, borrowing or modelling successful strategies saves many wasted years in an already short lifetime.

Blueprints for excellence

The models we identify will not necessarily provide standard blueprints for excellence, although, when based on the very best subjects (exemplars), they seem to offer universal benefits – for example, in sport and leadership. To start with, people use quite different strategies to attain a certain kind and level of expertise. This may relate in part to their sensory preference. A motivation strategy, for instance, can comprise any combination of representation systems and submodalities. Of course, we can achieve much with models or blueprints, whether standard or not. We aim to replicate behaviour or results, rather than adhering strictly to a model. You may make a strategy more effective by adopting your dominant representational system, for instance. On the other hand, however strange it seems, an unfamiliar strategy may produce better results.

If you can find a subject with a similar sensory profile to yourself – and better still, some degree of common values and beliefs – you may successfully model at a higher chunk level. In modelling specific skills, depending on the behaviour modelled, it may help also to have a similar physical build. Even in the case of a fairly standard strategy like spelling, you can do much to enhance the effectiveness, for example by adding your own preferred modality to a dominantly visual strategy (such as special sound effects), and adding visual submodalities that work best for you (like bigger or brighter).

The NLP pioneers did not model *people*, but rather the *strategies* they used to do what they did so well. The non-standard nature of human beings results in the unique variety of strategies we all use. They modelled experience as a structure and process. Emulating success depends on emulating experience, and this includes whatever 'experience' comprises. This includes the total state of the person you model, rather than just the visible, external movements. It doesn't require magic. It involves the well-known scientific processes of thinking and trying and testing.

Although modelling came early in the history of NLP, for most people it doesn't come first in the process of learning. Nevertheless, many opportunities lie in the area of modelling, and you can do plenty of personal change work to test your skills and achieve rapid results. In NLP, as we have seen, we first need to adopt a few presuppositions. We then learn about the NLP model of how we all represent things structurally, in our beliefs, values and feelings, and convert these back into the real world as behaviour and more feelings. With such a foundational model, you can achieve a lot from your own resources. You have a treasury of empowering memories and skills that you can draw on before resorting to outside models of experience (other maps). The subject receives relatively little attention in most NLP training programmes (compared to advertising copy), but we could benefit from some new developments in modelling above the simple sensory level.

The modelling process pulls many aspects of NLP together. It translates a theoretical model of subjective experience into personal behaviour and achievement that can influence a person's life in important ways. However, we need to emphasis *model-creation* and development, rather than techniques to apply existing models. A few, such as John McWhirter and Robert Dilts, seem to have addressed this issue.

In modelling excellence, we have an outcome the consequences of which we can hardly imagine. When you can *model* new skills theoretically, and replicate and apply them practically in different contexts, you will start on a very special road to discovery and personal fulfilment. From that point, you can start to think of (to borrow from a great American communicator, or his talented scriptwriter) 'not what NLP can do for you, but what you can do for NLP' and its novice adherents. Meanwhile you can *presuppose* (or pretend, if you like) that 'anything he or she can, I can', or you probably wouldn't set off down the modelling road anyway.

NEW MODELS ON THE BLOCK

NLP has created a few basic models, notably the Milton and Meta Models described earlier. The Meta Model, probably the one most widely adopted, classifies language for therapeutic purposes, based on earlier work by Chomsky and others, including his model of Transformational Grammar. Unusually, in view of the fundamental presuppositions of NLP and its basic cybernetic, or goal-achieving, precepts, that model has remained almost unchanged. Even its modellers, it seems, anticipated some expansion, if not redesign.

On the other hand, a few new models of human experience and perception have evolved since then. John McWhirter's Integrated Language Model exemplifies such a neo-NLP (my term – John has his own trademarked descriptions) model. He claims that this effectively replaces the Meta Model and more. His work, spanning several years, and that of any serious contenders, has shown that modelling experience requires more than a sensory, or 'first-order', approach. It concerns values, beliefs, and identity, for instance – concepts we understand in abstract or nominal rather than sensory terms. These also represent a higher neurological order of experience (check, if you need to, on Dilts' Neurological Levels Model). We can all try out these new models in our own situations, along with sensory-based techniques involving modalities and submodalities, and the familiar Meta Model questions. The *doers* have plenty to do while the *knowers* learn more. True modellers, however, remain a minority.

'AW, IT'S NOTHING.'

The talents and skills we observe as 'excellent' come in as many varieties as the people who display them, but one feature seems to apply to them all. People possessing 'natural' expertise often don't recognize their own talent in the way that those around them do. In particular, they don't know *how* they do what they do. If they do, they may not communicate it well. Top sports players don't necessarily make the best coaches, for instance.

NLP has focused upon what we term 'unconscious competence', and the idea of human cybernetic processes described at the beginning of this book. In other words, the masterminding process happens, not in the limited left brain of conscious, logical, rational purpose and will, but in the holistic, unconscious part of us. Here (for our present purposes anyway) habits, motor skills, 'autopilot' behaviour, and vital life functions reside. Little surprise, then, that something we don't give a moment's thought to seems unremarkable.

Despite this, talented people will equally remark on the skills they witness in others, and which to them seem equally remarkable. Have you ever seen a young nursery nurse mesmerizing a large group of children using natural storytelling skills? She didn't, like so many of us, abandon a universal childhood skill when no longer a child. That makes her special. We tend to notice and envy other people's abilities, just as children always envy their friend's toys, or we wish we had chosen the dessert a fellow diner chose. Mental arithmetic seems like wizardry to a person who displays extraordinary literary skills, for instance. Or a musical virtuoso marvels at another person's physical and sporting prowess. Try telling a lifetime non-swimmer, 'Surely everybody can swim, it just happens naturally.' They won't thank you. Tell a 50-year-old who never managed to learn how to cycle that cycling doesn't rank as a worthy modelling subject because anybody can ride a bike. The secret of excellence, paradoxically, lies in the fact that you don't recognize it in yourself. So you don't need to think about it. So your thinking doesn't interfere with inherently unconscious competence.

This means that we can all provide modelling subjects for somebody. We all have something we do enviably well. If you can't think of anything you do well, that probably proves the point. No doubt your nearest and dearest – or an objective work colleague – will readily vouch for some field of human excellence that you shrug off as 'Aw, it's nothing.'

'STARTING THE DAY' STRATEGY

Because of this blind spot about the nature of excellence, we tend to limit the scope of behaviour eligible for, or worth, modelling. A young man attending a seminar boasted no talents or special skills whatsoever, and so contented himself with offering his aptitude for getting out of bed in the morning. Apparently, he always arose full of health and optimism, just raring to start the day. With limited academic success and material worth, it emerged that after such a start, he went on to enjoy his day. How many successful people would swap a dozen of their modellable competences in return for even one such dawn in a week? Feeling good about yourself sits quite high up in terms of the Neurological Levels Model and 'meta meta modelling'. However, it turned out that he followed a specific sensory syntax each morning, conducting much of his strategy even before opening his eyes. This exemplifies the simple, discrete, behavioural strategies that we can successfully model.

Traditionally, we think of genius and virtuosity in the musical field of a Bach or the mathematical world of an Einstein. Feeling good about yourself (which eluded some of these geniuses) doesn't rank so high. In fact, it lies high up the hierarchy of human happiness and fulfilment that proved inaccessible even to the greatest of history's minds. Untapped scope lies in the everyday small-chunk behaviours, at strategy (VAKOG) rather than 'meta' level. Together, a few such changes (like feeling good every morning) make for an altogether better life.

Nature versus nurture

Genes provide a handy self-limitation for some people. They explain away all kinds of superior behaviour by accidents of birth. Because someone did not fare so well in the genetic lottery, they have little faith in whatever vestigial resources they happen to have. We don't know much about the role of genes, other than that we tend to overstate it. We know, for example, that parental encouragement and positive role models during childhood dramatically affect a person's self-image, and can lead to extraordinary achievement. Moreover, this early booster can originate from the most innocuous remark or circumstance. Self-belief follow self-fulfilling spirals – whether virtuous or vicious. Maxwell Maltz's little book *Psychocybernetics* makes the case for the power of self-image eloquently. 'Conditioning' – to use a catch-all term that includes just about anything except genetic pedigree (nurture, as opposed to nature) – accounts for remarkable success, whatever the pessimistic evidence of a person's family tree.

Modelling in chunks

The logical levels set out in Chapter 10 described behaviour and capability as different levels of psychological experience. We have seen that modelling applies best at the level of an activity, behaviour or specific skill, rather than to a capability or more general aptitude. You may need to break even a specific skill down into component parts so that you can elicit a sufficiently detailed strategy to copy, and in due course teach to others.

An artist may require skills in drawing, perspective, tone, applying washes, scumbling, glazing, form and so on. Each of these contributes to artistic capability, which starts to involve less sensory and more abstract characteristics – such as 'creativity' or 'appreciation' of form. The capability, however, *emerged* from a collection of smaller-chunk, mainly habitual behaviours. In the same way, the particular skills of turning and finishing wood form part of the capability of a woodworker. Hence the need to chunk down skills to a modellable level. For instance, reduce the skill of 'drawing' to discrete but useful strategies, like producing lines and shapes with different instruments, observing a subject, identifying and representing contrast, cross-hatching, and so on. You could probably cite examples of such important foundation skills from your own hobbies and interests.

Having said this, in order to model a skill or activity, you may have to access higher logical levels *in addition* to the specific behavioural activities. For instance, a person may need self-belief and self-confidence to achieve more than mere basic competence. An artist may need an appreciation of art and the subjects portrayed and maybe a love of nature, or fascination with the human form, to give full expression to their skills. Neurological changes happen at different levels, not least so that congruent, aligned behaviour results. The boundaries or critical aspects of change tend to occur at the higher levels, just as goals such as happiness subsume relatively shorter-term goals like making money or getting fit. Hence the importance of an ecology check, which usually affects higher logical levels of experience, even in the case of 'low-level' activity modelling. Even if you cannot model the higher-level influence, you will at least *identify* where a person draws upon other outside 'systems' that may explain their success.

EXERCISE 18.1

MODELLING

You can use different processes when modelling, and a typical example follows, with some comments to explain the process. This refers to a short-duration activity of the sort that requires dexterity and physical co-ordination.

1   Choose the skill, activity, process or state you want to model.

2   Choose a subject to model. You only need to look for the *skill*, rather than finding some superhuman genius. Some people just do one thing really well, which suffices for this purpose. You need not emulate the person in any other capacity, such as temperament or lifestyle, other than in so far as (a) those other factors affect the way they do what they do (such as confidence and self-belief), and (b) *you can adopt these factors ecologically*.

3   Observe the subject. This means having reasonable access to them, although a video recording will sometimes suffice. You may need to do all this without the person knowing. As we saw earlier, unconscious competence seems to dissolve into self-consciousness when

the conscious mind becomes involved (as in demonstrating how to tie a necktie to a group). If you can't arrange this, just bear the factor in mind.

4 Otherwise, observe from different perspectives, perhaps on several occasions. Don't try too hard. Do it as a child would do it – naturally.

5 You can interview the person to elicit a description, and use sensory acuity to detect unconscious strategy VAK representations.

6 See yourself as the subject, but in a dissociated state – seeing yourself from the outside.

7 Then take 'first-person' position, trying to enter inside your subject to fully associate the experience. This time you see, hear and feel what they do. In other words: become the person.

8 Practise the same sequence in your mind a few times. You may have to re-check anything that seems unclear.

9 Carry out the activity yourself (in 'first person'). Don't analyse it – just do it. Maintain the sensation of becoming one with the subject, especially in feelings, frame of mind and self-belief about the particular skill and your ability to master it.

10 Finally, make adjustments according to feedback. Feel free to improve the activity, just as your subject has done from time to time. You have the extra knowledge and skill to make changes at submodality level.

11 Practise your new skill. Practice – with the right strategy – makes perfect.

You may never arrive at excellence. Your modelling subject has the advantage, perhaps, of years of actual experience. But that need not affect your own potential. After all, we often overtake people who once outperformed us. 'Non-arrival' in modelling relates to quite different factors: first, the fact that you can keep learning and cybernetically improving, as the Four-stage Achievement Model in Chapter 3 illustrates; second, human excellence tends more to the infinite than the finite, as perpetual Olympic record-breaking seems to indicate.

19 *Frames and Reframing*

NLP uses the term 'frame' to describe the way we look at something. We put different items into different frames to see them from a different point of view. Reframing refers to seeing things from a different perspective or viewpoint, and can help to change how we feel about something, and identify creative solutions to problems. In this chapter, I will illustrate the process and use of frames and reframing.

Linguistic frames

You can use a frame as a linguistic device for more effective communication. This might apply to a meeting, interview or consultation, for example. It can help to make the scope, content, parameters, relevance conclusions and so forth of a meeting more meaningful or specific. It can help you to keep to an agenda and time limit, and to achieve your outcomes for a meeting. The following section describes some useful types of frame and some well-known applications. Once you have grasped the idea, you can apply frames yourself to these and other situations.

'OUTCOME' FRAME

'Outcome' frame simply means that you think in terms of what you want. You need to establish agreement on your purpose or outcome, typically at the beginning of a communication or meeting. This equates to the criteria in the well-formed outcome exercise in Chapter 4, but allowing for the group context. You can ask questions such as: 'What specifically do we want from this meeting/item?' You identify the purpose, hoped-for result, or aim. This provides a yardstick against which to measure success, as well as a clear target for everyone to aim for.

'AGREEMENT' FRAME

The 'agreement' frame establishes 'what we've agreed'. By using specific points of agreement (pacing), you can direct people to a common outcome. You can ask, for instance: 'Shall I summarize what we have so far agreed?' List what you have agreed in as much detail as possible, as a record of the consensus, correcting and amending and gaining full agreement as you go. However simplistic, this can avoid all sorts of problems later. You can, of course, apply this in one-to-one communication as well as in a group.

'AS IF' FRAME

Using the 'as if' frame, you try to encourage a group into the same frame of mind *as if* they had achieved the outcome. You learnt about the importance of sensory evidence when we addressed well-formed outcomes for individuals (see Chapter 4). You will need to ask questions according to the context and content, and also make allowances for those who have no knowledge of NLP, or the idea of future pacing. Otherwise, this works like a group visualization process.

You can ask, for instance, 'What exactly do we want to see?', and guide the person or group towards sensory evidence:

- What's the report going to look like? (content, scope, format and so on)
- Who else do we need to involve? (engage imagination)
- How will this sound to the Board?
- How will the changes affect X department?

Good outcome and agreement frames will have already framed the 'finished product' outcome in visible, tangible terms.

'RELEVANCY' FRAME

Keep to the outcome or agenda item by challenging irrelevant contributions. Success in framing relevance will depend upon having a well-framed outcome to start with. You can ask how X (the comment or question) relates to Y (the outcome we have agreed). Remember to use 'soft front ends' (see Chapter 12), as some people construe relevancy questions negatively.

'CONTRAST' FRAME

With the 'contrast' frame, you contrast the desired outcome to something else – such as the present situation or an alternative already considered. This creates choices (including doing nothing), and thus improves the quality of a final decision. Ask, for example: 'What's the difference between what you suggest and so-and-so?' (an alternative solution or opportunity), or 'How will that change the situation? How will that improve on the present position?' Making contrasts will give a better, truer perspective on the issue.

'BACKTRACK' FRAME

You can summarize what you have discussed as a reminder of factors or options, points for action, or in order to progress to a new topic, make a decision or maintain agreement: 'Let me summarize the points made, and what we have decided.' Backtracking can range from a succinct summary to a more or less word-for-word reiteration. At different points in a meeting, backtracking will facilitate an agreement frame.

Reframing

You can reframe any situation, issue or problem to gain new perspectives. We use the term 'reframing' generally to refer to 'seeing things in a new light', 'getting a new perspective' and so on, so it does not have the specific connotations of the individual frames above. Reframing will usually also change your feelings, and throw up creative ideas and insights for solutions. It can generate choices, and identify new or 'root' problems and causes. The more frames you can identify, the more choices you will generate, and the greater your chances of a successful outcome. A major reframe will sometimes change a person's attitude or beliefs at a high, neurological level, rather than at a sensory level as in the case of fast submodality switching. The new perspective or 'way of seeing things' engages the logical left brain as well as the sensory right brain, or unconscious mind.

CREATING CREATIVITY

The creative right brain works largely unconsciously, but we can do much consciously to foster greater awareness and see different perspectives. I will make some practical suggestions. Notice that these can affect lifestyle, and involve much more than techniques or formulae. Creativity requires an attitude, self-belief and a way of life that includes variety, novelty and plenty of 'downtime' (see Chapter 13) periods. Try the following:

1   Change your **identity or role**. Act (or at least think) like someone else – anyone else, for example a four-year-old child, the Queen, a decorator, a farmer, a vicar, Einstein, Peter Pan. See things from outside yourself.

2   Change **what** you do. Take up some new hobby or activity. Change your focus of attention in your work. If an avid reader, give yourself a break from reading for a few days, or read something completely out of character. If a non-reader, read a paperback by a target date. Do something you have never done before. Change an electrical plug, plaster some gaps in the wall or make a soufflé.

3   Change **where** you do things. For example, change your lunch venue and meet people in a different location. Perhaps rearrange your office or home furniture until it feels like a different room.

4   Change **when** you do things. Move regular appointments to different times in the day. Change your sequence of daily routines so that you do things at different times. At weekend, switch a regular Saturday visit or routine to Sunday, or vice versa. Notice what appears and feels different. Miss your regular Sunday lunch, or have it in the evening. Work through the night now and again when you don't have work the next day.

5   Change **why** you do things. Act in accordance with some reason other than the present one. Invent new reasons, and behave accordingly. Give yourself some secret agenda, for instance:

    – to make people smile
    – to notice beauty around you in the world
    – to learn ten entirely new things
    – to become more healthy.

Notice how you feel and behave differently when you change your purpose.

6 Change **how** you do things. Conduct some everyday task in a different way. For example, work from the bottom of a list rather than the top. Do something freehand that you would have used a tool or machine for. Carry out a small job very slowly, concentrating as you never have before, and notice the result and how you feel. Make up the extra time you spend by doing something else in one-third of the time it usually takes. You needn't choose life-or-death goals or do this during a particularly busy time.

We have a natural tendency to see things and do things in familiar ways. Most belief system issues arise when we find ourselves in situations of change. Although it starts inside, reframing means change. This can affect the 'content' of a situation, such as the identity or role perspective (point 1 above) or the 'context', such as where it takes place (point 3 above). Both reframes may change the 'meaning', and thus the effect it has on us.

Initiating and managing this process of change involves:

* wanting to change (or to accept help)
* knowing how to implement the behaviours and skills required for that change
* creating or grasping the opportunity to apply them in a context that will actually produce the desired outcome.

Sleight of mouth

The term 'sleight of mouth' alludes to the magician's sleight of hand. It applies to a reframing model that has gained some currency in NLP. However, like the ubiquitous references to magic in NLP literature, such a label does not always communicate well in the pragmatic business and professional world, so you can call it what you like, and to a large extent, you can use it how you like. This simple model helps to reframe a problem or issue and produce an insight, solution, or new line of enquiry.

Robert Dilts introduced the idea, bringing together several well-known ways of seeing an issue, such as the chunking process considered earlier. As a technique, it helps to stimulate multiple perspectives, or points of view, on any issue or problem. It suggests simple questions, much like those in the Meta Model. Most of the points of view will seem familiar, and indeed people have used them for many years in creative problem-solving and different aspects of communication such as negotiating and mediation. Some appear in other NLP models, and some, like chunking, have their own special significance in several aspects of NLP.

As an illustration, I have applied the model to a 'problem statement' from the field of training and development, but you can try the technique on any specific problem, unwanted behaviour or issue you face. You can use this tool either in individual problem-solving or as a group technique like a brainstorming exercise. I have used it successfully to tackle major corporate issues, both strategic and operational. It will adapt to opportunity search as well as problem-solving, so it can cover a range of marketing applications such as product development.

THE PROBLEM STATEMENT

Before applying the technique, draw up a clear problem statement. This simply sets down the problem succinctly in words, and you need to do this carefully. In doing this, you may need to identify a root problem, as often only a symptom presents itself (the 'presented' or 'presenting' problem). Otherwise, even if you solve the 'problem', it may recur. The Sleight of Mouth Model will also tend to redefine the problem, so you can re-run it using the new problem statement.

Figure 19.1 illustrates the model using as a problem statement: 'There's far too much work to handle.'

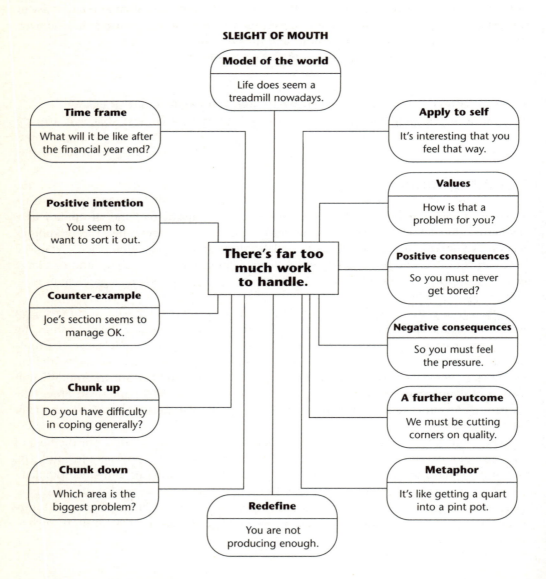

Figure 19.1   The Sleight of Mouth Model

CHALLENGING PERSPECTIVES

As Figure 19.1 shows, you then suggest responses, in the form of statements or questions, from the different perspectives or points of view. The power of the technique lies, first, in the range of perspectives brought to bear on an issue in a concerted way, and second, in the fact that, with a little right-brain creative thinking, you can generate any number of response comments or questions, and thus potentially scores – or even hundreds – of perspectives on any issue you care to address.

You may recall that the brainstorming technique involves aiming for volume rather than quality or credibility. It leaves criticism, analysis or refinement until later. The same principle applies here. Any one of these reframes might offer the breakthrough solution you seek, so don't discard any prematurely. In any event, by comprehensively reframing the issue, you will certainly change *the way it affects you*. Often, this alone solves the problem, especially in the case of a personal issue.

REFRAMING TIPS

Bear a few considerations in mind when using this and other reframing techniques:

- You don't have to produce solutions or definitive answers at this stage, although some may well occur as you formulate responses. If you could produce answers in such a glib way, the problem would not really qualify as a problem in the first place. Rather, seek to generate new, creative perspectives by intuitive association, new relationships and the odd 'Eureka!' Any single question may produce the critical 'aha' moment that leads to either a better definition of the problem, another question, or a solution. As in brainstorming, try to generate as many ideas as possible. As ideas emerge, keep going – you may prompt more, which means more choices.

- The more responses you can create from each perspective, the greater the chances of overcoming a problem or issue, so expect to go round the model a few times, generating new responses on each pass. For instance, a large number of metaphors may present themselves. You can draw on all you learnt in Chapter 14 about metaphors. What might seem naïve to you might 'click' with someone else who has a different personal map of experience and thus makes different associations.

- Don't worry if you cannot think of responses from a particular viewpoint. Don't use this as an exhaustive or logical left-brain technique with fixed rules that produce black-and-white answers. It just helps to stimulate your creative unconscious mind, which knew the answers all the time.

- Every situation differs, and these suggested perspectives, although not exhaustive, provide a memory-jogger that usually helps. Think of some more if you can. In most cases, you will think of at least one apposite question or comment on most of the 13 perspectives on a problem, and usually many more. More often than not, one or two of these will move you towards a solution. In other cases, an idea may come later, unexpectedly, but clearly triggered by treating the problem in this way.

- Finally, you cannot avoid doing some thinking – and creative thinking at that. The more creative your responses, the more choices you will produce, and the better your eventual solution. Quality solutions come from quality thinking, and quality thinking calls on both sides of the brain.

You can apply this technique to literally any problem statement – a specific human relations matter, a departmental or functional issue, something of corporate importance, or a personal matter, even a technical problem, provided you or your colleagues have the necessary technical knowledge to add to your creative insight. In any case, make sure you choose a genuine problem, preferably an intractable one requiring a creative breakthrough. If a spreadsheet or computer program will give the answer, you don't need to resort to your right brain, and a manager should delegate such a routine function anyway. But we can't solve most real-life problems in this way – hence the need to reframe them.

Having familiarized yourself with the model and response process, you might start by thinking of three pressing issues that you want to tackle. Express them as simple problem statements – a little practice at this helps – then have fun working your way round the model, perhaps with a colleague or group who 'own' the problem.

Points of view

The 'Points of view' technique will work in similar situations requiring creative thinking and a change of perspective. This works particularly well in interpersonal situations when people hold different points of view, so it can help in conflict-resolution. We often use expressions like 'She just doesn't understand' or 'I simply can't get through to him.' Using the 'points of view' language device, you construct simple sentences using words that provoke a different point of view: good, bad, right, wrong, stupid, smart, better, worse.

Using the simplified example 'She doesn't understand' and slotting these words into a standard syntax, we can derive the following sentences:

- *It's good* that she doesn't understand, *because* she might not be able to face things.
- *It's bad* that she doesn't understand, *because* it's ruining our relationship.
- *It's right* that she doesn't understand, *because* she doesn't have all the facts.
- *It's wrong* that she doesn't understand, *because* that's what she's paid to do.
- *It's stupid* that she doesn't understand, *because* she is suffering as a result.
- *It's smart* that she doesn't understand, *because* she can't be held responsible.
- *It's better* not to understand *than* to do what she does out of malice.
- *It's worse* not to understand *than* not to listen.

As in the previous technique, you can suggest several 'points of view' using each triggering word. You may struggle to think of any in particular cases, or it may seem stupid and pointless. Again, the model will stimulate creative thought, but you will have to call upon your own insight and ingenuity in devising different points of view to bring about change. You can use or discard a technique as you wish. Adhere to the principles, however – in this case, the need for other points of view to help understanding and increase your options.

With practice, you will soon find reframing an intuitive way of thinking, more effective in achieving your outcomes than analytical problem-solving techniques.

Reversals

I have used other approaches in business contexts which, while not strictly NLP techniques, help with problem-reframing and opportunity search. In the case of *reversals*, start with a problem statement just as in the 'sleight of mouth' technique, but then completely *reverse* the statement.

Many trainers, and most general managers, cannot put a value on a training event to the satisfaction of all the parties involved, including – especially – those responsible for funding decisions. This creates a dilemma, which you could 'brainstorm' using the 'sleight of mouth' technique, as an application of its problem-solving power.

'We can't measure the value of training.' should suffice for our 'reversals' example. In practice, it might apply to an actual programme or course, or a more specific aspect or part of the training. In fact, the model can apply to any problem or issue, or as a brainstorming tool to generate ideas and grasp opportunities. Once you learn the technique, you will probably find your own uses for it.

First, you *reverse* the problem-statement, 'We can't measure the value of training' to create a new statement or 'truth', such as: 'The value of training can be easily and accurately measured.' *Presupposing* your new statement as 'true', you then exercise your creative mind in thinking of issues the new statement raises, or what might follow from it. For instance:

- We can design and conduct training according to rational criteria.
- It could compete with other business investments on the basis of the returns it gives.
- We can allocate financial and other resources objectively.
- We can sell training more easily to trainees on the basis of value to them as well as the company.
- We can subject different kinds of training to standard evaluation.
- Training managers can convince top management of the effectiveness of particular training and its payback.
- Rather than ask 'Do we (or can we afford to) train?', we can ask 'What training will offer the best value, given our mission and culture?'
- We will find out which training to discontinue, and where to direct resources more effectively.
- Training personnel would receive important feedback as to their own effectiveness.
- We can standardize training provision, with corresponding economies of scale on the basis of consistent high returns.
- We can compete for scarce funds even in difficult economic times on the basis of profit centres rather than cost centres.
- Operational divisions will see training as a profit-earner alongside mainstream products and services.
- The annual training budget round will lose some of its politics.
- We will have a better basis for comparing internal and external training provision.
- We can plan capital investment, such as building and training equipment, on a sound, standard economic basis.
- The professional standing of the training and development function and its staff will improve.
- We can expect a Board-level training and development appointment, and greater influence brought to bear.

To elicit such issues from a reversal statement, act in 'as if' frame. Notice the language 'can' and 'will', rather than 'could' and 'would'. Then consider each issue or consequence of the reversal to search for further spin-off issues, consequences, questions or opportunities in a brainstorming way.

Notice that having framed things positively, we have left the problem mode behind. A more upbeat appraisal usually follows, in the belief that *a solution exists*. Let your creative mind move from one idea to another, developing as well as introducing new perspectives and scenarios. You can never exhaust right-brain ideas and insights. For example:

- Measurable training might suggest, for instance, that we should devote far more attention to evaluation techniques, rather than addressing the subject on a piecemeal basis, or when faced with a budgetary crisis.

- Presupposing evaluation possible, we will no longer use subjectivity as an excuse for not evaluating.

- Given that we need more research into evaluation methods, the issues thrown up by reversal (rather than the long-known problem) will generate fruitful lines of enquiry and greater focus than hitherto.

- In cases where certain specific training lends itself to accurate evaluation (such as shorter-term skills training for selling, debt collection, production processes, measurable product or service quality), we might channel more training funds in fair competition with other financial demands.

- We might abandon certain types of training or fund it as a known cost for wider business purposes, in open competition with other cost centres.

Note that you can subject any one of the 'angles' that emerge from the issues raised by 'reversals' to further reframing using the 'sleight of mouth' or other techniques. Simply rephrase the 'reversal' as a new problem statement, such as: 'We need stronger Board-level support for training and development.' Responses require 'content' or technical knowledge, of course, as in my example. But usually such knowledge forms part of the problem itself – you know quite well the implications of a personal problem, and similarly one concerning your job at work. In the latter case, you may have the advantage of several brains contributing.

Creative rather than analytical techniques can have unexpected value. You often identify and solve other problems, and discover opportunities you never even considered when you first defined your problem. These afford a welcome bonus.

Reframing sets no limits on possibility. It always increases choices. The reversal technique can be applied to any problem statement, and will often elicit ideas when a more marginal rethink does not work. You can use it for strategic rethinking in a world of changing markets and technology where only original, radical thinking will keep you competitive.

20 *Change Techniques*

This chapter describes some of the more popular techniques that draw upon the NLP presuppositions, models and core skills set out in Part 1 of this book.

Fast phobia technique

The successful treatment of phobias exemplifies one of the outstanding achievements of NLP. Practitioners achieve permanent cures in minutes rather than in what previously might have taken weeks or months. Once you understand the concept of association and dissociation, and reprogramming at a structural level – creating new neural networks – the consistent results seem less remarkable. Indeed, phobias offer just one example of change processes, although the often extreme nature of the condition makes the change seem more dramatic.

A phobia provides an ideal example of anchoring (see Chapter 16). This technique involves dissociation from such a highly efficient anchoring process. In cases of extreme symptoms, we need to take special care not to stimulate the phobia, with its unpleasant consequences. But the technique has the in-built safeguard of 'double dissociation', and also works well if self-administered. Several techniques fulfil the fundamental dissociation requirements for phobia cure and produce lasting results, and I have included the following as one of the more popular.

EXERCISE 20.1

OVERCOMING A PHOBIA

It helps to familiarize yourself with the process first, using a 'moderately phobic' experience from which you can learn. Therefore, choose a situation that makes you a little afraid, but not over-emotionally, and certainly not pathologically, so – for example, having to give an impromptu speech, being summoned to your boss's office, flying, and so on:

1   Identify a situation that would provoke the fear – without associating the feeling. This may have occurred in the recent past, or you can choose an upcoming event. Choose an intense example of the state – perhaps one that sticks in your memory.

2   Conduct an ecology check (see Chapter 4), to identify any positive intentions behind the behaviour.

3   See yourself as a still picture on a large cinema screen, at the moment just before the fear occurred, from a position seated in the theatre, maybe halfway towards the back – but you can sit where you like, and move if you want to.

4   Now leave your body, and imagine you can see yourself watching yourself on the screen from the projection booth right at the back of the theatre. It has a soundproof glass panel through which you can watch the movie.

5   As you watch yourself watching yourself, run a black-and-white movie of what happens, starting just before the fear sets in, right until the end of the experience. Nothing can harm you in this safe position. After the whole experience finishes, stop the film to make it a still picture again.

6   Now step into the movie screen as the person in the still picture. Run the whole movie *backwards* – in colour this time – as quickly as you can. Reverse everything until you return to the point of the first still picture. Do this several times as rapidly as possible, until you can rewind it in a couple of seconds, just like a very powerful video player.

7   'Break state' by physically moving around and thinking of something entirely different.

8   Now recall the memory just before the fear would have set in, and notice your new response – rate it 1 to 10 if you like. If any fear remains, run the whole sequence again, and notice that the fear has now either gone completely or reduced in severity.

9   Finally, test your cure in the real world. Do this gently at first. For instance, if you used to fear heights, check your responses progressively from windows at different storeys in a multi-storey building. You can then advance to the upper storeys of an outdoor car park, and so on. If you feared spiders, and you previously could not even look at a picture in a book, use a book as your test rather than a real spider initially.

Use your common sense. Remember that you can re-run the cure at any time to remind yourself of your victory over the phobia while at the cinema. In fact, if you follow the simple process carefully, you will not need to. You will have changed completely. This happens – as we saw earlier – in the actual neural networks of your brain. The more you expose yourself to what you once feared, the more confident you will feel about your permanent cure.

After a successful moderate cure, you can go on to tackle your worst fears, confident of your ability to apply the process.

Swish patterns

'Swish patterns' enable us to overcome negative emotions and unwanted, habitual behaviour. The technique varies widely, so I have given two quite different examples.

EXERCISE 20.2

SWISH PATTERN A

1   Think of a time in your life when you lacked self-esteem and failed to achieve some important goal. Associate into the experience, seeing it through your own eyes. Recall all the sights, sounds and feelings intensely. Notice what you feel in your body, and also notice any other things you see in your mind's eye. Recall whatever you say to yourself, or other sounds – anything that may associate with this unpleasant memory.

2   Next, come out of that memory or 'break state'. Do something that demands you use your conscious brain in 'uptime' – add all the digits of your birthday together, or something silly like that.

3   Now create the image of yourself you would prefer on a screen right in front of you. You have conquered the lack of self-esteem and sense of failure. You have changed into a different person. You have solved what used to trouble you. You no longer consider the problem an issue. You now have resources with which you overcome what used to get you down. You now have more choices. But you keep your identity. You still have your sense of humour. The person you see knows that you will succeed, because you already have.

4   Make the image large, colourful and attractive. Feel drawn to this person – Someone you really want to emulate. Change the pictures and sounds in any way that makes your image even more compelling, desirable and convincing. Give it sounds, brightness, movement. Hear the words, 'I feel good about myself.' Ask yourself, 'What would this new me look like if even more compelling?', and make whatever changes you wish – you have total control over your creation.

5   Make the whole image into a tiny dot, then see it quickly grow and become life-size again, filling the screen. Hear again the words, 'I feel good about myself.' Now see a blank screen. Then, once again, from a tiny spot, see the image grow and fill your view. Do this several times until it happens instantly and easily.

6   Now recall the unpleasant image you started with, and put the tiny dot right in the middle of that image.

7   Watch the unpleasant image become smaller and dimmer as the dot grows and finally fills your mind, replacing the old picture completely. Say, 'I feel good about myself', or something that makes you feel good.

8   See a blank screen again, and again recall the unpleasant image you started with. Do it all again: see the dot grow quickly and replace the old image. Say the words: 'I feel good about myself.' Hear them clearly in your mind. Make the screen blank again, and repeat the process. Do it several times, more quickly each time, until just by saying 'swish' you can instantly replace the old you with the compelling new person. Blank out the screen between each swish. Do this as many times as you like – it happens so rapidly that you can do it in moments. Hear the constant flow of empowering words coming from somewhere deep inside yourself, saying: 'I feel good about myself.'

9   Now see these compelling self-images multiply, stacking up way ahead of you and behind – all around you. They fill your life – past, present and future.

10 'Break state' with your birthday trick again, or spell your children's names backwards. This will bring you back to here and now.

11 After a few minutes, try to imagine the unpleasant memory you recalled at the beginning. You probably can't. Instead, you see a dot transformed into the new 'you', or just the new, empowering image. If your old memory appears, it will quickly turn into the new image that has taken its place. If not, simply carry out the 'swish' process a few more times, or do that anyway, just as insurance of a permanent change.

12 Check again tomorrow morning. If you ever feel the way you used to again, you know what to do. Say the words, 'I feel good about myself', and see a little dot in your mind's eye.

EXERCISE 20.3

SWISH PATTERN B

1   Identify when and where you feel stuck or out of control, and want to change some well-established habit. Where and when would you like to respond differently to the way you do now? Check that you really want to make the change.

2   Identify the first 'cue picture'. This stage involves identifying what you see or experience immediately before you begin the behaviour that you would like to reject. We have already encountered this in some of the earlier techniques. When carrying out this stage, make sure that you *associate*, which means seeing things through your own eyes. Sometimes, you will need to carry out the behaviour – inducing the actual habit pattern (like taking a chocolate bar from the cupboard) – to identify what stimulates it. We usually run on 'auto-pilot' when we practise these stubborn habits.

3   Create an 'outcome picture' of how you will see yourself differently when you have already accomplished the change. At this point, make the picture dissociated. See yourself from somewhere other than through your own eyes (remember how we manipulated submodalities in Chapter 9). Watch this picture, and adjust it to make it really attractive.

4   Now the swish. See the first cue picture big and bright. Put a small, dark image of the outcome picture in the bottom right-hand corner. Make the small, dark image grow big and bright to cover the first cue picture as it in turn grows dim and shrinks away as fast as you can say 'swish'. Then blank out the screen, or open your eyes. Carry out this swish routine four or five times, eventually taking a second or two each time, and blanking at the end of each one. You can test the change by a future pace (see Chapter 7). Picture the first image you imagined, and notice what happens. If the swish pattern has worked, you will find it difficult to call up a clear image of your first picture. It will tend to fade or change into the new picture. If not, do a few more swishes and carry out the process again.

Changing your personal history

If you have unpleasant memories that still cause a negative impact, you can transform them into positive memories. You can do this by recalling the memory and adding some resources.

EXERCISE 20.4

TRANSFORMING NEGATIVE MEMORIES INTO POSITIVE ONES

1   Go back into the memory you want to change. Then go further back in your memory to detect the first recollection of this kind (as in Exercise 11.3)

2   Now dissociate from it. In the light of what you now know, identify the resources that you would have needed in that situation to change it to a positive memory, and a satisfying experience. You can name the resource, such as 'security' or 'peace'. You will have known this resource in your life in some other context.

3   Anchor these resources and test your anchor (see Chapter 16).

4   See the memory as if you already had the resources you needed to make it a positive memory (while remaining dissociated from it). Notice how this changes the experience. Add any resources you need to make the memory positive.

5   Next, step inside the experience (associate). Use your positive anchor – and again notice the change. Dwell in the experience for a while, and notice, for instance, other people's reactions and comments. Explore each modality in turn – sights, sounds and so on. You can repeat this stage and the previous one to add more resources as you wish.

6   Holding your resource anchor, travel back into the present and check that each memory you meet along the way no longer elicits the old feelings. Add further resources as you need to.

7   'Future pace' to confirm that it will never happen again unless you choose.

Creating empowering beliefs

We have already seen how beliefs and attitudes affect all our behaviour as a two-way process. Our actions also create beliefs. In effect, we make excuses for everything we do, and justify them, creating the necessary beliefs in the process. Depending on your interpretation of your actions, the beliefs you form can either empower or disempower you in achieving your outcomes. I suggest below another exercise that will help you to turn actions into empowering beliefs.

EXERCISE 20.5

TRANSFORMING ACTIONS INTO EMPOWERING BELIEFS

1   Think of something you would like to believe about yourself, but which you can't really call 'true'.

2   State this desired belief in a positive form, just as in the goal-clarification exercise in Chapter 4, when we turned outcomes into a positive mode. Check also that you can do something about your desired belief, rather than having to depend on other people or circumstances outside your control to make it 'true' (the 'control' well-formed outcome criterion). Then carry out an ecology check (if necessary, refer to the checklist of questions in Chapter 4) to make sure that in this new belief you respect your family, friends, work colleagues and so on – people you want to take account of.

3   Ask yourself what sort of things a person with this desired belief would instinctively do. Imagine and make a list of all sorts of actions that match the belief.

4   Think of some particular time and place in the future when you would like to have this belief.

5   From your list, select an action or kind of behaviour that provides evidence of your desired belief, appropriate for the specific future time and place you have chosen.

6   Now visualize yourself in this future situation, carrying out the chosen action. Watch the whole scene as if on a movie screen, with you carrying out the actions. You might need to do this two or three times to make a clear and positive scene.

7   Start the scene again from the beginning, but this time stepping right into it as though part of it – seeing through your own eyes, and hearing and feeling everything around you through

your own senses. In particular, notice your *feelings* when you carry out this activity according to your desired belief. Say out loud your new belief with conviction as you carry on through the scene to the end.

8   Now repeat steps 4 to 7 a few more times. You can select different, appropriate actions from the list you made to illustrate your desired belief each time. Choose a different future time and place as an example of each. Each visualization will reinforce your new belief. You can convert actions which you may have already carried out in the past, and which you can now carry out if you wish in the future, into powerful beliefs. These beliefs will in turn produce more positive actions that will help bring about your outcomes.

Let me remind you that clear visualization enables you to change beliefs and feelings, as well as actual behaviour. The brain simply does not differentiate between the electrochemical changes resulting from external sensing, and those we create internally – or imagine. Both, however, constitute 'experience'. *Don't* treat these NLP techniques as games – they change the very landscape of your brain. Depending on the neurological level of change, they can fundamentally affect your life.

Generating new behaviour

The exercise below will help you to generate changes in your own behaviour. You can use it either to generate completely new behaviours, or to make modifications to existing, unsatisfactory behaviour.

EXERCISE 20.6

NEW BEHAVIOUR GENERATOR

1   Identify the new behaviour you want, or the change that you want in some existing behaviour.

2   Describe to yourself the new behaviour you want, asking yourself: 'How would I look and sound if I were doing that behaviour?'

3   In your imagination, watch yourself producing the behaviour you want in whatever context you want. Notice any other people involved in this, and their response to your changed behaviour. If you cannot imagine yourself with your new behaviour, then imagine watching somebody else doing it, then put yourself in the place of that person.

4   When satisfied with your own new behaviour, step inside yourself in the image and run through it yourself – become associated. Now, as you go through the motions, pay particular attention to how you feel, as well as to what you see and hear, and also to the effect on people around you.

5   If you want to change anything, go back to step 3, and change your own behaviour, getting back 'into yourself' to check how it feels.

6   When satisfied with your imagined performance and the feelings that accompany it, ask yourself: 'What signal will I see, hear or feel, internally or externally, that will let me know when I can usually adopt new behaviour?'

7   Finally, imagine that signal happening, use your new behaviour, and then become aware of your feelings of satisfaction.

You will probably find this 'new behaviour generator' a useful self-help tool in personal and professional development. Like any skill, the more you use it, the faster and easier it becomes. Aim to use it automatically and unconsciously, however self-conscious the process initially feels. Whenever you have a less than satisfactory experience, you can process it through your 'new behaviour generator', or you can apply it to longer-standing habitual behaviour. Gradually, you will take control of your behaviour, and thus the outcomes you achieve.

As well as techniques for controlling how you feel and replacing unwanted limiting beliefs, you now have the ability to change your behaviour. By making changes to the structure of how you think, you can bring about permanent change. Use your own creativity as you think of ways to apply these techniques personally and professionally.

The power of pertinent questions

Almost any statement includes one or more presuppositions. Indeed, we could hardly communicate and get on with normal life without them. Presuppositions have an effect on us in so far as we accept them (which we usually do) and incorporate them into our perception, or how we represent things. However, it seems that questions have an even greater effect on us than statements in activating our inner senses. 'What did you do on Thursday?' involves a series of 'sensory searches' it seems we cannot consciously prevent. Even if we don't answer a question, or if we try not to think about it (such as a query we overhear on a train or in the street), we go through the *mental process*. It works like the strange negative outcome phenomenon described when considering outcomes at the beginning of this book. To respond to the injunction 'Don't drink that!', we have to first understand the question – and that means in the only way we can: by sensory representations. And sensory representation means picturing, or thinking about, drinking.

To understand a question, we have to go through the same sort of process. A question can therefore have a powerful effect, just as the injunction 'Don't spill!' paints the picture, 'Spill!', and 'spilling' behaviour follows. All this illustrates the ubiquitous human desire for classification, patterns and meaning we noted in the first few chapters. Nothing can remain unresolved. No question can remain unanswered, including the question: 'Shall I answer it?'

This questioning efficacy gives the Meta Model set out in Chapter 12 its power. Whatever response questions elicit, the questions themselves, like 'Who says so?', or 'What, specifically?', will stimulate a sensory search, and do their change work unconsciously and efficiently. Eye movements and other cues let the questioner know of these neurological happenings more effectively than the person's verbal responses.

However, questions have more universal utility in personal change work. The self-question 'Why do I always act so stupidly?' possesses plenty of suggestive punch. Repeated randomly in the context of real experiences (each time you act in a remotely 'stupid' way), it will just about guarantee a 'stupid' self-belief.

Typically, this will apply in a particular context, such as in money matters, impulse buying or whatever direction the vicious self-belief spiral takes. However distorted or generalized the interpretation, eventually some neural dirt will stick, and a person's physical brain topography will change to reflect a 'stupid' question. Thoughts, attitudes, feeling, values and beliefs, as appropriate, follow in its wake. By structuring questions for specific purposes, as when challenging Meta Model language violations, you can concentrate and direct the suggestive power of questions.

Fortunately, questioning works both ways – to empower as well as to disempower. 'I wonder how soon I will master this?' will have an equally powerful, positive, helpful effect. The presupposition 'Some time soon' (or at least 'Some time') slides past the conscious, rational mind and does its seminal, suggestive work. 'Some time' means it *will* happen.

As a device, this works both personally and in communication with others. As a self-administered technique, it surpasses positive affirmations, especially over-ambitious, patently 'out of character' ones of the 'positive thinking' kind. The canny, conscious mind will question any unlikely truth about someone it knows only too well (its owner): 'No way – it'll never happen. How many times have you said that before?' Meanwhile, the subtle presupposition 'some time soon' slips through the cognitive filter, and a person's future changes for the better.

The questions in the well-formed outcome process, especially those that related to ecology, incorporated this suggestive phenomenon. In that case, the questions elicited unconscious outcomes, positive intentions and 'secondary gain' – in other words, they identified or *released* unconscious meaning. In this case ('How soon will I master this?') the question *installed* unconscious 'meaning', and produced the behaviour that followed. Each involved intrapersonal intelligence, and self-awareness of the *system* for changing perception and behaviour.

CARTESIAN COORDINATES

The Cartesian coordinate questioning technique helps to identify many perspectives in an issue. The form of the questions will seem like some of the ecology questions in Chapter 4 and the Meta Model questions in Chapter 12. The quadrant diagram in Figure 20.1 shows the logical relationship between the questions, but for most purposes the questions themselves will suffice.

You will have to think carefully about the non-mirror-image reverse question. In this case, what may seem a paradoxical or impossible approach will help to bring issues to the surface that would not have succumbed to reasoning.

CONVERSE	THEOREM
'What wouldn't happen if you did?'	'What would happen if you did?'
NON-MIRROR-IMAGE REVERSE	INVERSE
'What wouldn't happen if you didn't?'	'What would happen if you didn't?'

Figure 20.1   Cartesian coordinate questioning

Use these change techniques in addition to the models and techniques described throughout Part 1. I will list just some of these change processes. The bold numbers refer to the relevant chapter:

- Change of State Model – **3**
- Four-stage Achievement Model – **3**
- Life Content Model – **3**
- Timeline – **3**
- Well-formed outcomes – **4**
- Belief change – **5**
- Value-elicitation – **5**
- Pacing and leading – **7**
- Submodality switching – **9**
- Identifying roles and parts – **10**
- Inner Interpreter – **10**
- Inner team – **10**
- Neurological levels – **10**
- Meta Model – **12**
- Milton Model – **12**
- Post-hypnotic suggestion – **13**
- Metaphors – **14**
- Meta programs – **15**
- Anchoring – **16**
- Strategies and modelling – **17** and **18**
- Reframing – **19**.

You can apply these Part 1 models and techniques in accordance with the examples given, and practise your NLP skills to apply them more widely. Use them in conjunction with the presuppositions you have learnt, or apply the presuppositions as principles in your own way. Part 2 describes some applications in specific areas of business and personal development.

Selected Applications

Introduction to Part 2

You will have realized the wide range of NLP applications from the examples given in Part 1. These cover just about every aspect of communication and business – and human life. For Part 2 I have chosen to focus on a few key areas of application that illustrate the principles and techniques of NLP, providing a summary of how to use NLP in these areas, in which many readers will work or have an interest. This will remind you of the different ways you can approach a particular topic, such as public speaking or selling, and provide you with a convenient reference point back to the detail in Part 1.

Notwithstanding the earlier references to each of the application areas in Part 2, I have avoided repetition by either giving different illustrations and ideas to try out, or by adding guidelines – many from professionals practising in these areas.

The principles and techniques you have already learnt apply in most of these differing applications in one way or another. Some, such as the communication presuppositions (see Chapter 2) and techniques for controlling your state of mind (see Chapters 8 and 9), apply almost universally. For example, in the latter case, different people experience the same sort of unhelpful state when:

- standing before a group
- communicating bad news to a colleague
- disciplining a member of staff
- called unexpectedly to the boss's office
- awaiting the result of a biopsy
- starting an examination
- facing a critical five-foot putt.

Similarly, in every personal interaction the communication presuppositions apply, as do the various techniques for achieving rapport.

In the same way, you can make any goal more effective – or more likely to happen – by using the well-formed outcome criteria set out in Chapter 4. This applies to all the techniques described in Part 2. Some criteria will prove more appropriate than others, of course, and you may need to tailor them to different circumstances, but that just requires common sense. Outcomes occur in every walk of life, from personal and career ambitions through business objectives to the many unarticulated desires and hopes that every person harbours.

Because of these common features, none of the application areas demands very special treatment. Even in the case of a specific topic like anchoring, you will find it difficult to identify an area of business, relationships or self-development where you can't apply the technique in some useful way.

This means that you can learn enough from Part 1 to start using NLP, in almost any context other than, perhaps, professionally. Nevertheless, practising counsellors, therapists, trainers and other communicators will certainly think of ways to add NLP ideas and techniques to their present work with few risks other than those I spelled out as we went along. Whatever your particular needs, Part 2 will give you more ideas for applications, and the extra examples will reinforce your learning.

For these reasons – as well as to keep the book to a manageable size – I have omitted some major areas of application, such as education, sport and therapy. However, you can learn a lot from the illustrations throughout Part 1 drawn from these areas. In any event, you can readily *adapt* the application areas that I decided to include. You will recall, for instance, that several illustrations relate to children, and these have immediate relevance to education. Similarly, you can easily apply some of the modelling and state control examples to a sporting activity, or the Milton Model and anchoring techniques to therapy.

I concentrated in Part 1 on presenting the key presuppositions, not as rules or precepts, but as a holistic way of thinking or philosophy of life. The typical techniques described allow you to try all this out for yourself. It should prove easy to develop ways to exploit the presuppositions and techniques widely once you have used them in a *live setting* – whatever your area of work or personal interest. Thereafter, you will find that applications appear everywhere, and you hardly need ideas, just the genuine problem or desire for change, and the curiosity to try things for yourself and learn as you go.

Too much prescription doesn't help in lasting learning, as we sometimes miss the underlying principles when just applying techniques – or following rules in rote fashion. I have tried to strike a balance by making the presuppositions clear and credible as well as relevant to your everyday life, as these will form the foundation of your NLP. Much of NLP training focuses on techniques in an attempt to emphasize its practical nature. In fact, given an understanding of the basic models and presuppositions (see Chapter 3), the best practical investment lies in *core* skills, such as:

* accessing states – Chapter 9
* switching submodalities – Chapter 9
* achieving rapport in communication – Chapter 7
* using 'downtime' purposefully – Chapter 13
* formulating outcomes ecologically – Chapter 4.

In any event, simple *acceptance* of a presupposition as 'true' will immediately influence a person's behaviour, such as in the way we allow for other people's feelings and instinctively use matching to gain rapport, so don't underestimate the transformative power of the principles – or presuppositions – *themselves*.

In fact, you can make a few important changes in your life and solve a few problems from the earliest stage as you study each chapter in Part 1. In this way, the fundamental models and seminal 'core' skills quickly pay dividends. Fortunately, many of these core skills concern *intra*personal rather than *inter*personal activities, so you don't have to subject the rest of the world to your early learning blunders, or take big risks.

Rushing headlong into techniques will not produce the best results, for which you require a foundation of knowledge. Without such understanding of the operating principles, or presuppositions, you may not progress far in your NLP, especially if you wish to use it professionally. So, to repeat the point made at the beginning of the book, Part 1 – which I hope meets this learning need painlessly – comes *before* Part 2. In an effort to prevent you falling prey to the dangers of 'a little learning', I will frequently refer back to the various Part 1 topics and techniques. You will need to practise these before trying them out on unsuspecting friends and colleagues. Some of the techniques and ideas will require further explanation and background. Part 2 provides:

- a handy summary of NLP applications in your own discipline, such as selling or training, or one you wish to know better
- a checklist of ideas for personal development such as in relationships and goals
- some guidelines and less obvious applications for readers specializing in these areas
- further depth for those who want more details.

21 *Training*

Training embraces many of the aspects of NLP already covered, and it serves as a good example of an important application. The highest NLP qualification (Master Trainer) has more relevance to training than to, say, therapy or business. Whilst this level of aptitude largely involves passing on NLP skills to practitioners, the training skills offered apply far more widely, in one-to-one situations such as coaching as well as to groups. The presuppositions and methods described in Part 1, and the extra tips in this chapter, will provide an important resource even for trainers with no NLP affiliation. You will notice that some of the applications techniques also apply to sales presentations, public speaking and other topics dealt with in Part 2 – and vice versa. I have spread some of these common NLP applications throughout Part 2 to maintain some balance, so you may pick up useful information by dipping into chapters outside your immediate area of interest. For the Part 2 chapter headings, in the absence of any standard format for training or any other application, I have kept to words like 'outcomes' and 'rapport' that you can easily link to ideas familiar from Part 1.

Outcomes

Formal training objectives, such as for a course or programme, rarely take account of individual needs. We saw from the Life Content Model in Chapter 3 that we all approach our outcomes differently, and I gave the examples of *doing* a training course, *getting* a qualification, getting to *know* a subject, or *being* something or somebody. Even if desirable, trainers could hardly build such personal variables into standard programme content.

However, you don't need too much ingenuity to make training flexible enough for each trainee to gain from it their own outcomes. This will mean communicating 'core' information – basic knowledge – that trainees may not possess. (Some programmes assess learning style early in the course, but rarely apply this information to individually targeted learning.) This 'information' aspect of learning, or technical content, will probably not vary much, as people usually train for what they don't know, so each will have little or no prior knowledge. But that part of learning rarely accounts for the crux of a training programme anyway, nor the basis for its success. You can learn such information cheaply from a book or well-designed notes.

Worthwhile training outcomes should also consider the *application* of 'syllabus' knowledge (say, back at work), the skills and motivation to use it, and self-beliefs that will support the new learning – in other words, seek to train people to achieve better outcomes themselves in a particular area. Most trainees will agree to this sort of general outcome, for which training represents a means to that end, rather than an end in itself. But the specifics of a training outcome will vary a great deal, especially in its transference to the workplace or day-to-day life and the different 'resources' of the trainees.

MULTIPLE TRAINING OBJECTIVES

Trainers soon realize the variety of outcomes when starting with the customary opening introductions that include: 'What do I want to gain from this?' After allowing for diffidence, a herd instinct and a lack of mutual trust at the outset, these individual objectives vary greatly. But, however well planned the teaching, *learners* rarely subject their goals to the sort of well-formed outcome checks we addressed in Chapter 4. Setting their own well-formed objectives as part of the training process will enable trainees to increase their eventual, longer-term success. Clear goals will ensure the training's effectiveness at an individual trainee level. Given a clear cybernetic target (see Chapter 3), a lot of 'DIY' learning will follow. A trainee can draw on whatever resources the programme makes available, such as:

- the knowledge and experience of the trainer
- written notes and other handouts
- demonstrations and exercises
- the combined knowledge and experience of the participants.

LEARNING VERSUS TEACHING

This makes the trainer a facilitator. It places the emphasis on learning, rather than teaching. Responsibility for learning lies with the learner. Responsibility for *facilitating* learning, or making resources available, lies with the trainer – the one, in this case, who 'owns' the training outcome. Each, however, will have *communication* outcomes – the trainer to communicate knowledge, skills and any *effects* of the sort we have discussed (see Chapter 6), the trainee to communicate their learning needs and questions (trainers cannot mindread) – but also comments and other inputs that will add *synergistically* to the overall training through 'give and take'. This puts control in the hands of the (usually) paying customer undertaking training.

Paradoxically, perhaps, this allows for a variety of needs, styles and specific outcomes as each person draws on resources and learning relevant to themself. It means that a training programme can achieve multiple individual outcomes, and thus a much better overall outcome.

It doesn't mean that every trainee will have their training goals (once clarified) fulfilled. Some might lie outside the resources offered. Furthermore, some trainees will not take full advantage, say by questioning and participating. Some may have enrolled on the wrong course. In any event, without a well-formed outcome for such an event, they have far less chance of meeting their own needs.

INVESTING IN OUTCOMES

Setting individual training outcomes will probably justify 10 per cent of the programme, as a time investment. Bear in mind that by incorporating the well-formed outcome process into group work (for example, eliciting positive intentions from each other, and mutually stimulating new outcomes not considered before the training), a trainer can make use of time otherwise spent on undirected 'icebreakers' and other content not geared to identified trainee needs. Trainers can ask the ecology questions in Chapter 4 among themselves, in smaller groups or pairs, and apply evidence tests and other criteria. All these can fulfil the function of introductory icebreaking, familiarization and team-forming sessions while adding a vital dimension. With a net time investment of close to zero, the well-formed outcome-setting process therefore repays itself manyfold.

Depending on the duration and nature of the training, a values-elicitation process (see Chapter 5) will also repay the time and effort:

- It will reveal problems and needs that the training might well cater for, once identified.

- It will increase learning motivation. *Potential* learning – and its benefits – falls within each person's hierarchy of experience and identity (see Chapter 10). New values, beliefs and 'meaning' imply new ways to achieve higher-level outcomes (see Chapter 5).

- Values will impinge ecologically on success in training outcomes, as they do any personal goal. By *incorporating* rather than just allowing for values (what's important), the chances of success increase.

- As we saw in Chapter 5, *values themselves* may constitute 'outcomes', and a training event (on whatever topic) offers an environment where such changes can occur.

In some cases, all of these processes tell trainees that they have booked the wrong course, and NLP faces such eventualities squarely as part of its pragmatic approach. But such information will have more value on the first morning than when hindsight reveals the wasted time and money. Putting the customer's interest first will also do more for the training organization's reputation. In my experience, after initial well-formed goal-setting directed towards the benefit of the trainee, withdrawals rarely happen. For a trainer, honest, open self-questioning on the part of trainees constitutes a risk well worth taking. And even someone averse to introspection will admit to value or utility – and more often an important life experience – in medium-term hindsight. Mid- or end-of-programme evaluation 'happy sheets' have lost credibility even with orthodox trainers. One- and three-month follow-ups will identify the power of NLP interventions.

PERSONAL VALUE FROM TRAINING

Just as we all read our own meaning into a story or analogy, in the same way people can usually obtain value from just about any training than puts them at the centre, and focuses on learning and lasting outcomes rather than teaching. Long-term recollection of training events usually involves the food, friendships formed, the environment such as gardens, the social aspects, a humorous episode, or information gathered from participants. Rarely do the formal objectives of the organization or trainer feature. So much for communication outcomes and the presupposition that the response, or result, counts most.

By concentrating on important, long-term results and self-development *purposely* (such as rapport skills, outcome-setting and establishing one's values), training will begin to justify the expense in a way that it has not often managed to do. In other words, we will add beneficial lifetime learning to the food, venue and fellow participants that stay in the memory (if anything does) long after a training event.

A training event offers an important life experience and turning point. This can apply as much to a corporate topic such as creative marketing as to a personal topic such as time management or communication skills. The learning *discovery* process creates the memorable experience and lasting personal value.

EVIDENCE AND MENTAL REHEARSAL

The Evidence criterion of a well-formed outcome (see Chapter 4) increases the chances of success in any outcome. Where training involves physical or manual skills, multi-sensory mental rehearsal pays particular dividends. Mental rehearsal offers several advantages over conventional practice, which can sometimes make skill learning a long, drawn-out affair:

- You can achieve more in a given time. Mentally, we can speed up processes and attain the same imprint, or memory record, as when doing it at real-life speed.

- Often, we carry out an activity perfectly, but then have difficulty repeating it consistently, if ever – a type of beginner's luck. That 'perfect' mind-body record offers you an ideal resource for mental rehearsal. Re-run it while it remains fresh in your mind. Do it a few dozen times and you will simulate the effect of lots of success experience – *evidence* for your mind.

- You can 'monopolize' the system to eliminate worry and negative visualization. The cybernetic 'system' works perfectly anyway, so you may as well use it for conscious purposes. In short, fill your mind with what you want, rather than what you don't want; what you enjoy, rather than what you don't enjoy. Then, when acting purposely, start with a good blueprint, or model – aim for the best.

- You don't fail – or you don't need to. One of the main problems when learning a skill involves carrying failure memories with you. Every action carves out its own neural pathway, and typically, these more than outweigh successes. This produces the strange phenomenon of becoming worse the more you practice. You just confirm the dominant brain imprint, and it grows stronger with each 'miss' in a vicious downward spiral. By not 'missing', your mental rehearsal *experience* adds to your positive, success memories. This increases your self-belief in that particular skill or activity. Once again, you enjoy the *evidence* of success, which even your rational left brain accepts as valid.

- In sports training, we usually face the practicality of travelling to and from a practice ground or building, so this process and other preparation takes longer than the time spent actually practising. Mental rehearsal offers the most efficient means of creating neural networks. In this case, practice literally makes perfect, but it does this amazingly quickly when every try leads to a perfect result. Holing dozens of long putts in a row, or taking a succession of sales orders, would produce the same sort of emotional highs and self-esteem.

The mental skill consists of making the representation as realistic as real life – back to core NLP skills. Maybe you will not achieve 100 per cent reality – but a few more dozen 'hits' might well lead to the same effect. Remember that in most sorts of skills training, you can never attain 100 per cent success (say, in a tennis serve, or darts throw) – it just doesn't happen, unless you have chosen a rather simple skill. We need a few failures to learn from, but not so many that we identify ourself as a loser. The trick lies in tipping the balance of *perceived hits* (internal or external) so that you create a self-fulfilling cybernetic spiral of success.

Rapport in a group

As we saw in Chapter 7, the characteristics of achieving rapport differ slightly when communicating with a group. In a small group, you can often communicate on a person-to-person basis as well as collectively, for instance by pacing and leading. One or two people in rapport act as allies in a group situation. In other words, they will reinforce the rapport and unwittingly support your communication outcomes.

In a training event, you will probably have a group outcome, so in one sense you need to cater for the majority rather than the minority. On the other hand, a single difficult member can spoil things for the rest of the group, let alone the trainer. Often professional trainers spend a good deal of effort in winning over 'difficult' participants. In fact, you have more chance of persuading two or more *uncommitted* people to develop rapport and mutual support. Peer pressure will then act more powerfully than individual rapport skills focused on a resistant person, and in any case more effectively than even the strongest logical argument (if you ever want to 'win' an argument – which you probably won't succeed in doing, even though you might think you have – do it in private).

We have considered examples of the way you can apply pacing and leading skills successfully to extremely irate customers, so do not doubt the effectiveness of the techniques. You need to think more about maintaining your own appropriate state – so that you don't become flustered, act defensively or try to win a point – rather than doubting well-tried communication techniques. Even if you never achieve rapport with one or two people, letting that deflect you from your quest for your outcome can only make matters worse.

If you need to communicate to one person in particular – say, because of their attitude within the group – treat this as a *separate* communication outcome. In this way, you will consider the important factors more clearly, rather than confusing that outcome with your overall aim for the training. Your subsidiary outcome may involve, for instance, securing greater co-operation, or at least a neutral non-involvement, removing the person from the course, and so on. For a well-formed outcome, you will also have other considerations, such as leaving the person satisfied, feeling vindicated, or open to further training of a different sort. The method you choose might involve a chat on your own, a refund of fees, or the tacit co-operation of one or two of the other trainees. In other words, treat the matter as a communication outcome in its own right, and apply what you learnt in Chapter 6.

I have found that in such situations, I can actually gain a long-term friend. This works much like an irate customer who eventually obtains satisfaction, and finishes up more loyal to the company than before the complaint. People want you to show interest in and respect for them, and often our own obstinacy impedes a straightforward communication task.

Anchors

Once you grasp the principles of anchoring covered in Chapter 16, you can apply the process to all kinds of communication, including training programmes. I will offer a few ideas, but you can apply your creative mind to develop anchors that fit your kind of training and personal style.

COLOURS

If you discuss pros and cons, good and bad and so on, use a standardized colour scheme on flipcharts and overhead projector transparencies. This will reinforce the message at the time, and the extra submodality – in this case, a colour – will help to improve recall. When participants contribute, say, to a list of suggestions, swap markers depending on which category the list falls into. Many models comprise three or four elements – such as the 4 Ps Marketing Mix – so you can make use of more than two colours in these cases. If you revisit a particular topic, even days later, use the same colour.

Similarly, use colours for themes or key points, expanded hierarchically onto further transparencies or flipcharts. Edward de Bono uses coloured hats to denote thinking styles – more anchors.

ALLITERATION AND MNEMONICS

Many models use alliteration, such as the Marketing Mix or 4 Ps (Place, Promotion, Price, Product) I have just mentioned. In this case, the initial letter forms another anchor (like colour), and will aid memory. Almost any group of topics or subject headings will lend itself to alliteration with a little creative thinking and reference to a thesaurus while you prepare. Mnemonics, or any memory device, act as anchors, so use them to full advantage. For example, you may have used the SMART (Specific, Measurable, Achievable, Realistic, Timely) goal criteria model that covers some of NLP's well-formed outcomes, and the TOTE (Test, Operate, Test, Exit) described in Chapter 17.

PLACE

When drawing up lists, as well as using colours, you can keep to a consistent position or pattern – say, negative on the left and positive on the right, or bottom and top of a flipchart respectively. Accentuate the anchoring effect further by physically moving to each side of the flipchart as you write down the items. You will thus also anchor the floor space, or position in the room, at either side. When discussing respective elements or topics, along with switching colours, by physically changing your position you will help to anchor the point and promote learning.

Remember that unconscious anchors tend to have a greater effect than conscious ones (such as black = negative and red = positive). I sometimes use two flipcharts (for other reasons), and take the opportunity to use them as left–right anchors just as with two sides of a flipchart or transparency. This means you need to use even more floor space in acting out a place anchor. You introduce a *literally* different viewpoint or perspective, as well as keeping the audience's visual sense alert through movement across the room.

You can use place or position in many ways. Let's say you take up a seat at one end of a U-shaped layout to tell a story by way of illustration, and it elicits a very good response from the trainees – enthusiastic acceptance, humour or whatever. You can return to precisely the same position for your next illustration of that sort, and so anchor a positive state within the group. The same tactic will apply to any position in the room. Bear in mind that you can also anchor your own empowering states to those situations.

Position and posture, as distinct from place, can also act as an anchor, so you can reserve a sitting and standing mode respectively for certain kinds of communication. Sitting on a table can have a different effect than sitting on a chair for instance, perhaps to introduce some informality. Certainly, standing or sitting *inside* a U-shaped seating layout – close to the participants and in easy eye contact range – can lead to very different effects.

Moving across the room will help to maintain visual attention. Movement forms an important aspect of vision, and without movement people may soon lose attention. Professional speakers will walk across the stage from time to time, which exercises the audience's visual sense and attracts attention. People's eyes automatically follow movement, so if you remain immobile for long periods, movement from within the group, outside the window or from another source will probably distract your audience. Moving towards and away from the group also helps – switching from close-up contact to a more formal position at the front. Make these movement changes from time to time, rather than continuously. Aim to maintain attention and motivation, rather than tiring people out.

EQUIPMENT AND SILENCE

Switching on an overhead projector acts as an anchor. Without saying a word, you will draw attention to the screen. A few moments of silence often reinforces the visual message on the screen – undistracted by you and your voice. By staying consistent in the way you allow periods of pregnant silence, you can use this to great effect. Make sure you don't ruin the anchor with a silence resulting from uncertainty, disorganization (while you turn a transparency the right way up, or replace it with the right one) or a memory lapse, for example, otherwise you will anchor any negative emotions to the silence, and vice versa. You cannot stop people making unconscious associations, so make it your job to direct them towards your outcomes.

Apply the same silence tactic using a flipchart. In this case, turning to a new prepared page will attract attention and take time for the audience to absorb. Always allow plenty of time before rushing on – you probably know the subject inside out, but your audience doesn't. For timing, and also to gain rapport, place yourself in the audience's position as though seeing the material for the first time, as will apply to most of your group.

Timing forms an important part of the whole training, from the length of time for which you display a transparency to the lengths of sessions and frequency of breaks. Take a typical flipchart sheet. If you use, say, three main headings with a couple of subheadings each, the first ones in the group will absorb everything, but the slower ones will only read the main headings (set in capitals, which usually associate with a main topic newspaper headline or title – another common anchor). The very fast ones will think about the topics, read 'between the lines' or ruminate on a metaphor or analogy you have incorporated into the words. Generally, the slower trainees set the pace, and you can allow for this by keeping your presentation simple and multi-sensory.

Switching the overhead projector off will usually turn the attention back to you – usually your face. In this case, prepare to make your next point, rather than losing attention temporarily. If not quite ready, leave the projector switched on with the message doing its job. People don't mind having a little time for topics to sink in, and will always occupy their mind anyway. Turning it off will provide your cue for the next point or section of the training. You achieve the same transfer of attention when you turn over the flipchart to reveal a blank sheet – they return their attention to anything central to the occasion.

METAPHOR

A metaphor, or any sensory word, can act as a strong anchor. Sometimes, a group relates particularly well to a metaphor, story or analogy, although you cannot always predict this. It may have relevance to the company, the profession or function of the participants, a topical news issue and so on. Observe carefully the effect of metaphors, illustrations, puns and so on, and use them as anchors during the rest of the programme. This will take their minds back to the earlier material, or training content, to stimulate memory, but, perhaps more importantly, it will anchor the positive state of mind – such as humour, curiosity or fascination – associated with the metaphor.

STATE

You can anchor a positive state in almost any situation, but get ready to grasp the opportunity when it comes. We can rarely predict the effect of a spontaneous, innocuous happening, mistake, word, anecdote, cartoon or exercise on a group or individual. In the case of a useful state, as we saw with metaphors, it pays to anchor it for future use. In this case, the word, metaphor, cartoon or whatever can form the anchor. You can reinforce this to make it more memorable:

- by simple repetition
- by adding another modality, such as writing a word or apposite symbol, drawing a simple diagram (visible) or creating a distinctive sound
- by making a particular gesture or facial expression while saying the word.

Follow the basic criteria for anchoring given in Chapter 16. In a training context, you will need to integrate anchoring techniques into the content and style of the training, rather than making it seem contrived. You will also need to trust the power of anchors, and this comes with experience. To recapture the state, you do not have to repeat a story, but simply refer back to it in an appropriate context. For example, 'Remember the chicken?' will immediately associate listeners with the chicken story or incident, its meaning, and especially the state it produced. In some cases, the tiniest gesture or mannerism will anchor the 'chicken', which in turn anchors the original happening or meaning, in all its sensory detail. Thus, you will produce the same laugh, groan, smile, sigh or other response your anchored communication first produced. This gives us another reason to keep to sensory communication, rather than abstract words and concepts, whenever possible. When you need to refer back to them, you capture the memory much more easily.

Although anchors work well when applied quite mechanically – just like physical matching to create rapport – in practice you can achieve a far stronger effect by using your own creativity, ingenuity, and especially spontaneity – in other words, grasping the right opportunity both to set an anchor, then to use it (fire it) to gain a useful effect later. This comes with experience, of course, but once you start to trust your unconscious mind to 'feed' you with insights, ideas and appropriate mind pictures, you may surprise yourself with your creativity. Anchored graphic metaphors can stay in the memory for years, even after the trainees have long forgotten the subject of the course.

22 *Selling*

Selling on a one-to-one basis draws on many aspects of NLP, and successful salespeople, knowingly or unknowingly, use some of the techniques as a matter of course. Similarly, what we describe as a 'personable' or 'charismatic' character, or 'positive chemistry', often indicates someone who practises the principles of matching and rapport. Selling involves getting inside the customer's mind, or what NLP calls their mental 'map', where the key to success lies. Success also requires self-belief on the part of the salesperson, as well as clear goals and a positive state of mind when faced with inevitable setbacks. This means you need not depend on luck or genetics – the most unlikely people have produced remarkable sales results. You can make the necessary changes, and achieve big improvements, using the principles and techniques of NLP.

In the case of sales presentations to a group, you will find that much of what we covered in the previous chapter will apply. Similarly, visualization has added an important dimension to sales success. Anchoring techniques apply almost universally in interpersonal communication, including selling, and I revisit the topic briefly in this chapter.

Outcomes

Use the 'well-formed outcome' criteria in Chapter 4 to set your personal selling goals. The well-formedness checks will fit any personal goal, including those in a work setting. The usual area of conflict when setting work goals concerns the degree to which we 'own' or identify with the company's goals, a job description, monthly target or suchlike, but you will usually uncover this when carrying out the various 'well-formed' tests. When achieving professional or organizational goals, pay special attention to:

- the ecology questions (see Chapter 4) and the indirect effect of professional success or failure on other parts of your life, and people other than the bosses to whom you report

- different 'positive intentions' that might bring personal values and outcomes into conflict with professional duties and organizational loyalty (see Chapter 5)

- values, such as ethical considerations of products and services, or the common dilemma of sharing your life and time between work and home (you can conduct a values inventory of the sort described in Chapter 5)

- material 'having/getting' goals that may conflict with 'being' goals (see the Life Content Model in Chapter 3)

- maintaining personal control, and not agreeing to personal performance commitments that depend upon other people or factors outside your control (one of the 'well-formedness' criteria in Chapter 4).

OUTCOME OWNERSHIP

To realize the benefits of well-formedness, you need to 'own', personalize or internalize a sales outcome. Unless you *make it yours*, a goal hardly constitutes an outcome in the sense we have used the term throughout this book. Personal outcomes may include:

- keeping your job
- keeping your boss happy
- making the best of an impossible target
- beating a colleague
- playing the system
- keeping the peace at home.

Any selling outcome will have to fit with your personal inclinations, conflicting family interests, values and loyalty. This may involve the product or service you sell, the benefits you cite, the things you know but don't quote, how and to whom you sell, how you relate to your boss, and so on. Once you 'adopt' a handed-down goal as a true, personal outcome, the well-formedness criteria will apply, of course. But, importantly, you will also identify any *non-outcome*, such as an 'impossible' sales target you have not personally accepted, or a particular product you refuse to promote on ethical grounds.

You may then face more fundamental decisions about your present job, values and other outcomes, all of which the processes in Chapters 4 and 5 will tease out. Even an apparently minor sales task can fall foul of conflicting or counteractive, but more important (to you), personal outcomes. In short, to allow for these non-outcome 'losers' (which, because of their nature, attract failure), apply the well-formed outcome tests rigorously. If you can *renegotiate* your work-related sales outcomes – fine. But if it involves an important life decision, you will need to reorder your hierarchies, both of outcomes and values.

SALES PLANNING

As a sales manager or in a sales planning role, you will find several NLP adaptations to setting organizational, divisional or team sales plans. As we have seen, the NLP approach applies more to personal and interpersonal situations than to organizational ones, but analogies abound, such as in the neurological levels model (see Chapter 10). Of course, an organization does not have the neurology of a person, and the idiosyncrasies of the unconscious mind (in fact, it mirrors a low-capacity left brain), but the people who run it, including salespeople, do.

With a little adaptation, outcome-setting similarities abound. For example:

- Your plan will fit systemically into a larger one – say, a corporate plan – that will include other and bigger factors, such as other divisions or profit streams and capital resources.

- The 'positively stated' rule applies. For instance, a strategic plan to avoid the low end of the market, the African continent and so on would gain from expressing it in the positive. Ask: 'What, in that case, do we specifically *want* to achieve?'

- On the face of it, a single organizational goal cannot mirror the different roles and intentions of key people, such as the CEO, sales director, salesperson and so on – let alone the many workers who make up the business. Each ploughs their own furrow, whatever the mission or published corporate plan. This mainly affects the 'control' criterion. Tests for specificity, evidence and so on remain valid with a little adaptation. But even here, the analogy between multiple roles and 'parts' (see Chapter 10) makes much of the NLP approach applicable. For instance, an inanimate business simply has more visible 'parts' to reconcile.

- Corporate 'vision' (a buzzword once in vogue that we still use) can hardly exist other than through individual imagination. Companies don't have vision or imagination. Indeed, management science usually attributes this visionary or 'seer' role to the chairman or CEO.

- The inherent measurability of a business in the form of profit, ratios, employee productivity and suchlike, in contrast to many personal goals, lends itself to the 'evidence' criterion and quantifiable outcome features.

- Sales and other business planning policies increasingly emphasize individual accountability, such as for a budget, key client, product group or region, thus personalizing an organizational or functional goal in formal terms. In this case, hierarchical responsibility and contractual accountability will still need to pass the 'ownership' test. In other words, making a person accountable doesn't mean they will act that way. Only *perception* counts with individual outcomes, or what the person takes on board in holistic, mind-body terms. The 'control' criterion can and should form part of any accountability in a job specification, as much from the company's as from the individual's point of view. Personal failure, on the part of anyone on the payroll, damages the company, so misguided unilateral allocation of accountability will quickly backfire.

- Corporations know the importance of personal motivation, and design rewards and incentives to foster it. Unfortunately, these usually consist of material rewards, and fail to recognize the different individual Life Content (Chapter 3), Convincer and motivation strategies (Chapter 17) – and indeed meta programs (such as towards and away from) (Chapter 15). Apart from running ineffective compensation systems, companies waste valuable human energy they could unleash given knowledge of employees' motivational 'hot buttons'.

Self-belief

An individual's self-image and values will have a major bearing on success. As work occupies such a large part of our life, it will contribute a great deal to our self-beliefs. In this case, the belief will apply mainly *as a salesperson*, or in the function of selling (affirmed in 'I see myself as …'), rather than overall 'self-esteem'. Use the techniques in Chapter 5 to identify relevant beliefs and values (particularly disempowering ones), and to change them.

You can decide not to change a self-belief, of course, which will usually prove negative, or disempowering *in terms of a particular outcome* – in this case, selling as all or part of your job. We saw earlier that you cannot confine well-formed outcome criteria to work or any distinct part of your life. They know no boundaries. Therefore, you may have to face questions about whether you want to stay in your present job or position. This forms an invaluable mid-life 'square peg in round hole' check-up. In my experience, people discover that they occupy the wrong job about a decade too late. Once you accept the holistic application of NLP, you may need to make choices sooner than otherwise. You can always choose to stay put, so 'choice is better than no choice' anyway.

Convincer strategy

The Convincer strategy described in Chapter 17 has special application to selling. With those techniques, you can:

- identify a person's strategy
- identify your own strategy
- use it as a matching feature, such as in the language you use
- allow for it, and/or use it positively in your sales process.

It helps to determine your own Convincer strategy anyway. You may then wish to adapt your sales strategy and processes to match your decision-making inclinations, or change your Convincer strategy. For instance, the nature of the particular selling situation might not allow for time or deferment (on your part), such as when negotiating a price or agreeing to special conditions.

Brain hemisphere language

We considered some examples of the use of right-brain/left-brain language in sales promotion in Chapter 15. The respective characteristics of right- and left-brain thinking have their own language – we talk the way we think. A left-brain thinker will talk about detail, analysis, component parts, logic, cause and effect, necessity and suchlike. A right-brain thinker, on the other hand, will use spatial and visual terms, and refer to the big, holistic picture, hunches, intuition, brainwaves and 'possibility' rather than 'necessity'.

Right–left brain language appears frequently in marketing, whether for strategic positioning or promotion such as advertising. Left-brain strategies involve the use of 'justifiers' – or sound reasons to buy – such as statistics, product features and attributes, measurable benefits, credible endorsement, practical usefulness and value for money. We need to justify, both to others and ourselves, buying behaviour, and make remarks such as:

- I really needed a new dress.
- Well, it was on special offer, so it was worth it.
- A bargain like this won't come round again.
- It will last forever, so it's good value in the long run.

The left brain likes a sound, logical reason. If it doesn't have one, it invents one. Right-brain strategies, on the other hand, appeal to emotion, aspirations, the senses, the present moment, 'belonging' and worthy 'causes'. A dominant 'right-brainer', for example, will:

- experience the thrill of anticipation
- enjoy novelty and discovery

- value the present moment and a new 'experience'
- accept uncertainty and risk, including when buying
- bring emotion into decisions and buying behaviour, and need to 'feel right'
- want to express their identity when choosing a supplier, brand or product.

These marketing strategies translate into promotional copy and selling techniques, of course. In essence, they involve the NLP processes of getting into the mind or mental 'map' of the customer, then 'matching' it for rapport and 'perceived likeness'. In mass marketing, or when you don't know the bias of a customer, the secret lies in appealing to *both* heart and mind. One advertisement for personal loans ran 'You might find that life's little pleasures become a lot more affordable', subtly combining right-brain indulgences with left-brain economics. A right-brain approach might run 'Can you see yourself ... just imagine ... go on, spoil yourself', but the left brain will probably object before any chequebook appears. You will therefore need to add a left-brain justifier like 'it makes sense ... you deserve it ... it's excellent value' to tip the balance and secure dual-brain acceptance.

You can also apply brain dominance language in person-to-person selling. Use it as a communication matching technique for rapport (see Chapter 7), and also as a route to the other person's own meta program (see Chapter 15). As with Convincer strategy and any other meta programs, identify your own strategy first. Even if you occupy the opposite end of the continuum, you can use this knowledge to achieve rapport in a purposeful way. As we have seen, you can change a program or strategy if you wish to. You have control. In practice, as a professional, flexibility or adaptability (an important meta program in its own right) will stand you in good stead in most communication situations, including selling.

State

Attitude and self-belief account for a large part of success, but a salesperson will also succumb to day-to-day feelings as much as anyone, if not more, due to the pressure of securing results. Personal circumstances may also account for these swings of temperament, but all too often they have neither rhyme nor reason. Use change techniques such as 'swish' patterns (Chapter 20) and anchoring (Chapter 16) to recall empowering states. For instance, use them, in conjunction with submodality switching techniques (Chapter 9), to change negative associations, such as the effect a particular client or colleague has on you. The anchoring techniques in Chapter 16 have special application to high-speed state changes, and most successful salespeople have developed effective anchors of their own. You only need a couple of winning resources – such as vivid memories of specific achievement or a state of mind – to form the basis of a successful state-of-mind strategy. Remember that you need not restrict your resources trawl to specific selling memories. You have probably experienced the state you want in other areas of your life, or when younger, so don't underestimate your innate resources.

Anchors

I have referred to the use of anchors in accessing states, and they apply equally to many areas of selling. You can anchor a positive *customer* state, for instance, based on a past successful sale, a previous meeting that went well, or even an earlier part of a sales meeting. You don't need to waste useful customer states you have already 'won'. You will have learnt enough in Chapter 16 to apply anchors in this way. Anchors follow simple principles, and any limits lie only in your ingenuity when using them. The simplest gesture, like touching the customer's arm, can anchor their emotional state at that time, or you can use a particular phrase or form of words, or both. The state may related to a particular product feature or benefit, so again you have an anchor you can trigger by way of reminder, even if through a tenuous link in a future sales meeting. You can't predict these positive occasions, of course, so you need to have your anchoring skills at the ready.

In the remaining chapters of Part 2, you will find some other aspects of selling applications, such as negotiation and presenting to a group. Don't rely on one particular technique, but if you must, at least don't restrict yourself to just one or two specific applications. Mix and match.

23 *Negotiating*

Much of the earlier material in Part 2 also applies to negotiation. Negotiation forms a large part of some sales functions, for instance, depending, among other things, on level of seniority and the nature of the product or service. Here, I will cover some particular aspects of negotiation.

Interim outcomes

Larger-scale negotiations may involve stages, or interim outcomes. Often, professional negotiators set out to move just one step nearer their goal at a meeting or session, rather than trying to achieve their ultimate objective. The same well-formedness criteria you learnt in Chapter 4 apply to each objective. You can then compare the ultimate negotiating objective to the higher goal (say, happiness, fulfilment) towards which an interim, or stepping-stone, outcome usually aims.

You may need to chunk down your negotiating objective to a greater extent than normal. This stems from the fact that, by nature, your outcome in the communication will have to cope with an *opposing* outcome of similar importance to the other party. You have different goals, otherwise you would not need to negotiate. Ascertaining the reality of this difference, and using it for your purposes, will form part of the negotiation process.

'Stage' outcomes reflect not the value or scale of a negotiation, but rather the need to make changes at the appropriate speed. Remember that you need to influence *perceptions* – 'reality', according to the NLP model, plays little part in person-to-person communication.

A step-by-step approach also recognizes the different Convincer strategies at work, and – even more important – the universal human resistance to change. In the case of a top-league negotiation, most corporate mergers fail *culturally*, and often result in a later demerger. This confirms how even the most professional operators underestimate the human aversion to change. As well as the sheer practicalities of organizational level changes, negotiating incremental outcomes will accommodate the complex, opposing perceptions of the parties more effectively.

You will not gain anything by aiming too high – we saw in Chapter 4 the importance of the perceived size of an outcome. Nor will you gain by aiming too low, either in your interim or overall objectives. However, in this case, the judgement does not just relate to you and your motivation threshold, but to the other party, and the nature and circumstances of the negotiation. Clearly, the 'content-free' NLP characteristic does not apply in negotiation, when you will usually require intricate knowledge of your subject. Communication and negotiation skills simply help you to make better use of your knowledge and resources. Nevertheless, the *principles* of good communication, and the basic interpersonal skills you have learnt, do not alter with variations in content or scale. Expert communicators can therefore, with adequate briefing, apply their skills to other forms of negotiation, such as mediation.

Convincer strategy

The Convincer strategy applies particularly in negotiation, and thus in a far wider range of applications than selling. For instance, it will apply in conflict-resolution between management and workers, company and union, in various mediation processes, corporate mergers and demergers, supplier and partnership arrangements, family feuds, generational battles and so on – in short, wherever individuals with different needs and desires wish to reach a mutually acceptable outcome.

Notice how the Convincer strategy will suggest interim (or stage) outcomes, regardless of the factors we have just considered. Think, particularly, how the time-period factor might affect people in very different ways. For this reason, macho last-minute pressure and phoney deadlines may backfire. People tend to keep to their strategy whatever the logic.

CREATING PERCEPTIONS

In protracted negotiations or mediation, you will usually have time to elicit Convincer strategies. By taking account of this as a communication as well as a specific negotiation feature, you can add an important dimension to matching and rapport. In other words, 'perceived likeness' in decision-making – say, between two rapid decision-makers, or parties who both need plenty of time – will afford an important rapport match. Remember, for matching purposes you do not need to match innately – in terms of your preferred convincer strategy, as if trying to match blood types. Rather, as with physiological or sensory matching, you need to transmit the perception of 'likeness': speak the other person's language, whatever your own.

Convincer strategy itself can create conflict, of course, just like any differing meta program. For example, one person might want to come to an immediate decision, while another, needing time, feels unduly pressurized – regardless of the terms or content of the negotiation. Each party may then wrongly question the intentions or integrity of the other party. In fact, you can apply negotiation skills to resolving any conflict, including negotiation style or organizational processes – you can negotiate *anything* – including whether and how to negotiate.

For instance, it sometimes helps to agree explicitly to a decision 'schedule', and maybe to conclude within a certain period. Alternatively, an agreed schedule could allow for more than one meeting to cover different milestones or components, together with telephone and e-mail contact, and so on. Such a preliminary schedule may itself demand negotiation. However, if it happens overtly, it will allow for the different Convincer strategies at work, and will engender trust. At the same time, a simple pre-agreement, such as venue and timing, will also give opportunity for a 'chunked-up' consensus very early in the process. In other words, the more you can agree on (about anything) the better. If both parties run 'automatic' strategies and want to reach a conclusion quickly, a decision frame (see Chapter 19) can save much time and effort, and avoid unnecessary conflict.

Chunking

All the principles of rapport and good communication apply in both selling and negotiation. Sometimes, you need more than a yes/no decision. This might apply in the case of negotiation, where you cannot foresee the topics you will address, or when the sale does not follow a predictable sort of process. In such cases, the need for rapport increases, as you will probably have to venture further into each other's 'maps'. But the process will probably take longer anyway, so you will have more opportunity to pace and lead, identify meta programs, and apply your communication skills in general.

CHUNKING UP

Chunking also has many communication applications, and negotiation provides a good example. The 'sleight of mouth' technique in Chapter 20 illustrates the almost limitless scope for chunking. By chunking upwards, you will usually gain *agreement*, even though of little or no financial or material value. For example:

- We all want to come to a successful conclusion.
- We all agree on the importance of honesty and mutual respect.
- We all have rights.
- We all have busy lives.
- We all have to make a living.
- We want a long-term relationship.

This helps to maintain vital rapport, and can provide a way out of an impasse. Remember, for every 'yes' you secure, the next one usually comes easier. A succession of positive nods can have an unstoppable effect, so relatively minor 'yes' answers can add up to produce a major negotiating advantage.

CHUNKING DOWN

On the other hand, chunking down can often move a negotiation on and prove valuable – for example, focusing on a specific product feature, or particular terms such as availability, delivery, back-up, service, warranties and so on. A fairly minor agreement, even if you have to concede something, can give a great boost to the overall negotiation. For example:

- I'm sure we can agree on that.
- What specifically bothers you?
- What can we clear up quickly?
- I can do something for you on …

We don't all value things the same, or logically or consistently, so an innocuous, low-value point conceded on your part may have disproportionate value to the other party. Your observational skills will help to identify these values by the body language they produce. 'Soft' Meta Model questioning (see Chapter 12) usually helps to tease out the specific items of value.

Part of a win–win negotiation strategy will involve *synergistic* trade-offs. Each party wants certain things that the other party doesn't, and these often constitute items low in monetary value. Conceding specific items also offers a face-saving opportunity that may have great *negotiating* value in maintaining progress and rapport. Synergy exists anyway, in the very nature of negotiating 'give and take'. It therefore pays to identify any such items, even if you have to divide their value two ways to arrive at a true win–win outcome.

Chunking up and down will usually create these opportunities. Check back on 'sleight of mouth' language patterns (see Chapter 20) for examples. The Meta Model in Chapter 12 also includes examples of chunk-down questions. The Milton Model language patterns (also in Chapter 12) can help to chunk up, as can metaphor (Chapter 14). However formal a communication, people remain subject to suggestion through appropriately vague language. Similarly, given appropriate questions or 'responses' we all respond to Meta Model questioning, and will readily divulge deep meaning (literally, what we have *in mind*) that can have value in negotiation.

Group negotiation

For group negotiation, refer back to the group aspects of communication covered in Chapter 6, and pacing and leading individuals in a team or group in Chapter 7. As we have just seen, you can also exploit the different Convincer strategies in play (see Chapter 17).

In any group negotiation or sales presentation, try to determine the real decision-makers and influencers, or you risk discharging all your ammunition in the wrong direction. In one sense, you cannot negotiate with a group – just with individuals. In the same way, you cannot negotiate with an organization or legal entity, just their representatives as *people*. However, as with training outcomes, your overall outcome may influence tactics and techniques at one level. Often, for example, you can exploit ranking differences, animosity and political in-fighting within a negotiation group (setting one against another), so set outcomes at both levels – group and individual – or have multiple outcomes, such as applied to the formal decision-maker, a key influencer, the financial executive or purse-holder, an important doorkeeper, and so on. You may need to set a different objective for each, as subsidiary objectives to your overall negotiation outcome.

Frames

We saw in Chapter 19 that frames have special uses in meetings. This applies especially in negotiation, where recording decisions, tracking agreements, maintaining progress within a time schedule and keeping to material matters can assume special importance. Check back if you need to for details about different types of frames, such as 'agreement' and 'outcome' and how you can incorporate them into a negotiation meeting.

24 *Interviews and Appraisals*

In this chapter, I shall deal mainly with job interviews, but you can easily relate what you learn to any one-to-one interview, such as with a supplier or client. In the case of a job appraisal, you will probably know the other person well, and may also have knowledge of meta programs and other useful characteristics – or you can identify them prior to an appraisal or similar important meeting (see Chapter 15). 'First impressions' only happen once, of course, so this factor will apply in most job interviews. But even this high-speed, intuitive phenomenon depends on the nuances of body language, voice and the factors of rapport and 'perceived likeness' covered in Chapters 6 and 7, so the communication principles fit specialized forms of communication such as these very well.

Proxemics

Chapter 7 explains the importance of positioning, or proxemics. Consider this before any important person-to-person meeting, such as an interview, appraisal session, confidential chat or formal warning. Of course, achieving optimal position works best when in your own office or on your own patch, when you can exercise control and make any preparations necessary. However, we sometimes have a choice in other situations ('Where would you like to sit?'), so you can think about which position might best help your outcome. Position in relation to the other person can have importance for both the interviewer and interviewee. You can probably apply some of the positioning factors in Chapter 21 relating to training.

Outcomes

What you have learnt about outcome setting, mostly from Chapter 4, will apply in almost any situation. In the case of an interview or appraisal, you will normally have the time to decide on a specific outcome, unlike many less formal or spontaneous communications. Otherwise, the principles apply consistently. Take account of the *effect* you want to achieve, as well as any other communications outcomes, such as to transfer knowledge or understanding. In such a planned situation, you may find that a checklist helps – what you need to find out, information you need to impart, and so on. Why not memorize it, and devote your 'uptime' attention to important observation?

Consider the effect you want to create as integral to your outcome, rather than a separate outcome from, say, obtaining and giving information. For example, you may want the interviewee or member of staff:

- to feel you have treated them fairly and respectfully
- to feel you will act impartially towards other candidates

- to feel they have all the information they wanted about the job and the organization
- to feel comfortable about asking sensitive questions, such as to do with salary and conditions, or the ethical policy of the company
- to feel you have given them whatever time they needed
- to sense that you take a genuine interest in them as a person
- to sense that you value their opinion, whatever their age and experience.

Usually, such positive feelings will help you to elicit full and honest information, as well as portraying the organization positively – usually part of the job interview intention in a two-way process. If you want a person to feel angry or pressured, say, to see how they react, treat that outcome separately and don't let it affect the rest of your aims, not least your outcome for the overall meeting or communication.

SCENARIO FUTURE PACING

Other aspects of outcomes may require more of a right-brain approach. In a job interview, you may wish, for example, to determine whether a person will get along with an existing team, a particular middle manager, your typical customer and so on, or whether they will command the respect and loyalty of subordinates. We usually carry out this sort of judgement intuitively as a visualization process, 'seeing' the person in the sort of situation they might encounter. It may happen by default in 'first impressions'.

Normally, an interviewee cannot do this in respect of the hiring company, as they will not know the people, culture or environment, so formal questioning will rarely help. No formula exists for this 'reading' or future pacing process, on either side. It requires trust in your own unconscious processes. We assess people all the time, and especially on our first meeting. We sometimes make errors, although it seems that women usually do better than men. This underlies the importance of core skills like visualization. Some people seem to weigh people up very easily, but in any case we know that 'neuro-skills' improve with practice.

You will rarely have to make an instant decision at an important interview or appraisal meeting. Indeed, unless for very special reasons, we can rarely justify a hasty decision about such a major investment on the part of the organization. Often, we gain an intuitive feeling about a person a little *after* the first meeting – maybe after work when thinking about something quite different, or before dropping off to sleep that night. So you don't need to force an instant judgement – even if you could. Knowledge of your own Convincer strategy furnishes you with choices about appropriate decision-making policies in light of the nature of any communication. Any long-term investment will usually justify a commitment of time (say, a further less formal meeting with the candidate), even if contrary to macho management fashion, and maybe your own comfortable Convincer strategy. By keeping your *outcome* in mind, you will get these intuitive judgements right much more frequently.

RAPPORT

The greater the importance of a communication, the more you need to gain early rapport. A staff appointment, at any level, can have serious consequences for an organization, and a large financial investment usually goes into making the right decision. The length and format of a job interview allows concerted matching, in interests and values as well as physiology and voice. This means that your NLP rapport skills will reap dividends. If you wish, you can encourage a person to relax, open up or let their hair down, using pacing and leading techniques. You have the tools.

Conversely, you will not get far without rapport skills. Sometimes, we don't hit it off with a person, yet could have avoided a lack of rapport by simple body, voice and language matching.

An interviewer's or appraiser's objectives will usually include objectivity, which you can best achieve from a position of rapport. Even if you don't like a person, you will achieve the communication outcome more effectively. In most job interview cases, you will not work with the person yourself anyway. Your understanding of the NLP model and individual maps will help you avoid the worst pitfalls of prejudice and mindreading (see Chapter 12).

Finally, check back on techniques for breaking rapport in Chapter 7. You may find this useful to end an interview or extended appraisal meeting.

Values and self-beliefs

You will probably wish to learn as much as possible about a potential employee. This includes their self-beliefs, values, ambitions and suchlike. The questioning process for ascertaining values in Chapter 5 provides a sound basis for eliciting this information. Combine this with sensory acuity, and core observation skills. You will build up these skills over a period by consciously watching, listening, and thinking about your interpersonal dealings.

Remember that a couple of negative self-beliefs can ruin a person's potential for learning and achievement (look at the list of examples in Chapter 5). People can change if they want to, of course, but you may need to decide whether you wish to invest time and effort in change in the case of a newly hired member of staff. Given a shortlist of technically suitable candidates, you may well achieve the 'values match' you want in the organization without practising mental surgery. The person will undergo enough early learning and changes anyway. Keep your 'people risk' to a minimum.

Cultural change usually happens over time, but a change-averse person with conservative meta programs (see Chapter 15) may give you more problems than you bargained for if cultural adherence falls high in your priorities. In fact, cultural mismatch poses the main problems in corporate mergers, long before human resources staff introduce their formal communication policies. You will probably find the above scenario future pacing skill the most appropriate for judging cultural 'fit' at the interview stage – but meta program techniques don't come with a warranty.

You now have powerful ways to elicit values (Chapter 4) and outcomes (also Chapter 4). Ask successively: 'And what is important to you about ...?' This will usually take the candidate into 'new territory' – they will have to address personal issues they may not have considered for a long time, if ever. Similarly, after identifying personal goals, follow up with: 'And what then?' This will also extend their thinking and draw upon their (unprepared) unconscious mind. Aim to get beyond any façade, or rehearsed script. Meta model responses offer a powerful tool for gaining access to 'deep structure' information.

The effect of this values-elicitation process varies greatly. Some people love talking about themselves, however personal and revealing the questioning. Others resent the intrusion, and feel vulnerable and intimidated. From a position of rapport, however, you can usually overcome conflict. In any event, by means of a few well-designed questions you can probably find out pertinent information that you could not have gained from pages of form-filling.

A popular tactic for interviewing involves inducing in the candidate a perturbed or wrong-footed state so that their true character emerges. This can sometimes take a brutal, or at least 'unecological' form – characteristic of the unenlightened, macho management vogue. Unless you have a 'positive intention' to impress, bully or whatever, if you want to produce honesty and spontaneity, the values-elicitation process will achieve your aim more effectively.

25 *Coaching*

Almost all the NLP one-to-one communication techniques described in this book apply to personal coaching. In particular, modelling and mental strategies account for much recent interest and success, whether in sport, business or any other area of personal coaching. Unlike group communication, such as applies to training, you will need very little fine-tuning to apply all your Part 1 learning to coaching. This confirms once again the universal application of NLP principles and their adaptability within the general field of interpersonal communication.

We have also seen a rapid evolution of these models and methods in comparison with more traditional communication theory and with management science. Enthusiastic NLP practitioners and novice readers of NLP books and articles constantly seek out new applications in their many different fields of work, and bring their functional knowledge and skills to bear. In the light of this, I want to emphasize the need for *creativity* and *ingenuity* (a right-brain approach), *flexibility* (as in the Four-stage Achievement Model) and *originality* (drawing on your unique 'map' of experience resources), rather than to portray coaching – or any other of the communication applications covered in Part 2 – as in any way 'special'. 'There is nothing new under the sun' anyway, not least when it comes to human communication. However, by understanding how your mind works – including feelings, values and beliefs – you can perform more effectively – in fact, in NLP parlance, with *excellence*. This applies especially to the many kinds of activities that we do well *naturally*, or cybernetically, as we saw in Chapter 3, albeit, perhaps, with some relearning, or redrawing of our mental map. None the less, personal coaching does have a few peculiar characteristics that deserve particular attention, and in this chapter I shall confine myself to these.

Personal outcomes

I cannot overemphasize the importance of well-formed outcomes in any aspect of personal achievement. Most top sports coaches seem to achieve more through their ability to maintain motivation and discipline than their ability to identify and improve technical skills – a basic coaching requirement, but not one that accounts for excellence. Many top sportspeople do not have the ability to pass on their technical skills, let alone their strategy for motivation. Conversely, some of the best coaches did not reach the highest level in their specialization. Anyone who hires a coach will probably have ambition to start with. The role of the coach will therefore involve turning desires, dreams and hopes into well-formed, realistic outcomes – in other words, ensuring they happen. This makes NLP, with its emphasis on change and practical results, ideal for successful modern-day coaching. The outcome process in Chapter 4, in particular, has proven effective in coaching as well as state-control (for example, see switching submodalities in Chapter 9) and many other applications. For the coach themself, *communication* outcomes – to enter right into the person's mind – will sit higher in their priorities.

As it happens, sports coaches used visualization techniques for many years before they started to appear in business and other forms of training. For many top sportspeople, visualizing success and the dream of medals and fame go right back to childhood, and form a large part of their lives. This compares with others who have not grasped the core processes of realistic sensory representation – serious dreaming, if you like – although they clearly possess the technical skills. Such a person may repeatedly come close to winning a championship, or clinching a business deal, then seem to throw it away without explanation. Something gives way. Effective coaching needs to include mind control (your own, rather than others) in precisely such situations.

Strategies

'Natural' champions operate effective control strategies anyway, but often don't know how they do it. This means that in the event of a lapse, they don't know what action to take, and might wrongly attribute their failure to a technical weakness. Typically, months of technical correction follows, their natural style and skills become compromised, and a long wilderness period may ensue. By understanding your own success strategies, you can first ascertain what has changed mentally to account for the change in results, but you can also *make* changes at this level – in fact, to submodalities. This means that you can purposely improve mental strategies as well as technical, physical ones. Some top sportspeople assert that the 'mental side' accounts for 80 to 90 per cent of success. The coach plays a big role in this area, whether training for DIY change techniques, guiding through the processes to 'install' changes, or using 'artfully vague' Milton language patterns (see Chapter 12) to reach the unconscious mind.

Content-free coaching

Although belatedly, NLP methods have now taken their place in managerial and 'executive' coaching, especially at Board and CEO level, where, presumably, the earnings potential – as with top sportspeople – justifies the investment. In some cases, psychology coaches cover both sports and management, and use largely the same methods. The content-free characteristics of much NLP training makes this apparently incongruous practice credible. As we have seen, facing a large audience has remarkable similarities to facing a little golf ball in certain circumstances. By focusing on the brain networks that run our state in *any* situation – understanding and changing the map – we avoid having to fully understand the content or technicalities of a behaviour. The recent emphasis on emotional intelligence has made NLP change techniques a more important factor in coaching. Interpersonal or 'people' skills have benefited from intrapersonal skills and self-knowledge based on the NLP model. At the same time, the communication presuppositions (Chapter 2) and techniques (Chapter 7, such as pacing and leading) have revolutionized classic communication theory.

Modelling

Coaching has direct links to the modelling strategies you learnt in Chapters 17 and 18. Identifying a client's strategies will provide a good foundation for change work. In the case of an extended coaching programme, you can probably make changes at a higher meta program level – refer back to the main meta programs in Chapter 15, almost all of which will apply in a coaching situation. When eliciting these programs, by following the strategy questions (see Chapter 17), you will find that you also identify values and beliefs (see Chapter 5). Success often occurs at this level, rather than in the form of outward behaviour we can mechanically replicate. As with outcomes, your client can identify and change values and beliefs using the specific patterns and techniques in Chapter 5. In practice, just a couple of negative self-beliefs may account for a major blockage in performance. Usually, no degree of technical or behavioural improvement *whatsoever* will overcome the effects of such a self-belief meta program.

On modelling, the 'special resource' we usually want to model consists of what we usually term 'natural talent', or 'unconscious competence'. The coach works on a factor that the subject already possesses, but wishes to develop. The danger lies in interfering with this natural talent in the belief that a physical weakness or technicality accounts for poor results. The 80 to 90 per cent mental part becomes ignored. It stays out of sight, takes much more knowledge and skill to do anything about, and even the best coach finds it hard to 'sell' anyway. Amidst frustration and incomprehension, the natural talent gets driven out by technical interference with strokes, swings and posture. Well-meaning sports coaches (almost always ex-players) strive to make an essentially *unconscious* skill *conscious*. Self-consciousness and a newly surfacing negative self-belief kill the vestige of true talent. Scores of household-name sportspeople have followed this wilderness route, and in very few cases have fully recaptured their lost innate talent.

In executive coaching, in place of scientific swing and stroke analysis, managers face conditioning in systems, measurement, case studies, analytical techniques, buzz concepts, and the trappings of management science. In the process, they may lose their natural people skills, feelings and gut instincts. You can identify all this by applying the outcome criteria and beliefs and values checks to your client, who unconsciously *knows* wherein success lies. True skill happens easily, comfortably and *naturally*. In contrast to basic skills training, true coaching usually means releasing resources that already exist, and adding right-brain mental skills to do full justice to physical talents and left-brain intellect.

All of NLP concerns modelling. Everything in Part 1 will help you to successfully model the excellence around you. Holistic modelling seeks to identify and emulate all the factors of success that our extraordinary mind-body system comprises.

Communication

Coaching calls for a special relationship. If part of a programme, this shares the same sort of problems as any close relationship. In this case, clear, common objectives will go a long way towards maintaining the necessary rapport. Remember, however, that effective communication need not imply continual consensus and agreement between the parties. The trick involves making important changes, perhaps in beliefs and attitudes, whilst maintaining moment-to-moment rapport, and certainly a continuing relationship. You will need pacing and leading skills, for instance. Coaching does call on advanced NLP skills, but you will find no effective limit to the changes you can bring about.

Usually, the relationship relies on positive chemistry, and a good coach tends to economize on words, and certainly injunctions and criticism that interfere with a person's natural talents. Except in the case of people of just such a temperament, this does not happen by accident, so you need to deliberately choose the nature and style of your communication. As usual, in NLP no hard and fast rules exist, but, as usual, a clear outcome, especially regarding the communication effects or 'responses' you want to achieve, a solid understanding of the communication presuppositions, and trust in your own unconscious mind, will all but guarantee success.

26 *Speeches and Presentations*

Tips and techniques

All the applications for training (see Chapter 21) apply to other forms of speaking to a relatively small group. In this chapter, I summarize techniques and tips that will prove useful, beginning with the following:

- Set a well-formed outcome for your communication, including the effect you want to achieve (see Chapter 6). Spend time ensuring the ecology is right. This process may also identify values and beliefs pertinent to your outcome (see Chapter 4).

- Enter an appropriate state for your specific communication outcome (see Chapter 6), and make full use of positive anchors (see Chapter 16) to achieve this dependably and consistently. Draw upon helpful previous states, whether connected with public speaking or not.

- Visualize, or 'future pace', your speech in 'associated' state (seeing as if through your own eyes in as much realistic sensory detail as you can).

- Rehearse what you need to grow familiar with. That doesn't mean practising in front of a mirror – the only perspective you will find it impossible to recreate on the day without your mirror. If you do this, you will only see what the audience sees. In fact, what *you* see – the audience – accounts for the typical public speaker's stage fright. Mental rehearsal involves making your behaviour seem familiar, and avoiding surprises like a 'sea of strange faces'.

- Practise mentally repeatedly. Do anything a few times and it becomes easier and more enjoyable. You do this by making repeated memory imprints of sights, sounds and feelings, as realistically as you can. As we have already seen, you can practise mentally many times faster than in real life. Also you don't (or needn't) make mistakes that remain as negative memories.

- Become 'familiar' in any other way you can by sensible preparation. For instance, it may help to visit the venue and get a feel for the place from where you will stand, even if just for a few moments during a coffee break. Real life includes not just every sense, but every happening, as well as the people and surroundings. If you cover this sensory preparation well, on the day of your speech you will have a sense of *déjà vu*, and the confidence that only comes from having 'been there, done that'. Your mind doesn't know the difference, provided you future pace realistically.

- Incorporate into your mental rehearsal any notes you will use (see below on the use of notes), or a verbatim script if custom requires this. You won't realize what can go wrong with following notes when making a speech (a great deal) unless you have used them a number of times – in other words, unless you have experience. If your normal job doesn't involve this, you will need to *create* this, and any other 'detail' experience, by mental rehearsal.

- Respect and like your audience, and incorporate this into your mental rehearsal. To help achieve these states, feel free to switch submodalities and re-create 'content'. For example, make each face the respective colour of the rainbow, make the average height of your audience four foot six, or add a helpful musical background.

- The technique consists of anchoring an empowering state, by doing whatever you have to do mentally. You will not need to change much anyway. For example, you can leave them all with stony faces and half-closed eyes, but make the stone the best marble, the faces truly classical, like rows of Greek busts, and the sleepy eyes bespectacled with cheap frames. Anchor all this (see Chapter 16), and you can almost guarantee the association on the day, and the state it produces.

- Don't annoy or embarrass people. Most audiences start out on the speaker's side. Who in an audience likes to feel embarrassed, make enemies of complete strangers and waste valuable time? Only when *you* create embarrassment, annoyance, a feeling of discourtesy and so on will you suffer the consequences. However, an audience makes up its mind quickly (first impressions – hence the importance of your opening), and does not forgive readily once wronged. Remember the communication presupposition concerning the responsibility of the communicator. It means you can't blame the audience, however tempting. With no one else to blame, you may as well do it properly from the start.

- Stand up, shout up, and then shut up. The biggest problem for amateur speakers comes when they have to shut up and sit down, so it pays to mentally rehearse your closing remarks. People remember how you start and how you finish, and not much in between. A speech can therefore hinge on grabbing early attention through your introduction, and leaving a lasting impression through your conclusion. I suggest you *memorize* your closing words, then you can move to these with confidence when you know you have to stop. This means you will project your message more clearly to your audience, and not grind to a halt. Better to leave them wanting a bit more than feeling they have had too much.

- Check that any self-beliefs, in the specific area of public speaking you want to succeed in empower rather than disempower you. Using what you learnt in Chapter 5, you can identify and change such beliefs.

- You can use anchoring techniques of the sort described in Chapter 21 for training a group. In a fairly short speech, consider anchoring, say, your key points (experts recommend keeping to three), and an introductory statement. Refer back to these in your conclusion to bring the whole presentation together. As we saw, you can anchor a word, a question, a statement, a quotation, a metaphor and a positive audience response state – in fact, anchor anything you can use as a resource to reinforce your communication and make it more memorable.

- If you do not use visual aids, you can add visual contact by gestures, facial expression, posture and movement around the floor space (all the matching possibilities covered in Chapters 6 and 7). Bear all this in mind if you have choices, such as using a lectern, standing or sitting, using a microphone and so on. Often, you will have a good deal of freedom, so aim to create plenty of choices and exercise control.

- The shorter your notes, the better. Long notes may tempt you to read them, and you then risk losing your place. Consider using symbols and little pictures to remind you of key points (my book *Say it with Pictures* covers this in detail). A picture paints a thousand words. This avoids verbatim monologues, saves much paper (an A4 sheet can serve for a long speech if you prepare your subject well), and avoids the familiar experience of words blurring into a mass of nothing, or simply losing your place. By working from key words or symbols that anchor a topic, illustration, joke or whatever, you will not depend unduly on your notes as a crutch. By avoiding the need to read out a script, you will not have to look down – you have no excuse to. Basic courtesies of this sort will improve your audience ratings, whatever you actually say.

Cybernetic outcomes

We often consider skills in oratory a gift. However, few gifted 'natural' speakers could begin to describe their secrets of success, let alone train other people. In fact, we all have strategies that operate in this way to produce what NLP terms 'unconscious competence'. These operate in the cybernetic way described in Chapter 3. This model applies to every aspect of outcomes, from achieving a certain self-belief through carrying out a physical activity on 'autopilot' to entering the appropriate state for the job in hand. You can apply these aspects of cybernetic goal-achieving to any of the main applications in this part of the book, but I will cover them here in the context of public speaking.

In each application of a skill or competence, we harness the elements of a mind-body cybernetic or goal-achieving system. Self-image forms an unconscious target in specific areas such as public speaking, drawing, playing a sport or suchlike. As we saw in Chapter 5, self-belief, or self-image, affects everything we do, and may well constitute the single most important factor in human success. As a nominalization, belief – and self-belief – comes high up the neurological levels, towards Maslow's self-actualization and the identity in most models of human need and motivation. A low self-belief in public speaking will often account for the majority of success or failure.

The cybernetic system requires a *sensory* target. You can achieve this by expressing either your belief, or what comprises, supports or gives evidence of your belief. One belief change pattern (see Chapter 5) involves visualizing more than one behaviour or experience that provides this support or evidence. Sensory experience usually works in a very common-sense way. In this case, your behaviour defines you – your values, beliefs, identity and so on. A person who gets on well with people, can empathize and easily make friends will find it hard to resist the 'people person' or 'good communicator' self-belief. The behaviour supports and *proves* the belief.

Even the critical, self-doubting conscious (left-brain) mind will in the end submit to evidence or rational argument. The unconscious mind simply registers the sensory pictures – or behaviour memories – and categorizes them according to previously held beliefs and values. This works in a hit-and-miss way, forming either a virtuous or vicious, self-fulfilling spiral of behaviour – hence people with irrational 'can't do' beliefs and people (not so many) with equally irrational 'can do' beliefs.

SELF-BELIEF

The crucial negative self-belief factor in public speaking (far more than in training and selling) justifies a few further remarks. Let's remind ourselves of a typical self-belief origin. We covered this briefly in Chapter 5. Valerie, a six-year-old, overhears a favourite aunt saying to her mother: 'Isn't George bright? Fancy reading all those words and doing sums.' Valerie knows what 'bright' means, as she has heard this before about some of her classmates, but until now didn't link her brother George with 'bright'. Now she thinks: 'I wish I was bright.' Seeds of doubt grow, as further random comments at school and playing with friends in the following days seem to 'fit' this idea. Then a friends calls her 'stupid'. A self-fulfilling spiral begins to gain momentum as a tender self-belief, 'I'm not very bright', takes root.

In her mid-forties, Valerie still considers herself 'not very bright'. Indeed, she does have difficulty with 'academic' subjects, reads more slowly than other people, tends to lose her train of thought from time to time, and so on. Now, even when her behaviour and exam results in an Open University course give evidence to the contrary, she still justifies her self-belief, making what to close friends seem like silly excuses for her fluke success in anything 'academic'.

The unconscious mind keeps this bandwagon rolling. Mental filters interpret any sensory experience according to well-entrenched beliefs and attitudes that, amazingly, *reinforce* the unfounded belief, rather than causing doubt and a will to believe differently.

Repeated visualization of empowering experiences will tip the balance even in the case of a powerful self-belief. Self-talk also helps. In this case, you reaffirm with your conscious mind (the language side of the brain) the abstraction (belief) that the sensory experience – through visualization – unconsciously confirms.

The other belief-change pattern described in Chapter 5 will also serve this purpose. In this case, you change belief incrementally, 'walking' through the different stages of doubt, then 'open to change' that belief change usually involves. You need to *want* to believe, however. Often, a person reaches this important turning point when convinced about the random origin of self-beliefs in general. Better still, they expose the shaky foundation of their *particular* disempowering belief, often remembering its childhood origin.

Awareness of the NLP 'filter' model will also prepare the way for changes that we would normally not entertain. I emphasized in Part 1 the importance of establishing a grounding in the principles and presuppositions, rather than launching into techniques that, without that foundation, would probably not work.

CONGRUENCE

'Congruence' means communicating holistically, in such a way that every 'part' of you (see Chapter 10) believes and pursues the same outcome. Incongruence happens when some part of you has a different agenda, perhaps unknowingly. This usually reveals itself in body language, voice or some aspect of your words and physiology. People don't need to understand communication theory to detect such incongruence – children do so from an early age. But incongruence doesn't improve rapport or communication, or the communicator's state of mind.

You can use Exercise 10.1 to overcome any basic parts problems. However, the well-formed outcome process in Chapter 4 usually weeds out possible conflicts, and you can change or abandon outcomes as you wish.

Congruence may also concern the different neurological levels we discussed in Chapter 10. Typically, a higher-level belief or value will conflict with 'lower-level' behaviour. For example, a self-belief 'I'm hopeless (or great) at speaking in front of a group' will conflict with the actual behaviour of speaking in front of a group. Usually, the higher level wins – in this case the self-belief, which sabotages the behaviour. As we have seen, you can change this at the belief level (see Chapter 5), or often by simply accruing successful public speaking 'experiences' through multi-sensory mental rehearsal.

Glossary of NLP Terms

Accessing cues
The strategies we adopt to tune our bodies by breathing, posture, gesture, voice and eye movements to think in certain ways. These cues can indicate which representational system a person uses. *See also* **Eye accessing cues**.

Analogue
Continuously variable between limits, like a dimmer switch for a light. In NLP, it refers to the use of sensory representations when thinking.

Anchoring
The process by which any stimulus or representation (external or internal) becomes connected to and triggers a response. Anchors can occur naturally, or we can set them up intentionally.

'As if' frame
Pretending that some event has happened, thinking 'as if' it had occurred, encourages creative problem-solving by mentally going beyond apparent obstacles to desired solutions.

Associated
Inside an experience, seeing through your own eyes, fully in your senses.

Auditory
To do with the sense of hearing.

Backtracking
Reviewing or summarizing, using another's key words and tonalities.

Behaviour
Any activity that we engage in, including thought processes.

Beliefs
The generalizations we make about the world and our operating principles in it.

Calibration
Accurately recognizing another person's state by reading non-verbal signals.

Capability
A successful strategy for carrying out a task.

Chunking (stepping)
Changing your perception by going up or down a logical level. Stepping up means going up to a level that includes what you are

studying. Stepping down entails going to a level below for a more specific example of what you are studying. We can do this on the basis of member and class, or part and whole.

Complex equivalence

Two statements considered to mean the same thing, such as 'He is not looking at me, so he is not listening to what I say.'

Congruence

State of being unified, and completely sincere, with all aspects of a person working together towards an outcome.

Conscious

Anything in present-moment awareness.

Content reframing

Taking a statement and giving it another meaning by focusing on another part of the content, asking: 'What else could this mean?'

Context reframing

Changing the context of a statement to give it another meaning by asking: 'Where would this serve as an appropriate response?'

Conversational postulate

Hypnotic form of language; a question interpreted as a command.

Criterion

What you consider important to you in a particular context.

Crossover mirroring

Matching a person's body language with a different type of movement, such as tapping your foot in time to their speech rhythm.

Deep structure

The complete linguistic form of a statement from which we can derive the surface structure.

Deletion

In speech or thought, missing out a portion of an experience.

Digital

Varying between two different states, like a light switch that must be on or off. In NLP, it refers to the use of non-sensory symbols, such as words or numbers, when thinking.

Dissociated

Not in experience; seeing or hearing events from the outside.

Distortion

The process by which we inaccurately represent something in internal experience in a limiting way.

Dovetailing outcomes

The process of fitting together different outcomes, optimizing solutions; the basis of win–win negotiations.

Downtime	In a light trance state with your attention directed inwards to your own thoughts and feelings rather than the immediate world around you, as in daydreaming.
Ecology	A concern for the relationship between a being and its environment. Also used in reference to internal ecology; the relationship between a person and their thoughts, strategies, behaviours, capabilities, values and beliefs. The dynamic balance of elements in any system.
Elicitation	Evoking a state by your behaviour. Also gathering information either by direct observation of non-verbal signals or by asking Meta Model questions.
Epistemology	The study of how we know what we know.
Eye accessing cues	Movements of the eyes in certain directions which indicate visual, auditory or kinaesthetic thinking.
First position	Perceiving the world from your own point of view only, in touch with your own inner reality. One of three different Perceptual positions, the others being second and third position.
Frame	A context or way of perceiving something, as in outcome frame, rapport frame, backtrack frame, and so on.
Future pacing	Mentally rehearsing an outcome to ensure that the desired behaviour will occur.
Generalization	The process by which one specific experience comes to represent a whole class of experiences.
Gustatory	To do with the sense of taste.
Identity	Your self-image or self-concept. Who you take yourself to be. The totality of your being.
Incongruence	State of having reservations, not totally committed to an outcome. The internal conflict will emerge in the person's behaviour.
Intention	The purpose, the desired outcome of an action.
Internal representations	Patterns of information we create and store in

our minds in combinations of images, sounds, feelings, smells and tastes.

Kinaesthetic

The feeling sense; tactile sensations and internal feelings, such as remembered sensations, emotions, and the sense of balance.

Lead system

The representational system that finds information to input into consciousness.

Leading

Changing your own behaviours with enough rapport for the other person to follow.

Logical level

Something occupies a higher logical level if it includes something on a lower level.

Map of reality (Model of the world)

Each person's unique representation of the world, built from their individual perceptions and experiences. The sum total of an individual's personal operating principles.

Matching

Adopting aspects of another person's behaviour for the purpose of enhancing rapport.

Meta

Existing at a different logical level to something else. Derived from the Greek, meaning 'over and beyond'.

Meta Model

A model that identifies language patterns that obscure meaning in a communication through the processes of distortion, deletion and generalization, and specific questions to clarify and challenge imprecise language to connect it back to sensory experience and the deep structure.

Metacognition

Knowing about knowing: having a skill, and the knowledge required to explain how you do it.

Metaphor

Indirect communication by means of a story or figure of speech implying a comparison. In NLP, metaphor includes similes, parables and allegories.

Milton Model

The inverse of the Meta Model, using artfully vague language patterns to pace another person's experience and access unconscious resources.

Mirroring

Precisely matching aspects of another person's behaviour.

Mismatching	Adopting different patterns of behaviour to another person, breaking rapport for the purpose of redirecting, interrupting or terminating a meeting or conversation.
Modal operator of necessity	A linguistic term for rules ('should', 'ought', and so on).
Modal operator of possibility	A linguistic term for words that denote what we consider possible ('can', 'cannot', and so on).
Model	A practical description of how something works, designed to be useful. A generalized, deleted or distorted copy.
Modelling	The process of discerning the sequence of ideas and behaviour that enables someone to accomplish a task; the basis of accelerated learning.
Model of the world	*See* **Map of reality**.
Multiple description	The process of describing the same thing from different viewpoints.
Neuro-linguistic programming	The study of excellence, and a model of how individuals structure their experience.
Neurological levels	Also known as the different logical levels of experience: environment, behaviour, capability, belief, identity and spiritual.
New code	A description of NLP that comes from the work of John Grinder and Judith DeLozier in their book *Turtles All the Way Down*.
Nominalization	The linguistic term for the process of turning a verb into an abstract noun, and the word for the noun so formed.
Olfactory	To do with the sense of smell.
Outcome	A specific, sensory-based, desired result that meets the well-formedness criteria.
Overlap	Using one representational system to gain access to another: for example, picturing a scene and then hearing the sounds in it.
Pacing	Gaining and maintaining rapport with another person over a period of time by joining them in their model of the world. You can pace beliefs and ideas as well as behaviour.

Parts

Sub-personalities with discrete intentions, sometimes conflicting.

Perceptual filters

The unique ideas, experiences, beliefs and language that shape our model of the world.

Perceptual position

The viewpoint we are aware of at any moment can be our own (first position), someone else's (second position), or an objective and benevolent observer's (third position).

Phonological, ambiguity

Confusion between the sound of a word and its spelling: for example 'The difference is plain/plane to see/sea.'

Physiological

To do with the physical part of a person.

Predicates

Sensory-based words that indicate the use of a particular representational system.

Preferred system

The representational system that an individual typically uses most to think consciously and organize their experience.

Presuppositions

Ideas or statements that have to be taken for granted for a communication to make sense.

Punctuation ambiguity

Ambiguity created by merging two separate sentences into one.

Quotes

A linguistic pattern in which you express your message as if stated by someone else.

Rapport

The process of establishing and maintaining a relationship of mutual trust and understanding between two or more people. The ability to generate responses from another person.

Reframing

Changing the frame of reference around a statement or event to give it another meaning.

Representation

An idea: a coding or storage of sensory-based information in the mind.

Representational system

How we code information in our minds in one or more of the five sensory systems: visual, auditory, kinaesthetic, olfactory and gustatory.

Requisite variety

Flexibility of thought and behaviour.

Resource

Any means applicable to achieve an outcome: physiology, states, thoughts, strategies, experiences, people, events or possessions.

Resourceful state

The total neurological and physical experience when a person feels resourceful.

Second position

Perceiving the world from another person's point of view, in tune and in touch with their reality. One of three different perceptual positions, along with first and third position.

Sensory acuity

The process of learning to make finer and more useful distinctions about the sense information we obtain from the world.

Sensory-based description

Information that is directly observable and verifiable by the senses. The difference between 'The lips are pulled taut, some parts of her teeth are showing, and the edges of her mouth are higher than the main line of her mouth' – a description – and 'She's happy' – an interpretation.

State

How you feel: your mood. The sum of all neurological and physical processes within an individual at any moment in time. The state we experience affects our capabilities and interpretation of experience.

Stepping

See **Chunking**.

Strategy

A sequence of thought and behaviour adopted to obtain a particular outcome.

Submodality

Distinctions within each representational system; qualities of our internal representations, the smallest building blocks of our thoughts.

Surface structure

A linguistic term for the spoken or written communication that has been derived from the deep structure by deletion, distortion and generalization.

Synaesthesia

Automatic link from one sense to another.

Syntactic ambiguity

Ambiguous sentence where a verb plus 'ing' can serve either as an adjective or a verb: for example, 'Influencing people can make a difference.'

Third position

Perceiving the world from the viewpoint of a detached and benevolent observer. One of three different perceptual positions, along with first and second position.

Timeline	The way we store pictures, sounds and feelings of our past, present and future.
Trance	An altered state with an inward focus of attention on a few stimuli.
Triple description	The process of perceiving experience through first, second and third positions.
Unconscious	Everything not in your present-moment awareness.
Unified field	The unifying framework for NLP: a three-dimensional matrix of neurological levels, perceptual positions, and time.
Universal quantifiers	A linguistic term for words such as 'every', and 'all' that admit no exceptions; one of the Meta Model categories.
Unspecified nouns	Nouns that do not specify to whom or to what they refer.
Unspecified verbs	Verbs that have the adverb deleted; they do not say *how* the action was carried out.
Uptime	The state where the attention and senses are directed outwards.
Visual	To do with the sense of sight.
Visualization	The process of seeing images in your mind.
Well-formedness criteria	Ways of thinking about and expressing an outcome which make it both achievable and verifiable: the basis of dovetailing outcomes and win–win solutions.

Sources and Resources

Further reading

Alder, Harry, *NLP: The New Art and Science of Getting What You Want*, Piatkus, 1994. One of the early British-authored titles that risked using the then little-known term 'NLP' in the title. A painless introduction that has remained popular over the years and has been translated into many languages.

Alder, Harry, *NLP for Managers*, Piatkus, 1996. One of several books applying NLP to a wide area, and taking a business rather than therapy approach.

Alder, Harry, *NLP in 21 Days*, Piatkus, 1999. An introduction covering the recommended international syllabus for NLP practitioner training.

Andreas, Steve, and Faulkner, Charles (eds), *NLP: The New Technology of Achievement*, NLP Comprehensive, 1994. From the Nightingale-Conant/NLP Comprehensive stable, so best regarded as part of their training marketing. Although all standard NLP, the format and language seem less orthodox and more user-friendly than in most such books.

Bandler, Richard, and Grinder, John, *Reframing: Neuro-linguistic Programming and the Transformation of Meaning*, Real People Press, 1982. Included here because written by the founders of NLP. Reframing applies to almost any area, such as business problem-solving and negotiation, although you will usually find more succinct coverage as a single chapter in the average introductory text. As with some of their other books, this one includes large chunks of material transcribed verbatim from live training programmes – which you either like or you don't.

Bourland Jr, David, and Johnston, Paul D. (eds), *To Be or Not To Be*, International Society for General Semantics, 1991. This book brought E-Prime to the NLP community. Written in E-Prime language, of course, and for that reason alone it will interest language enthusiasts.

Grinder, John, and Bandler, Richard, *Frogs into Princes*, Real People Press, 1979. One of the 'original' or 'founder' NLP texts, mainly consisting of seminar transcripts on reframing and anchoring. Somewhat outdated in terms of the techniques described, and in terms of reader 'accessibility', but historically part of the NLP canon, so its bibliographical position remains secure.

Grinder, John, and Bandler, Richard, *The Structure of Magic, Volumes I and II*, Real People Press, 1975 and 1976. These two volumes describe the Meta Model – a large part of early

NLP – and apply NLP theory to non-verbal communication. Although now far from the best introduction, the authors deserve inclusion here because of their seminal importance to the NLP phenomenon.

James, Tad, and Woodsall, Wyatt, *Time Line Therapy and the Basis of Personality*, Meta Publications Inc., 1988. Essential reading about timelines, as this book popularized the topic. It covers much more than the timeline concept (which some introductions deal with succinctly anyway) and includes meta programs.

O'Connor, Joseph, and Seymour, John, *Introducing NLP*, HarperCollins, 1994. A British introduction to the subject that has stood the test of time. Bookish and in some respects outdated, but still as good an introduction as you will find.

Robbins, Anthony, *Unlimited Power*, Simon & Schuster, 1986. The book that launched Tony Robbins into the public eye. A punchy, extremely positive style for those who can stomach it, a million miles from some contemporary NLP writing, but this is NLP all the same, on which Robbins cut his teeth. Along with other entrepreneurs in the movement, Robbins has tried to create his own trademarks and branding, although nothing has acquired the historical significance of the term 'NLP' in the public consciousness.

Professional Association

The Association for Neuro-Linguistic Programming (ANLP) is a registered educational charity serving as a point of information for the general public, and fostering interchange among all those interested in NLP in the United Kingdom.

The Association of NLP (ANLP)
    PO Box 5, Haverfordwest, SA63 4YA
    Tel. 0870 870 4970
    The Association publishes the journal *Rapport*.

NLP online

Readers connected to the World Wide Web can access additional NLP resources. The NLP community seems quite computer-literate, and a general search on the term 'NLP' will usually produce hundreds of sites, albeit of varying quality. Unfortunately, Web sites come and go, and defunct sites can cause as much frustration as out-of-date *Yellow Pages* entries. Moreover, new sites appear continuously. Therefore, I shall not waste your time with a list of recommended addresses. Far better to do your own simple search – say on 'NLP' – and browse through those sites that seem interesting. In particular, watch out for 'links' to explore. Soon you will notice that certain addresses keep recurring, and you can bookmark the ones you might wish to visit in the future. Enrol yourself on e-mail lists, and join chat rooms if that takes your fancy. If you ever run short of responses, you can use a multiple-browser search facility such as Copernic (free download from <http://www.copernic.com>).

You will find many commercial organizations offering training, books and all manner of products and services for NLP buyers. Each has some axe or other to grind, and objectivity just doesn't exist. So, unless you wish to buy, you may wish to conduct a more specific search. For instance, try 'NLP articles' (which you can download to your heart's content) or – better still – specific NLP subjects you now know about, such as anchoring, meta programs or spelling strategy.

As ever, you need to take anything on the Internet with a few pinches of salt. An attractive, credible-seeming site will often deliver pure nonsense. Unlike books, no publishers' filtering process or quality control applies, and you may not even be able to identify the real person – credentials or no credentials – responsible for a comment or article. Anonymous 'experts' write, review, pontificate and advise with impunity.

On the other hand, you will come across articles published by learned journals, doctoral theses on NLP topics and the like. Similarly, your search will uncover some non-profit NLP associations with published standards of practice. So, with patience and increasing skill in navigating the Web, you will find reliable sources and a few jewels in the process. In short, although it doesn't offer the convenience of a book, cyberspace abounds in useful material. After a while, you may enjoy making a contribution to NLP yourself by publishing your own ideas online.

NLP training organizations in the UK

The following list of training organizations does not imply ANLP or any other accreditation.

A D International
Sherwood House
7 Oxhey Road
Watford
Herts
WD1 4QF

Tel. 07000 234683

Advanced Behavioural Capabilities
30a Main Street
Prickwillow
Ely
Cambs
CB7 4UN

Tel. 01353 688 533

Advanced Neuro Dynamics, Inc Hawaii

Tel. 001 808 596 7765

Advanced Neuro Dynamics, Inc
Rosedale House
Rosedale Road
Richmond
Surrey
TW9 2SZ

Tel. 0208 9399007

Ark Management Resources Ltd
Grasleigh House
63 Bargrove Road
Maidstone
Kent
ME14 5RT

Tel. 01622 671472

Artesion Group Ltd
37 Cavendish Avenue
Finchley
London
N3 3QP

Tel. 0208 349 2929

Back on Track
39 Hawkins Street
Rodbourne
Swindon
SN2 2AQ

Tel. 01793 533370

Beeleaf Communication Training
Beeleaf House
34 Grove Road
London
E3 5AX

Tel. 0208 983 9699

Brian Morton Associates HRD
Flat 4 'Braidley'
31 Cliff Drive
Canford Cliffs
Poole
Dorset
BH13 7JE

Tel. 01202 708095

Calabor
48 St James Road
Carlisle
CA2 5PD

Tel. 01228 599899

Carol Kinsey and Associates
8 Derby Road
Cheam
Surrey
SM1 2BL

Tel. 0208 715 3607

Developing Company
9 Southwood Lawn Road
Highgate
London
N6 5SD

Tel. 0208 341 1062

Dominic Beirne School of Hypnosis
The Stables
Welcombe Road
Stratford upon Avon
Warcs
CV37 6UJ

Tel. 01789 261620

Dr Susi Strang Associates
Sun Dial House
29 High St
Skelton
Saltburn
Cleveland
TS12 2EF

Tel. 01287 654175

DS Training (Development Steps)
2 Prescot Green
Ormskirk
Lancs
L39 4US

Tel. 01695 580288

Evolution Training Ltd
3 Wythering Close
Bognor Regis
West Sussex
PO21 4XX

Tel. 01243 268249

Excellence for All
53 Warwick Street
Haslingden
Lancashire
BB4 5LR

Tel. 01706 600886

Frank Daniels Associates
103 Hands Road
Heanor
Derbyshire
DE7 7HB

Tel. 01773 532195

Hexagon Training Company
78 Ivy Park Road
Sheffield
S10 3LD

Tel. 0114 2302753

Hidden Resources
21 Wood View
Birkby
Huddersfield
HD2 2DT

Tel. 01484 549515

INLPTA Hampshire

Tel. 01329 285353

Inspire Partnership
Bark Barn Cottage
West Dean
Salisbury
SP5 1JA

Tel. 01794 340480

Integration Training Centre
12 Prince of Wales Mansions
Prince of Wales Drive
London
SW11 4BG

Tel. 0207 622 4670

International Teaching Seminars
19 Widegate Street
Spitalfields
London
E1 7HP

Tel. 0207 247 0252

Janus Pim
Dale View
Head Cragg
Kirkby-in-Furness
Cumbria
LA17 7TB

Tel. 01229 889633

John Seymour Associates
17 Boyce Drive
Bristol
BS2 9XQ

Tel. 0117 955 7827

Key 2 Potential
34 Victoria Road
Uxbridge
Middlesex
UB8 2TW

Tel. 01895 255063

Kite Courses
34 Park Hall Road
East Finchley
London
N2 9PU

Tel. 0208 444 0510

Lambent Training
4 Coombe Gardens
New Malden
Surrey
KT3 4AA

Tel. 0208 715 2560

Lazarus Consultancy Ltd
37 Cavendish Avenue
Finchley
London
N3 3QP

Tel. 0208 349 2929

Link Fortune International Ltd
3 Stoutsfield Close
Yarnton
Kidlington
Oxon
OX5 1NX

Tel. 01865 847711

Marlin Management Training & Marlin Institute of NLP Psychotherapy
Marlin House
2 Coppice Close
The Street
Takeley
Nr Bishops Stortford
Herts CM22 6QB

Tel. 01279 873494

Neuro-Energetics
2137 Embassy Dr.,
Ste 212
Lancaster PA 17603
USA

Tel. 001 717 293 8803

NLP Academy
35–37 East Street
Bromley
Kent
BR1 1QQ

Tel. 0208 402 1120

NLP International
4 Ravenslea Road
London
SW12 8SB

Tel. 0208 933 8199

NLP North East
Bongate Mill Farmhouse
Appleby in Westmorland
Cumbria
CA16 6UR

Tel. 01768 351934

NLP University
Dynamic Learning Center
PO Box 1112
Ben Lomond
CA 95005
USA

Tel. 001 831 336 3457

Northern School of NLP & Associated Studies
22 Painterwood
Billington
Clitheroe
Lancs
BB7 9JD

Tel. 01254 824504

Optimum Performance
7 George Street
Carleton
Nr Skipton
North Yorks
BD23 3HQ

Tel. 01756 791110

Organisational Healing Ltd
48 Walton Road
Stockton Heath
Warrington
WA4 6NL

Tel. 01925 861600

Pathways To Change
Flat 4
2 North Park Road
Bradford
West Yorks
BD9 4NB

Tel. 01274 545948

Pegasus NLP Trainings
9 Ridley Road
Bournemouth
Dorset
BH9 1LB

Tel. 01202 534250

Performance Enhancement Ltd
1 Manor Court
Barnes Wallis Road
Segensworth East
Fareham
Hampshire
PO15 5TH

Tel. 01329 285656

Performance Partnership Ltd
11 Acton Hill Mews
310 Uxbridge Road
Acton
London
W3 9QN

Tel. 0208 992 9523

Pilgrims
Pilgrims House
Orchard Street
Canterbury
Kent
CT2 8BF

Tel. 01227 762111

Postgraduate Medical & Professional Education
PO Box 506
Halifax
HX1 5UF

Tel. 01422 343165

PPD Personal Development
30A The Loning
Colindale
London
NW9 6DR

Tel. 0208 201 3333

Q Learning
Cedar Court
9–11 Fairmile
Henley-on-Thames
Oxon
RG9 2JR

Tel. 01491 414202

Q-OPD International Ltd
PO Box 3810
Bracknell
Berks
RG12 7YE

Tel. 01344 484634

Quantum Libet
160 Gloucester Terrace
London
W2 6HR

Tel. 0207 724 1163

Realisation at Stenhouse
36 Plasturton Gardens
Pontcanna
Cardiff
CF1 9HF

Tel. 029 2037 7723

RYP Training and Development Ltd
37 Cavendish Avenue
Finchley
London
N3 3QP

Tel. 0208 349 2929

Sensory Systems Training
162 Queens Park
Glasgow
G42 8QN

Tel. 0141 424 4177

Sue Knight Books and Talks
Great Oaks
Green Lane
Burnham
Bucks
SL1 8QA

Tel. 01628 604438

Thorpe Institute
Thorpe Hall
Thorpe Constantine
Tamworth
B79 0LH

Tel. 017712 175 989

Tina Boyden Associates
69 Goddard Place
Off Monnery Road
London
N19 5GT

Tel. 0207 281 9663

Training Changes
7 Spencer Avenue
Cheltenham
GL51 7DX

Tel. 01242 580640

Tranceformational Change
Hawthorn Farm
Corner Drove
Ware
Nr Ash
Kent
CT3 2LU

Tel. 07711 036182

Transformation Training Ltd
59a Greenside Road
London
W12 9JQ

Tel. 0208 743 3064

Vievolve
Bix Manor
Broadplat Lane
Henley-on-Thames
RG9 4RS

Tel. 01491 577244

Washington School of Clinical & Advanced Hypnosis
Richmael House
25 Edge Lane
Chorlton
Manchester
M21 9JH

Tel. 0161 882 0400

zetetic
6 Florin Walk
Harrogate
HG1 2SN

Tel. 01423 527909

Index